ETHICS, POLITICS, AND EDUCATION

*

ETHICS, POLITICS,
and
EDUCATION

*

by

I. B. BERKSON

University of Oregon UBooks
EUGENE, OREGON
1968

Copyright © *University of Oregon 1968*

Contents

Preface

THE TRANSFORMATIONS that have taken place since the earlier part of the twentieth century—in science, in economic processes and world politics, in psychological knowledge and in general climate of opinion—demand a reformulation of the pattern of beliefs which served as guiding ideas during the modern era under the aegis of liberalism. As is evident in current discussions, the changes in society and politics, as well as in theories of knowledge and in philosophic outlook, are having a profound effect on educational conceptions and on school policies. This book attempts an analysis of ideas and issues which bear on the educational problem and presents a statement of the author's position on major lines of school policy. Pedagogical questions receive incidental consideration, but the discussion relates primarily to the broader issues in science, economics, and politics of general public interest and is addressed to the general reader as well as to the student and teacher of education.

The discussion in Part One, which provides a brief review of scientific thought, is intended to point up the limitations of science and scientific method for the construction of moral theory. The position upheld is that the source of moral ideas lies in the historical experience of mankind, not in science or in scientific method. Analogies between scientific method, as employed in the natural sciences, and the methodology of the social studies are so general as to be without essential significance and if taken literally would actually be misleading. The data and conclusions of the behavioral sciences may aid in the realization of ethical ends, but the ends themselves are to be sought in the cultural heritage—in the insights and conceptions revealed in literature, philosophy, and religion.

The Western ethic is rooted in a synthesis of the Judeo-Christian, Hellenic, and Roman thought. Its history reveals a continuing struggle between a spiritual-moral-rational ideal, on the one hand, and the established economic and political institutions of each era, on the other. One major task of philosophy in relation to education is to make explicit the enduring principles and ideas—the ideals of justice and compassion, of reason and law, of equality and freedom, of personal dignity and community loyalty, of the uniqueness of each individual and the unity of mankind. However, principles, ideas, and ideals proclaimed in the abstract are likely to become mere expressions of sentiment, ineffective in their influence on social life, even evasive in the face of urgent problems of economic and political organization. The other task of educational philosophy is to apply the enduring ideals to contemporary social issues.

In accord with this approach, the second part of the book is devoted to an analysis of major contemporary social isues and to an exposition of the principles of democracy conceived as the modern humanist manifestation of the evolving Western ethic. On the domestic front, the problems discussed include the establishment of civil rights, the achievement of equality of opportunity and of status for Negroes, the elimination of poverty which conditions the other deprivations. In the field of foreign relations, the problems are the strengthening of the United Nations, the expansion of its educational, social, and economic agencies, the growth of international law, and the organization of collective security. In both areas of concern, it is of the essence that the concept of equality be joined with the concept of liberty as an activating idea. In furthering international organization as well as within the national life, the directing principles are to be found in the ethics and politics of democracy. But it is of crucial importance to recognize that in the emerging era we shall be living in a pluralistic world order in coexistence with several diverse socioeconomic and political systems. The overshadowing problem of the immediate future is to achieve a *modus vivendi* with Communist nations in the interest of promoting world peace.

In the discussion of education, in the concluding chapters, I deal with issues treated in current educational literature, keeping in mind the ideas developed in the body of the book. I follow the view that a philosophy of education must begin in the field of education; it is not the application of a metaphysical principle to education although assumptions of the nature of reality are indirectly involved. I conceive educational philosophy in terms of a consideration of major education problems in the light of a democratic social philosophy and system of government. Educational philosophy has a three-sided frame of reference: the individual person—child, youth, or adult; the society in which the individual lives; a configuration of standards and values.

The school has functions in transmitting the cultural heritage, in nurturing personal growth, in adjusting the individual to society, in promoting the social good. In all of its activities, its work implies a pattern of ideals and a relation to community life.

The two-fold frame of reference—the historical and the contemporary—has implications for the program of teacher education. First, it implies as a prerequisite a basis of liberal education—a core of classical literature, history and humanities, a study of the ethical and political ideas of Western civilization. It means restoring the history of education to its essential place. The other indispensable aspect is concern with contemporary social thought and problems. The underlying purpose of the book is to bring the ethical-political category into the focus of the study of educational philosophy—to give a central place to political and economic theory in the preparation of teachers and other educational personnel.

The book is intended to reflect contemporary views rather than to present a novel conception. At the same time it may be regarded as an expanded essay on "This I believe," supported by references in recent writings in science, economics, and political theory, but nevertheless a personal affirmation of convictions and conclusions. It represents an elaboration of my *The Ideal and the Community* in which the thesis of the tension between ethical values and social organization was set forth and the need of continuous and persistent effort to implement our ideals in the institutional structure was expounded. In the present endeavor, there may be noted a greater emphasis on political realism and on the economic conditioning of social organization.

Perhaps an *apologia* is in order for attempting to deal with, and to express opinions on, so wide a range of topics. The justification is that some indication of position on the various issues discussed is necessary to give relevant meaning to the general point of view advanced. It is imperative in these critical times to formulate our beliefs, to make explicit our assumptions, to clarify our aims—and, above all, to apply them to current problems in society and education at the points of controversy.

I acknowledge indebtedness, first, to Professor Martin Fleisher of Brooklyn College of the University of the City of New York for bringing to my attention recent literature on politics and economics and for what I learned through our many discussions on these subjects. Thanks are due to Professor Ernest Nagel of Columbia University for reading the sections in Chapter Two on scientific explanation and for making several corrections in the interest of precision of statement. This acknowledgement of indebtedness, I wish to emphasize, does not carry with it any implication of his agreement with my rather negative estimate of the value of scientific method for moral theory. I am grateful to Dr. Ordway Tead for reading the first draft of the book while it was still in process and for contributing to the clarification of my ideas. Greatly do I appreciate the friendly assistance given me by Mrs. Polly Reichenbach who prepared the original typescript and who helped through her interest, her factual knowledge, and her perceptive understanding. A word of appreciation is due also to Mrs. Catherine Lauris of University of Oregon Books for her felicitous editorial suggestions and her contribution to the artistic design of the book.

To Professor Keith Goldhammer—with whom I had the privilege of teaching and exchanging ideas at the University of Oregon—I owe a special acknowledgment for his appreciative reading of the final manuscript which led to its publication.

I. B. Berkson

Eugene, Oregon
July 1967

PART ONE

SCIENCE, VALUES, AND SELFHOOD

CHAPTER ONE

INTRODUCTION: THE NEED

AND NATURE OF BELIEF

Our Changed World of Events and Ideas

Liberalist Doubt and the Need of Reaffirmation

The Scope and Core of Belief

Our world is disintegrating inwardly,
as it is outwardly, because it has neither a
structure of thought nor an ideal of life
in things basic to men's experience on
this planet. JOHN HAYNES HOLMES

1·

Introduction:
The Need and Nature
Of Belief

OUR CHANGED WORLD OF EVENTS AND IDEAS

D URING the last half-century, the world has undergone a transformation that has changed it more radically than in any other
period during the previous half-millenium. We live not only in "a
changing world," as the phrase goes, but in one that has already
changed. Our period is characterized by extraordinary developments
in science and technology and by unprecedented political upheavals;
it is remarkable for new conceptions of the nature of the universe
and for novel views of the mind of man. We stand on the threshold
of a new epoch in world history as different from the modern age as
that period of dynamic change was from the medieval—perhaps it
would be correct to say, as different as the Christian was from the
Graeco-Roman era which preceded it. The interplay of new forces
and new conceptions demands a reconstruction of major beliefs of
the modern epoch now in the process of passing.

The most striking manifestations of the vast transformation are
connected with the remarkable advances in the natural sciences. The
sensational achievements in nuclear fission and in rocket propulsion,
which have given to our era the popular designations of the "atom
age" and the "space age," hold promise for constructive civil use. At

the same time, the fantastic inventions of recent decades fill us with a sense of anxiety and cast a shadow of foreboding on all our thoughts and activities. Airplane, radio, and now telstar, have made neighbors of all the peoples of the earth, but the improvements in transportation and communication have accomplished little toward international understanding—have increased rather than lessened destructiveness if war should come upon us. Even the wholly salutary advances in medical science have had their problematic consequences, as in the reduction of infant mortality and lengthening the lifespan with the concomitant of "population explosion."

The advances in science have monstrously aggravated the problems of the contemporary era, but they are not, in themselves, the causes of the widespread disturbances of our age of crisis and quandary. The changes resulting from the scientific achievements must be seen in their interaction with the wide range of factors, social and ideational, as well as material. In our contracting world there are powerful driving forces: of economic change, of the struggle between democracy and communism, of anti-colonialism and the demand for racial equality. Three revolutions are simultaneously at work in the world: the industrial-technological, the political-economic revolution of communism, the anti-imperial, national, and racial revolution of suppressed peoples.

For half of a millenium, economic change has been proceeding at an accelerated rate, first advancing from an agricultural base to an industrial stage, now entering a thoroughgoing technological phase. Beginning in Western Europe, it has spread throughout the world, invading areas still under tribal forms of social organization. In the United States and in European countries, automation in manufacturing, mechanization in agriculture, substitution of synthetic goods for natural products, have proceeded steadily at an ever rapid pace. In the Soviet Union and in Communist China, the change from largely feudal conditions to industrialized technological society has been accomplished in a relatively short period through the use of drastic, coercive means. The underdeveloped countries in Asia, Africa, and South America must likewise—whether by gradualist or revolutionary processes—undergo radical economic reconstruction if a decent standard of living is to be achieved for the poverty-stricken masses of their peoples.

In each region, in the advanced countries of the West as well as in the less-developed nations, the transformations in the economic system have ramifying political and social consequences. Large-scale organization of production, corporate or collectivist, necessitates an

6

expansion of the role of government in the coordination and direction of the national economic effort. The innumerable products of science and technology, together with the change in the mode of economic organization, have many-sided effects on social life—on the structure of the agricultural community, on the character of urban environments, on the status of women, on the form of family life. On the domestic front, the new forms of economic organization with their correlated changes in the institutional structures affect the most intimate human relationships. On the international scene, in the disparity of the rate of economic change, as between the highly industrialized nations of the West and those still held down by primitive agriculture carried on under exploitive political regimes, is rooted the portentous political struggle of the day between democracy and communism.

In the political sphere, the entrenchment of communism in Russia and its spread to other parts of the world have critically altered the balance of power and influence in international relations. The Communist countries—the Soviet Union, the Chinese People's Republic, with their satellites and sympathizers—represent in population, raw materials, and military potential an array of forces comparable, in broad terms, to that commanded by the Western nations living under some form of democratic polity. The eruption of disunity as a result of national rivalries and policy differences between the U.S.S.R. and the Chinese People's Republic is of importance in lessening the danger of Communist domination, but it does not alter the major fact that the West no longer occupies the position of hegemony in world civilization.

Within the Western alliance there has, likewise, been a weakening of solidarity, as strikingly demonstrated by the secession of France, under de Gaulle, from the NATO structure, and by her refusal generally to subordinate her national interests to the unity of the alliance and to accommodate her foreign relations to American policies. The leadership of the United States has also been challenged by Fidel Castro's adoption of a line oriented to communism. The *detente* effected by President Kennedy's resolute action in 1962, eventuating in the removal of Russian offensive weapons from Cuban soil, eliminates the threat of effective communist aggression in the Western hemisphere. But the fact that a communistic political economy has gained a foothold in Latin America is a fact of lasting import.

Alongside the economic-political revolutions—communist and noncommunist—in the underdeveloped countries of the world is a determined rebellion, now almost completely successful, against the imperialist domination of European powers. Throughout Asia and

7

Africa there is an awakening, an irresistible effort to organize national life on lines of political independence. Associated with this awakening is a powerful drive on the part of colored peoples everywhere—black, brown, yellow, olive—to eradicate once and for all the symbols and practices of racial discrimination. Within the short period since the second world war, there has been an irreversible reduction in the relative position of the Western European nations in power and prestige. With the decline has come the beginning of the end of white domination, and, it may be added, of Christian supremacy as the Afro-Asian nations take their place in world civilization.

We are well aware of these great changes which have been briefly summarized—every day brings added evidence of the vast transformation. Our tendency has been to emphasize the material factors as determinative and to give less attention to the intellectual assumptions and to the social philosophies—to the ideas that have played a part in bringing about the revolutionary changes of our times. And the power that ideas, clearly defined and firmly held, can have in shaping future events, if not wholly neglected, is greatly underestimated. Here is a crucial problem confronting the Western world. Advances in science have been readily accepted and securely embodied for good and for ill in material instruments. But the reorientation in our intellectual and moral attitudes needed to understand, and to cope effectively with, the new social and political situation in the world is a more subtle and difficult process. In the formulation of ideas and values we lag behind. Liberals as well as conservatives—perhaps more than conservatives—rely on beliefs and attitudes remaining over from nineteenth-century thought. The progress in science and technology has tended to mask the disintegration of the system of ideas and values that had been the basis of the West-European conception of life.

Already at the beginning of the twentieth century, many forces had combined to weaken the synthesis of Christian faith and classic reason which had for an extended period in European history provided a foundation of intellectual unity and a sense of spiritual security, and, it should not be forgotten, afforded support for a stable political socio-economic order. The humanistic and individualistic tendencies initiated by the Renaissance, the separation of church and state brought about by nationalism and republicanism, the Darwinian evolutionary theory which shook the confidence in the teachings of the Bible—these several forces worked together to undermine the authority of organized religion. In addition to its rejection of supernaturalism, the scientific movement, with its empirical imprint and its exaltation of change as a primary assumption, challenged the logic and metaphysics of Aristotelianism which had hitherto served as groundwork for those who endeavored to support faith by reason. The rise of capitalism interacting with the intellectual and political tendencies promoted an individualistic cult of material success which was, in R. H. Tawney's sharp indictment, "the negation of any system of thought and morals which can, except by metaphor, be designed as Christian." An air of disingenuousness pervaded the Victorian era in the heyday of liberalism which concealed class and imperialist exploitation under a thin veneer of moral and religious pretensions.

In the last half-century, crushing blows have been dealt to the already attenuated traditional pattern of intellectual and moral assumptions. Quantum theory and relativity imply a departure from the conception of a completely designed and predetermined universe which for Isaac Newton was secure evidence of the existence of God as creator and preserver of the order of the world. Marxism and Freudianism from opposite standpoints and in different ways have played their part in destroying the traditional image of man as easily amenable to rational control. But more shattering than the changes in the universe of thought were the horrendous events of the two world wars which have brought us down from the high optimism of the era of liberalism to the dark mood of anxiety reflected in the current existentialist philosophies.

The murders and obscenities of fascism in both Catholic and Protestant countries have exposed the ineffectuality of Christianity as a social-moral force, whatever significance it may still have for individual psychological adjustment and for identification of the faithful with a community of ideals. The capitulation of Britain and France to Adolph Hitler at Munich revealed how far the ethics of calculated expediency can seduce statesmen to dishonor and bring their nations to the verge of destruction. The eruption of Nazism in Germany, land of philosophy and education—the widespread acceptance of fascism by a large part of the German people and the readiness of leading democratic nations to appease it—cannot be explained away by attributing it to the aberrations of a power-crazed Fuehrer. These phenomena, culminating in the mass murders of the gas chambers, were the excrescences of the disorganization of the conditions of life and the dissolution of the patterns of thought that marked the end of the modern era in European civilization.

LIBERALIST DOUBT AND THE NEED OF REAFFIRMATION

The springs of Western intellectual and moral conceptions have not dried up; their sources lie deep in the ground of human history. The major moral and political ideas—as well as the scientific knowledge and technology—that are changing the world have their roots in Western thought: in the Hellenic search for reasoned truth and for ordered government, in the Stoic conception of a rational universal law based on equality, in the Judeo-Christian aspiration for human dignity and brotherhood, in the democratic demand for personal and national freedom. The predicament of the Western world is in part caused by the ineluctable difficulty of maintaining ideals in the face of the struggle for existence, by the problem of creating the means needed to fulfill envisaged ends, by the inevitable lag between aspirations and their institutional embodiments.

But there is another contributing factor to the disturbed condition of the Western world: we have not elaborated a unified conception to take the place of the classic-religious synthesis which is no longer tenable in its basically medieval form. As a result of the swift march of revolutionary events in the last half-century and the extraordinary transformations in the realm of thought, the Western world finds itself in the throes of conflicting views, with no agreement on fundamental issues. We have maintained ourselves for the most part by working compromises, and have made of "pragmatism," in the popular expedient sense, a principle of action.

The struggle for world leadership between East and West, as we constantly proclaim, is not merely a struggle between contending blocs of powers but a war of ideas and values, a battle between communism and democracy as philosophies of life. However, whereas the principles and objectives of communism are boldly stated, what we mean by democracy suffers from a diversity of meanings and from mutually contradictory interpretations. In some instances, democracy is defined restrictively as a matter of government only; in others, it becomes a general humanitarian outlook. On the one hand, the principle of "inalienable rights" is made the cornerstone; on the other hand, the "sovereignty of the people" is made an absolute. In the former case, racial equality in all aspects of social life would be a categorical imperative; in the latter, enforcement of desegregation against the will of the white majority is accounted as "undemocratic." Even the freedom of the press, a leading American educator contends, is "only an assigned one" that could be rescinded as well as modified by the people who, it is implied, originally established it.[1] The question, posed at the end of the first world war by the late Ralph Barton Perry with reference to democracy, still stands: "We

[1] See below, chap. VIII, pp. 263-265.

have repeatedly professed this creed on many solemn and public occasions. Do we *really mean* it? And if so *what* do we mean by it?"[2]

The idea of a formulation of beliefs runs counter to the temper of progressive nineteenth century thought. Liberalism, as we properly call its guiding thesis, distrusted general concepts: it entertained a certain diffidence toward the definition of ends as smacking of religious dogmatism and of the imposition of absolutist systems of thought. Empirical and individualistic in approach, liberalism regarded flexible adjustment to change as the mark of scientific intelligence and moral wisdom, as well as the means of social progress. Freedom of the mind, its key concept, tended to be interpreted as emancipation from doctrinal and institutional authority. The emphasis was laid on inquiry, on observation of facts without recourse to a priori assumptions. The essence of science, in accordance with some versions of liberalism, was not to be found in the carefully organized bodies of verified knowledge which it provided, but in its method, in its reliance on experience, and its readiness to challenge existing beliefs.

The liberalist outlook was the culmination of a movement of revolt begun during the period of the Renaissance against the absolutism of Christian dogma and the intellectualism of scholastic philosophy. An attitude of mind which had begun as a rebellion against abstract universals assumed to represent eternal truth ended in a negative orientation toward belief as such, toward any idea of enduring truth. Doubt became a guiding principle, not doubt in the Cartesian sense— which was a philosophic pose, a preliminary to the establishment of a system of thought—but a sceptical principle of magnanimous tolerance and wholesale open-mindedness. A widespread liberalist attitude finds reflection in the following declaration: "It surprises me to find out in how many areas of life I have unanswered questions rather than beliefs. It surprises me even more that in many of these areas a change of doubts and questions to beliefs would feel to me like a change for the worse, not for the better."[3]

Doubt is a first step in freedom of the mind and is often constructive. It plays a part in initiating inquiry. But we cannot remain suspended in doubt with reference to basic issues. All genuine thinking, not to speak of effective action, implies presuppositions and assumptions, goals and ends. Intellectual freedom is not a natural right to think as one pleases: it is an arduous discipline. It involves the responsibility

[2] Ralph Barton Perry, "What Do We Mean by Democracy?" *International Journal of Ethics*, XXVII (July, 1918), 449-464.

[3] Bonaro W. Overstreet *This I Believe*, Edward P. Morgan, ed. (New York, 1952), p. 129.

of setting forth new assumptions for thought and new principles of action when old doctrines are abandoned; its proper exercise results in rational belief as a basis for moral commitment.

Liberalism's contributions to the progress of thought were due not to its doubts but to its positive beliefs. In its eighteenth century seminal form, it arose as a clearly conceived pattern of political beliefs and social ideals nurtured in the Western philosophic and religious tradition. The Declaration of Independence was grounded in truths considered to be self-evident, on inalienable rights with which men were believed to have been endowed by their Creator. In the background of the English conception of a Bill of Rights and of the French Declaration of the Rights of Man, as well as of the Jeffersonian pronouncement, there was the classical-medieval conception of "natural law," of a law which required human legislation for its interpretation and realization but which no assembly of men could rightfully abolish.

In the deistic view of the eighteenth century, freedom implied government by reason and law as against the arbitrary power of a personal sovereign. In the nineteenth century, a variety of influences combined to give the idea of freedom a voluntaristic connotation. Laissez-faire capitalism required unregulated competition. Protestant, nonconforming sects made individual conscience the guide of ethical judgment. The Darwinian theory of natural selection merging with Spencer's doctrine of the survival of the fittest gave a transcendental sanction to the "shouldering aside of the weak by the strong." Whereas the earlier liberalism reflecting the Stoic-Christian tradition had endowed nature with a quality of justice, now nature in the raw, as exemplified in the "tooth and claw" struggle for existence, became a model for human ethics. In practice, the harsh individualism of British thought was moderated by a strongly rooted respect for traditional law and by a system of education that stressed scholarship and discipline. In the United States, a spirit of independence stimulated by successful rebellion and strengthened by an open frontier put a premium on nonconformity—encouraged the idea that individual judgment was an adequate guide in morals as in politics.

There were countervailing, socially-oriented tendencies within the mainstream of liberal thought and these gained ground at the end of the century. John Stuart Mill acknowledged the necessity of government intervention and favored cooperative projects as means to counteract the excesses of individual enterprise. T. H. Green, in his advocacy of "positive freedom," made the well-being of the community prerequisite to individual liberty. In the United States the attack against "social Darwinism"—initiated by Lester Ward and reflected in the writings of John Dewey—was accompanied by the promotion of cooperative endeavor and community-centered concerns. Nevertheless, there remained embedded in American liberalist thought a conception of the primacy and the autonomy of the individual to which an antinomian attitude and a voluntaristic temper adhered.

An individualistic psychology persisted in the conception of the nature of the self and remained dominant in progressive education despite its apparent stress on the social aspects of personality. Self-realization was conceived in terms of growth in analogy with the development of biological organisms. The obvious fact that the human being can realize himself only through definitely structured institutions was overlooked. Cooperation was conceived as interaction among individuals; that individuals must work together within given social organizations was largely left out of consideration. "Thinking for oneself" was regarded as the great achievement of intellectual freedom; that effective thinking requires a critical awareness of assumptions and a clear definition of ends received little attention. Insofar as the individual was to be restrained, it was through "intelligent self-control," through consideration of others, and concern for the general welfare; the part that identification with actual communities and loyalty to consciously-held principles and ideals play in the guidance of life received no emphasis.

In the century and a half after the American and the French revolutions, when liberalism was at its height as an intellectual movement, the institutions of Western society still provided standards, values, purposes. The family retained its position as the organic cell of society, the churches provided ethical and spiritual resources for the greater part of the people, the democratic political system stood unchallenged. The schools, the colleges, the universities, even the most liberal of them, still regarded "the transmission of the cultural heritage" as an indispensable part of their work. Within each area of acitvity—of political thought, of religious belief, of philosophic outlook—there were divergences of opinion; nevertheless, there did exist a general consensus on fundamentals. In a period when the basic assumptions of the social order were not seriously threatened, liberalism could do its work of criticism of dogmatic belief and of emancipation from rigid convention with fruitful results for the enrichment of life and for social progress. Nor was it necessary, perhaps, in an age of gradual change, to insist on the formulation of beliefs; we need not make explicit what is generally agreed upon.

Whether the social liberalism of the early twentieth century could

13

have evolved into a well-grounded philosophy of politics and education remains a question. Time was not given for its elaboration and for its communication to a wide public. The first world war intervened and brought about its undoing. It was fought, as Woodrow Wilson proclaimed, "to make the world safe for democracy"; in its consequences, it sowed the seeds of totalitarian revolution. With the rise of fascism and communism, the weak side of liberalism became apparent. The lack of a clear body of principles made of it a house divided against itself as it faced communism. Its undiscriminating tolerance prevented it from denying the right of free organization to fascoid groups, despite their rejection of the whole fabric of the Western ethic, the Christian, the classic, and especially the liberalist. In its diffidence toward clearly formulated beliefs, it offered no counterforce to the aggressive philosophies which aimed to destroy it.

In the present era of vast transition—of bemusement and discouragement—it becomes urgent for the Western world to declare the beliefs on which it takes a stand and to define the goals it aims to promote. It is important to reaffirm the enduring values of the Western tradition and to restate them in application to current problems. We need not shrink from using the word "ideal." For the liberal, the word "ideal" was suspect; he tended to look upon it with misgiving as utopian, as ineffectual, or even hypocritical. It is true that ideals may be impotent either because they are the stuff that dreams are made of or, on the other hand, merely preserve the verbal skeletons of ancient vital conceptions. At times ideals remain inert, limited to the universe of thought, not because they are invalid but because the conditions of life are not suitable for their implementation. But when ideals express the needs, the strivings, the visions of communities of men and are related to actual possibilities of action, they have immense power in mobilizing energies for the achievement of great ends. As Ralph Barton Perry has written: "As something to live by, the ideal gives a nation its stability, its monumental greatness, its place in history; while to the individual it gives a sense of membership and participation."[4]

A clarification of assumptions and a definition of ends is necessary for giving direction to national policy. It is essential if we are to extricate ourselves from the morass of conflicting views and evasive neutralisms in the field of education. The need of a formulation of ideas and ideals to give direction in public affairs merges with the need of a system of values to guide the personal life. The sense of

[4] Ralph Barton Perry, *Puritanism and Democracy* (New York, 1944), p. 61.

14

insecurity which pervades the consciousness of the intellectual class is no doubt related to the breakdown of religious beliefs and traditional moral attitudes. But it is also closely connected to the disenchantment with liberalism as an effective saving philosophy of life. The vagueness of definition which it encourages leaves much room for "bad faith" in the sense that Jean-Paul Sartre has described it, "hiding a displeasing truth or presenting as truth a pleasing untruth." Such self-deception easily becomes a rationalizing apologia for failure to implement our democratic pronouncements.

There is a growing realization in American literature of the need of a formulation of beliefs and of a commitment to a scheme of values. We are told, as the advertisement of one recent collection of statements urges, that "men and women will lead richer lives if they deliberately decide what they want from life—what they want in material things and the relative importance of moral and spiritual things."[5] This utilitarian approach, however, misses the point. A decision on ends can never be made on the calculus of pleasure and pain; it may, and generally will, require sacrifice. It can never be a merely private, individual choice; it must include a communal reference. A formulation of belief is necessary not primarily for those who seek the life abundant in the drive for status and success. It is essential for all of us who seek to live a rationally grounded, meaningful life, and to achieve peace of mind. Pleasures give joy, may be humane, bring moments of spiritual enhancement. But the sustained happiness of *eudaimonia* can be attained—as the philosophers and the religious have understood—only through commitment to a way of belief and a way of life to which our minds and our consciences give approval. This is true, whether we call the faith we choose the "Life of Reason," or the "Will of God."

THE SCOPE AND CORE OF BELIEF

In the current literature which reflects increasing awareness of the need of clearly defined values and purposes, the term "belief" still carries with it mainly a connotation of faith in the religious sense. In *This Is My Faith*, twenty-five leaders of American thought in various fields of endeavor, in philosophy and religion, in education and social work, have gven expression to the quest for a consciously formulated

---

[5] From the publisher's statement introducing *This I Believe, op cit.* The book itself is a fine collection of statements of "the personal philosophies of one hundred thoughtful men and women."

scheme of beliefs within a cosmic frame of reference.[6] Some of the viewpoints represent a world outlook within the bounds of a theistic conception; others speak for a naturalistic humanist approach. Both types of view, as Stewart G. Cole, the editor, interprets the problem, represent "a search for religious convictions," and "a quest for profound values to sustain human beings in adverse times." The book grew out of the hope for a reconciliation between the two types of search for basic values, the church-centered and the secular-oriented. The major concern of the study was "to assess the impact of the Judeo-Christian religions, the world-view of modern science and value-structure of democracy, upon man in his search for a valid faith."[7]

A fully integrated philosophy of life will include a stated or implied reference to the nature of the universe and the place that man has in it, involve some assumption of the degree of freedom that man has in shaping his destiny. Intellectual integrity demands an avowal of a cosmic point of view whether one believes, as does Stewart G. Cole, that the cosmos provides a support for man's spiritual aspirations or whether one holds, as does this writer, that the universe is not concerned with man's "highest well-being." However, in the outline of the point of view to be presented in the following chapters, the core of interest is in the social implications of belief and not primarily in their cosmic sanction.

A statement of belief adequate for meeting the perplexities of our times must be more than an assertion of religious faith, however broadly the term "religious" is used, whether in the supernatural sense or in the humanist meaning. Nor does a conception become valid by inclusion of a reference to "the scientific world view," a dubious idea as applied to ethical and social matters—certainly questionable when it is averred that "modern science is introducing us to a universe which is boundless and beautiful, creative and conservational." Closer to the focus of ultimate concern is the emphasis on democratic values—on human dignity, on social improvement, on freedom joined with responsibility—but this too remains abstract and possibly empty in the cosmic-centered outlook. A statement of belief must include a conception of the good society, defined in terms both of ideas and of political organization. Crucial to the definition of the political structure is a determination of its economic basis.

[6] Stewart G. Cole, ed., *This Is My Faith: The Convictions of Representative Americans Today* (New York, 1956).
[7] *Ibid.*, p. 7.

Much of the discussion between theists and humanists echoes the eighteenth- and nineteenth-century conflicts between state and church and between religion and science. A clarification of the antinomies—the natural versus the supernatural, experience versus revelation, state power versus church right, is still essential for the formulation of a comprehensive point of view. But with all this, the religious question no longer occupies the center of the stage either as an intellectual problem or as a power struggle: a measure of reconciliation has been achieved. The major conflicts of our era are in the field of social philosophy—between nationalism and internationalism, between racialism and human equality, and in the overarching struggle which we epitomize in the antithesis: democracy versus communism. In the war between social philosophies, questions of ethical, spiritual, and religious import are certainly involved. A consideration of social philosophies will necessarily lead us into the realms of the moral and the ideal. On the other hand, making the religious and the spiritual aspects of human experience the major subject in the discussion of belief is apt to lead to the neglect of the critical social issues. Often it proves to be a way of a subconscious avoidance of the actual problems which we must face.

Conceptions influenced by German idealism make communion with cosmic reality a central element in the development of the ethical consciousness. On the surface, the emphasis on values in contrast to the maintenance of creeds and rituals of organized churches would seem to indicate a rational and social approach. But the moral aspiration that invests the cosmic-centered Weltanschauung tends to become sublimated into a pious sentiment, and to evanesce in transcendental emotion. To be told that love is an essential element in human relations, that universal peace has been the eternal longing of man, that we must retain our faith in humanity, may lift our spirits for the while, but such general pronouncements can have little effect in resolving the problems of family life and social organization, of justice in the economic life, and of order in international affairs. Edifying but not effective is the belief which asserts that "if the ethical and spiritual values of religion . . . were universally emphasized—in place of doctrine, ceremony, and cult (which tend to divide rather than to unite men)—racial discrimination and international suspicion and hatred would dissolve as does snow in the rays of the sun."[8]

Values are not abstract entities that descend from a heavenly sphere

[8] Paul Arthur Schilpp in Cole, *op. cit.*, p. 201.

17

to become incarnate by their own spiritual force. Values inhere in the many-sided affairs of life, in activities as well as in attitudes, in political and economic organization as well as in personal relations. Ethical judgments do not constitute a separate ethereal realm. They are evaluations of feeling and behavior, arising as distillations of experienced appreciations. It is only when we attempt to indicate how the conceptualized values are to be implemented that we recognize the difficult problems involved in their realization. Relating values to activities will quickly disabuse us of the proposition that, "As all truth is one, so we believe, all values are one . . ."[9] Values are plural and they may conflict with each other; therein lies the necessity of choice at the heart of the ethical situation. Moreover, it needs to be added that ethical choice can never be of single items of value, the choice is always a commitment to a *way* of belief, to a *pattern* of values, to a *style* of life.

To neglect the activist social implications of belief is to fail in the obligation that is placed upon us by the ineluctable fact that man is by nature a political animal. To do so would fail to deal with the conditions prerequisite to the moral and spiritual life. However, the criticism of the cosmic-oriented outlook is not intended to justify the view that human personality can fully be realized in the social dimension alone. To confine values to social activities would leave our lives impoverished in spiritual quality. The growth of personality requires cultivation of the self through the humanities, through art, and through music. It is nourished—here lies the valid insight of cosmic-oriented idealism—by the elevation of the spirit through the deeply personal experience with an all-embracing reality. Democratic humanism need not disregard the "cosmic-matrix" although it does not accept it as the "spiritual undergirding" of the moral life. Self-transcendence is compatible with a homocentric, culturally and historically conditioned philosophy of life. What is denied is the validity of any religious or philosophic outlook which turns away from a central concern with the political and economic issues of our time.

A meaningful faith must have a finite object, an active social reference. A "pure faith" is apt to be a passive psychological state of acceptance, of submission to things as they are, or a lapse into irrationality. Faith suggests unrealized possibilities, connotes a dissatisfaction with the present, holds out hope for the future. We retain faith in human nature despite evidences of its corruption; we have faith that racial discrimination will ultimately be abolished although

[9] Cole, *op. cit.*, p. 55.

it is still widespread; we build our lives on faith in democracy despite its rejection today by a large part of the world and our own lagging and faulty implementation of it.

Faith confronts the existential facts of life but does not yield to them; it recognizes that active effort must be applied if the envisaged ideal is to be brought nearer to realization. Faith is compatible with truth but it must not be confused with it. Herein lies a primary difficulty, for faith in the mind of the believer tends to assume the garb of truth. The word "truth" is notoriously ambiguous—in common parlance it signifies any belief in which we place our trust, whether on the basis of authority, on intuition, on self-evidence, on reason, or on scientific verification. In general discourse, we may speak of moral truths or religious truths or artistic truths. But such usage tends to endow beliefs or insights which we regard as valuable or significant with the sanction of objectivity and certainty.

Truth, significance, value, and faith are much intermingled in the conduct of life's affairs, but clarity of thought demands that we remain aware of what distinguishes them in discourse. The term "truth" is relevant to events, implies a relation of agreement between statements and the existences which they describe. It is appropriately used with different degrees of precision in common-sense statements of facts and with reference to the conclusions arrived at by carefully devised methods of inquiry in the sciences. A true statement is always potentially significant, but it may also be trivial, or, in particular instances, be "incompetent, irrelevant, and immaterial." The sphere of significances and values is wider than the province of truth, may contribute more to the enrichment of life's experiences. Nevertheless, significance and value must respect the claim of truth; we must ever be on our guard not to confuse them with truth. Faith goes beyond ascertained truth. Still it dare not be based on untruth. Faith lives in a world of possibility but at the same time abjures the existentially impossible.

The term belief extends over the whole range of human judgments from those we acknowledge as true to those we accept on faith. Beliefs vary in degree of certainty: a belief may be an unchallenged assumption taken for granted, it may be a hypothesis tentatively held as a basis for inquiry as well as a scientific conclusion, experimentally verified. Beliefs are conative as well as cognitional forms of kinetic and potential energy. Scientific beliefs primarily concerned with knowledge and explanation are nevertheless closely linked to human endeavor. Beliefs about values may represent aesthetic judgments only, but they are, even more than scientific beliefs, directly concerned with implications for conduct.

We may, therefore, accept the definition suggested by Charles S. Peirce that a belief is a general principle or idea "upon which a man is prepared to act";[10] but we should add the reservation, "when action is called for." A belief may remain dormant; it need not prescribe beforehand every action for every instance as in religious systems of casuistry. But it should supply sufficiently clear guiding principles for individual conduct and for social policy. A general belief properly allows consideration of circumstances but at the same time sets bounds to what is permissible. It may employ strategy in implementation, taking into account factors of time and place, but the sacrifice of principle to expediency nullifies the essence of belief.

The beliefs to be outlined in the following chapters will relate to the various aspects of thought—the scientific and philosophic, the ethical and the religious, the political and the economic. The discussion will be organized around three areas: the nature of science and its relation to values; aspects of a humane ethic; the reconstruction of the economic and political order. Underlying the present exposition is the idea that a philosophy must be seen in its totality, particularly in its reference to these critical issues. However briefly each area is touched upon, to discuss them all is necessary in order to make the point of view evident. This is particularly true for the discussion of education, the subject of the concluding section, on which all cultural and social influences converge. In the course of the presentation, the metaphysical position will be indicated. But the unity of thought as far as it may be attained is not to be regarded as the deductive consequence of an ontological premise. In the pattern of conception to be here proposed, it is the social phase—particularly the ethical-political core of human organization—that will be kept in the foreground. It is part of the thesis that no complete harmony can be achieved in the actions of the existential world or, for that matter, in the universe of thought that deals with existence. The ideal and the actual are ever in a state of tension.

---

[10] Peirce reports it as "Bain's definition of belief;" see "Pragmatism in Retrospect: A Last Formulation," in *The Philosophy of Peirce*, Justus Buchler, ed., (New York, 1940).

Only a malignant end can follow the
systematic belief . . . that all truth is one
truth; that all experience is compatible
with all other; that total knowledge is
possible; that all that is potential can exist
as actual. J. ROBERT OPPENHEIMER

2.

Scientific Explanation and Moral Judgment

THE DIVERSITY OF KNOWLEDGE

EVERYTHING that man knows or could possibly know, we may grant, is a product of human experience. Our beliefs about nature, our ethical ideas, our metaphysical systems, our visions of God, no doubt, are impregnated with man's creative imagination. Conceptions asserted as scientific truth as well as creeds acknowledged as matters of faith may be viewed as having been worked out by men in their doings and reflections, in their struggles and aspirations, in their sufferings and enjoyments in the course of the affairs of life. As a corollary, the validation of our beliefs must be affected by human experience and judgment.

However, of itself, the broad assertion that our beliefs are the product of human experience and are subject to human judgment yields little positive guidance. The word "experience" which plays so large a part in modern philosophic discussion is a slippery concept, a "weasel word," as it has been called. In the German subjective idealism of the nineteenth century—and in its English and American counterparts—"experience" denotes inner states of consciousness. It implies that intuition is a valid mode of grasping truth, of gaining insight into the nature of the universe, of achieving communion with an Absolute

23

that transcends the existential world. It favors and supports the religious, the spiritual, the metaphysical. On the other hand, in British empirical thought, the term "experience," on which it rests, maintains that sense impressions are the ultimate basis of knowledge. Its affiliations are with science, its connotations are secular and commonsensical; it abjures the a priori and distrusts the speculative. In the Deweyan philosophy, in which the factor of "mind," central to idealism, is grafted on to the British empirical stock, the concept of experience becomes even more difficult as it is made the source and criterion of all forms of knowledge, of scientific thought, of personal ethics, and of social policy.

A first step in the endeavor to develop a pattern of defensible beliefs is to abandon the idea that there is a single principle, of substance or of method, adequate for all kinds of understanding. We must rid ourselves of the metaphysical temptation to explain this pluralistic universe of ours through one of its aspects alone—be this matter or spirit, unity or diversity, change or Being. Equally must we deny that there is a primary way of knowing, a methodological master-key that will open the doors of the many mansions in the grand estate of knowledge. This cautionary admonition applies to the rationalism which holds that an absolute a priori is the foundation as well as to the empiricism which bases all on experience. It certainly applies to the intuitionalism which believes that the most significant truths are revealed to us in a flash of immediate insight. The rejection of a monistic metaphysics appertains to the conception that locates reality in the individual instance, in the given sense-data, as well as the philosophies which begin with universals, with general assumptions, and transcendental absolutes and educes all reliable knowledge from such premises. Not to be excepted from this criticism is "the method of intelligence," the Deweyan interpretation of scientific method, when this is put forward as the all-sufficient instrument of ethical judgment and social reconstruction as well as a means of furthering inquiry in the natural sciences.

To maintain that the several realms of inquiry are distinct is something different from holding that there are walls of separation dividing them or that there is no interaction or interrelation among them. Conceptions overflow and penetrate different areas of understanding. The religious aspiration for unity has been a factor in the scientific endeavor to formulate uniform laws of nature. Psychological findings as to the relation of native impulses to environmental influences may make our moral judgments and our penal codes more humane.

Elements of experience, of reason, of intuition enter into all phases of knowledge in various v.　　　　　　　　ferent proportions. There are persistent common problems ﹏　　　y effort to ascertain warranted belief, e.g., the relation of common observation to scientific inquiry, of the individual to the collective judgment, of strict inference from data to imaginative exploration of hypotheses, of the relevance of each particular of truth to "the background which is the unbounded Universe."[1] There are no wholesale answers to these many aspects of inquiry; in each area, there is a different configuration of crucial questions and of possible answers. Nor can we expect to achieve the same kind and the same degree of certitude in all spheres of human understanding. Aristotle, who, it will be remembered, was not indifferent to the problem of the unity of knowledge, noted in the *Ethics*, "We must be content in each class of subjects with the accuracy of such a kind as the subject matter allows and to such an extent as is proper to the inquiry."

Every formulation of a general method of knowing unrelated to the distinctive content of the phase of experience under investigation, when not so general as to be fruitless, is likely to mislead. In this chapter comment will be made on three areas of scientific inquiry—mathematics, physics, and a third realm in which the problem of purposes, values, or ends is involved, e.g., biology, psychology, sociology. This analysis will serve as a foil for the discussion of the relation of science to ethics. The thesis is that while findings in biology, psychology and anthropology may modify our moral conventions in some respects, affect the treatment of deviates, and aid in the better realization of accepted ethical standards, neither science nor scientific method can determine or greatly affect the basic ethical aims of a society. The chapter will conclude with a sketch of several polarities of thought within which the present exposition is framed.

THE MATHEMATICAL GROUNDWORK

From classic Greek times until the nineteenth century, when non-Euclidean geometries were invented, mathematics was regarded as the science which provided certain, necessary, absolute, ideal truth. Long before, as early as the second millenium B.C., practical knowledge of numerical relations—as in determining the calendar, surveying land, and keeping accounts—had been highly developed in Babylonia and in Egypt. It was the Greeks, however, who created mathematics as a theoretical science, made of it an instrument for the understanding

---

[1] Alfred North Whitehead, "Mathematics and the Good," in *The Philosophy of Alfred North Whitehead*, Paul Arthur Schilpp, ed., (Evanston, 1941), p. 670.

of nature. Their evaluation of its significance as a key to knowledge is indicated by the name they gave to the study of arithmetic and geometry, namely, *máthema*, that is, "learning." The arithmetic proportion between the hypotenuse of right-angled triangles and its sides was known well enough for use in measurements a thousand years before Pythagoras of Samos devised a proof for it. Perhaps the famous theorem in geometry was connected with the name of this religious mystic because of his great concern for its philosophic implications. He saw in it a confirmation of his belief that "Number rules the universe," an idea which was to have a decisive influence on the whole character of Western scientific thought.

The communitarian brotherhood established by Pythagoras was an ethically-centered philosophic society. It was devoted to religious contemplation as much as to mathematical speculation. Mystical ideas characterized much of the doctrine of the Pythagoreans in the latter as well as in the earlier period of their organization. The Pythagorean doctrine was, nevertheless, a movement away from the purely emotional, darkly orgiastic, tendencies of earlier Greek sacred cults. It introduced an element of reason, of measure and proportion, of boundary and form, as a means of understanding nature and of ordering the conduct of life. In thus exalting the rational aspects, the Pythagoreans aimed not only to contain the demonic impulsions but also to counteract the conceptions of those atomists who regarded the universe as a fortuitous combination of material particles. The Pythagorean strain is evident in Plato who regarded the universe as mathematically constructed, as manifesting a rational-spiritual design, which was at once a principle of order that redeemed the world from chaos and a pattern of perfection that offered a model for the idea of the good.

The mathematical Weltanschauung contained an intuition, "that only through number and form could man grasp the nature of the universe."[2] This Pythagorean-Platonic insight, at times with mystical overtones, played an essential part in the modern scientific movement that began with the Renaissance. Copernicus arrived at the heliocentric theory by picturing a simpler pattern for the paths of the heavenly bodies than that postulated in the Ptolemaic system, one which he believed to be more in accord with the Pythagorean outlook. To the mathematical defense of his theory he added the aesthetic consideration that it exhibited "the admirable harmony in the world." Tycho Brahe, who collected a vast amount of accurate astronomical

[2] Tobias Dantzig, *Number: The Language of Science* (New York, 1930), p. 43.

information and who emphasized the importance of careful observation, maintained, nevertheless, that some hypothesis of a patterned world system had to be assumed if any intelligent observation were at all to be made. Johannes Kepler, who "reduced to order the chaos of data" left by the great Danish astronomer, was impelled, even more than Copernicus, by a quasi-religious fervor, by a "passion to uncover the magic of mere numbers and to demonstrate the music of the spheres."[3] It was his mathematical genius which enabled him to discover the three laws of planetary motion and to substitute the postulate of elliptical planetary movements for the time-honored belief in the uniform circular motion of the heavenly bodies. Kepler's achievements would not have been possible without the advances in astronomical observations; on the other hand, he could not have made the discoveries if he had not been seeking geometric forms into which the observations could be fitted.

Between the seventeenth and nineteenth centuries, as attention was focused on terrestial mechanics, experimentation came to be increasingly recognized as a necessary component of scientific investigation. However, the mathematical perspective remained an integral element both in the theory of scientific method as well as in the actual conduct of inquiry. The popular view that Galileo relied primarily on observation and experiment is a half-truth. He was indeed a perceptive observer and carried on experiments to verify his hypotheses. As in his interest in improving the telescope, he recognized the importance of instrumentation as a means of accurate observation. He certainly rejected the position that general propositions could be asserted as true on purely logical grounds when there was no evidence to support them. But in the first instance his investigations were directed by the Platonist insight that nature was ordered on mathematical lines. His observations took on form in his mind through quantitative arrangement and geometric patterns.[4] He solved problems by mathematical analysis as much as by experimental demonstration. He was at pains to show that a principle derived from the observation of a relatively small number of cases could be used to ascertain new facts "without the need of recourse to experiment." Assuming the necessity of verifying predictions by subsequent observation and experimentation, Galileo laid emphasis on the demonstrative and constructive value of

[3] Herbert Butterfield, *The Origins of Modern Science* (London, 1951), p. 56.

[4] Galileo engaged in "thought experiments" which he never tried out. He discusses what would happen if a stone were dropped from the mast of a moving vessel and arrives at the correct answer which was only many years later confirmed by actual trial (Butterfield, *op. cit.*, pp. 71ff.).

mathematics along several lines: for the induction of general principles from particular observations, for the resolution of apparent discrepancies in observed phenomena, and for the extension of knowledge beyond that already obtained through observation.

The mathematical-experimentalist approach exemplified in the work of Galileo became the accepted method for the study of nature in modern times. Francis Bacon, who "wrote on science like a Lord Chancellor," popularizing a one-sided view of experimentation, nevertheless recognized that mathematics had a role to play in the physical sciences. His distrust of it, like his prejudice against scholastic disputation, arose because in the past it had been used, along with logic, to restrict knowledge instead of serving as an instrument for its advance. René Descartes, on the other hand, magnified the office of mathematics: he believed that God had created the world in accord with predetermined laws which could be accounted for mathematically, could be deduced with precision from the simple ideas of motion and extension. In his view, experimentation had some part to play in ascertaining which of the possible variations of the general law of nature God had chosen to adopt. Isaac Newton brought the movement of uniting mathematics and experimental method to a culmination. In his work on optics, he employed experimentation extensively. He was suspicious of speculative hypotheses not deduced from phenomena, considering the inductive method of drawing conclusions only from observation and experiment the only true scientific procedure. But his greatest achievement, the formulation of the universal law of gravitation, resulted from a feat of mathematical demonstration. Burtt summarizes Newton's conception of science, *"as the exact mathematical formulation of the processes of the natural world."*[5]

In the synthesis elaborated by Immanuel Kant, the mathematical component retained primacy. Starting from the assumption that science implied absolute, necessary, universal truth and impressed by David Hume's argument that experience could never provide such truth, Kant believed that he had found a way out of scepticism by building on man's perception of time and space which he conceived to be mathematical in nature. Arithmetic and geometry, respectively the sciences of temporal and spacial relations, together provided the a priori structural frame which made indubitable knowledge a possibility. However, science required content as well as form, and content, he agreed, could only be supplied by experience. Thus scientific

[5] E. A. Burtt, *Metaphysical Foundations of Modern Physical Science* (New York, 1925), p. 223.

knowledge resulted from the incorporation of empirical findings into the intuitive rational principles of knowledge—of the primary forms of time and space, and the auxiliary categories, e.g., universality and casuality, quantity and quality, relation and modality. For Kant, as Collingwood summarizes, "natural science is essentially an applied mathematics."[6] However, in Kant's view, scientific judgment applied only to the phenomenal world of nature; it could give no secure knowledge of "the thing in itself," of the reality that lay behind experience. Nor could science provide a basis for ethics, for the belief in freedom, in reality, or in God. These aspects of knowledge involved an act of faith and a resolution of commitment.

The carefully reasoned Kantian construction was erected on presupositions which stood in harmony with the mode of scientific investigation in astronomy and in physics during the seventeenth and eighteenth centuries. It broke down under the impact of development during the nineteenth and twentieth centuries. There were changes in social and religious thought which weakened the idea of a pre-existent original truth and turned attention away from the search for an a priori metaphysical foundation. Within the field of science, mathematics lost its dominating position as the role of experimentation increased in chemistry and biology. In these areas of investigation, inductive classification played a relatively large part and empirical verification prevailed over mathematical demonstration. The discovery of new geometries brought with it the realization that the time-honored axioms of Euclid were not intuitive truths about the nature of space; they were assumptions required for the systematization of theorems which, in the first instance, had been suggested by experience. Of similar import were developments in arithmetic which implied that number was not the result of our innate perception of time but a highly developed form of logic.

Two contrasting views as to the nature of mathematics gained currency during the nineteenth century. The positive empiricist continued to believe that mathematics provided truth about the physical world, although he regarded such truth as derived, like all other forms of knowledge, from partial and piecemeal experience. John Stuart Mill, for example, went so far as to suggest that in a universe constituted differently from our own, two plus two might not equal four. The other point of view held that mathematics comprises a formal set of symbols inwardly consistent but devoid of factual knowledge, that its theorems are deductions from the axioms of pure logic. In the

---

[6] R. G. Collingwood, *An Essay on Metaphysics* (Oxford, 1940), p. 250.

logical positivist interpretation, a mathematical proposition is an analytic proposition whose "validity should follow simply from the definition of the terms contained in it."[7] In the more extreme conceptions of philosolphical analysis and linguistic philosophy, mathematical operations consist of manipulating symbols, playing a logical game under defined rules of inference. In fine, according to the schools of thought which regard it as a purely formal science, mathematics, erstwhile considered the very foundation and perfect figure of truth, gives by itself no truth at all, if the term truth is meant to apply to the existential world!

A reconciliation of the two views—the one that asserts that mathematics provides knowledge, even though imperfect, of the actual universe and the other which regards it merely as a purely formal science—may be effected, as Morris R. Cohen has suggested, by making a distinction between applied and pure mathematics.[8] Pure mathematics comprises a highly developed system of logically consistent propositions. It deals with a realm of possible perfect orders, with a universe of ideal existences whose features have no *necessary* relation to the world of actualities. In pure mathematics, every proposition or theorem may be deduced with absolute certainty from its axioms or postulates. However, whether the axioms or postulates are true in the sense of correspondence with experienced phenomena cannot be determined by mathematical operations alone. The task of determining the existential truth of any given axiom or of any proposition is the function of applied mathematics which brings us into the realm of physics. To ascertain whether any mathematical statement is true we must apply it to the actual world to which it refers, and examine it with appropriate instruments under defined conditions. As we pass from pure mathematics to its applications, we must sacrifice the Kantian "apodictic certainty" and content ourselves with the degree of reliability that empirical investigation warrants.

Although there is no absolute concordance between any particular mathematical system and the natural world as we know it through experience, common sense and science concur in the assumption that the agreement is close. As Santayana, recognizing that mathematics only makes explicit essential relations between certain terms, notes: "And yet, notoriously, mathematics holds true of things; hugs and permeates them far more closely than does confused and inconstant human perceptions."[9] The history of science bears witness to the inti-

---

[7] A. J. Ayer, *Language, Truth and Logic* (London, 1950), p. 82.
[8] *Reason and Nature* (New York, 1931), pp. 171-173.
[9] George Santayana, *The Realm of Truth* (New York, 1938), p. 2.

mate interconnection between mathematical thought and knowledge of the world. Euclidean geometry was not drawn fully elaborated as a coherent system from the resources of pure mind; it was the fruit of a long historical development which began with the need for land measurements, as the term "geometry" indicates. The marvelous advance in scientific theory during the Renaissance, pervaded though it was by a mathematical outlook, was, nevertheless, stimulated by concern with problems in architecture, shipbuilding, and particularly by interest in military engineering. Galileo wrote to a friend that it was the problem of the flight of projectiles that led him to study the gravitational pull of bodies, and he opened the discussion in the *Discourses on the Two New Sciences* by noting that the Venetian arsenal provided a large field for investigation, particularly in the field of mechanics. The same interplay between practical needs, experimentation in physics, and mathematical concepts is illustrated in the development of the theory of relativity furthered by interest in optical and electro-magnetic phenomena and facilitated by the advance in mathematics during the nineteenth century.

Mathematics, in consonance with observed phenomena, is also a powerful instrument of discovery. It points to possibilities, creates expectancies which may be verified by future findings. At its higher levels, mathematics involves an element of creative imagination disciplined by ordered thinking. Mathematical propositions are products of thought, mental constructions, but they are not mere figments of the imagination.[10] They refer to orders, patterns, configurations that exist or could exist in the natural and social world; they describe relations of *things*, not just relations in general. Since its generalizations are inductions by inference from observed phenomena, it is, at the same time, a means of eliminating the purely fanciful. Mathematics thus has a two-sided function: it organizes empirical observations into a coherent logical system; it offers an instrument of extending valid knowledge to ever wider ranges.

It is abundantly clear in our day of nuclear energy, of missiles and rocketry, of electronics and cybernetics, that both pure and applied mathematics are essential for the understanding of nature and for

[10] Ernst Cassirer, *The Problem of Knowledge*. (New Haven, 1950), pp. 61-62: "Mathematical thought can never be a mere cogitation, for no bounds could be set to such a process; given free rein it might pass over into pure fantasy. Hence even in pure mathematics we cannot speak of "free creations" of thought without endangering its content of truth. There must always be *a fundamentum in re;* it must always be related to some given factual content with which its ideas correspond and which it will bring to expression."

its control. With all due recognition of the part that empirical observation and experimental verification have played in achieving knowledge of the physical world, it is necessary to realize that without the mind's intuitive capacity to grasp relations, to see forms and figures, science would never have risen above the purely practical level of its condition in early civilization. The study of mathematics is, in itself, an immensely fascinating activity as is the game of chess for those who have a talent for it. Taken alone, as a system of manipulating symbols, it has as little significance for life as has the game of chess. But united with empirical and experimental inquiry, it has power that surpasses the magical.

A reservation is in order at this point. The knowledge that the mathematical-experimental method can give is knowledge of the world of nature; to what degree it is applicable to human behavior and to ethical questions is another matter.

THE NEW PHYSICS AND CHANGED CONCEPTIONS

With the enlargement of the role of observation and experiment in scientific work, "experience," in the empirical connotation came to be regarded as the source of all valid knowledge. This was true especially of British thought which occupied a leading position during the nineteenth century. In practice, mathematical and logical treatment of the data of experience continued to be an integral element of scientific research. But the experimental component captured the focus of attention and exercised a major influence on philosophy as well as on popular conceptions. The power of yielding certain demonstrated truth formerly attributed to logic and mathematics was now transferred to the realm of experimental physics. Experience based on sense-perception and experimentation, it was thought, provided general truths, universally applicable; the laws of nature inferred from the observation of many invariable sequences revealed an underlying uniformity of a mechanistically determined cosmos. If scientific generalizations did not accord with newly observed facts, the fault lay in improper formulation, in the inadequacy of the observations, or in the inaccuracy of the measuring instruments. That there might be indeterminacy in nature was not admissible in the predominent nineteenth-century mode of thinking.

A disturbing note entered philosophic discussion with David Hume's criticism of the idea of causation. He did not attack determinism directly. But his view that our sense of causation was merely an idea in the mind, derived from the experience that certain antecedents were regularly followed by certain consequences, robbed the concept "cause" of its coercive force, divested it of the power to compel the effects with which it was associated. From this, it followed that although experience could provide us with workable knowledge it did not give assurance of certainty. We had no other recourse but to base our actions on experience, but we could not be sure that the future would repeat the past. Only in mathematics and logic could we have conclusions that of necessity followed from axioms and premises, but such truths told us nothing about the actual world in which we live.

John Stuart Mill was influenced by Hume in holding that experience was the basis of our knowledge of causation, and pressing the doctrine of experience to an extreme, he maintained that mathematics and logic, as well as physics and politics, rested on experience. He straddled the issue raised by Hume—whether cause implied a necessary and compelling connection between experienced events or represented merely an invariant sequential relation. He assumed that causation was a universal principle underlying all phenomena and that it was amply varified by experience; in effect his outlook was conditioned by the Newtonian principle of mechanistic determinism. While he assumed that knowledge gained through experience was, at any given time, partial and imperfect, he believed that if all the factors at work were empirically known, then it would be possible to predict the subsequent development with certainty. In Mill's philosophy, the element of possible contingency in nature is not recognized any more than it was in the traditional cosmological outlook.

The conception of the nature of the physical universe that has been taking shape during the last half century under the impact of the revolutionary concepts of field, quanta, and relativity differs decisively from the presupposition of a perfectly ordered, mechanistically determined universe postulated in the classical Newtonian position. The physical universe, heretofore regarded as constructed of solid bricks of matter now appears to be composed of volatile energies. What was conceived to be empty space turns out to be a field of energy whose structure is as important in determining the laws of magnetism and electrical phenomena as are the properties of the particles contained within it. Matter and energy are regarded as interchangeable: matter is concentrated energy and energy is dispersed matter.

The atom is liberated from its Newtonian incarnation as a "solid, hard, massy, impenetrable" particle; it resembles rather a magnetic field with a nucleus around which electrons revolve. It no longer moves mechanically in accordance with compelling laws: its elementary components taken singly seem to be free-wheeling. Only when the elementary units of matter-energy are dealt with in large aggregates can predictable regularities be discerned, and then only with a calculated degree of probability. The ideas of absolute motion and absolute space are abandoned; motion is always "*relative* motion of one object with respect to another." Throughout modern physics relations among things are as significant as the properties of things; one might say, "relations are 'the thing'."

The new conceptions suggest that, as the ancient Lucretius believed, there is radical contingency in nature. It should be borne in mind, however, as the philosophers of science assure us, that the Newtonian principles may still be considered as true, although in a carefully defined sense. They are fully applicable to terrestial mechanics where tangible masses move with ordinary velocities, i.e., the earth rotating on its axis or revolving in its orbit around the sun. Only when velocities are extraordinarily great in comparison with infinitely small masses, as in light radiation and in electro-magnetic phenomena, do the Newtonian principles falter—they do not apply, or they do not apply with sufficient accuracy to explain the phenomena observed. The newer conceptions associated with relativity theory and quantum mechanics do not invalidate the classical laws as working principles in the delimited field of their application. They provide refined conceptual instruments serviceable in the realm of experience to which the Newtonian principles refer and, in addition, are applicable also to the more intricate nuclear world and vaster astronomical realms with which modern physics deals.

The realization that Newton's principles, as traditionally formulated, are not valid for the explanation of subatomic processes has led to the belief, in some quarters, that radical indeterminism pervades the universe, that the time-honored laws of causation can no longer be maintained. The Heisenberg "principle of indeterminacy," it is sometimes loosely said, "opens up to us a glimpse of nature that may at bottom be irrational and chaotic."[11] Far-fetched conclusions concerning ethics and religion have been drawn in popular writings from the allegedly "acausal" behavior of protons, neutrons, and electrons; and fundamental questions with reference to chance and determinism have been raised in serious philosophical discussions. However, mod-

[11] William Barrett, *Irrational Man, A Study in Existential Philosophy*, Doubleday Anchor Book (Garden City, N.Y., 1962), p. 38.

ern physics gives no warrant for a definitive wholesale answer to this ancient metaphysical problem. The hypothesis of "uncertainty relations" refers to atomic events, not to nature in its entirety, and even in this sphere it is only one factor of a highly complex analysis.[12]

On the implications of quantum mechanics for the question of a general theory of causation there is no unanimity. The majority of physicists in the field of quantum mechanics tend to assume the hypothesis of an inherent indeterminism in nature and to believe that the observed regularities can be explained statistically, i.e., "that quantum theory deals with laws referring to crowds and not individuals."[13] Einstein, however, never gave up his belief that the present quantum theory was temporary and would be replaced by another that did not involve the assumption that "God was playing dice"; he retained faith "in perfect laws in the world of things existing as real objects." Ernest Nagel, in his thorough review of the problem, "Causality and Indeterminism in Physical Theory," concludes: "the question whether these processes are absolutely fortuitous is not an issue of scientific moment, for . . . quantum theory is compatible with either alternative."[14]

Whatever the metaphysical implications of modern physics may be, in total effect—despite the terms "relativity theory" and "uncertainty principle"—the contemporary conceptions increase the possi-

---

[12] The Heisenberg hypothesis of "uncertainty relations" holds that in subatomic processes it is not possible to determine *simultaneously* both the velocity and the position of a particle with *arbitrary high accuracy*. It was a factor in resolving the problem of the "dual nature" of subatomic entities which could be characterized either as "waves" (continuous emissions) or "particles" (intermittent bombardments). The attempt to explain these atomic events by Newtonian principles led to contradictions. Heisenberg's hypothesis was compatible with the theory of "complementarity" put forward by Niels Bohr which allowed the use of both models, the wave and the particle, without contradiction.

The significance of the hypothesis of "uncertainty relations" outside of the sphere of atomic processes is questionable, to say the least. As Heisenberg notes, "quantum theory is only a small sector of atomic physics and atomic physics is only a very small sector of modern science." Although he believes that quantum theory involves a change in the "concept of reality," Heisenberg does not use it as a key to the understanding of human affairs. On the contrary, he stresses the inadequacy of the concepts of physics, either Newtonian or quantum theory, for explaining all aspects of reality.

For a popular presentation of Heisenberg's conceptions, see his *Physics and Philosophy*, (New York, 1958). A critique, including a linguistic analysis, is presented in Ernest Nagel, *The Structure of Science* (New York, 1961), pp. 293 ff.

[13] Leopold Infield, *Albert Einstein, His Work and Its Influence on Our World* (New York, 1956), p. 110.

[14] *The Structure of Science* (New York, 1961), p. 335.

bility of accurate prediction of physical events in a wider range of phenomena than was possible under classical assumptions. There is no return to the doctrine of rigid determination which it was assumed underlay the Newtonian world view. The assumption—that simple causes inevitably lead to simple effects and that a given combination of causes necessarily leads to a known complex of effects—yields in current thought to the statistical conception that certain groups of factors are generally followed by other groups with a calculated degree of probability. We can never make unerring statements about individuals; and in the judgment of aggregates, no absolute certitude can be assumed. Our ability to predict depends on a multiplicity of factors and on a context of conditions. Nevertheless in a wide range of physical events we may achieve a high degree of predictability, a virtual—though not an absolute—certainty that anticipated results will be realized.

The change from the Newtonian view of the nature of the physical universe has been accompanied by a radical revision of the associated positivist attitude of mind which dominated the conception of scientific method for the greater part of the modern era. Positivism, following Newton's premise that principles of science "are deduced from phenomena and afterward made general by induction," regarded scientific propositions as generalizations arrived at by the study of the properties of things known to us through the senses—either by direct perception or with the aid of instruments. The work of the mind came *after* the data had been collected: its task was to give "comprehensive and condensed reports on our observations and nothing else." It rejected a priori assumptions as interfering with freedom of judgment and also deprecated speculation as likely to lead to fruitless argumentation. In the earlier stages, sharing Newton's mistrust,[15] positivism was suspicious of hypotheses, although in later developments, tentative generalizations—made on the basis of past observations to be checked experimentally—became recognized as legitimate and necessary. Underlying was an assumption that the world could be known in the raw without the mediation of thought-forms.

Contemporary philosophy of science based on the new physics takes a different turn. It emphasizes the part played by concepts, symbols, and models in scientific thought, recognizes the need of a

[15] Newton took the word "hypothesis" to mean a conjecture not deduced from phenomena or supported by experimental proof. Using the term in this sense, he advised, "one should abstain from contemplative hypotheses, as from improper argumentation." He admitted the use of hypotheses insofar as they furnished experiments to explain but not to determine the property of things.

basis of presuppositions and of a conceptual framework of theory, appreciates the creative part played by "ideal experiments."[16] It remains in line with empiricism in its insistence on verification by experience. But in some respects it reintroduces, in a reconstructed form, the idea of the reality of universals that had found expression in classic and medieval thought. It makes a critical analysis of the relation of laws of nature to facts of nature, of hypotheses to established principles, of the descriptive to the explanatory tasks of the scientific enterprise. It takes cognizance of the diversity of levels and realms of knowledge, of the difference between science and the common understanding. It recognizes the limitations of science as well as its potentialities. In total effect, it represents a new pattern of ideas and makes for a different outlook on the nature of human thinking than that which dominated the modern age. Some of the salient features of the current conception of scientific explanation are summarized in the following section.

FEATURES OF SCIENTIFIC EXPLANATION

All sciences represent logically unified bodies of knowledge. A distinction, however, needs to be made between descriptive sciences, e.g., minerology, botany, and geology, on the one hand, and the theoretical sciences, e.g., physics, chemistry, and biology, on the other. The former, sometimes described as science in the "natural-history stage," answer to the definition of science as "organized" or "classified" common sense. Explanation plays a part in the descriptive sciences, but in the main, they exemplify the conception that scientific generalizations represent carefully organized, accurate summaries of facts observed. The theoretical sciences likewise have their source in everyday experiences—as in physics, that water freezes and evaporates, that bodies fall and move when pushed, that the sun gives light and casts shadows. Moreover, they include and rely on organized classified knowledge. However, the primary function of the theoretical sciences is to *explain* the phenomena observed, not alone to describe them.

The distinctive goal of the theoretical sciences is to formulate

---

[16] Leopold Infield traces the beginning of Einstein's special and general theories of relativity to early speculations during youth, the former to wondering about a man running after a light ray, the latter, to imagining a person's behavior in a falling elevator. (Leopold Infield, *Albert Einstein*, New York, 1950, pp. 48ff.) Heisenberg notes that quantum physicists often fruitfully discuss "ideal experiments" carefully designed to clarify critical questions. (Werner Heisenberg, *Physics and Philosophy*, New York, 1958, p. 36.)

comprehensive systematic principles of explanation which will account for the observed regularities and facilitate accurate prediction in a wide range of phenomena. The great triumphs of science result from the extraordinary explanatory power of theoretical analysis. Physics, generally assumed as offering a model for scientific method, is a prime example of a theoretical science. Its laws and principles are formulations of patterns of relations, conceptual frameworks within which facts can be embraced and understood. They represent idealized statements theoretically of universal validity in the realms of subject matter to which they refer. In practice, however, the scope of applicability, though wide, is always limited: any statement of the law or principles must be accompanied by supplementary conditional provisions.

As Stephen Toulmin expresses it: "Physics is not the natural history of the inert." It stands at a far remove from common sense modes of observation and explanation. The science of physics isolates certain properties usually found together in nature and brings together under a single principle matters which ordinarily seem very different, e.g., Newton's law of gravitation assimilates the behavior of tidal waves to falling bodies, Einstein's theory of relativity makes mass and energy interchangeable. Physics creates new terms and uses old words in new meanings. Such terms as points and lines, particles and waves, forces and masses, when used by the physicist are subtle abstractions, the product of highly defined intellectual activity. They have but a distant resemblance to the analogous common sense objects; they are justifiable inferences arrived at by complex chains of reasoning, not primary sense-data. What they mean can fully be understood only through mathematical symbols.

What a physicist means by an "experiment" has little resemblance to the "trial and error" procedure with which it sometimes is confounded in popular opinion and in educational literature. In physics, the construction of apparatus as well as the experiment itself must be strictly controlled by prior knowledge and by reference to theory. Without a clear conception of the problem and what to look for, as Toulmin says, "One might manipulate apparatus for a lifetime, and accumulate all the observations one cared to, without ever spotting what form the law should take."[17] The organization of the experiment requires a hypothesis, an idea of a possible solution, and the hypothesis can have meaning only in the framework of established

[17] Stephen Toulmin, *The Philosophy of Science*, Harper Torchbooks (New York, 1960), p. 64.

principles. Physics makes use also of prior mental exploration, of "thought" and "ideal" experiments which are carefully developed logical inferences, not random guesses. Modern physics emphasizes established knowledge and theoretical assumptions, as well as speculative exploration and projection of hypotheses, as prerequisite to the verification function of experimental activity.

The science of physics has not grown by collection of data or primarily by the addition of new facts. Advances in theory are based on earlier theory either as extensions, modifications, or rejections accompanied by a new formulation of theory. Changes in physical theory may result from various causes—from a new way of looking at the phenomena, from conclusions of experimentation, from the discovery of new facts. However, the addition of facts cannot, of itself, produce a new conception. As Conant points out: "A theory is overthrown by a better theory, never merely by contradictory facts. Attempts are first made to reconcile the contradictory facts to the existing conceptual scheme by some modification of the concept. Only a combination of the new concept with facts contradictory to the old ideas finally brings about a scientific revolution. And once this has taken place, then in a few short years discovery follows upon discovery and the branch of science in question progresses by leaps and bounds."[18]

Even when the new theory results in a radical reformulation, its significance can be understood only in contrast with the old. The laws and principles of physics represent a continuous development when viewed in historical perspective. But physical theories do not change every day. For long periods of time, once established, they remain "absolute presuppositions" prerequisite for the investigation of new problems. They become postulates whose truth or falsity is not, for the time being, an issue in dispute. Every scientific system has two parts: the one consists of the body of principles considered as well established; the other, the propositions which are regarded as being in the stage of "hypotheses." in the case of the former, the question raised is whether the law or principle applies to a particular instance, that is, whether the law or principle "holds." The question, "Is it true?" properly refers to the hypotheses but not to the framework of accepted theory.

The hypothesis, moreover, is never a random suggestion: it is organically related to the established body of knowledge and prin-

[18] James B. Conant, *On Understanding Science*, A Mentor Book (New York, 1951), p. 48.

ciples. It represents one element in a constellation of propositions and it cannot be either verified or overthrown by reference to isolated facts. The meaning of the hypothesis, the questions to be asked and the experiments to be devised to test it, all depend on accepting the established conceptual scheme as a basis. In the conduct of inquiry, the established principles are logically prior and prerequisite to the formulation and testing of the hypothesis. If verified, the hypothesis becomes part of the established body of theory.

It is not possible to question everything at once; something must be left standing. If one conceptual scheme is abandoned, another must be adopted before productive inquiry can be reinstituted. However, to assert that scientific laws and principles are not subject to question during a particular project of inquiry does not, of course, imply that they are never to be questioned. The scientist, as it is said, "must be prepared to challenge all preconceptions," that is to say, when there is scientific ground for challenge. Furthermore, although the truth quality of scientific laws and principles is not the issue in their role as postulates, they are not, as logical assumptions, merely the work of pure mind. Their validity in the last analysis derives from the fact that they have been developed in the course of investigation of definite problems and are empirically verifiable. Verification lies at the heart of the natural sciences.

The foregoing analysis is designed to counteract the notions that an experiment is a sort of trial-and-error operation, that scientific method and "thinking for oneself" are synonymous, that knowledge can best be advanced by independent inquiry without regard to established principles. It is intended to deny the view that *all* scientific propositions are hypotheses to be held tentatively, that all are equally subject to change, that "continuous inquiry" is the chief mark of the scientific attitude. On the contrary, the analysis indicates that the virtue of a conceptual scheme in the sciences is due to its being so well grounded in cumulative experience, so carefully formulated and so thoroughly tested in expertly devised experiments, that it remains serviceable as a basic presupposition for an extended period of time and for a wide range of phenomena.

LEVELS AND LIMITS OF SCIENTIFIC INVESTIGATION

There is a deeply rooted tendency in Western culture, inherited from Greek philosophy, to seek in nature the ground principles of all knowledge. For an extended period, the Pythagorian-Platonic view that mathematics reflected the essential order of nature domi-

nated the philosophy of science. In the centuries immediately preceding our own, physics gained pre-eminence as the basic science,
and under the influence of the Newtonian conception, mechanistic
determinism became widely accepted as a primary characteristic of
the cosmos. The "reductionist" thesis was advanced—the idea that
complex phenomena of human behavior could be broken down to
simpler levels: social phenomena could be reduced to the psychological, to the biological, and finally to the chemical and physical. The
same habit of thought, of regarding physics as a key to the nature of
the universe, has led some writers in recent years to the opposite
fallacy, to a reductionism in reverse. The suggestion of indeterminism
in the realm of atomic physics is made the ground for the belief that
free-will has an origin and a sanction in cosmic nature.

"Physics," "nature," "science" are often used interchangeably—a
tendency abetted by the derivation of "physics" from the Greek
word *physis*.[19] But physics, in the modern sense is only one branch
of the study of nature, and there is no warrant for the view that it can
provide either the basis or the method for all fields of study, not to
speak of serving as a key for the understanding of the cosmos as a
whole. The laws of nature, of which physics speaks, are not total
explanations of the universe at large, but statements referring to
defined areas of investigation. Even with reference to the relevant
areas, the principles of physics, however wide their range, always
have a limited application in practice. The concepts of new physics—
of field and probability, of the interdependent, relational character of
causal factors—imply the necessity of viewing phenomena in context,
of thinking in terms of levels and realms of existence.

Principles of explanation drawn from one sphere of investigation
cannot be automatically applied to other spheres; passing from one
branch of physics to another, or from physics to chemistry, requires
giving new meanings to old terms or the invention of new terms. It
means utilizing different types of diagrammatic representation, different instruments of observation and measurement, different modes
of mathematical treatment. The fact that each branch of science has
its body of knowledge and specialized personnel should make it evident that no easy transfer of principles is possible. Insofar as concep-

---

[19] In Greek thought, *physis*, like our word "nature," had a many-sided meaning in addition to its underlying connotation of "the intrinsic and permanent
qualitative constitution of things." It signified origin, cause, process of growth,
divine law, the totality of things. (See William Chase Greene, *Moira, Fate, Good
and Evil in Greek Thought*, Harper Torchbooks, New York, 1963, pp. 221-228;
also Appendix 27, p. 410f.)

tions are applied from one field to another, comparisons will have the character of analogies in which recognition of similarities will depend on the insight of the investigator rather than on logically necessary conclusions deduced from general principles.

The considerations which qualify the possibility of utilizing principles from one branch to another within the field of inorganic phenomena should lead to the abandonment of all vestiges of the "reductionist" conception. The major areas of investigation—the physical-chemical, the biological in its great divisions of plant and animal life, the human in its psychological and social dimensions—represent different patterns of organization, not only ascending orders of complexity. The more complex or higher levels are, to be sure, conditioned by the lower; the biological depends on physical and chemical processes, the human being as a living creature is conditioned by biological needs and impulses. Nevertheless, the higher levels can never be broken down into lower components as may be done in the inorganic field. Each level of organization represents an autonomous system of relations and can be understood, in last analysis, only through direct observation, in terms of its characteristics and in the framework of conditions under which it can maintain and fulfill its ends. Biological facts must be viewed with reference to biological functions; social facts must be examined in relation to human needs, purposes, and values.

As soon as we reach the level of living things, the physical and chemical factors must be seen in relation to the maintenance of the organism as a whole. Whether we characterize living things as "functional," as "purposeful," or as "teleological," it is evident that vital processes are controlled by discernible ends built into the organism. The biologist interests himself in physical and chemical processes in the measure that they facilitate or obstruct the life processes of self-preservation, growth, and reproduction. He is concerned with living things as *distinct* from nonliving. It is not enough to concede, as is sometimes done in defense of the reductionist position, that explanations drawn from physics and chemistry must be "supplemented by additional principles." The whole way of looking at the object of investigation must be altered as we pass from the realm of the inorganic to the organic. The presuppositions, the problems, the methods of study in the field of biology must be drawn from the field of biology; the types of experiment must be limited by the need of keeping the creature alive. These considerations apply with ever greater force as we move from plant to animal life, where consciousness and choice operate in varying degrees, and as we proceed through the range of animal life from fish to mammals, and from marsupials to primates.

When we come to the sphere of human life, to the fields of psychology and social organization, the experimental method—which plays the crucial role of verification in the inorganic sphere and remains an important feature in biological inquiry—can serve only as an auxiliary mode of investigation. Apart from the danger of injuring the subject of investigation, experimentation with human beings must be narrowly limited since this requires the isolation of variables, the possibility of repeated trials, and the creation of ideal laboratory conditions. Human beings must be studied in relation to social conditions and institutional arrangements under which they live or could possibly live. Given certain defined objectives, as in the field of learning, e.g., the problem of teaching children to read, experimental investigation may have a part to play. Although even here, the superiority of scientific method, in its strict experimentalist interpretation, over empirical inference by trained teachers or common sense analysis is far from apparent. One factor in the problem is that in human affairs we are concerned with each individual and not only with average performance of large groups.

In the study of personal behavior, it is necessary to rely on various types of investigation other than experimental. The "case study" method for instance, as in clinical psychology and psychotherapy, may offer greater promise, although it depends to a large extent on the insight of the investigator and leaves much room for subjective interpretation. In the study of society, in economic and political questions, experimentation is obviously impossible, since this would involve periodical resetting of interrelated institutional arrangements including basic changes in the legal and educational systems. Scientific method in psychological and social studies needs to be broadened to mean "controlled empirical inquiry," using a phrase suggested by Professor Nagel.[20] Perhaps even this concept requires qualification. In the social sciences, investigation must rely largely on descriptive studies, comparisons of different cultural environments, statistical analyses. At times it must be limited to post-mortem diagnosis of factors at work in historical change. Such forms of study have value as reliable knowledge when a degree of consensus among trained investigators is achieved. At present, this is far from the case. Studies in psychology and sociology, in economics and politics, provide informed judgments that may profitably be taken into consideration.

[20] *Op. cit.*, pp. 450ff.

But the use of the term "sciences" with reference to psychological and social studies may be questioned, since they lack a basis of agreed-upon principles and a dependable mode of validation.

The difficulties attending the application of the methods of the natural sciences to psychological and, especially, to social phenomena are compounded by the problem of values—a broad term which covers ethical conceptions, political philosophies, and economic theories. Inorganic phenomena exhibit properties, but reveal no purposes that need be taken into consideration. Biological phenomena have recognized functions to which inquiry is related. But human affairs are marked by conflicting interests and divergent value patterns as well as by different conceptions of the institutional forms required to realize common ends. As in the natural sciences, descriptive factual inquiries have their place in the social studies, but they would be of little significance if unrelated to specific needs and to the value systems of definite societies. Psychological and social studies are rightly and unavoidably related to human purposes, just as biological studies are properly related to the functions of living creatures.

In the behavioral sciences and in the social studies, the assumption of definite value-oriented points of view is as legitimate as it is unavoidable.[21] But the transfer to the field of attitudes developed in the study of physics, where the question of ends does not enter, has frequently led to the illusion that social science can and should be "neutral." As a result, the value orientation is driven underground. Notoriously, unavowed value-commitments affect the organization of research as well as the stated conclusions. The danger of misleading bias would be lessened if the ethical and political presuppositions were made explicit. As it is, much in the study of human affairs, particularly in the social area, is either disingenuous, pretending to an impossible neutrality or of trivial significance consisting of unrelated collections of factual materials. To make clear the value implications of social theory—of economic, political, and educational conceptions—is particularly important in our day of stark conflict in ideologies.

Neutrality is not objectivity. The one connotes noninvolvement,

---

[21] As Gunnar Myrdal states: "There is no way of studying social reality other than from the viewpoint of social ideals. A 'distinterested social science' has never existed and, for logical reasons, cannot exist. The value connotations of our main concepts represent our interest in the matter, gives direction to our thoughts and significance to our inferences. It poses the questions without which there are no answers." (*An International Economy*, New York, 1956 Appendix, p. 336. See also, Preface, p. x and chap. I, pp. 14, 15.)

passivity, perhaps indifference. Objectivity means submitting one's point of view to evidence, considering alternative positions fairly, viewing issues from a wider perspective than originally held, adopting a new point of view when this is warranted. It implies disinterestedness in the sense of dispassionate judgment, not lack of interest in the results of investigation. The natural sciences are not "neutral" with reference to the theoretical and practical problems presented in their fields of study; they are concerned with finding solutions in their fields of inquiry. In the natural sciences theory is both explanatory and directive; even when not immediately applied, theory is always relevant to possible practice. The same is true in the social studies, but there the relation of theory to practice is closer. In the social studies, theory is always a directive of practice, always related to furthering human interest and purpose. To attempt to improve human life is not a hindrance but a help to the psychological and the social sciences. The social theorist cannot avoid being both scientist and ethical philosopher, and he should be aware that he plays both roles so as not to confuse them with each other.

To summarize: the principles and methods of the physical sciences cannot serve as models for all fields of investigation. Each broad division of study, the physical, the biological, the social, is sufficiently different to warrant considering it autonomous—remembering that autonomy means a degree of independence within a wider frame of reference. Although some very general attitudes and modes of procedure may be discerned in all scientific activity, each area of investigation has its body of knowledge and principles, each its unresolved problems, each its special methods of study. This does not mean that science is advanced by narrow specialization; creative work in any field is stimulated by knowledge of related fields. At the same time, it is essential to bear in mind that each area of investigation gives us only an aspect of knowledge, not a key to the totality of knowledge. If this is true of the natural sciences, it applies with greater force to the social field where ethical evaluations are involved. To merge all types of controlled inquiry under the category of science, and to make all scientific method coincident with experimentation, is tantamount to obscurantism in reverse. It is as futile to attempt to derive ethical ends from physics, either Newtonian or Einsteinian, or from biology, either Lamarckian or Darwinian, as it is to attempt to understand natural phenomena from the study of anthropology or the history of culture.

Scientific inquiry implies attitudes of mind, a demand for logical consistency and objective verification, a "disinterested passion for truth," as is often said. At its highest levels, it involves an aesthetic impulse, an urge for ordered explanation, a striving to disclose a "pre-established harmony" in the universe. But attitudes alone cannot produce a science. Three factors are necessary to warrant calling any area of study a science. First there must be a body of verified knowledge and a consensus of principles on which to build. All scientific developments have grown out of criticism of earlier knowledge and assumptions. In the second place, scientific study demands special instrumentalities for observation and testing, requires accuracy of measurement and quantitative analysis. Not least, the pursuit of science requires specialized personnel, men competent in knowledge and skilled in the use of the instruments of investigation. Within each field in the highly developed sciences of our day, moreover, a considerable division of labor is required—research workers, teachers, theoreticians, and, perhaps one might add, philosophers. Every established science is a historically developed social institution, with its body of knowledge, accepted basic assumptions, and international corps of workers.

To reduce scientific method to a general mode of procedure or to a broad attitude of mind robs science of the characteristics responsible for its success—concentration on certain aspects of knowledge to the exclusion of others, slow accumulation of bodies of knowledge, invention of special techniques for study, subjection of the results of inquiry to the scrutiny of a competent body of investigators. The limitations on the transferability of scientific method to the general affairs of life are inherent in its nature. The definition of science as organized common sense has a certain merit in that it indicates that science is not a world apart, unrelated to ordinary experience and to common needs. Nevertheless, science, particularly physics, in its theoretical aspect on which its marvelous utilitarian success ultimately depends, represents a type of interest and of knowledge which is as far removed from common sense as can well be imagined. Science is specialized, it abstracts features of phenomena from their concrete embodiment, it is unconcerned with immediate application. Science yields a different sort of knowledge than that which common sense gives. But it should be emphasized that although it is different, science is not necessarily superior in all instances. Critical common sense which takes a large number of factors into consideration may well provide better judgments in the concrete existential problems which face men in daily life. This brings us to the question of the relation of scientific inquiry to ethics.

46

SCIENCE AND ETHICS

With the weakening of religiously sanctioned ethical conceptions and the coincident rise of trust in science as a source of secure knowledge, the belief gained ground that moral issues could be resolved by modes of inquiry that had proven effective in the study of nature. The movement to relate ethics to science represented a revolt against the restrictive moral absolutism and the inherent dualism of the theologically grounded traditional systems. It embodied an attempt to restore unity between men's beliefs about the forces at work in nature and conceptions of value. It embraced the hope, common to all ethical philosophy, of transcending parochial loyalties, national chauvinism, and racial prejudice, by a universal ethic, by a common human morality based on reason.

The experimentalist philosophy expounded by John Dewey is an outstanding example of the faith in scientific method—conceived broadly as "intelligent action." He regards it as significant for the establishment of ethical ends as for the achievement of reliable knowledge. Underlying the judgments made in the course of resolving practical and moral issues that arise in daily life, on the one hand, and in the most carefully conducted scientific inquiry, on the other, according to Dewey, there are the common essential elements of reflective thinking—the initiation of thought by a problem, the formulation of a proposed solution, the subjection of the hypothesis to the test of action, the final judgment by the consequences. He recognizes that science is not the only kind of valid knowledge and he emphasizes that in the practical application to life's affairs there needs be an interaction between the "refined products" of scientific inquiry and the "coarse everyday experience." But he makes the experimentalist method of the natural sciences the model for genuine knowing "because the operations of physical knowledge are so perfected and its scheme of symbols so well-devised."[22]

In this fusion of cognitional and moral judgment, Dewey was motivated primarily by a supreme concern with the problem of values. The application of the operational procedures as in experimental science, he believed would lead to ending the gap between thought and action, the contrast between profession and deed that has characterized much of Western civilization. It would resolve the sharp dualisms between the spiritual and the material, between the end and the means. Moreover, centering attention on the consequences of prospective action instead of basing judgment on precedents, would

[22] John Dewey, *The Quest for Certainty* (New York, 1929), p. 250.

lead to a new liberating orientation—to a future-centered outlook. He believed that the "method of intelligence" held the key to social reconstruction demanded by the democratic promise in interaction with new economic forces. In a summary statement of his view, he went so far as to attribute the crisis in contemporary life to the imbalance created by our systematic use of experimental method in determining the material conditions of social life while he continued to rely on custom, external authority, and on "so-called absolute ideals and standards" in the realm of moral values and social ends.[23]

Endorsement of Dewey's liberal, ethical, and social aims does not need to carry with it any agreement with his confident reliance on the scientific method as the primary means of advancing them. To attribute the moral difficulties experienced in personal affairs and the revolutionary upheavals in social organization mainly to the lag between traditional ideals and scientific modes of thought seems, on the face of it, a gross oversimplification. The belief that the primary remedy for our troubles is to be found in a new mode of inquiry savors of the ancient faith dear to the heart of the philosopher that knowledge is the sufficient key to virtue and to power.

In any case, Dewey's conception of scientific method is one-sided. Although on occasion he gives explicit recognition to the importance of "principles worked out in the past," in total effect he underplays the contribution made by the heritage of knowledge and of theory. In the interpretations of exponents of the experimentalist doctrine, particularly in the field of education, Dewey's moderating comments are generally left out of account. Scientific method becomes a synonym for "the open mind," criticism is translated to mean nonconformity, an invidious contrast is drawn between intelligence and tradition. Much that characterized experimentalist philosophy as usually interpreted seems to be drawn, not from a study of scientific method, but from the revolt against the domination of the church in moral and intellectual matters. It is an echo of the conflict between science and religion.

A balanced view of scientific method as applied to ethics would lead to quite a different emphasis than that implied in the experimentalist interpretation. It would make the traditional heritage of moral values the foundation on which to build further. It would bear in mind Oppenheimer's dictum: "knowledge rests on knowledge; what is new is meaningful because it departs slightly from what is known

[23] *The Philosophy of John Dewey*, Paul Arthur Schilpp, ed., (Evanston, 1939), p. 591.

before." It would give consideration to the idea that every new discovery or theory in science is an element "within the framework of vaster, unanalyzed, unarticulated reserves of knowledge, experience, faith, and presuppositions."[24] Divergences from established principles would require at least a modicum of consensus among students of ethical theory before they could be approved as valid directives for action. Deviations from accepted modes of conduct could not be justified merely on the basis of individual experience or the claims of spontaneity . A modification of the voluntaristic impression conveyed by the usual experimentalist exposition could be achieved, if the appreciation of the cultural heritage and the community framework, latent in Dewey's philosophy, were to receive more explicit consideration. But the major difficulties of applying scientific method to moral issues—in any interpretation, experimentalist or other—would still remain.

The ethical conceptions and moral codes of any society or any period are not sacrosanct. Like scientific theories and procedures, they are products of human thought and experience and are subject to criticism and revision. The question is whether the revision can be made by methods drawn from the field of science. The biological, psychological, and anthropological sciences may be of great help in fulfilling purposes already determined on, and in maintaining and improving existing institutions. Where a humane attitude exists, research may be of significance in the treatment of the retarded, of sexual deviants, of the socially maladjusted generally. Some broad parallels may be drawn, as indicated, between criteria of scientific thought and ethical judgments. However—this is the main point—scientific inquiry cannot establish the principles and ends by which the individual and society need to be guided.

The two areas of inquiry, the scientific and the ethical, deal with two different aspects of the quest for knowledge; perhaps it would be better to say two different sorts of knowledge. The one aims to understanding the world as it is, its possibilities and limitations; the other seeks to formulate a pattern of values by which we ought to direct our lives. The common view of mankind holds with Einstein, "that knowledge of what *is* does not open the door directly to what *should be*."[25] Scientific knowledge may suggest a modification of an accepted moral convention but the crux of the matter is that it can

[24] J. Robert Oppenheimer, *Science and the Common Understanding* (New York, 1953), pp. 49, 90.
[25] Albert Einstein, *Out of My Later Years* (New York, 1950), p. 22.

never be decisive in the determination of ethical aims. However broadly we interpret the term science, whether as certified knowledge or as valid method, it affords no basis for the moral life. The failure to distinguish the theory of the nature of the world from ethical theory "with sufficient clarity," as Bertrand Russell concludes in his survey of Western philosophy, "has been a source of much confused thinking."[26]

Apart from the problem discussed above concerning the difficulties in the transfer of knowledge and methodology from one field to another, especially from the natural sciences to human affairs, there is the critical question of the possibility of validation. Conclusions drawn from scientific inquiry can be objectively verified, but ethical conceptions can not. The formulation of scientific principles may be affected by the nature of the human mind, but the processes by which they are reached eliminate individual subjectivity. The fact that scientists reach a large measure of agreement on major questions, that hypotheses and conclusions are operationally verified, that a high degree of accuracy in prediction is achieved, argues that scientific laws and principles are controlled by events outside ourselves. Although the determination of scientific conclusions involves communication and discussion, the agreements are, by no means, the result of a consensus reached by mutual persuasion. The investigators are *compelled* to agree by the evidence of experimental test and by the irrefutable chain of reasoning. Science does not permit free will within its domain; it demands acceptance by the individual of the logically, experimentally, communally determined findings.

"To judge by the consequences," a recurrent theme in experimentalist philosophy, provides no resolution of moral dilemmas. We cannot know the consequences of our ethical decisions with any degree of certainty as we can in scientific matters. This, however, is incidental; the essential element in the moral situation is the necessity of taking responsibility for consequences of our actions that we had neither willed nor foreseen. As in marriage, we make our moral decisions "for better or for worse." The main difficulty of the doctrine of consequences is that it fails to make clear the criteria by which the consequences are to be judged.

The doctrine of "judgment by consequences" arose as a criticism of the formalism which demands that we follow principles blindly and mechanically—that we must not lie even to protect the innocent—

26 Bertrand Russell, *A History of Western Philosophy* (New York, 1945), p. 835.

as unfriendly critics questionably interpret the Kantian view. Ethical principles unrelated to consequences, it is true, are likely to lead to fanaticism when they are not totally ineffective. But there is an indispensable element in the Kantian doctrine: to take a stand on principle is at the very heart of the ethical situation. We must consider the consequences of the principle while we maintain the principle; in many instances, we must take a stand on principle despite untoward consequences. The Kantian doctrine is not an empty formalism. In making good-will a supreme principle, it retains the moral substance of the Western religious tradition, and, in the imperative that every human being should be treated as an end, it anticipates the democratic social ethic. The application of a moral principle to practical situations involves an element of individual judgment, but a criterion of principle is prerequisite and indispensable.

Ethical decisions cannot be made one by one without some reference to an accepted pattern of values—a conventional code, a religious or philosophical system, a chosen style of life. In this respect, in the need of a prior principle, ethical judgment resembles scientific judgment. But there is an unbridgeable gap between the two types of judgment. The principles controlling scientific judgment are verifiable by reference to the range of phenomena which they describe and explain. But in the moral situation we can, in final analysis, have recourse only to human opinion which is diverse and conflicting. The moral situation allows—and by the same token—necessitates personal choice and deicsion.

In every community there are minimal decencies and social practices, protected by legal penalties, whose acceptance is dictated by prudence. In societies above the primitive where a measure of freedom obtains, there will be a variety of ethical patterns, some highly praised, others permitted with genial tolerance. Above the level of the legal and prudential morality, and strictly speaking not even there, it is not possible to prove the superiority of one way of life over the other, although persuasive arguments may be adduced. It will, perhaps, be generally admitted that it is impossible to have absolute proof of the superiority of the life of the saintly Francis of Assisi over that of the Epicurean philosophies, of the Puritan over the Pietist way of life. But truth to tell, it would be difficult to demonstrate the superiority of the life of the saintly Francis of Assisi over that of the sinful Casanova of Seingalt. It is not possible to disprove the lugubrious pronouncement of the Preacher when he avers that "the day of death is better than the day of one's birth." The ethical attitude presupposes a reverence for life and a regard for human beings. As in art and in music, there is an element of beauty in the good life which requires a sensitive personal responsiveness.

The nature of the moral problem is obscured when one thinks of it as a question of choice between a recognized unambiguous good and a clearly recognized evil. The ethical choice is between a lesser and a greater good, and perhaps as often between a lesser and a greater evil. The ethical situation is permeated with actual or potential conflict, not only between desire and duty as the conventional formulation has it, but between one duty and another. There may be a conflict between the ethical ideal and the mores of the community, between a loyalty to one's country and a universal religious aspiration. Our ethical tendencies are nurtured by the pronouncements of statesmen, the wisdom of philosophers, the vision of the prophets, the insights of poets, the example of the saints. They are cultivated by the study of history and literature, of philosophy and religion. Our moral conceptions are supported by national traditions, by religious communities, by regional cultures. Such guidance as we can have in moral matters arises out of human experiences; it is in the nature of human testimony and connot claim to be certain knowledge which has a basis in a "universal and objective order of worth."

In final analysis, the ethical life requires a conscious choice of a principle of action and of a way of life, it demands affirmation and commitment. To say that ethical judgment involves a personal choice does not by any means imply a light-hearted preference. Ethical choice represents a decision which carries with it obligation, self-discipline, and sacrifice. It is because of the difficulty of making ethical decisions that men have sought to strengthen their convictions by attributing to them a supernatural sanction or the authority of a self-evident truth. In the turn to a knowledge of nature for support of ethical theory, there remains a vestige of men's need of an extra-human sanction for their convictions and aspirations.

Nature does not provide man with a system of values. Least of all, does physics give a basis for ethics or politics. As Heisenberg points out, the concepts developed in the field of physics do not automatically apply to the other natural sciences, not to speak of the sphere of morals. His view is that the discovery of the limitations of the Newtonian principles, which are valid for mechanics but not for all realms of physics, should make us "less inclined to assume that the concepts of physics, even those of quantum theory, can certainly be applied everywhere in biology or other sciences."[27] The precise language of

[27] Werner Heisenberg, *Physics and Philosophy* (New York, 1958), pp. 199ff.

science refers only to "a very limited part of reality." The concepts of ordinary speech, of "natural" language, "vaguely defined as they are, seem to be more stable in the expansion of knowledge than the precise terms of scientific language derived as an idealization from only limited groups of phenomena." The concepts of natural language, Heisenberg believes, "are formed by the immediate connection with reality"; they represent a wide range of reality and incorporate the essential values of human life which have been the object of traditional religion.

The view that "natural," ordinary speech, not the terminology of scientific investigation, discloses the realm of human values is congenial to the line of thought presented throughout this chapter. But the idea that the concepts of common language "touch reality" is ambiguous; it may imply that men have a direct intuition of a moral order subsistent in the universe. This does not follow. Common language gives better clues to values than scientific language, not because it offers an immediate connection with a wider range of reality, but because it reflects a closer and richer contact with human experience, with needs, aspirations, and ideals. The emphasis of language as a carrier of values calls attention to the social matrix of thought; ordinary language, more than the scientific forms of expression is permeated with cultural influences.

The main conclusion of this chapter is that an ethical conception must be based on a study of man's cultural and institutional history; it cannot be derived from scientific inquiry into the character of nature. Morality, it is true, is not only social; it is individual and, as Henri Bergson has said, also "human." Nevertheless, every actual ethical system whether personal or political is rooted in the way of life and in the beliefs of definite communities—national cultures, religious fraternities, regional civilizations. In every community, there are divergencies between practices and professed beliefs, between conventional morals and the ideals proclaimed by thinkers and statesmen. There are features that are local and temporal, and ideas that are perennial and universal. It is philosophy's main function to make a critical analysis of the culture of a period and to formulate the major presuppositions, principles and ends of an ethical conception to serve as a guide to personal conduct and as a basis for social organization.

Underlying the present study is the belief that Western civilization —despite conflicting strains of thought, divergent philosophic schools, differing religious denominations—embodies the basic elements of a humane ethic. Dewey regards the problem of restoring integration between our beliefs about the world we live in, on the one hand, and our beliefs about values and purposes on the other, as the deepest problem of any living philosophy. He reads the history of European thought as reflecting a struggle between the forces of advancing scientific knowledge and the inertia of institutional beliefs. Without underestimating the importance of achieving a measure of accord between a philosophy of nature and a theory of morals, the main concern in the present attempt to outline a pattern of values lies in the problem of the conflict between ethical ideals and their institutional embodiment. This is the problem around which the contemporary crisis in the world revolves.

Ethical philosophy today has a twofold task: to make clear the enduring principles of the Western tradition in their bearing on the contemporary social conflicts, and to give some indication of the kind of policy which promises to advance the realization of the principles in the light of current possibilities.

POLARITIES OF THOUGHT

The ideals, values, purposes of man's life must be drawn from his social, cultural, and historical experience. Nevertheless, man's life is conditioned by the world of nature which preceded him. It is framed within a created universe not of his making. The universe that serves as man's abode is many-sided and can be viewed from various perspectives and apprehended in different moods. The science of physics represents only one way of knowing, concentrated as it is on descriptive and explanatory statements about one aspect of the phenomenal world. However, every study has implications for understanding beyond its immediate sphere; this is especially true of the study of nature. The analysis of scientific thought has overtones of general import for the understanding of human affairs. In concluding this chapter, a number of ideas garnered by the writer from the philosophy of science are presented, partly as a review of the discussion, partly as a personal interpretation of a number of philosophic issues.

Science and Reality. Does the pursuit of natural science depend on a belief in an objective order of truth in the universe? The scientist-qua-scientist may excuse himself from giving an answer. He may aver that his concern is only with phenomena of experience, that he reports what he finds in his limited area of investigation, and that his statements of truth are always conditional. He may plead that he is not called upon to say whether there is any reality behind appearance, let alone describe its nature. The scientist is not compelled to adopt the correspondence view of truth as conformity to a pre-existent realm of objects or the experimentalist conception that ideas are instruments for the understanding and direction of human experience. He may refuse to decide to what degree the nature of the human mind has entered into the formulation of scientific theories and propositions.

Such diffidence would be a leaning backwards in caution. The scientist certainly assumes that the things and events he studies have a real existence, that the regularities he observes are there to be discovered. The phenomena which are the objects of his attention are no mere figments of the investigator's imagination since they can be observed by others. If there is any bias in a verified scientific statement, it is the common bias of the human mind, not the subjective bias of the individual observer. The fact that scientific investigation results in virtual unanimity on major issues is reasonably decisive evidence that the techniques of study have largely eliminated the refractive distortion of human interpretation. We may accept the view that scientific conclusions are objective in the sense that they reveal an actually existent aspect of the universe of nature with great, if not perfect, fidelity.

A philosophy which respects science can reasonably take the Aristotelian position of the reality of universals[28] in the sense that general laws, propositions, and theories arrived at in scientific inquiry are not mere creations of the human mind. There is a correspondence between the scientific statements and the realities they represent although the likeness may be touched up by human coloration. However, it is essential to remember that each science reveals to us only a limited aspect of reality and that all the sciences together do not give us total truth.

A map has a certain correspondence with the lay of the land, enough to prevent us from losing our way, but it does not tell us much about the country through which we are passing, of its natural beauty, of its inhabitants, or the social and economic conditions of the area. The concept "reality" may not be necessary for specific scientific inquiries but it impresses upon our consciousness that existence is prior to, and richer than, our knowledge of it, and that exact and verified knowledge is only a small part of the vast, diverse, infinitely subtle

[28] Some, but not all asserted universals are real. As Charles S. Peirce notes: "Of course, nobody ever thought that *all* generals were real; but the scholastics used to assume that generals were real when they had hardly any, or quite no, experiential evidence to support their assumptions: and their fault lay just there, and not in holding that generals could be real." (*The Philosophy of Peirce*, Justus Buchler, ed., New York, 1940, p. 364.)

realm of possible understanding. Moreover, the belief that universals are real does not imply that particulars are unreal. The universal and the particular are complementary perspectives.

Thus, finite and infinite attain meaning through each other. As Whitehead explains: "The notion of the complete self-sufficiency of any item of finite knowledge is the fundamental error of dogmatism. Every such item derives its truth, and its very meaning, from its unanalyzed relevance to the background which is the unbounded Universe." And conversely, "infinitude in itself is meaningless and valueless. It acquires meaning and value by its embodiment of finite entities. Apart from the finite, the infinite is meaningless and cannot be distinguished from nonentity."[29]

Relationalism and Probability. Every thing, every idea, every person that can be discerned is to be seen as a location in a wider frame of reference. The particular, however unique, is never an isolated entity, it is always a focal point in a system of interactions and relations. The particular instance has no *recognizable* existence outside of a defined position in time and space; it cannot be *understood* except in terms of relation to other particulars within a frame of reference. This is the "principle of reason" as formulated by Morris R. Cohen: *"Everything is connected in definite ways with definite other things, so that its full nature is not revealed except by its position and its relations within a system."*[30]

The word "definite" should be underscored: science does not make the assumption that everything is connected with, or relevant to, everything else in the universe. It seeks ever wider frames of reference but its quest stops short of ultimates, and of "all-embracing Being." It does not deny the existence of a universe which transcends our powers of intellectual cognition—a universe to which poetry and religion, expressing a common intuition of mankind, bear testimony. It allows a place for mysticism, not as a rival of scientific knowledge, or as superior to it, but as a significant aspect of experience. But it would deny that we can *know* the cosmos. Verifiable knowledge, as science uses the term, is always limited, however wide in scope and however systematically unified it may be.

Associated with the concept of relativity—or "relationalism" as it perhaps should be called—is the concept of probability. We need not hold that everything in the universe is mechanically determined in a strictly causal relationship. It is theoretically possible that radical con-

---

[29] Whitehead, *op. cit.*, pp. 670, 674.
[30] *Reason and Nature* (New York, 1931), p. 150.

tingency obtains in some spheres of existence as mechanism does in others. Contemporary science, in the study of phenomena, steers clear of a dogmatic reliance on either horn of the dilemma; it postulates a relative determinism that must be ascertained at various levels of existence. In physics and chemistry, prediction approaches practical certainty, but even in these fields, every law, although theoretically uniform, must be accompanied by a statement as to the range of applicability. In the biological field, prediction is far less reliable. but dependable conclusions can be formulated within limits of statistically stated probabilities. In human affairs, prediction becomes hazardous; in personal and social life, the factors are numerous and complex, inner motivations as well as external conditions must be reckoned with, experimental and controlled inquiry are narrowly limited. Diagnosis becomes an art rather than a science. But the more that conditions can be brought under control in relation to designed ends, the greater the chance of effecting desired results.

Polarity and Conflict. The problem of the relation of the particular to the universal, of determinism to contingency, is illustrative of the principle of "polarity"—the idea that opposing terms of scientific and philosophic discourse involve each other, e.g., unity implies diversity, the ideal has reference to the actual, the temporal can be discerned only in the background of the enduring. Polarities may merely signify marked points in a pattern of relations as in the designations of "north" and "south." They may represent complementary entities reciprocally interactive, as in the case of "individual" and "society." Or they may define mutually exclusive existential situations, as in the fateful distinction between life and death. Purely intellectual contradictions may be resolved by precise statement or by logical analysis, but all application of opposites to existential situations involve difficulties and contraditions. In both nature and society, there are ever elements of friction and tension, of struggle for survival of one form of existence over another.

The polarity principle guards against two misleading philosophical tendencies. One is the metaphysical tendency to oversimplify the manifold of reality by assuming either change or being, form or matter, the psychic or the physical, as the primary process or substance of existence. The imposition of any single principle on reality is generally a case of special pleading; it prevents free examination of existential situations which always include a mixture of factors and a variety of aspects. The polarity concept should warn against wholesale debate on change versus constancy. Change can only be discerned from a fixed point of reference, changes are plural and of different kinds. In any concrete situation, the nature, the direction, and the rate of change need to be considered. Change may be cyclical, continuous or discontinuous, progressive or reactionary. Moreover, only if we have some definite conception of values can we decide which social changes to support and which we should try to prevent.

The other philosophical tendency that we must guard against is to attribute reality only to rational and spiritual values while the existential difficulties and evils of the world are relegated to the limbo of "nonbeing." Faith in reason and an aspiration for harmony are essential elements in the Western religious and philosophic heritage. But to dismiss the factor of conflict and contradition as illusory, to minimize the travail and tragedy of life, to convert suffering into an instrument of salvation, transforms a moving faith into a passive complacency. Idealistic philosophies have generally been written in an optative mood, transmuting the aspiration for an ideal good into a supporting already existing good, too easily converting a partial possibility into a completed reality.

We are not called upon in the manner of theodicy to justify the ways of Reality to man. A philosophy which is in the spirit of science bids us face phenomenal existence as it impinges on us with its rational and irrational elements, with its material as well as its spiritual aspects. To extend the realm of the satisfying, of the rational, and of the spiritual is possible. But it requires great effort; we cannot rely on destiny, on evolutionary progress, or on a power in the universe not ourselves making for righteousness. In the best achievement, there remains a struggle between the vital energies and the structural forms, between the perfect idea and the institutional embodiment, between experienced existence and ordered thought. There remains the need of reconciliation, and in the individual life, not infrequently, of the wisdom of resignation.

Experience and Metaphysics. The overarching polarity in the realm of knowledge may be expressed in the antithesis suggested by "experience" and "metaphysics." Each of these terms has several significances and sometimes they are merged. In modern idealism experience is associated with the intuition of, and communion with, a transcendant Absolute. Broadly speaking, however, the terms "experience" and "metaphysics" reflect contrasting approaches to the problems of knowledge. In the one, immediate cognition, sense-impression, active response to life situations, are regarded as sources of genuine understanding; the individual instance, the changing, the diverse personal

58

judgment, lie in the focus of attention. In the other, thought begins with unified principles, with enduring frames of reference, with ideal standards of judgment. In traditional metaphysical systems, both truth and value are regarded as having their support in an objective ultimate reality.

Common to the experience philosophies is the view that structured thought comes after, that it is a consequence and not a priority, that action, feeling, sensation, precede thought. Making experience primary was a reaction against classical metaphysics which enthroned logically ordered thought, making it a superior type of knowledge not amenable to correction by ordinary human experience. It included a protest against intellectual elitism and against the authoritarian cast of mind. In the empirical and experimentalist versions, moreover, the doctrine of experience included a protest against the time-honored dualism by which the pleasures and pains of everyday life were assigned to the inferior realm of the temporal world, while the ascetic virtues were clothed with the attributes of spirituality and eternality.

With the pluralist and humanist implications of the experience philosophies, the present analysis is in full accord. Particularly significant in the Deweyan philosophy is the emphasis on relating critical thinking to moral action. However, it is necessary to counterbalance the nominalistic and individualistic tendencies of the experimentalist philosophy by giving proper consideration to the complementary aspect of thought—the universal and enduring principles which have found expression in the traditional metaphysical approach "which looks toward Plato and Aristotle." Metaphysics is subject to criticism when it attributes a supernatural origin to its universals and makes them superior to human experience, but its abandonment would undermine the foundations of Western thought. Science and ethics in their higher forms are the result of the Hellenic impulse to weave experience on a frame of reason, to base knowledge and action on a foundation of conceptual principles, to guide them by an envisaged design.

The errors of metaphysics are the excess of its virtue. They arise out of the quest for a consistent view of nature and the moral life. But the universe can only be known, at any one time, from a certain perspective. The virtue of metaphysics lies in the endeavor "to see life clearly and to see it whole"; the error creeps in when an unavoidably one-sided perspective is asserted to be the only true one, when a point of view appropriate to one situation has been made into a compelling universal truth. The excess of the principle of unity has led to the fusion of the idea of the good with the idea of the truth. We must keep in mind the disparate sources of scientific knowledge and moral wisdom—the one based on objective impersonal verification of observed phenomena, and the other supported by social consensus and by personal testimony. Once the ethical ends are determined, then scientific knowledge becomes indispensable in harnessing natural impulses to human aspirations and creating the conditions necessary for their realization.

In the Aristotelian metaphysics, two tendencies came together. One was the recognition of the indispensability of "first principles" as a basis for science and as a means of giving direction to moral life. The other was the search for an overarching unity of Being, an eternal and secure cause from which all subordinate causes could be derived.[31] We need to retain from the Aristotelian thesis that all thinking and all moral activity must be based on clear and firm principles. But we need not regard the principles as eternally fixed truths; they are to be held as enduring presuppositions that undergo modification periodically as civilization develops, as new scientific advances are consolidated, and as human sympathies broaden. At the same time, it is necessary to bear in mind that when new content is poured into old conceptual forms there remains a core of essential ideas: in science, the concepts of cause and effect, of the uniformity and diversity of nature, of classification into types, of the need of formulation in laws and theories; in ethics, the ideas of justice and compassion, of freedom and law, of the secular and the sacred, of the temporal and the spiritual, of the unique person and the unity of mankind.

The metaphysical concept of Being reflects man's intuition that a Unity pervades the universe. Aristotle tried to make this "Something that transcends the limits of human experience accessible to the critical understanding."[32] Herein lies an error—for it attempts to articulate the ineffable, to say in prose that which can only be suggested in poetry and may be experienced in religious worship. When we are not too much harassed by the pressure of wordly affairs, a sense of the unity of the universe may persist in the background of our consciousness; when we are at peace in moments of contemplation we may apprehend it in communion. But when we convert the aspiration for unity into a definitive ontological statement, we confuse a partial view with our sense of the whole; a quest is frozen into an existence, a creative impulse may become a restrictive dogma.

[31] Collingwood, *op. cit.*, chaps. I, II, III.
[32] Werner Jaeger, *Aristotle* (Oxford, 1934), p. 378.

The universe, as experienced in its existential impact contains an inexhaustible diversity of beings and forces. Within this plenitude are attractions and repulsions, antinomies and consistencies, harmonies and conflicts. Every way of looking at a situation must be subjected to its polarity. Change can be measured only from a point of constancy, unity is the counterpart of diversity, the particular can be seen only in the perspective of the universal—the infinite is the finite unbound. The antithetical terms have no *existence* in their absolute forms; they are conceptual boundaries within which we come to *know* as well as to experience existential reality. Albert Camus quotes Pascal: "A man does not show his greatness by being at one extremity, but rather by touching both at once."

Within the structure of knowledge erected with such enormous effort over the long period of human history, there lies the antinomy of experience and ordered thought. Thought demands that we view each moment in a conceptual frame of reference wider than the immediate situation in which the experience occurs, to evaluate it in the perspective of enduring time, and in the background of an enlarged living space. Still every experience is unique, bringing with it an accompaniment of joy or sorrow, of hope or of despair, of the warm stir of life or the chilling premonition of dissolution. The radiance and the poignancy of the existential event are lost in the endeavor to grasp its lasting meaning, to understand it and to judge it. Philosophy and religion attempt to preserve enduring significances; poetry and the arts reflect the essence of spirit in the unique experience. Reasoned knowledge, instructive and useful though it may be, is always partial, ever a compromise as it constrains vital moments within the measuring instruments of time and space.

CHAPTER THREE

ASPECTS OF A HUMANE ETHIC

Nature, the Nature of Man, and Human Nature

The "Problem of Man"

A Threefold Conception of Selfhood: the Community, the Ideal, the Person

Existentialist Alienation and Philosophic Detachment

The Institutions of Community: Family, Church, and Nation

Ethics and Politics in Western Thought

In all past history there was a self-evident bond between man and man in stable communities, in institutions, and in universal ideas. Even the isolated individual was sustained in his isolation. The most visible sign of today's disintegration is that more and more men do not understand one another . . . that there is no longer any reliable community or loyalty. KARL JASPERS

3.

Aspects of a
Humane Ethic

NATURE, THE NATURE OF MAN, AND HUMAN NATURE

DEEPLY rooted in the Western tradition—in religion, in philosophy and, to some extent, in science—is the belief that the
Universe is concerned with the destiny of man, that the Cosmos is
governed by a moral and rational principle. There have been troubled
queries and sceptical opinions in ancient days as well as in modern
times. Job finally recognized that God's ways were not man's ways:
he came to understand, as Horace Kallen interprets, that if man was
determined to maintain his integrity and to realize his nature as man,
"this is to be accomplished in a world which was not made for him,
in which he shares his claim on the consideration of Omnipotence
with the infinitude of its creatures..."[1] In a lighter mood, Epicurus
reconciled himself to the idea that the gods lived in a world apart.
Supremely happy themselves, they were indifferent to the weal and
woe of men; if they did not reward him for his virtues, at least they
did not punish him for his misdeeds. However, these views are exceptional; in the mainstream of the Western tradition runs the current of
belief that the Cosmos—call it God or Nature—supports man's ethical
ideals; there is, as George Santayana has phrased it, "the fond delusion
that man and his moral nature are at the center of the universe."[2]

[1] Horace M. Kallen, *The Book of Job as a Greek Tragedy* (New York, 1959),
pp. 76-77.
[2] George Santayana, *Three Philosophical Poets*, Doubleday Anchor Book
(New York, 1953), p. 185.

The faith that the cosmos is concerned with man's destiny has expressed itself in a variety of forms and with different intents. In the Old Testament account, the earth and the heavens were brought into being for the sake of man, the final achievement of God's creative effort. Plato, discoursing in the high terms of philosophy, places his Idea of the Good in an eternal realm which exists apart from man in an unchanging sphere of reality. Stoic philosophy and Christian theology differed in a crucial respect: the former granted man the power of self-control through living in harmony with a universal Reason; the latter denied such spiritual autonomy, holding that man cannot achieve redemption without the help of revealed faith. But both were at one in regarding the universe as ruled by a Providence concerned with the destiny of man.

Modern thought continued to assume a harmony between cosmic processes and man's good, but with a different, generally with a reverse, connotation. In the traditional view, the cosmic-oriented outlook was associated with restraint over natural impulse, with resignation in the face of evil fortune, with subordination to the authorities of state and church. In the modern age, the cosmos in the guise of nature is seen as the source of man's vital energies and of his aspiration for liberty and justice. The appeal to nature is in support of the rights of man; it serves to defend nonconformity and to justify revolt against kings and clerics. Naturalism becomes a force for institutional reform, for reconstruction of the political order, for radical change in the aims and methods of education. Thomas Jefferson proclaims the nation's right to independence on the basis of the Laws of Nature and of Nature's God. For Emerson, for Thoreau, and for Walt Whitman, nature is permeated with moral quality and spiritual beauty; from nature men derive the will to freedom, the right of the individual conscience, the warrant for civil disobedience. But nature has also been called upon in defense of raw instinct and passionate emotion, in extenuation of the irrational and the demonic. In Nietsche, nature sanctions the amoral superman and his absolute will to power. Hitler aimed to replace the "humanity of the individual" by the "humanity of Nature which destroys weakness in order to give its place to strength."

The teleological, anthropomorphic interpretation of nature persists in the doctrine of evolution and has its tender-minded and tough-minded exemplifications. The theistic-humanist holds: "In the light of the fact that man himself is a natural product of nature, it seems wholly unwarranted to say that 'nature is indifferent to man' or to his interests." With this goes the assumption, "in human and even in social behaviour, the same orderly and causal lawfulness applies which works in the rest of the order of nature." The fact that nature is at times disorderly and that man at times sinks into savagery, it is suggested, really testifies to man's innate natural capacity for moral and spiritual greatness! Since we could not recognize light if there were no darkness, Professor Schilpp avers, there is a sense in which "evil, so far from being a problem at all, is actually a blessing."[3] In this idealistic view of evolution, nature is made over in the image of moral man. In the nineteenth century interpretation of Darwinism—which celebrate's nature's alleged law of the survival of the fittest—man was made over in the image of the lower animals; the theory of evolution became a means of rationalizing harsh exploitive competition. Both views—the one which endows the cosmos with moral, rational, and spiritual character, and the other that finds a sanction for man's inhumanity to man in nature's ruthlessness—reflect man's moral aspirations or attempt to rationalize social policy.

Awe of the cosmos is indeed the beginning of wisdom, and regard for nature's laws is a condition of understanding. But it is a grandiose "pathetic fallacy," in Santayana's sense, to seek support for moral action in the universe which is disclosed to man in diverse manifestations. The universe out of which man has evolved seems as little concerned with man's destiny as is the earth with the growth of the tree in which it is rooted. The most that can be said is that nature on our own planet evinces a benevolent neutrality toward man's existence. Nature gives man vitality and endows him with potentialities for development even though, at the same time, it sets limits to his life span and to his achievements. The universe which is man's abode is not unfriendly to man's survival and self-realization—provided that he does not upset the balance too violently by his inventions as we may perhaps be doing by our intensive exploration and use of atomic energy. But the purposes of human life cannot be found outside of the sphere of man's life—in the cosmos, in the universe, in nature— whichever term we use. Human ends must be determined by man himself who, in the ultimate meaning, is "the measure of all things"— that is, the measure of all things moral.

The ethical problem revolves around the nature of man. But it is necessary to bear in mind that there is a vast difference between the term "human nature" as the biologist might study it, and "the nature of man" as the theologian and the philosopher use the phrase. In the

[3] Paul Arthur Schilpp in *This Is My Faith,* Stewart G. Cole, ed., (New York, 1936), pp. 202, 203, 208.

latter instance, moral assumptions are always implied. As the title of Reinhold Niebuhr's Gifford lectures suggests, the discussion of the Nature of Man is a prelude to the interpretation of the Destiny of Man. The central theme of the religio-philosophical tradition until modern times was the conflict between the essential nature of man and human nature in the creaturely sense. In the traditional view, essential man is conceived as a moral, rational, spiritual being, as a special creation set off from the rest of nature. In this interpretation, man's nature is dual, composed of an animal-like body and a divine-like soul. His distinctive character, pervaded with spirit, is ever at war with his animal incarnation dominated as it is by appetite. Not all of the classical and the Judeo-Christian philosophies required an ascetic suppression of desire and passion. The major religious as well as the philosophic views in Western tradition have allowed, indeed have counseled, a golden mean conformable to a rule of reason. But there was always the assumption that man could not attain to lasting happiness through the satisfaction of his natural instincts; the good life implied the acceptance of a way of belief and the practice of a code of conduct requiring self-control and self-restraint.

The naturalistic outlook of the modern age rejected the dualism which set the moral good against man's native impulses. The philosophies which assumed a favorable view of human nature were at times political and social theories in the guise of psychological expositions. They represented attack on absolutist regimes, reflected aversion to formal religious doctrine, expressed revolt against hypocritical social conventions, were motivated by opposition to harsh penal codes. In its most discerning versions, the naturalistic conception revealed the vital roots of ethics and of religious faith without which their ordered doctrinal forms become withered branches on the tree of life.

In some of its influential versions, naturalism attempted to construct an ethic on the basis of man's animal drives and satisfactions. "Social Darwinism" closed the gap between human and animal nature and modeled man's morality on a one-sided view of natural selection. The more moderate utilitarians who built their moral theory on the profit system of the surplus of pleasures over pains took account of the satisfactions of the mind as well as of the body in their calculus. Exemplifications of naturalism which were touched by philosophic idealism assumed an impulse of sympathy in the repertoire of man's natural endowment and brought to the fore the social aspects of personality. But in the main, the naturalist theories tended to blur the distinctions between desires and aspirations, between wants and values, between the pleasures and joys which may be derived from creaturely satisfactions and the sustained happiness that comes in the pursuit of an ideal. They tended optimistically to underestimate the conflict between the satisfactions of the animal needs, the demands of social organization, and the fulfillment of human aspirations.

The naturalist bias like the supernaturalist exhibits an imbalance when it attempts to derive an ethical conception from outside the realm of social and cultural life. We can understand man only in the light of his distinctive human activities, through the arts and sciences he has created, through the institutional systems he has constructed, through the ideals to which he aspires. It is true that our animal endowment is indispensable to our moral and spiritual achievement as well as necessary for our survival and creaturely satisfactions. However, notwithstanding the mythical forms of thought in which the traditional religious conceptions are wrapped and the antique language in which theological doctrines are couched, they reflect the imperishable insight that man is a special creation and represents a distinctive being made in the image of the Divine. There is a real struggle within man among the several aspects of his nature. The ethical problem is centrally connected with the ever-present, never completely resolved, conflict in man's complex, ambivalent nature.

THE "PROBLEM OF MAN"

Man's difference from the animals is comprised of three major interacting aspects. Man has an exceptional ability to adjust himself to a variety of conditions, on the one hand, and to modify the environment to accord with his needs and conceptions, on the other. His great power to control his environment is made possible by his ability to invent tools combined with his power to communicate through speech, and to transmit his skill and knowledge from generation to generation. The ability to adjust to and control the environment has been marvelously increased by the power to abstract and generalize which has raised practical skills to the level of scientific technology. But these capacities of adaptation and environmental control which the naturalistic analysis tends to emphasize would, taken by themselves, make man an ingenious animal; they would not define him as a human being or suggest his moral problem. We come nearer to a recognition of man's character when we focus attention on the social aspect of man's original endowment which implies the necessity of mutual aid, the regulative function of the mores, and the constraint of law. The social nature of man would itself make him a distinctive creature and endow him with a moral dimension. But this delineation of man remains faulty because it does not give adequate consideration to the ideational aspect as the essence of man's character. Man is a biosocial-ideal creature in which the aesthetic, rational, spiritual tendencies are the directive factors, the "final causes" of his being.

More significant than his social nature, for the ethical as distinguished from the moral, are the characteristics that arise from the *psyche*, from that aspect of man's nature suggested by the words, "mind," "soul," "spirit." At all times, in the earliest stages of culture and under the most difficult conditions of life, man has striven to give expression to his psychic nature—to endeavor to understand the world he lives in, to create things of beauty, to relate himself in justice and in kindliness to his fellow men. Man is impelled by aesthetic sensitivity to surround his physical activities with manners; he mingles his partaking of food with rituals and amenities, devises seemly ways of courting and mating. Man reveals a need for intellectual order, an impulse to seek the truth, an aspiration for righteousness. Some men are willing, one might say are impelled, to forego the ordinary satisfactions of life in order to realize their creative energies in art and in science, or to devote themselves to social and religious causes. History affords examples of men who have starved themselves to achieve spiritual communion.

The aesthetic, the intellectual, the spiritual tendencies interact with the physical and biological wants in complex ways; and the physical and biological drives are transformed through their interaction with social tendencies and institutional structures. But the psychic-spiritual expressions do not arise out of the natural-biological as sublimations of natural desires, or compensations for frustration. Biologically, man may be regarded as of the race of animals, as a product of a long evolutionary development in the history of living forms. But he represents an extraordinary qualitative mutation. Man's body-resemblance to the animals is misleading and the similarity of some of his behavioral responses is deceptive. "We may readily admit," as Cassirer says, "that the anthropoid apes, in the development of certain symbolic processes, have made a significant forward step. But again we must insist they did not reach the threshold of the human world."[4] Man is as different in psychic organization, in his moral, intellectual, and esthetic sensitiveness from the highest of the animals, as mammals are from birds or fish.

The distinctive faculty of *homo sapiens*, classically referred to as "reason," is better suggested by the word "imagination." It is man's

[4] Ernst Cassirer, *An Essay on Man* (New Haven, 1944), p. 68.

power of imagination that liberates him from the confines of the sensory and the motor experiences. Man can live in a wide dimension of time and space transcending his existential limitations. He can in his mind transport himself to other places and to other times; he can see himself as living in the past and in the future. He can universalize, view the individual event within a system, conceive the concrete instance as the application of a general law. He can detach himself from his immediate experience and see himself *sub specie aeternitatis*. He can dramatize himself and put himself in another person's place; more, he can identify himself with others, with their joys and their sufferings. He can think of himself as part of humanity.

Imagination unbound creates mythology; pruned of its exuberance it becomes reason; united with reason and with sympathy it leads to enlightened ethics and to rational religion. Implicated in the conversion of the free imagination is another feature of man's image-making power—the faculty of discerning forms in things, of grasping orders in movement, of constructing idea-concepts. Man can conceive designs and proceed to carry them out, to envision utopias and endeavor to move the world toward them. In his distinctive responses man does not react to his physical environment directly; he confronts the world through the mediation of language and structured thought, through the interposition of symbols. His liberating imaginative power joined with his form-contriving tendency enables him to create conceptions of life which serve as models by which to live.

The three aspects of man's character—the biological, the social, the ideal—affect each other in mutually supportive and productive interations. But a factor of tension, and often of conflict, persists among the three levels of organization both in the life of the individual and of society. As a living creature, man is impelled to preserve himself and to reproduce his kind. Social organization increases his ability to fulfill these vital needs; it provides security, facilitates economic production, protects stable marital relations conducive to the nurture of the young. Along with the realization of objective needs, social organization offers opportunities for the cultivation and satisfaction of the emotional concomitants that attend the fulfillment of the vital drives; for love in the conjugal and parental manifestations, for companionship and conviviality, for self-identification with group purposes.

At the same time, social organization unavoidably channels and constrains the natural impulses, involves suppression of combative tendencies, control of sexual urgencies, regulation of economic motivations. Interpenetrating all social life are judgments of right and

71

wrong which in part reflect necessary practical arrangements and in part result from a comparison between the actual situation with an envisaged ideal of human relations. The actuality ever appears to fall short of the claims of justice and the perfection of beauty. As civilization advances, the creaturely needs may be more adequately met for a greater number of men, but the tension among the several levels of being and selfhood does not disappear; indeed the gaps between the biological, the social, and the ideal seem to widen with the growing complexity of civilization.

Man has multitudinous problems to meet in his effort to survive, to fulfill his vital impulses, to develop adequate social institutions, to satisfy his tendencies to intellectual and artistic creation. There persists "the problem of man" in the sense that the philosopher and the theologian use the phrase. There remain the tension and conflict between man's nature and needs as a living creature on the one hand, and his nature and aspiration as a rational and aesthetic, as a moral and spiritual being, on the other. Social organization mediates between these two ultimate poles, but it can only achieve a compromise between the vital forces and the ideal forms. Man has a twofold problem, the one which we may call moral-social, the other ethical-spiritual. The former relates to the necessity of conformity to the conventionally approved customs and mores; the latter goes beyond the moral and upholds the ideal values proclaimed by philosophers and poets, by prophets and religious teachers. The twofold struggle of impulse against socially structured forms and against conceptual ideals becomes exceedingly complicated by the fact that man is highly individualized. Men vary greatly in the pattern of their native endowments, in the relation of their egocentric drives to their social sensibilities, in their power of imagination and abstraction, and in the ways in which these characteristics are related to each other. The native differences are enormously modified by the forces of acculturation and education and by exigencies in the circumstances of men's lives.

Man does not have by nature a narrowly fixed, completely determined, mode of behavior. His moral and spiritual problem arises out of the plenitude, the diversity, and modifiability of his native endowment. He himself must create the institutional structures, the intellectual principles, the value-systems necessary for the realization of his potentialities. His effort is at every point made difficult and his character rendered ambiguous by the struggle between the biological, the sociological, and the ideational aspects of his nature.

A THREEFOLD CONCEPTION OF SELFHOOD:
THE COMMUNITY, THE IDEAL, THE PERSON

In the foregoing, attention has been directed toward the structured character of existence: living creatures are organisms, societies are marked by ordered relations, ideas imply conceptual forms. This emphasis on organization at various levels has significance for moral theory and involves a criticism of two different views encountered in current approaches—one that sets out with a given set of values, the other illustrated by the Deweyan pragmatist conception which turns away from judgment by prior standards.

The value-oriented approach begins with a list of virtues, e.g., truthfulness and honesty, duty and responsibility, piety and reverence, love and chastity. Basing ethics on such general traits is subject to the criticism of vagueness, or arbitrariness, or ineffectiveness in application. The bare injunction to be honest whatever happens, as Dewey says, gives little indication to what it means to be honest in particular situations; it leaves to "chance, to the ordinary judgment of the individual, or to the external authority to find out just *what* honesty specifically means in the given case."[5] The concept of "love," which plays so large a part in both Christian and humanist statements of the present day, may serve as a case in point.

Love can mean all things to all men—things evil as well as good. As Richard McKeon interpreting Plato says: "There is an order of loves that runs from the divine love inspired by the highest values, dimly discerned and rarely approximated, to the lowest degradation and perversion that man can suffer in lust and madness."[6] Love may mean *eros*, or *agapé*, or *philia*—boundless desire, Christian fellowship, humane friendship. It may refer to conjugal and parental affection, to the amiable *amour* of a Don Juan, to the obscene passion of a Marquis de Sade. For Martin Luther, as Reinhold Niebuhr points out, all-encompassing and transcendant love of God was compatible with the absolute subordination of the subject to princely authority and with brutal suppression of the serf by the master.[7] "Love thine enemies" may lead to an inverted social ethic; the doctrine of nonresistance may become a means for denying the claims of justice.

The Deweyan thought has no confidence in statements of moral goals in terms of broad concepts. But it does not propose to remedy

[5] John Dewey and James H. Tufts, *Ethics* (New York, 1936), p. 305.

[6] Richard McKeon, *Thought, Action, and Passion* (Chicago, 1954), p. 37.

[7] Reinhold Niebuhr, *The Nature and Destiny of Man* (New York, 1943), Vol. II, p. 194.

the vagueness of the value-oriented approach by prescribing definite codes of conduct. On the contrary, it deprecates the use of "unchanging moral rules" or of casuistical determination of the right thing to do on each occasion.[8] Such constraints on the judgment of the individual, it is held, result in formalism and legalism, in subordination to external authority, in maintaining the static present, in preventing personal and social growth. The objection to any fixed moral system is especially strong among the educational exponents of the pragmatist view. As John L. Childs expresses it, "Living requires no ends or standards other than those which its own ongoing movement provides."[9] William H. Kilpatrick says that judgment of the advantages or disadvantages of any institutional arrangement "must be left to the exigencies of the situation."[10]

The choices of values and the decisions on action are to be made, the educational pragmatist maintains, by the method of "critical intelligence," by careful consideration of the probable consequences for himself, for all concerned, and for the general welfare. In Childs' formulation, the right is that which is in harmony with the personal and social good, and the good is that which makes for richer experience, for all-round growth, and for social progress. In Kilpatrick's phrase, the goal is "the life good to live" which includes a wide range of "satisfactions," physical and mental, aesthetic and moral, personal and social. Throughout the educational pragmatist's presentation runs the social theme—a recognition of the social nature of selfhood, an emphasis on social responsibility, a concern for social welfare. It echoes Dewey's summation: "The moral and the social quality of conduct are, in the last analysis, identical with each other."[11]

With all its regard for the social nature of personality, the Deweyan moral theory is subject to criticism on several grounds. The notions of "continuous growth," "richer experience," and "better society" fail to satisfy the need of a definite criterion of judgment. Moreover, it exaggerates the degree of freedom that the individual has in making choices and decisions, however intelligent and well-disposed he

---

[8] It should be pointed out, however, that Dewey differentiates between fixed moral rules and "true moral principles." The latter have value as tools of analysis, as supplying "stand points and methods which will enable the individual to make for himself an analysis of good and evil in the particular situation in which he finds himself." For a discussion of his conception of "The Nature and Office of Principles," see *Ethics* (*op. cit.*), pp. 304-314.

[9] *American Pragmatism and Education* (New York, 1956), p. 111.

[10] *Philosophy of Education* (New York, 1951), p. 50.

[11] John Dewey, *Democracy and Education* (New York, 1916), p. 415.

may be. Moral decision usually involves a choice of a lesser evil in a limited situation rather than a choice of greater satisfactions either for oneself or for others. The most serious objections attend the doctrine of "judgment by consequences." In the first place, it is, to an extent, circular in its argument, as Dewey at times appears to recognize: it implies an intelligent moral person to begin with.[12] Furthermore, the moral problem, more often than not relates to unforeseen and unwanted consequences rather than to anticipated consequences resulting from voluntary choice. Moral issues are involved in the relation of parents to an ill-born child, in what to do when a marriage has proved disappointing, in honoring a business contract which has become unprofitable. Then there are the situations in which the individual's decision has played no part but in which he is nevertheless deeply involved. Are we to fight for our own country in a war we consider unjust?

The pragmatist view, as generally interpreted, underestimates the element of real conflict involved in moral choice, both in the life of the individual and of society. It resolves the problems of the moral life too easily and too optimistically. The traditional view which emphasizes the need of restriction and sacrifice, of reconciliation with adversity, of resignation in the face of the inevitable cannot be left out of account in the statement of the moral problem. In total effect, the cencepts of intelligence, of growth, of judgment by satisfying consequences, taken by themselves, have less to offer in the way of guidance than the inculcation of the virtues of duty and honesty, of justice and compassion, reverence and piety, even though we may grant that these concepts may remain ineffective, and even misleading, if not defined in terms of, and applied to, concrete situations.

Both approaches—the one that posits definite criteria of value and the other which makes judgment by consequences the central consideration—are necessary elements in a balanced elaboration of moral theory. But as they stand, both are "academic," in the unfavorable sense, as being inadequately related to the existential life situations which they portray. Underlying both, there is an abstract conception of the person as a discrete individual. The Deweyan view is closer to reality in its constant emphasis on the social nature of the individual and its insistence on the necessity of examining moral principles,

[12] See, Dewey and Tufts, *Ethics* (*op. cit.*), p. 264: "The more importance we attach to objective consequences as the standard, the more we are compelled to fall back upon personal character as the only guarantee that this standard will operate, either intellectually in our estimates or practically in our behavior."

such as justice, in application to specific institutions and in the consideration of measures of economic and political reform. However, despite the recognition that the individual is constantly subject to social pressures and that personality is greatly affected by institutional arrangements, the notion of a free independent individual still dominates the experimentalist analysis as well as the value-centered conceptions of the moral situation. Society is regarded as an association of interdependent individuals. "Society," it is said, "*is* individuals-in-their-relations."[13] The fact that the basic human relations are mediated by institutional arrangements does not play an essential part in the Deweyan moral theory, although this would be in accord with the cultural and social outlook if consistently carried out.[14]

The point made here is that the individual is a *sociological*, as well as a social being. Another way of stating it is that we play *roles* in society as members in families, as workers, professional men, or business managers, as citizens or governors of our country. There are moral traits, e.g., courtesy, consideration, mutual respect, that should apply to all social relations. But the actual concrete issues arise within the institutionalized social structure and each sphere of human relations has its distinctive moral problems. It is not enough to maintain that universal moral precepts, e.g., "thou shalt love thy neighbor as thyself," be concretely applied to the various aspects of life, to the economic and political, as well as to general personal relations.

Moral problems have their origin in the organized community life; it is in point to say that there is a family morality, an economic morality, a political morality. The distinctive moralities will be affected by a universal overarching principle, e.g., the principle of democracy or the Kantian imperative. But unless we focus our attention on the institutional context we shall not know what the problem really is, we shall not realize the difficulties involved in its possible solution. Keeping before our minds the fact that all social life is built around structured relations, we shall the more readily recognize that moral conduct requires rules as well as proper dispositions to guide behavior, that it involves substantive principles of action as well as methods of at-

[13] John Dewey and John L. Childs, "The Underlying Philosophy of Education," in *The Educational Frontier*, William H. Kilpatrick, ed., (New York, 1933), p. 291.

[14] See the strong statement in *Human Nature and Conduct*, (New York, 1922), pp. 166-167: "To view institutions as enemies of freedom, and all conventions as slaveries, is to deny the only means by which positive freedom in action can be secured . . . Not conventions, but stupid and rigid conventions is the foe."

tacking specific issues, that it implies obligations to be performed as well as satisfactions to be enjoyed.

We must go further before we reach the heart of the moral and political problem. For man is not only a social being standing in person-to-person relationship to others, and a sociological being playing various roles in a structured society. He is above all a *communal* being. It is his nature as a creature who lives in organized communities, bound together by common material interests, by common loyalties, by a common heritage of ideals, that is of central significance for the moral life—for the integrity of the person, and for the realization of selfhood as well as for the social good.[15] The moral problems of contemporary life are interwoven with the weakening of community ties and with the lack of a unifying principle for the major community institutions of Western life, the family, the cultural nationality, and the religious associations of church and synagogue.

A community differs from an ordinary association in several significant aspects. An association is organized for a specific purpose, as in the case of a trade union, a political party, or a scientific society. It is joined voluntarily and it may be left at will. Each association has its rules of membership, and an individual may be ousted if he violates them. An association may take on the character of a community for some of its members for whom it becomes a center of life interests. But in the usual case, membership merely implies interest in the specific purposes of the organization and its benefits. A community encompasses a wide range of concerns—of material interests, of customs and beliefs, of values and ideals. Moreover, crucial to the concept of community is the sense of attachment, of involvement in a common destiny. We may join a community, but ordinarily we are born into the communities with which we identify ourselves. Involvement in the life of a community brings with it responsibilities for its survival and security, and demands loyalty.

---

[15] This is the purport of the classic Greek conception usually quoted in the name of Aristotle, "Man is by nature a political animal," which Ernest Barker translates as "man is by nature an animal intended to live in a *polis*." To grasp the significance of the idea it needs to be remembered that the Greek *polis* was not merely a state; it was a community bound by ties of kinship, by common culture and religious heritage, and in Barker's words, "an integrated system of social ethics." Aristotle is at pains to make clear that while security and protection of the economic basis are prerequisites, the essence of the state-community lies in the moral and spiritual sphere—in ensuring the control of life by law and justice and in educating the young to virtue. See Ernest Barker, *The Politics of Aristotle* (Oxford, 1946), p. xlvii, p. 7, pp. 118-120. Also Edward Zeller, *Outlines of the History of Greek Philosophy* (New York, 1931), pp. 192-193.

A community usually has a contingent basis: it may rest on a territorial contiguity, on common ethnic origin, on identity of race. It may be conceived in narrow terms as in the Nazi doctrine of "the community of blood and soil." But the genuine community, though necessarily concerned with security and survival, is characterized by common values and ideals. Community life is the source of character development on two interactive but nevertheless distinct levels. Community life necessitates approved norms of behavior and requires mutual adjustment of interests. It provides opportunities for personal participation and for cooperation in common tasks. It induces consideration of the welfare of the community as a whole. It is the identification with the activities and concerns of the communities to which he belongs that the individual achieves an enlargement of selfhood. But, in addition—interweaving with the problem of the relation of the individual to the common tasks and the conventional usages of the community, which we may call the *moral* problem—is the *ethical* problem which relates to living in accord with the ideal aspirations and the universal values for which the community stands.

Life in society can be lived at various levels of adjustment and integrity. A large proportion of men seem to accept Solomon's counsel: "Be not righteous overmuch!" The conventional man follows a practical code without self-censure, may take advantage of loopholes in the law, regard the marriage vow, on occasion, with a degree of nonchalance, assume that ethical principles do not apply to business. He may justify this way of life on the grounds that "one must live" and that "everybody does it." He may accept the code of practicality in some aspects but not in others—evade paying taxes but act with strict honesty in private affairs. A second level of social behavior is represented by those who try to adhere to the professed morals of the community to which they belong, to fidelity in marriage, to the ethics of fair trade, to the duties of citizenship, and who are troubled by conscience when they are tempted or forced by circumstances to violate the customary norms. Genuine ethical behavior involves more than conformity to the institutionalized mores of a particular society. It requires commitment to an ideal conception of a way of life.

The moral life on each of its levels demands choice, not only a decision of what action to take in a particular situation, but in the first instance a choice of a principle of action, of a pattern of behavior, of a style of life. The inadequacy of the utilitarian ethics and of much that goes by the name of pragmatism is in the implication that moral judgments can be made one by one, without a prior determination of a general principle of action and a commitment to a code of conduct. It is not necessary to decide beforehand on every possible eventuality, but there must be some prior decision on major issues. Some boundaries must be set for what is permissible in the area of family life, in the economic sphere, in the political domain. The most important freedom is the freedom to choose one's way of life, not the freedom to choose one satisfaction as against another satisfaction. To leave all decisions to the individual judgment in particular instances nullifies any meaning that the terms "moral" and "ethical" may have.

The realm of the moral allows a greater range of freedom than does the sphere of law, but as in law, some basic agreement on principles and on some concrete applications is essential if moral theory is to be of any significance. Principles need to bend to circumstances, application must be revised in the light of changing conditions. One may take a holiday from one's usual way of life. But even if we do not repent us of our "lost week-end," we must be able to return to some regimen of life, to some haven of consciously held principle. We must be able to come home again from our wanderings. The casual, the unprincipled life is as unsuitable as the uncritical unexamined life which Socrates pronounced, *"ou biotos,"* unlivable for man. To be a free person, and an "inner-directed person," in David Riesman's phrase, means to be directed by a consciously held conception of life within a definite community.

We realize ourselves through our sociological relations—through the structured institutional life and through communal attachments.[16] This is, however, only one aspect of self-realization; another aspect, as has been emphasized, is the allegiance to a pattern of values. Along with the social self and the ideal self lives a third self—the private, intimate self. No involvement in the public life, however intense or many-sided, gives harmonious expression to the self—in public life, the self becomes both less as well as more than the private self. No rational or spiritual conception, however broad, can reflect the intimacy and the richness of individual experience. Despite involvement in social relations, despite identification with universal ideas, the

[16] Compare: "Granted that the development and growth of the individual is a worthy ideal of any society . . . its realization depends upon the nature of the conditions, social and cultural, within which one must live and work. This being so, self-realization is to be seen not as a goal but as an unearned dividend arising from certain kinds of structural connections in the public world." Solon T. Kimball and James E. McClellan, *Education and the New America* (New York, 1962), p. 237.

self retains a sense of its own unique identity. Each one has a private corner to which no other person, however dearly beloved and trusted, has access. Each one's attempt to communicate with another proves, in the ultimate meaning, a failure. As Karl Jaspers says, "something incomprehensible remains in the personality."

The self seeks realization in hours of contemplation, in reflective reading, in listening to music, in the unhurried appreciation of works of art. It may find active expression in crafts, in household duties, in gardening, in various hobbies. The self finds satisfaction in walking on the open road, in conversation with a friend, in small acts of kindness. Many are the ways in which the self finds peace of mind and joy in the uncoerced doings and dreamings of the daily life. Still we must remember the comment of D. H. Lawrence, who loved the "life of the little day, the life of little people," but who added: "Unless we encompass it in the greater day, and set the little life in the circle of the greater life, all is disaster."

EXISTENTIALIST ALIENATION AND PHILOSOPHIC DETACHMENT

The existentialist philosophies that have gained popularity in the period after the second world war reveal a significant insight in their emphasis on the autonomy of the moral person. There is value in their warning against allowing one's self to be swallowed up in the collective organism, in the state and in the industrial society, in the church and even in the institution of family. There is ethical import to the imperative that each one must take responsibility for his decisions in times of crisis. But the possible contribution of the existentialist confrontation is negated when it implies that moral judgment can be made and that selfhood can be realized without reference to a pattern of universal values or to the common concerns of a definite community of men. From this root of ego-centricity springs the sense of meaninglessness and anxiety, of loneliness and despair, that pervades so much of the literature currently written in the existentialist mood. A confusion pervades it between detachment and alienation. The self becomes alienated, feels itself alone, only when the individual has cut himself off from his community and has lost faith in its beliefs and values.

At first sight, Karl Jaspers, philosopher of detachment, seems to recognize the close relation between the individual's integrity and his loyalty to the community of which he is a part. He observes that in the past, when men were bound together in stable communities and were united by universal ideas, "Even the isolated individual was supported in his isolation."[17] But instead of turning thought to the task of restoring community attachment and rebuilding institutions in harmony with a reasoned conception of life, he calls on the individual to "rely only in himself . . . to find our way back to ourselves, and to help ourselves by inner action." In like manner he proceeds to make affirmations and then blandly to neutralize and vitiate them by contrarieties.

Jasper tells us that if our lives are not to be meaningful, "they must find their place in an order." Then he leaves us suspended in the nebulous transcendence of "the Comprehensive." He propounds the unconditional imperative of "decision lucidly taken out of an unfathomable depth." But, at the same time he warns against any definitive choice: the philosopher should take nothing for granted, should question everything, remain "floating in his situation." Philosophy, he recognizes, includes wonder and this leads to knowledge, but it also includes doubt which detects that our categories of human understanding are entangled in hopeless contradictions. The deepest source of philosophy is man's experience of the "ultimate situations"—the inevitability of death, the subjection to chance and suffering, the consciousness of guilt. He grants a saving grace to philosophy—"the will to authentic communication." But this remedy for all human ills turns out to be nothing other than that frail plant, "man's love for man"—which, as all European history cries out in anguish, is a broken reed when unaccompanied by justice and unprotected by law. In fine, devoid as it is of any support in a system of ideas and lacking rootage in a definite form of community life, Jaspers' philosophy evanesces in sentiment and deliquesces in the subjectivity of "the inner experience of Being."

Jean-Paul Sartre's philosophy of commitment reveals a firmer stance and a more constructive social orientation. There is no withdrawal from the affairs of life; he calls for involvement in political struggle, for active defiance of the oppressor. He is ever aware of the presence of others and of the need of mutual responsibility. As he starkly describes in *The Republic of Silence*, each member of the Resistance stood alone, was hunted in solitude, was arrested in solitude, was tortured in solitude, faced death in solitude. "Yet in the depth of their solitude, it was the others they were protecting . . ."—all their comrades in the Resistance, all Frenchmen who fought against the enemy, all men everywhere who rose in rebellion against tyranny.

---

[17] Karl Jaspers, *Way to Wisdom* (New Haven, 1951), p. 25. Most of the references to Jaspers are taken from this essay.

81

Sartre teaches "total responsibility in total solitude." There is a positive theme in his doctrine: in the extremity of death and torture, he preserves a seed of the essence of liberty—the power to say "no" to the torturer, to remain silent, never to yield—but to defy, to resist, and to fight to the bitter end. Some vestige of faith in victory over the conqueror remains.

Nevertheless, a heavy cloud of hopelessness hangs over Sartre's conception of man as an alien in the universe. Although sympathetic to communism, he sees no salvation in it any more than in any other social philosophy. Like Karl Jaspers, he regards man's life as tragically conditioned by the existentialist "ultimate situations"—by the feeling of being an alien in the universe, by the sense of forsakenness, by the belief that evil in the world is irredeemable. Resting on a one-sided view of human nature and distorted by an abstract individual psychology, Sartre's over-subtle analysis in his massive work *Being and Nothingness*, proves unproductive despite the many insights into character it contains. Failing to reckon with the fact that man is, inexorably, a social and political creature, and uninformed by any constructive theory of organized community life, the solution he offers, namely, "being as the synthetic fusion of the in-itself and the for-itself" leaves us in a no-man's-land between an obscure metaphysics and an indeterminate ethics.[18]

The note of despair that marks recent existentialist writings is understandable as a reaction of sensitive men to the horrors of Nazi dictatorship and the obscenities of the concentration camp. It reflects the intellectual's feeling of impotence in the face of brutal realities and reveals a sense of disillusion with European philosophy and with the Christian religion as sources of individual and social redemption. The failure of an era, the bankruptcy of a political system, the weakness of a particular religious tradition are projected onto man's condition. As Professor Heinemann notes in his discussion of Sartre's pessimistic analysis, "this temporary disgrace of Eurasia has here gained the status of metaphysical dignity."[19]

The existentialist confrontation has value as a counterweight to the too-easy solutions of rationalist and liberalist thought. It has significance in that it makes salient the human need of standing apart from the collective public life, as expressing "the courage to be as oneself," to use Paul Tillich's phrase. But it does not support the other aspect

[18] Jean-Paul Sartre, *Being and Nothingness* (New York, 1956), p. 626.
[19] F. H. Heinemann, *Existentialism and the Modern Predicament* (New York, 1953), p. 126.

of personality, the need of participation in community life, "the courage to be as a part." Whatever significance it has as expressing the character of an age, existentialism fails as a perennial philosophy. It lacks two essentials. It has no theory of political organization which is as indispensable for man's freedom and spiritual development as it is for his security and well-being. And, it lacks an ethical foundation in a definite system of values.

The original *Existenzphilosophie* of Sören Kierkegaard, despite its nonpolitical character, presents a profile quite different from the recent nonreligious and atheistic types. In contrasting Nietzsche and Kierkegaard, William Barrett points out: "Communication means community, and the adventurer into the depths would do well to have roots in a human community . . . Nietzsche lacked such lines of communication, for he had cut himself off from the human community; he was the loneliest man that ever existed. By comparison, Kierkegaard looks almost like a worldly soul, for he was solidly planted in his native Copenhagen, and though he may have been at odds with his fellow citizens, he loved the town and it was his home."[20] More needs to be said: from early in his life, as Kierkegaard testified, he strove to find the idea for which he could live and die. After struggling with the many alternatives of *Either/Or*, he took "the leap" of firm decision which brought him through conflict and the bitterness of estrangement to a haven of peace and joy. The idea he chose was Christianity: "his one thought was what it meant to be a Christian—in Christendom."[21]

There is, it is true, as Barrett indicates, a vestige of the sense of community in the background of Kierkegaard's thought. But he struggled against it, denying any moral or spiritual significance in allegiance to society. His major theme is "the single one." He asserts: "The formula for being a Christian is to be related to, to turn to, God personally, as a single person, quite literally, as a single person." He deplores the tendency of the apostles to conceive Christianity as a community—an idea which he believes "has been the ruin of Christianity." By the same token he regards celibacy—for the laity as well as for priests, for women as well as for men—an essential teaching of the New Testament. Marriage is a continuation of original sin, the chief hindrance to the realization of the spiritual ideal. The sanctification of marriage as a divine institution and the exhaltation

[20] William Barrett, *Irrational Man*, Doubleday Anchor Book (New York, 1962), p. 180.
[21] Robert Bretall, ed., *A Kierkegaard Anthology* (Princeton, 1947), p. xx.

of the family as an exemplification of the moral life he attributes to the failure of Christianity to renounce its link with Judaism which he holds to be its very antithesis.[22]

In its rejection of the bond of community, existentialism negates both its plea for individual responsibility and its call for moral freedom. Attachment and detachment are both indispensable for personal self-realization and in the fulfillment of the ethical life. Horace L. Friess quotes a fine passage from the writings of the fifteenth-century Indian religious poet, Kabir. Using the confluence of the sacred rivers, of the Ganges and the Jumma, as a symbol, Kabir says: "Through the human soul there are forever coursing the two rivers of attachment and detachment; and their confluence, their mingling, is the secret of the holy life."[23] The "stream of attachment," Professor Friess points out, can be interpreted in two ways—in the sense of attachment of family, neighbors, and friends, and in the sense of an attachment to an ethical aspiration, to a "broadened concern for the bonds of human fellowship." In the viewpoint outlined in this chapter, the central theme has been the indispensability of two forms of attachment—of loyalty to definite communal institutions, to the family, to the nationality, to the religious association, on the one hand, and to a body of universal values and ideals which grow out of the institutional life but at the same time transcend any particular society in time and place. In both senses, community and communication are interrelated. Communication and community can have no serious meaning without a common heritage of shared beliefs and values and without a common form of organized community life.

The humane life includes a degree of realization in three spheres of selfhood—participation in the life of the community, commitment to a framework of values and ideals, and expression of the private self in activities which relax the body and refresh the spirit. An equitably balanced and harmonious fulfillment of all three aspects of the personality is rarely possible in the life of the world. In extreme cases, the need for the direction of life by an ethical principle may lead to the establishment of a deliberately organized form of community life, e.g., the monastery or convent, the "backwoods utopias" in the United States, the *kibbutzim* or communitarian settlements in modern Israel. The need for an inner directed life may express itself in the philosophic detached way of life, as with Benedict Spinoza and

[22] Sören Kierkegaard, *The Last Years 1853-1855*, Ronald Gregor Smith, ed., (New York, 1965), pp. 67, 71, 73, 79, 81, 119, 258, 300, and *passim*.

[23] Horace L. Friess, "Our Invitation to Hope," An Address, May 8, 1960, The New York Society for Ethical Culture, (New York, 1960), p. 7.

Immanuel Kant. In their case, concern for the community found expression in their social and political theories despite their apparently abstract intellectualistic character of their vocations. But for the overwhelming majority of men, the "good life," the controlled and directed way of life, must be found within the sphere of the actual society in which they live and within the established institutional forms—with their possibilities and their limitations, their opportunities for self-expression and their restraints on freedom, their satisfactions and their disappointments, their successes and frustrations. A measure of adjustment and compromise will always be necessary. Nevertheless, it is essential to hold fast to some system of ideal beliefs. And it is necessary to give heed to the admonition of the Jewish Fathers, "Separate not thyself from the community."

THE INSTITUTIONS OF COMMUNITY: FAMILY, CHURCH, AND NATION

In former times, the village and the small town represented the chief centers of community life. Such face-to-face societies provided a basic unity of political and material interests and of religious and moral conceptions. For a part of the population in predominantly rural district this is, to some extent, still the case—with its detrimental as well as its positive aspects. However, with the shift of the growth of metropolitan areas and the conglomeration of diverse populations, the homogeneous society of the past no longer represents the major form of community life. Many associations—the professional organizations, the trade unions, social-class cliques, neighborhoods—afford some opportunities for communal expression, but these are auxiliary rather than essential. There remain three institutions, the family, the religious association, the nationality, which have the potentiality of playing crucial roles in moral development. These taken together represent the chief repositories of the Western ethic. Each embodies the concept of "community": each represents common needs, purposes, and ideals, each involves a sense of belonging and identification, each demands discipline and loyalty. The family, the religious association, and the nation, are structured forms of life that have possibilities and limitations, are constituted of freedoms and necessities. They represent communities of destiny that condition our course in life.

We are all members of families even though we may not marry or establish new lines. Connection with a religious organization is ostensibly a matter of voluntary choice. But even if we give up the faith in which we were born, its influence persists in our consciousness. Moreover, religious ideas and institutions pervade Western culture and, whether in agreement or disagreement, have an effect on our thought. Our nationality determines—through language, literature, and education—the form in which the Western cultural heritage comes to us, and gives to our social outlook the signature of democracy. Conditioning these major institutions is the political organ of society, the state, which serves as the framework within which all other associations and communities are contained and which both supports and constrains them. Within each of the pivotal communities—the family, the religious association, the nation and the state—there are innumerable problems of a practical, moral, and ethical nature. The integration of the personality requires finding some *modus vivendi* in the face of the conflicting demands of the several institutions.

The family is the most deeply rooted of all human institutions; it represents a highly complex organization of biological drives, sociological forces, and ethical ideals. Although sexual impulse supplies the initiating factor, the family is not the product of physical need in isolation from other factors. On the contrary, the libido in the broad sense of vital energy as well as in the narrow sexual connotation has always protested against the restrictions necessitated by the marriage institution. It is, rather, the long period of infancy, the enduring maternal instinct, the continued interest of the father in his mate, that have combined to create the human family. Through its concern for rearing the child, the family becomes the chief agency for cultural transmission, particularly in the sphere of moral and religious influence. Until recently, for a large part of the people, it was the agency of vocational training. Although it is no longer the primary unit of productive enterprise, the family retains a centrally important economic function in its responsibility of supporting itself and its obligation to take care of the children until they reach maturity. It is from the family needs and organizations, interplaying with the idealizing tendency of the human mind, that the Judeo-Christian ethic of the fatherhood of God and the brotherhood of man derives. From it also arises the attribute of compassion, which in Hebrew thought is coordinate with God's attribute of justice.

The discussion of marriage, in the celebrated work on *Ethics* by Dewey and Tufts, gives major consideration to the effect on family life of changes in modern society—the emphasis on the individual, the new significance of sex in personal relations, the emancipation of women, their demand for equality, their interest in a career.[24] The

[24] John Dewey and James H. Tufts, *Ethics, op. cit.* The quotations are from chap. XXIII, 'Marriage and the Family," pp. 489-517, written by Mr. Tufts.

general orientation is indicated by the statement that the trend of the age is "against institutions or modes of securing social ends which require sacrifice of individual life or happiness." Nevertheless, marriage and the family are warmly defended on the ground that in the long run "the partnership in the whole of life" affords a deeper and richer experience than the casual alliance in which "one can make and break relations as tastes and moods change." The gratification of sex—so it is urged—contributes more to the fullness of life when it is associated with the cooperative planning for the future of the children, with the sharing of the joys and sorrows of family life. We are told that "the friendship between man and woman which marriage affords when at its best, is more intimate, more beautiful, and mutually helpful than any other." Self-realization, it is agreed, must be adjusted to social claims, and this constitutes a problem "which each must work out anew." There is confidence that the family will not only be able to withstand the modern forces at work but will be enriched by them and be raised to a new level of high morality.

Another side of the story is suggested by William James who says: "See the unnamed and unnamable sorrows which the tyranny, on the whole so beneficent, of the marriage-institution brings to so many, both of the married and the unwed."[25] The glowing view of marriage presented in the previous paragraph may be defended on the ground that it represents an ideal toward which to strive and one that is in varying degrees possible to achieve by persistent and intelligent cultivation. However, the difficulty is far more serious: the whole way of posing the problem of marriage is deceptive. The option of marriage or mistress is not open to any large section of the population. But apart from this incidental point, the problem of marriage cannot be fruitfully discussed without reference to the total sociological context.

Marriage is not only an arrangement between a man and a woman for satisfaction in decency of sexual needs and for fruitful companionship, however significant and enriching these aspects may be. Nor is the definition of the family made complete by adding to its function the rearing and the education of children. The possibilities for moral growth inherent in family life as well as the difficulties that surround it are obscured when marriage is described as a matter of free choice. It is misleading to create the impression that the individual once married has any considerable range of freedom "to work out anew" the claims of his personal interest vis-à vis the claims of society.

Marriage and the form of the family are, in the first instance, pre-

25 William James, *The Will to Believe* (New York, 1917), p. 207.

scribed for us by the society in which we live. Family life is conditioned by legal provisions, social conventions, and moral codes. The adjustments in married life are not only to another person, but first of all an accommodation to a structured system of relations. The form of the family, the prevailing laws and conventions, may be modified, but, in that case, new laws and conventions must be adopted. It is always within the limitations of social forms that any degree of freedom may be said to exist in the marriage institution. However great the margin of deviation allowed, the essence of it is that family life means a transfer from the regime of maximum satisfaction to the regime of the primacy of obligation.

Marriage is a fateful crossing of the Rubicon into a new stage of life: it means adopting a new role, achieving a new identity. It means establishing a home as a center of life; it involves support of a household and perhaps financial aid to parents and other relatives. It means accepting membership in a family unit which, even in its modern attenuated state, includes grandparents as well as parents and kinfolk of various degrees of relation. Marriage implies a new focus of concern, it requires a transformation of ego-centric involvement with one's own satisfactions and development to an identification of the self with the family community.

It is in fulfilling obligations and responsibilities as well as in the realization of joys and satisfactions that the mature moral personality is formed. The ethics of marriage and of family life cannot be based either on an ascetic or a hedonistic moral theory. Nevertheless, the balance of emphasis, as in the traditional systems, needs to be placed on self-restraint, on devotion and on sacrifice. Family life cannot be sustained by "the marvel and the mystery of Love" which, we are told, transforms all relations between the members of the family and achieves "self-pervading communion of persons."[26] The sincerest affection must be supported by common material concerns, common cultural interests, common values, common involvement in a wider social community of neighborhood, social class or religious association. In marriage, the very meaning of love must be transformed, weaned from its primarily romantic implications and brought to its mature connotation of concern and solicitude. Marriage is "for better or for worse"; it brings in its train a commitment of comradeship in adversity—in the face of the loss of fortune, in the event of illness, in responsibility for a retarded child. Family life cannot rest on the morality of prudential wisdom in the sense of intelligent considera-

[26] Radoslav A. Tsanoff, *Ethics* (New York, 1947), p. 199.

tion of consequences; it demands a morality of acceptance of responsibility for unintended and unwanted consequences.

The institution of the family is subject to great strains under the impact of modern conditions and forces—the hectic pressure of life in metropolitan areas, the weakening of religious influence, the reduction of the functions and activities of the home. A major factor to reckon with is the entry of women into a great range of occupations which keeps the mother as well as the father absent from the home for a greater part of the day. The strengthening of family life involves problems in the economic area, in housing, in medical care, and in the expansion of social services and psychiatric aid. The unsettlement of the traditional codes of sexual behavior is a major problem.

The difficulties that have arisen as a result of complex changes in social conditions and moral attitudes cannot be resolved by the return to the prescriptive regulations of former days, which in any case were not as consistently practiced as we pretend. But even less appropriate to the need of our times is the view that gives major consideration to "the increased interest in sex," that depreciates sacrifice for social ends, that leaves final decision in all moral matters to the undirected judgment of the individual. The institution of the family is indispensable to Western civilization, as important to the individual as it is to society. However wide the latitude of permissiveness, the standpoint in moral judgment cannot be primarily the ambitions, the desires, or the opinion of the individual. What conduces to the integrity and welfare of the family community as the nucleus of social organization is a prerequisite consideration.

Supporting and complementing the institution of the family is the organized religious community which in its various forms—the historical Christian churches, Jewish synagogues, and the modernist types such as the Christian Science Church and the Ethical Culture Society—occupies a significant place in the social and cultural as well as in the spiritual and strictly religious phases of life. The religious community encompasses a wide range of concerns related to family life, to social welfare, to education and philosophic conceptions. Its approach to the activities and to the issues of life differs from that which prevails in secular institutions. In the family and in the economic and political affairs, the social arrangements and the moral regulations arise out of animal instincts and practical needs while the religious attitudes and endeavors have their genesis in the psychic impulses which are the distinctive attitudes of man. They grow out of man's imaginative power, out of his sensitivity to the spirit that hovers over the waters of life, out of his great need to see himself in relation of unity to the cosmos.

Although the religious community reaches out toward universal ethical values and transcendental aspirations, it is in the first instance an extension of the family connection. Affiliation with a religious community is not, for most people, the result of a preference for a congenial mode of worship or of a choice of a rationally convincing system of beliefs; it is rather a response to the need for community attachment, for belonging to a group with which one feels a consciousness-of-kind. We are born into religious communities as we are born into a line of families, and generally each one remains identified, in the minds of others as well as of himself, with his original religious community even when no longer attached to it.

Membership in one or the other of the major religious groupings in the United States is influenced by ethnic background. This is obvious in the case of the Jews; it applies, although in lesser degree, to the Irish, Italians, and Poles, who are predominantly Catholics. The ethnic factor is not absent in the case of Protestants whose family background can generally be traced to English, German, or Scandinavian origin. Conversion from one of the historical faiths to another is only rarely carried by a change of conviction. It is more likely to result from intermarriage or from a change in social status. In transference of allegiance to one of the newer religious associations, e.g., the Christian Science groups or to Ethical Culture societies, dissatisfaction with the traditional beliefs is more often the cause, but intermarriage and social status also play a part.

Affiliation with a religious community is, in itself, of psychological and moral significance, as enlarging selfhood and strengthening the sense of personal dignity. It tends, moreover, to lead beyond mere attachment into the sphere of cultural and ethical values. Viewing the religious associations as forms of community life points up their wide range of concerns and the many social as well as spiritual resources which they potentially offer. The organized religions include good works as well as articles of faith, engage in pastoral and charitable activities as well as provide houses of worship, are concerned with the temporal as well as the transcendent. Their rituals and ceremonies lend an overtone of sanctity, of radiance and of grace, to the crucial occasions of marriage and of birth; they support hope in illness, assuage the grief of mourners. The music of the religious service releases emotional stress, composes and lifts the soul. The traditional religions are custodians of the literatures on which they are founded, and encourage the cultivation of the classic humanities. They offer help in relieving the existential anxieties, in cleansing from sense of guilt, in giving meaning to life, in redeeming doubt and indecision by urging to commitment. The religious community opens a gateway to communion with the intangible and the imponderable essences that pervade the universe. And when the Western religions are true to their Judaic origin, they make service to fellow man an integral element of the love of God.

Not all the denominations lay equal emphasis on the various lines of activities, nor stress the social and the educational as well as the devotional and creedal aspects. Each religious community and each denomination within the major divisions represents a unique pattern of ideas, practices, social and world outlooks. It is upon the total effect of their ideas, services, and activities that the significance of the religious communities is to be adjudged. The attempt to find general values underlying the various religions is likely to result in the enunciation of a few vague moralistic truisms. As Horace M. Kallen says, in response to one such proposal, "to strip the Judeo-Christian religions, or any other of 'their divergent ethnic, doctrinal, and structural factors' would be to denature them."[27]

Appreciation of their contributions is not meant to conceal the negative aspects of institutionalized religions either of the past or of the present. The accusation that the traditional religions have tended to emphasize formal beliefs and rituals of worship rather than their moral and social purpose cannot be altogether denied. Notoriously, Christian churches, preaching love have at times practiced hate, have ministered to the rich rather than to the poor, have served the powerful rather than aided the oppressed. The theological defense of religion has often been marked by obscurantism and obfuscation. A grave intellectual error bedevils it, namely, the claim to possession of truth; worst of all is the pretense to possession of absolute truth. Religions may be better or worse—enlightened or superstitious, spiritually significant or dessicated by routine habit, socially beneficial or detrimental—but, as George Santayana has said, "never true or false."

Affiliation with a religious community has value in the measure that it is voluntary. The great merit of the separation of church and state is that it eliminates the coercive element in religion, that it allows each one freedom to associate himself with the religious community of his choice. There are important sections of the population who feel no need personally for a religious association, who express their moral

[27] Horace M. Kallen in *This Is My Faith*, Stewart G. Cole, ed., (New York, 1956), p. 150.

impulse in social causes, and who find resources for spiritual life in literature and philosophy. Nevertheless, for the majority of the American people affiliation with a religious community has genuine value, in sustaining them as persons, in sanctioning moral principles, in linking them with a historical and international community, in revealing for them the realm of transcendental experience. The traditional religions play a significant part in supporting minority groups in their struggle for civil liberties and in their effort to retain distinctive values in the ethnic cultural heritage. Religious leaders are playing an outstanding role in the struggle against poverty and discrimination and in efforts directed toward international peace.

The third institution of community, the nation, exercises a pervasive, in certain senses a decisive influence, on the personality. One may avoid marriage; affiliation with a religious community is voluntary. But we must be born in some nation, and only in the rarest instances can we sever our connection with it. The individual's sense of identity is linked with consciousness of belonging to, and being descended from, a national group. One's nationality determines one's language and cultural heritage; it influences the religious community with which one is likely to be associated. One's nationality affects one's security and freedom and conditions one's political philosophy.

There are two distinct meanings of the term "nation"—the cultural and the political. In its primary cultural meaning, nationality implies common language and literature, common history and traditions, common customs and ideals. The political meaning refers to the organization of the state as a territorial unit on the basis of the principle of nationality. The two conceptions are separable in application. The ancient Greeks represented one nationality but were divided into separate states; empires are multi-national states generally dominated by one nation, e.g., ancient Rome, the former British Empire. The union of nationality and statehood is a feature of the modern age in Western Europe and was associated with the rise of democracy. It is playing a decisive role in the organization of the newly developing countries in Asia and Africa recently liberated from colonial domination.

The principle of nationality in both its cultural and political meaning presents numerous problems in the domestic sphere as well as on the international front. Within the United States, there is the problem of the integration of the minorities into American life, the equalization of opportunities for individuals, and the recognition of the validity of their voluntary organization as communities. The crucial case is that of the Negro. Less exigent but still significant is the question of "cultural pluralism"—the right of minority groups, of other than "Anglo-Saxon derivation," to retain a sense of group identity and preserve their language and elements of their cultural heritage within the framework of American life.[28] There are unresolved issues in the relation of religious communities to the national culture and to the state; e.g., in the field of education, in the right of conscientious objectors to be exempted from military service, in the matter of the salute to the flag.

On the international scene, the principle of nationality implies self-determination and the protection of the autonomous rights of sub-nationalities in multi-national states. Overriding all other problems is the critical one of adjusting the economic and political interests of each nation to the developing international character of society. On the ethical plane, is the need of harmonizing loyalty to nation with the idea of the unity of mankind. It is in the area of national life that we find the gravest conflicts and tensions between the demands of security and material welfare, on the one hand, and the universal ideas of democracy for which America stands. But the problems cannot be resolved by resort to a cosmopolitan humantarianism. Nationality is an existential reality, significant from a cultural, psychological, and moral point of view, as well as fundamental to the political organization of a world order.

Within each of the pivotal institutions of community, the family, the religious association, the national society, there are problems of a practical, moral and ethical nature. Freedom must be adjusted to necessities, satisfactions to obligations, ideals to possibilities. In each area there is room for a degree of diversity and for a measure of choice. Nevertheless, in each, the maintenance of community life requires the assumption of principles and the definition of norms, some socially determined boundaries of right and wrong. The three institutions, family, religious community, nation, are interdependent. At the same time, they stand in a relation of tension with each other, support and supplement each other, and check each other. For the individual, there is a problem of achieving a workable reconciliation among the interests and ideals of the basic communal institutions. For moral philosophy, there is the task of formulating principles for the several institutions of community which may guide the judgment of the individual.

The moral life cannot be lived in the mental and spiritual realm. There is no salvation or justification by faith without good works. The affirmation of general ideas in abstract form, i.e., justice, love,

[28] See Milton M. Gordon, *Assimilation in American Life* (New York, 1964).

peace, is of little significance, although such value-concepts are indispensable as points of reference in application to their appropriate realms. Nor is it sufficient to say that morals are social; it is necessary to add that the chief problems of morality are not in the relation of abstract individuals to abstract individuals, but of person to person relations within the institutionalized and communal structures. This brings us to the final point. The institutions of community need the protection of the state. Ethics requires a politics to support it.

ETHICS AND POLITICS IN WESTERN THOUGHT

A concern with the relation of ethics to politics is a distinguishing mark of Western thought: "The great political theories grow out of and give expression to moral beliefs and sentiments. None of the important questions in political philosophy can be answered without reference to these beliefs; and no moral doctrine can be seriously estimated or criticized without full consideration of the political theory which derives from them."[29] Pervading the ethical-political conceptions also is a striving for rationality as conforming to an envisaged ideal. The Western conception of an ethically-based political community in harmony with reason has its origin in Athens and is exemplified in the writings of Plato and Aristotle. The spirit and substance of the ethical outlook of the West, however, was essentially derived from Hebrew sources which entered Europe through the Christian synthesis of Judaic, Hellenistic, and Roman thought.

Hebrew thought of the Biblical period contains, in aspirational mood, major themes of a universal and humane ethic. At its heart lies a sense of reverence and awe toward the universe, a high regard for all created things, an affirmation of the value and the sanctity of life. The monotheism of the Hebrew Scriptures is not metaphysical but moral: it connotes the unity of all mankind, the fatherhood of God and the brotherhood of man. Created in the image of God, each person is precious and unique; descended from a single ancestor, all men are equal in worth. God is Sovereign of the Universe, his law stands above the law of earthly kings. Justice and compassion are the twin attributes of deity. Throughout the Scriptures there is an undercurrent of protest against slavery and oppression of the poor. The prophets' denunciation of the worship of Baal and Ashtoreth is an expression of hatred against the lord of the land and of abhorrence of licentiousness. Hebrew thought, however, is never otherworldly; it knows that man does not live by bread alone, but it recognizes the need of bread

[29] T. D. Weldon, *States and Morals* (New York, 1947), p. 273.

as the staff of life. Peace is a pervading idea, the inner peace of mind, and peace in the world which in Isaiah's vision will come in the end of days.

"The example of the Hebrew nation laid down the parallel lines on which all freedom has been won—the doctrine of a national tradition and the doctrine of the higher law; the principle that a constitution grows from a root by a process of development, and not of essential change; and the principle that all political authorities must be tested and reformed according to a code which was not made by man."[30] Lord Acton's appreciative judgment states one indispensable aspect of the Western development. It is true that the teachings of Scripture— its sympathy for fellow men and compassion for suffering, its cry for justice based on human equality, its recognition of a morally inspired law, its proclamation of liberty to all the land and to the inhabitants thereof—have served as an ethical ferment, troubled men's consciences, even at times stirred them to revolutionary action in behalf of social advance. But the Hebrews lacked a constructive political conception. The envisaged ideal society was to be achieved by following the precepts of the Torah; it would come when the principles of justice, compassion, and peace were inscribed in the hearts of men, when the knowledge of the Lord would cover the earth as waters cover the sea. The nearest the Hebrews came to a political idea was in the hope for a messianic king, descended from the line of David, on whom would rest "the spirit of wisdom and understanding, the spirit of counsel and of courage, the spirit of knowledge and reverence of the Lord."

It is to the Hellenes, not to the Hebrews, that the West owes the political concepts prerequisite to the development of the good society. The definition, quoted in the name of Aristotle that man is a political animal, represented a general Greek idea underlying both the Sophist and Platonist interpretations of the classical Athenian view: it signified that citizenship in the state is indispensable to humanhood. Outside the *polis*, Aristotle held, man must either rise to divinity, that is, become a God, or revert to the animal state, that is, become a beast. In the classic Greek conception, although the state may have had its origin in the need of security and economic life, its final end, its true purpose, is the moral perfection of man. The education of the young to virtue is its indispensable function. Moreover, the full import of the idea that man is a political animal can be realized only when we

[30] Lord Acton, *Essays on Freedom and Power,* selected and with an Introduction by Gertrude Himmelfarb (Glencoe, Ill., 1948), p. 33.

bear in mind that the Greek city-state was a community, not merely an association of individuals. Citizenship was acquired by descent, it implied membership by birth in an organized community bound by a common system of law and conception of justice.

In the view of both Plato and Aristotle, the good state is prior, in the sense of being prerequisite, to the good individual. Private ethics and public ethics are different sides of one unitary conception. As Windelband summarizes: "For Aristotle like Plato was convinced that the moral excellence of man, since it always relates to activities which prosper in the life of the community can find fulfillment only in the life of a community; for him, too, there is ultimately no perfect moral life outside of the *state*, the essential end of which was considered by Aristotle also to be the ethical training of its citizens."[31] This insistence on the political and communal basis of man's life is all the more significant because both Plato and Aristotle regarded the highest values of life as residing in the realm of mind and spirit; with Plato, it rested finally in mystic religious communion, with Aristotle, in the intellectual contemplation of divinity.

Interrelated with the political idea is the other Hellenic principle: man is a rational creature. Reason in the classic Greek view implies the faculty of discerning orders, of conceiving universals within particularities, of setting up patterns—assumed to represent supersensible reality—as standards of judgment. Reason works two ways: it controls impulse and leads to an ordered way of life; it subjects traditional and conventional habits to the judgment of an ideal standard. In the life of the individual, reason leads to Socrates' conception of *askesis*, a discipline of rational control. As applied to the state, it signifies the rule of law approved by reason; it means establishing the state on a constitutional foundation embodying a conception of the good.

It is in the union of an envisaged ideal with the principle of law that the ethical and political come together in the Greek view. Plato's concept of the Idea of the Good serves as a directive for a reform of the state as a means of the attainment of the moral perfection of man. As Ernst Cassirer has interpreted Plato's view: "The soul of the individual is bound up with the social nature; we cannot separate the one from the other. Public and private life are interdependent... That was the fundamental insight by which Plato, from his first studies of dialectic, was led back to his study of politics. We cannot hope to reform philosophy if we do not begin by reforming the state. That is

[31] W. Windelband, *A History of Philosophy* (New York, 1919), p. 152.

the only way if we wish to change the ethical life of men. To find the right political order is the first and most urgent problem."[32]

There remains in the classical Greek conception, especially in Plato, a doubt whether the philosophic life can be lived within any actual political order. But the high evaluation of the speculative life does not lead to a diminution of concern with the political order. In the *Republic*, the philosopher-rulers, having served the state effectively and faithfully, are allowed, at the age of fifty, to spend most of their time in study, "to lift up the eye of the soul to gaze on that which sheds light on all things; and when they have seen the Good itself, take it as a pattern for the right ordering of the state and of the individual, themselves included." Even then, these elder statesmen must take their turn at public service, act as teachers of the younger guardians, and give counsel in times of trouble. Aristotle's views on politics are more down to earth: he recognizes several forms—monarchy, aristocracy, democracy, polity, or the mixed constitution—as valid in relation to economic and other factors. But, like Plato, he regards ethics as the guide to politics and maintains that moral education is a primary function of the state. Both of them regard the *polis* as the center of community life and as the model type of state organization.

In both Plato and Aristotle, there is a recognition that actual states fall short of the ideal and are ever liable to corruption. To live in accordance with the philosophic conception of *eudaimonia*—of happiness in the sense of composure of the spirit—requires a degree of detachment from worldly affairs. There remained, nevertheless, in their view, the basic assumption of Greek political thought, that social organization under state control is indispensable for the moral and spiritual development of man as well as for the satisfaction of his natural needs and for his security. In the Hellenistic era, in the period of political upheavals when the independent city-states organization gave way to empire, active interest in the reform of existing states declined and the belief in the possibility of a good state on this earth well-nigh disappeared.

The chief philosophies of the Hellenistic period, Stoicism and Epicureanism, did not reject the state in theory. In harmony with their rational and universal outlook, the Stoics set up an ideal of *kosmopolites*, of world citizenship that would embrace all men and women on a basis of equality regardless of race or nationality, and whether free or slave. Nevertheless, they regarded citizenship in the actual state where

[32] Ernst Cassirer, *The Myth of the State*, Doubleday Anchor Books (New York, 1955), pp. 73-74.

one lived as an obligation. The Epicureans likewise recognized the state as necessary for maintaining the minimum of social order prerequisite for carrying on the private life. They taught obedience to the laws of the state, if for no other reason than for the purpose of avoiding punishment. However, in both views interest in the state is secondary. The problem that was central in the philosophy of Plato and Aristotle, the reform of the *polis* in the light of an ethical ideal, was replaced by the personal problem of maintaining an ideal way of life in the face of the urgencies of physical desires and of the pressures of worldly affairs. Happiness could be achieved only in freeing oneself from everything that disturbed one's tranquility and composure. For the Stoics this meant, primarily, freedom from passionate emotion; the Epicureans emphasized freedom from the distractions of business and politics which interfered with the pursuit of cultivated enjoyment and gracious living.

The ethical philosophies of the Hellenistic period are usually represented as ushering in a new era marked by emphasis on the personality of the individual, by a turning toward the inner life and by withdrawing from social relationships. As applied to Epicureanism and Stoicism, particularly to the latter, this interpretation is likely to be misleading. The self-sufficiency of the Stoic and Epicurean is not achieved by alienation from society, but on the contrary, by identifying oneself with a community wider than the *polis*—a community bound together, not by ties of kinship or material needs, but by beliefs and attitudes. In both systems, friendship is highly valued. In this connection, it is well to remember that the ancient schools of philosophy were not only teaching institutions devoted to academic instruction. They were fraternities, with the juridical status of religious bodies, dedicated to the promotion of a way of life as well as to the pursuit of knowledge.

What is implied in the Stoic and Epicurean doctrines is not isolation from society or even from politics. The core of the idea is rather that the happiness of the individual is *not dependent* on the character of the state in which he happens to live, just as it is not dependent on good or ill fortune. Both philosophies, especially the Stoic, had at least a theoretical concern with the nature of the state and with the problem of justice as a basis of law. Although the Stoic conception of world citizenship was a sentiment rather than an effective political idea, its rational and universal principles had a great influence on the Roman jurists and became a part of the European tradition of natural law which embodied the idea that human legislation must be in accord with a higher moral principle.

In the ethically-based philosophies of the Hellenistic period there was a broadening of the sense of community beyond the confines of the city-state. But along with this went a weakening of concern with civic life and an underestimation of the part that political organization plays in the liberation or suppression of the ethical life. In the medieval Christian concept of "the two swords," the classic Athenian ideal of a unity of life within the city-state community was replaced by a theory of a dual loyalty—to the church and to the royal power. The prince exercised rightful authority in the temporal sphere, in maintaining order and administering the civil law. The church claimed supremacy in all matters that pertained to the moral and spiritual life, in defining doctrine and determining matters of faith and ritual prerequisite to salvation. As the many jurisdictional disputes during the Middle Ages evidence, the lines of competence were never clearly drawn and the division of authority not strictly carried out in practice. But both sides, the royal and the clerical, accepted the theory in principle, and employed it in defense of the scope of their respective authorities.

The doctrine of two powers—each with its own laws and organs of administration supporting each other—was designed by the churchmen who formulated it to preserve the autonomy of the religious interest and to extend its spiritual and moral influence over the secular arm. In practice, it served to enhance the power of government; the church fathers made obedience to the ruler a religious duty as well as a secular obligation. In some opinions, as in that of St. Ambrose, the church retained the right to rebuke an erring emperor on the ground that as a Christian he was "within the church, not above it." But he denied any right to resist the prince by force. St. Augustine likewise affirms that the royal power must be bound by Christian morality. But his concern is with the achievement of personal salvation through religious communion, not with the reform of the secular life. Gregory the Great is more explicit in his counsel of passive, uncritical obedience to government. He asserts emphatically that subjects must not only obey but also that they must not set themselves up as judges of their rulers. "For indeed," he says, "the acts of rulers are not to be smitten with the sword of the mouth, even though they are rightly judged to be blameworthy." In final analysis, the control of the secular power over the church authority was more effective than the spiritual influence of religion over the princes.

The religious teaching of the Middle Ages was oriented toward the enhancement of the inner spiritual life and toward the achievement of personal salvation in the world-to-come rather than toward the advance of justice on this earth. The mystically-minded Plato of the *Timaeus*, not the imaginative statesman of the *Republic*, engaged the attention of the churchmen of the Middle Ages. The vision of Isaiah dropped into the background; Jesus' pronouncement, "My kingdom is not of this world," became the central motif. Acceptance of one's lot, resignation to the evil of the world, submission to authority—these attitudes were made the better part of wisdom. Humility and piety, chastity and abnegation, were the esteemed virtues. There was a positive humane side to the medieval ethic in its encouragement of kindliness and of charity, of compassion and forgiveness. The depreciation of the worldly interests was a foil for the praise of the beauty of the inner life of spirit and for the commendation of the beatitude of the *vita contemplativa*.

Despite its very limited influence on the actual conduct of government during the Middle Ages, the doctrine of the "two swords" bequeathed to modern times the indispensable and distinctive conception that there is a realm of mind and spirit that lies outside the competence of the state. As George H. Sabine wrote, in concluding his discussion of the concept of the two jurisdictions: "This double aspect of Christian society produced a unique problem which in the end contributed perhaps more than any other to the specific properties of European political thought. Far beyond the period in which the relation between the two authorities was a chief controversial issue, the belief in spiritual autonomy and the right of spiritual freedom left a residium without which modern ideas of individual privacy and liberty would be scarcely intelligible."[33]

Toward the end of the Middle Ages, new social forces and changed ideas stimulated a strong interest in political theory among ecclesiastical and lay philosophers. The expansion of trade, the growth of cities, the emergence of a strong mercantile class and the stirrings of nationalism combined to emphasize the importance of the secular power. The renewed study of Roman jurisprudence and the increased knowledge of Aristotle led to an emphasis on the rationality and the universality of law. The effort of political theory was in the direction of creating an effective unitary social and political authority to replace the medieval conception of dual jurisdiction. At first, there was an endeavor to convert the spiritual and moral superiority of the church into the political concept of papal supremacy. In the end, the religious authority was deprived of all independent coercive power and subordinated to the sovereign national state.

[33] *A History of Political Theory* (New York, 1937), p. 196.

The discussion among the schoolmen in the ensuing period of transition contributed to the development of the principles of republican government and to the relaxation of doctrinal rigidity. Thomas Aquinas in the thirteenth century would make the Pope, as embodying the superior spiritual authority, the final arbiter of Christian governments. In line with the principle of dual jurisdiction, he would accord the emperor full authority in temporal affairs. But departing from the medieval mood, he abandons the attitude of passive obedience to the royal power. The monarch as well as his subjects must obey the law; the king holds office in the interest of the common good, and when he proves unfaithful in his trust, the people have the right to depose him. There are thus, anticipations of political liberalism in St. Thomas' views. But his thought is still bound to medieval preconceptions, as is evident in his acceptance of the church's severe attitude toward heresy.

Marsilius of Padua, in the next century, points more definitely toward the constitutional secular state. He gives the church a significant place in the body politic, but he drastically reduces its power through limiting its property rights, abolishing all its temporal functions, and confining its authority narrowly to matters of faith required for salvation in the after life. Moreover, although he holds that a common core of Christian belief is essential, this is to be determined by a General Council of the church, not by the pope or the hierarchy. And differing sharply from Aquinas, he would impose no penalty for heresy. Likewise, he denies arbitrary power to the head of the state; he conceives the executive as subject to a legislature in some measures representative of the community at large. The views of William of Occam are still more advanced in the direction of political and intellectual liberalism. He regards civil government as legitimate—as "natural" and "rational"—only when it is supported by the consent of the governed; he defends the right of minorities within the church to follow the dictates of conscience in the interpretation of Christian doctrine.

In the centuries intervening before the establishment of the constitutional state, absolute monarchy became entrenched and received the approbation of political theorists for a time. The monarchies rendered tangible services: they subordinated the church to the state, crushed the power of the feudal barons, united the nation, promoted the interests of the manufacturing and the trading classes. However, in the wake of the necessary—and, in the main, salutary—enlargement of the secular power, the classical conceptions and the medieval checks on arbitrary government were undermined. The idea of a natural law that stood above a civil law, the organization of local communes, the feudal compact between lord and vassal, the autonomy of the free cities—these concepts and institutions which limited the power of the princes in various respects lost their significance in political theory and their importance in practice. The church, deprived of its independent power, became a voluntary institution or an adjunct to the secular government. With the disappearance of the legal authority of the church, the modicum of moral influence on government implied in the claim to spiritual authority was further weakened.

With Niccolò Machiavelli, all pretensions to moral considerations in politics were abandoned. He confines himself to a discussion of the policies and the devices that are likely to strengthen or to weaken the secular ruler. Whatever the motives and purposes—whether he was an utter cynic or patriotic nationalist—he made a lasting contribution to political theory in bringing out into the open the indispensable part that power plays, for good or for evil, in the maintenance of states. Thomas Hobbes, likewise, recognized the necessity of coercive force and of a sovereign authority to exercise it. He sacrifices all qualifications to a severe consistency. His premise is that brutish natural man, dominated by self-interest and "a restless desire for power after power," is ever at war with every other man. Nevertheless, men have enough sense to institute governments for survival and protection of property. But, since "covenants without the sword are but words," government must have absolute coercive power to punish individuals who disturb the peace and interfere with the orderly carrying out the business of life. There are no good or bad governments, only strong or weak ones. Law has nothing to do with morality; it is the unrestricted command of the sovereign.

The recognition that government, indispensable for social organization, necessarily involves the use of coercive force contributed an essential element to modern political theory. However, traditional European conceptions that reflected the insight that man was a spiritual being and that a polity devoid of a moral basis could not long survive continued to act as a leaven, at the same time undergoing reconstruction in the light of the humanist and secularist tendencies of the modern world. Sir Thomas More, emulating Plato and interpreting him in the light of the communitarian principle of the early Christian church, fused ethics with politics again in his utopian vision of a cooperative commonwealth based on self-labor. Hugo Grotius, concerned with the relation between sovereign states, emancipated law from its dependence on religious sanction of the Catholic church. Natural law, basing its authority on "right reason," taken to reflect mankind's common view of what is just, is binding on all peoples whatever their religion, on rulers as well as peoples. Both More and Grotius point toward socialism and internationalism.

When absolute monarchy in England, grown arrogant—and no longer serving the needs of the expanding middle-class interests—was overthrown, John Locke produced a workable conception of republican government by means of a combination of the prevalent and traditional political ideas. The second *Essay on Government,* in which the major principles are expounded, has the appearance of a political tract in defense of a revolution already accomplished. But, as George H. Sabine, has pointed out, it reached far into the past: "Through Hooker, Locke was joined with the long tradition of medieval political thought back to St. Thomas, in which the reality of moral restraints on power, the responsibility of rulers to the communities which they ruled, and the subordination of government to law were axiomatic."[34] It is necessary to add that Locke greatly modified the traditional ideas and wove them into a new pattern. Natural law he interpreted in the sense of natural rights, inherent in the individual and inalienable. He specifies them as life, liberty, and property. His conception assumes an individual living in a national community. It is the nation which delegates power to the government, a power which is limited by long-standing conventions and by law which must be interpreted and applied by the courts. It is the nation which has the right to recall the government and to choose another when it fails to protect the inalienable natural rights. In the matter of the dual jurisdiction he broke with the medieval system altogether, divesting the church of coercive power, separating politics from religion. Even here, however, an important influence remained from the medieval tradition. As he denies to the church the right to interfere in government, so he denies to government the right to interfere in matters of belief.

Locke's conception was compromised by the central place he gave to property as a basis for participation in political life. His division of the community into two nations, the propertied and the propertyless, conditioned English politics for two centuries. In Jean Jacques Rousseau's interpretation of the social contract, political and social equality is made the foundation. Everyone, regardless of property qualifications, should have one vote and a vote of the same value. The paradoxical epigrammatic character of much of his writing has given rise to diverse interpretations: by some he has been denounced as the advocate of irresponsible individualism, by others as the forerunner of

[34] *Ibid.,* p. 523.

modern collectivist despotism. Neither of these accusations is justifiable in such extreme form. But there is more ground for the latter in his concept of the General Will, to which the individual must subordinate himself.

The crucial element in Rousseau's contribution is the restoration of the primacy of the community, of the Greek idea that man is a citizen by nature of his character as a human being. With this goes an explicit recognition of the interdependence of ethics and politics, the idea succinctly expressed in the *Emile*: "Society must be studied in the individual and the individual in society; those who desire to treat politics and morals apart from one another will never understand either."[35] As Ernst Cassirer has pointed out, the clue to the understanding of Rousseau's inner motivation and of the thread of consistency in his diverse writings is given in the Confessions:

I had realized that everything was basically related to politics, and that, no matter how one approached it, no people would ever be anything but what the nature of the government made it. Therefore the great question of the best possible government seemed to me to reduce itself to this: which is the form of government fitted to shape the most virtuous, the most enlightened, the wisest, and in short, the "best" people, taking the word in its noblest meaning?[36]

[35] Jean Jacques Rousseau, *Emile, or Education*, Modern Library (New York, 1911), p. 197.
[36] Ernst Cassirer, *The Question of Jean Jacques Rousseau*, Peter Gay, ed. and trans., (New York, 1954), p. 65.

PART TWO

THE ETHICS AND POLITICS OF DEMOCRACY

CHAPTER FOUR

TWO IDEOLOGIES: LIBERALISM AND MARXISM

The Conflict of the Two Worlds

The Ideology of Liberalism

Marxism as a Critique of Liberalism

Variations in Marxist Doctrine

Beyond Marxism and Liberalism

That was the fundamental insight by which Plato, from his first study in dialectic, was led back to his study of politics. We cannot hope to reform philosophy if we do not begin by reforming the state. That is the only way if we wish to change the ethical life of man. To find the right political order is the first and most urgent problem. ERNST CASSIRER

4.

Two Ideologies: Liberalism and Marxism

D URING the period from the American to the Russian revolution, liberalism, as an attitude of mind and as a concept of government, provided the activating force in European and American social and political policy. Its energies were directed against the ideas and institutions associated with the regime of the preceding centuries—of absolute monarchy in union with church establishment. On the positive side, it stood for the republican forms of government, for toleration of religious differences, for individual rights and national unity. In England, France, and the United States, where these principles were accepted as basic assumptions, there remained a struggle between liberalism proper—the actual pattern of operative ideas—and the growing demand for democracy. The former rested on the individualistic, property-centered conceptions of John Locke; the latter owed a greater debt to Rousseau's notions of the equality of political rights regardless of property qualifications and sovereignty of the people as an integral community. In the middle of the nineteenth century, a third conception, that of socialism, became an active political idea, and under the caption "communism" had already assumed the threatening form of "a specter haunting Europe."

109

Like liberalism and democracy, communism has roots in classic and medieval thought. As a moral attitude expressing itself in utopian visions, it had antecedents in Christian interpretation of Plato's *Republic* and of the Stoic conception of natural law. The patristic and scholastic writings are pervaded by the belief that riches are a hindrance to salvation, that great wealth cannot be obtained without injustice. The canonical commentators reiterate the opinion of St. Isidore of Seville that possession in common is "the sweetest of all things." In the medieval Christian view, the communistic society is to be achieved through self-reform by means of religious and moral discipline. In the early English communisms from the fourteenth to the seventeenth centuries—as illustrated in the teachings of Wycliffe, More, and Winstanley—the dreams of an ideal commonwealth begin to be more closely related to the need of change in economic and political organization.

With the ascendance of industrial capitalism in the nineteenth century and the deterioration of the condition of the working classes, socialist endeavors began to take on definite forms in a comingling of humanitarian sentiment with social theories and practical proposals. The nonpolitical Robert Owen, father of British socialism, established cooperative communities in England and in the United States. In France, there was a proliferation of socialist ideas in the conceptions and projects of Saint Simon, Fourier, Louis Blanc, and Proudhon. It was among Germans that socialism attained the position of a clearly formulated doctrine integrated with economic theory; to this development the scholarly Karl Rodbertus and the versatile, energetic Ferdinand Lassalle made significant contributions. Karl Marx, with the editorial assistance of Friedrich Engels, drew the various strands of socialist thought together in a comprehensive political philosophy and a revolutionary praxis which, despite diverse interpretations, still provides a theoretical basis for contemporary communism.

Toward the end of the nineteenth century, socialism became an organized political movement in England, France, and Germany. It exercised important influence in the promotion of cooperative ventures and trade union organization, in furthering social reform legislation, and generally in supporting progressive tendencies in liberalism. Wherever advances were made in the extension of the suffrage to the working classes, socialism tended to lose its revolutionary aspect and to rely on the gradualist methods of the democratic political process. However, in Russia, with the failure of liberalism to achieve power and the subsequent overthrow of the czarist rule under the leadership of the Bolshevist wing of the Socialist party, Marxism regained its revolutionary dynamic. It became a powerful force for change in the industrially undeveloped countries where democracy had failed to gain a foothold.

Before World War I, it had been taken for granted that the defeated German and Russian autocracies would be replaced by democratic parliamentary regimes on the Western model. After a brief period of wavering, Russia, under the leadership of Lenin, turned in the totalitarian direction, and any belief that the dictatorship would be temporary was shattered during the Stalinist police-state regime. The Chinese People's Republic followed the same road; the hope that it would act as a moderating force has been completely disappointed. The new nations of Asia and Africa indicate a tendency toward dictatorships combined with socialist programs, even though they may not accept the Communist model nor blindly follow Russian leadership. Whether Fidel Castro was a "Communist" in the strict ideological meaning before he gained power is a question. But now Cuba is definitely in the Soviet orbit.

In Germany after World War I, social democracy was tried in unfavorable conditions, the victorious Allies visiting the sins of autocratic, imperialist Kaiserdom on the young Weimar Republic. It took another world war to destroy the Nazi terror which had risen to power not without the support of influential groups in England who saw in the resurgence of Germany a counterweight to Communist Russia. The irony was that the defeat of Nazism was accomplished only with the aid of the Soviet Union which had been forced into the struggle by the demonic Hitler. There is a decisive deliverance from evil in the overthrow of fascism in Germany and in Italy. But the spread of dictatorships in various parts of the world, characterized by extreme nationalism, dependent on personal leadership combined with the use of military force and emotional propaganda, and supported or unopposed by large sections of the people, can hardly be encouraging to the belief that the liberalist form of democracy will soon prevail or inevitably be victorious.

In the countries of the West, where it was well established before the first world war, the liberal democratic form of government has been able to maintain itself despite attacks from the Right and the Left. However, the liberalist principles have not gone unscathed. In France, under de Gaulle, parliamentary government has been virtually abrogated for the time being. The electoral laws have been manipulated to reduce the strength of Communists' representation and to restrict their participation in the government. This happened to an extent in Italy also. In England, the liberalist component in democracy was subjected to criticism from several sides because of its close link to capitalism.

One line of thought attacked liberalism for its moral and religious neutralism, its lack of commitment to any definite pattern of values, its individualistic emphasis, its alleged worship of material success. Although this type of criticism—often associated, as by T. S. Eliot, with "The Idea of a Christian Society"—regards the spiritual basis of the national life as the paramount issue, it recognizes the importance of the economic aspect and inclines toward some form of socialism. A similar more broadly humanist conception is exemplified by R. H. Tawney's memorable denunciation of "The Acquisitive Society" and its "Religion of Inequality." Harold J. Laski's sharp critique of liberalism as "the Philosophy of a Business Civilization" remains in the background of thought even though his favorable judgment of "the Russian experiment" proved mistaken.

The disillusion of the European intellectuals with the course of events in the Soviet Union under Stalin has not brought them back to a belief in the adequacy of liberalism. Existentialism, despairing of any ultimate solution of the problem of man, appears in its major forms to imply indifference to political effort. Nevertheless, Jean-Paul Sartre, its most popular exponent, is apparently sympathetic to communism, although he recognizes its dangers. Communism is still a legitimate subject of discussion in European intellectual circles. In England and in the Scandinavian countries, membership in the Communist Party is not regarded as a mark of disloyalty. In France and in Italy, Communist parties attract a substantial proportion of the votes. In the United States, the intellectuals' faith in liberalism as an all-sufficient philosophy of life and politics remained firmer. There was less tolerance toward communism in any of its interpretations and less objectivity in the discussion of Russian affairs.

In a clear and brief account of its development, Professor J. S. Schapiro, a staunch exponent of liberalism as "the way of the inevitability of gradualness in the progress of mankind" maintained that there had been a continuous march of freedom in the United States from Jefferson's Declaration of Independence through Jacksonian democracy, to the New Deal initiated by Franklin D. Roosevelt. He pointed to the Supreme Court decision of May 17, 1954 as a decisive step in the resolution of the "American dilemma"—"as a great vindication of the liberal principle of equality." In summary, he acclaimed the United States as the world defender of liberalism: "History has thrust America forward as the most powerful and the most determined champion of the democratic way of life, first against the militarism of

Imperial Germany, and then against the totalitarian dictatorships of fascism. Since then the hopes of liberals everywhere rest on America as the leader of the free world in the ceaseless struggle against the totalitarian dictatorship of communism."[1]

For the better part of the last half-century we lived under the shadow of "The Conflict of the Two Worlds," to use the title of the opening chapter of George F. Kennan's *Russia and the West*.[2] The struggle, led by the United States, on the one hand, and by the Soviet Union, on the other, was described in terms of a many-sided opposition. The usual designation of the conflict as a struggle between East and West implied a geopolitical war between two regional groups of nations. Russia's proud identification of the Soviet regime as "socialist" and its disparaging characterization of the American system as "capitalist" disclosed the economic groundwork of the contest. Our own confrontation of the issue as a battle against totalitarian dictatorship reflected the long historical struggle for the idea of freedom, the central theme of Western political theory. The most complex difference was epitomized in the anti-thesis: "democracy *versus* communism" which conceived the conflict as one between two comprehensive philosophies of life—each with its presuppositions about nature, man, and society, each claiming universal validity.

Some reservation may be in order with regard to these conventional terms of opposition. The association of communism with the East and of democracy with the West is an incidence of the historical circumstance that communism first succeeded in establishing itself in Eastern Europe. Communism is, strictly speaking, a Western creation with roots in European religious and political thought. It still has, with its basis in Marxism, respectable intellectual advocates and a sizable number of party adherents in countries under democratic regimes. The sharp opposition between capitalism and socialism has been diminished by the development of mixed economic systems in the West and by modifications introduced in the state-controlled economic structures under communism. To formulate the struggle as a conflict between communism and democracy is a legitimate but nevertheless a partisan statement of the case. Both Russia and mainland China claim that they are genuine "people's democracies." Marxism regards the parliamentary system as a means of maintaining capitalism's exploitive rule over the working classes, but in theory at least,

---

[1] J. Salwyn Schapiro, *Liberalism, Its Meaning and History*, An Anvil Original (Princeton, 1958), p. 87. A more balanced critical account is presented in his larger work, *Liberalism and the Challenge of Fascism* (New York, 1949).

[2] (Boston, 1961).

it affiirms support of representative institutions as essential to democracy. Lenin wrote: "Without representative institutions we cannot imagine democracy, not even proletarian democracy; but we can and *must* think of democracy without parliamentarianism . . . "

During the last decade, with the proliferation of nuclear weapons and in the light of increased possibilities of coexistence, the tendency developed among political realists to play down the ideological aspects of the conflict and to represent it as a power struggle between national and regional blocs. The rift between the Soviet Union and the Chinese People's Republic, it was recognized, opened the way to an eclectic policy adjusted to the possibilities of accommodation and peaceful cooperation in each case. Within the Soviet Union, fundamental changes in the Communist line were in evidence. After the Twentieth Congress of the Communist Party in 1956, when Nikita Khrushchev in a secret speech had denounced Stalinism, there emerged a radical revision of outlook and strategy.[3] A reconciliation with Yugoslavia had been achieved; neutralist countries like India which maintained links with the capitalist world were no longer to be regarded as enemies; a *detente* with the United States to avoid a possible nuclear war became a primary aim. Although the Soviet Union continued to exploit revolutionary movements in Asia, Africa, and South America, it renounced its role as leader of the world revolution to destroy Western capitalism. "Peaceful competition" became the order of the day. Within Russia itself there was an easing of police pressures and terrorist methods in the interest of national unity and of economic efficiency. In the economic field, "material incentives" and other devices of capitalism were introduced within the framework of the state-controlled system.

Despite the better understanding and the sobriety of mood that gained ground in recent years among students of politics, uncritical propaganda continued to prevail in the public discussion of communism. This was true not only of the mass media and of the popular press, but also of educational writings, liberal journals, and responsible newspapers. Without regard to their differences in aim and character, communism and fascism were lumped together in a common denunciation as totalitarian dictatorships. In a book published in 1961, a liberal professor of education wrote: "The appeal of the communist movement today is at root the same as that of the ill-fated fascist

[3] Edward Crankshaw has summarized the main points of the new Soviet foreign policy: "Peaceful coexistence, different paths to socialism, revolution without violence, and the abandonment of the doctrine of the inevitability of war." See *Krushchev, A Career* (New York, 1966), p. 227.

movements of the 1930s and 1940s in Germany, Italy and Japan." Both totalitarian movements were explained as attempts to escape the responsibilities of freedom, to seek the securities of the totalitarian state in the face of the uncertainties and the "meaninglessness" of modern life.

In this wholesale condemnation of communism and Marxism, no distinctions were made between the programs of recognized Communist parties in democratic countries and the revolutionary groups fighting against reactionary oppressive governments. It was generally assumed that communism wins and maintains mass support by the use of force. When a Communist party made gains in free elections, victories were explained as due to the persuasive appeals of magnetic leaders who beguiled—as a *New York Times* editorial commented after the Italian elections in the spring of 1963—"the uneducated, the thoughtless, the rebellious, the materialistic" by "offering the well-tried lure of Marxist ideology."[4] The truth is that communism has a sympathetic following among Italian intellectuals and exercises an important influence on the trade unions.

No good purpose is served by these one-sided, defensive, self-deceptive presentations. The task we face is not negative but positive—not to fight communism but to strengthen democracy, to clarify its meaning as a political and social conception and to restate it in the light of the new situation in the world, of the much changed technological basis of the economy and of the emerging international world order. The criticisms of conditions and policies made by leaders of thought cannot be answered by a reiteration of traditional tenets of liberalism. The challenge of communism cannot be met by denunciation; it cannot be suppressed by military intervention.

As compared with the autocratic and aristocratic regimes of the post-medieval era, extraordinary progress was made under the auspices of liberalism—in the standards of living, in extension of educational opportunities, in the spread of religious tolerance, in the advance of individual freedom. But the day has gone when we can be satisfied with measuring progress in terms of amelioration of bad conditions in the past. In total effect, what is striking is not the progress made but the discrepancy between the promise, on the one hand, and the lagging fulfillment of asserted principles, on the other. A century after their so-called emancipation, Negroes are still struggling for elementary human rights in the South and for the elimination of discriminatory practice in the North. As a nation, we still present the profile of

4 *New York Times*, May 4, 1963.

a class society marked by extremes of wealth and poverty that contrast sharply with the doctrine of equality of opportunity. In foreign affairs, likewise, there are glaring discrepancies between the liberalist claims and the realities of our policies. We support reactionary dictatorships provided only that they oppose communism.

As a preliminary to outlining guiding principles for a reformulated democratic conception, it will be in point to subject liberalist theory to analysis—to distinguish between its valid enduring contributions and such assumptions as are no longer tenable. It will also be of service to indicate the major themes in Marxist thought which in its original form arose as a critique of nineteenth century liberalism. Marxism is a good instrument for detecting the weak spots of the liberalist position. The analysis of the Marxist ideology is not calculated to make it more acceptable to the democratic view. On the contrary, it will reveal the principles on which no compromise is possible. But there are also points that must be taken into consideration in the reformulation of the democratic conception in relation to the problems of the domestic economy and of international relations.

THE IDEOLOGY OF LIBERALISM

As a body of social and political thought, liberalism has undergone modification in the course of historical development and is subject to variations in interpretation. Beginning with the aristocratic liberalism of the English Revolution of 1688, it reached its characteristic middle-class form during the nineteenth century as "bourgeois" liberalism from which it has, in the recent period, been trying to emancipate itself. John Stuart Mill represents a transition from the rugged business-class type of the nineteenth century to the humanitarian social reform liberalism of the early twentieth century. During the last fifty years, it has been increasingly associated with the cause of labor in Great Britain and in the United States, and since the second world war has become a major support of the welfare state. In every period, it has had its more conservative and more progressive exponents. Despite its several varieties, liberalism constitutes an identifiable social philosophy —a conception of government, a pattern of values, and a theory of social progress.

In its broadest meaning, liberalism implies the directing principle of the whole modern era. Its key idea is freedom for the individual; it arose as a reaction to autocratic government and authoritarian religion, signified a movement toward humanism and toleration of diversity, expressed an affirmation of national independence as well as of personal liberty. In its political aspect, it conceived the state as the servant of human interest, set indefeasible human rights at the foundation of government. It laid down the principles of republican rule: the separation of church and state, the parliamentary system with its indispensable prerequisite of an opposition party, the division of powers as a check on the executive and as a means of maintaining the independence of the judiciary. In the essentials, of personal freedom, civil liberties, and constitutional government, liberalism remains an indispensable, distinctive component of democracy.

However, in important respects, liberalism and democracy were opposed to each other until the end of the nineteenth century and this opposition has left its imprint on contemporary conceptions of liberalist democracy in the United States. In its classical nineteenth-century embodiment, liberalism was inseparably associated with industrial capitalism and political laissez-faire. Its representatives fought for the extension of the suffrage to the upper ranges of the middle class engaged in trade and manufacturing, but resisted for a long time granting the franchise to those who lacked substantial property qualifications. Lord Macaulay in England, François Guizot in France, Daniel Webster in the United States employed their eloquence to warn of the dangers that threatened sound government and the general social welfare if the right to vote were given to the poorer classes. It was not until the end of the century that manhood suffrage—with only minor qualifications—was achieved in England and France. In the United States, universal white manhood suffrage came earlier; nevertheless, American history reflects a prolonged battle between the idealistic conception of democracy as based on human equality and the view embodied in the Constitution that good government must be founded on the rights of property. Although progressive liberalism has, during the last half century, lent support to social reform and to the welfare state, diffidence with reference to social equality, it may be said, has remained the hard core of the conventional liberal outlook in the United States.

Associated with the dominant middle-of-the-road liberalism—and in no small measure with the more progressive strains—is a pattern of beliefs about human nature and social methodology that have their roots in nineteenth century conceptions. In the center of thought is the concept of a free, autonomous, essentially rational individual as the unit of social organization. It is on the moral qualities, the critical intelligence, the alert participation of each citizen in political life allegedly that "the capacity of democratic government for great achievement depends."[5] Liberalism embodies a grand faith in educa-

[5] Rockefeller Panel Reports, *Prospect for America* (New York, 1961), p. 463.

tion as a means of developing good character and the power to think for oneself, of training for citizenship and for effective social adjustment generally. Education, public discussion, pursuit of science, and free inquiry are regarded as the main and generally adequate instruments of progressive social advance. When disputes arise, reliance on settling them is placed on negotiation, consensus, or compromise. By these rational methods—education, discussion and inquiry, consensus or compromise, joined with democratic government based on universal suffrage—current liberalism still maintains that the welfare of mankind may be advanced "steadily, continually, and inevitably to an ever better civilization."

A cursory examination of the historical record does not bear out the view that democratic government and social progress in England, France, and the United States have been brought about through rational, noncoercive processes. The course of the "inevitability of gradualness" did not run smooth even in England—where the claim that political and social change can be made without resort to force has a considerable measure of justification. The Glorious Revolution of 1688, generally referred to as the "bloodless revolution," was preceded, it will be remembered, by twenty years of ruthless civil war. It ended only with Oliver Cromwell's dictatorship under the Protectorate. In the final solution, the two sections of the aristocracy—the owners of landed estates and the affluent trading class—united to rule the country jointly instead of decimating each other.

The Reform Bill of 1832, hailed as a "second glorious revolution," brought about the transfer of political power from the landed gentry to the wealthy manufacturing and trading classes. This "peaceful" transfer of power from one class to another was effected in the atmosphere of working class demonstrations and riots; the Bourbon restoration in 1830 in France was fresh in mind and the memory of the dread terror of the French Revolution was still very much alive. Advocates of the Reform Bill warned that the continued exclusion of the main body of property holders from political influence would necessarily drive them to the side of the revolutionists. The relinquishment of the dominant power by the aristocracy was the result of a "compromise"—that is, an agreement between the two sections of the very upper class to extend the suffrage—but at the same time to limit it—to a relatively small portion of the population. The lower middle class and the factory workers, to whose support the victory of the bourgeoisie was in great measure due, failed to receive the vote. Instead, the workers were confronted by the Poor Law of 1834 which deprived the underpaid laborers of public assistance formerly given from parish rates and forced the unemployed into the workhouses where the pay was even lower than the minimum subsistence wage in the factories.

The ameliorative social reform measures enacted between 1832 and 1867, when bourgeois liberalism was in power, were pushed through with the aid of the Conservative Party. In this, "politics" as well as sentiment played a part. Lord Shaftesbury and his friends, who sponsored the Factory Laws of 1833 and of 1847, were undoubtedly inspired by humanitarian considerations. But the support that these measures received from Tories in Parliament was largely motivated by hatred of the Liberal Party whose general policies were undermining the position of the landed aristocracy. The extension of the suffrage to industrial workers was accomplished in 1867 under the auspices of the Disraeli Conservative government. Its purpose was to offset the strength of the Liberals and to unite the nation in pursuit of Disraeli's imperial policy. It was only in 1884 that the Liberal Party under William Gladstone's leadership joined, through the enfranchisement of the rural workers, in the movement of extending the suffrage. The social legislation at the end of the nineteenth century and the beginning of the twentieth—minimum wage, workers compensation, old-age pensions—resulted mainly from the increased working class strength and the use of the strike by the trade unions.

In England, after the Revolution of 1688, the transfer of the balance of political power—first from the aristocracy to the upper middle class and to a union of middle class and labor forces—was made by relatively nonviolent methods, although threatening demonstrations and strikes played their part. In France, liberalism had a turbulent career marked by revolution, coup d'etat, and dictatorship. The Reign of Terror, the military rule of Napoleon, the restoration of the reactionary Bourbons followed in rapid succession until the Revolution of 1830 brought bourgeois liberalism into power. A constitutional monarchy was established under the "citizen king" Louis Philippe; the parliamentary regime was restored and civil rights reinstituted; the suffrage extended by lowering property qualification. But as in England, the workers did not receive the right to vote despite the fact that they had mounted the barricades in Paris to aid in the revolutionary uprising.

François Guizot, who dominated the political scene from 1830 to 1848, continued obdurately to oppose any attempt to extend the franchise to the nonpropertied classes. He voiced the view common to the liberals of the period, in England and the United States as well as in France, that a propertyless electorate would undermine the stability and the prosperity of the state. The free enterprise system, he maintained, gave every capable citizen the opportunity of acquiring property and thus entering the ranks of the responsible ruling class. For the working class—suffering from unemployment, starvation wages, exploitive conditions—Guizot had nothing but contempt; he thought them shiftless or incapable. In the course of time, the bourgeois government became despotic and corrupt, opposition increased from those who wanted a more broadly based democratic republic as well as from socialistically-minded proletarian groups. The uprising in February 1848 which sent a revolutionary tremor throughout Europe ended the regime of bourgeois liberalism in France.

The Second Republic, hopefully established on the basis of manhood suffrage, was short-lived. An uprising of the Paris workers in June 1849, although quickly suppressed, aroused the fear of "the red spector of communism." By a coup d'état, Louis Napoleon, who had been elected president, overthrew the Republic in 1851 and in the following year declared himself emperor. Under the Second Empire a facade of democracy was maintained, but the candidates for office and parliament were controlled by the centralized government. Trade union activities and strikes were forbidden; the censored press became nothing but a mouthpiece for the government. The great advances in industry which enriched the bourgeoisie permitted some improvement in the lot of the workers; a number of social reform measures were introduced—old-age pensions, sickness insurance, and public works to ease unemployment. But poverty and pauperism continued to prevail.

After the defeat of France in the war with Prussia in 1870, the suppressed ferment of discontent burst into revolution. The resistance of the Paris Commune, which held out for a radical socialist regime, was finally broken, and after a period of turbulence the Third Republic was established through a united front of moderate Republicans against the Royalists. Despite many crises, the Third Republic maintained itself until the Nazi occupation during the second world war. It was followed by the Fourth Republic in 1946 which gave way to the so-called Fifth Republic under de Gaulle, who carries on without the benefit of parliamentary debate.

In the United States, republican government was brought into being under conditions favorable to democracy. Great estates were confined to the plantation country in the South; in the Middle West, cheap land was available to anyone who had the courage to brave the rigors of life of the open frontier. In the New England states or on the Atlantic seaboard, commerce and trade offered opportunities for entering into middle-class occupations. The Declaration of Independence was a manifesto proclaiming human equality; economic conditions in the new land and the influences emanating from eighteenth-century French thought were favorable to the idea of universal suffrage.

The framers of the Constitution, however, keenly conscious of the economic basis of politics, regarded the ownership of property as a prerequisite to the responsible exercise of the voting privilege. This was not only true of the avowed anti-democrat Alexander Hamilton, who represented the mercantile and banking interests. The moderate James Madison also opposed universal suffrage on the ground that "those who hold property and those who are without property have distinct interests in society."[6] He thought that the time might come when the mass of the people would be without property and, forming a majority, would use their power to infringe on the rights of property. However, recognizing that the Constitution might not be ratified if it contained specific property qualifications for voting, the cautious founding fathers left the issue to the states. As a counterweight to a legislature which might be unduly responsive to public opinion, they created the Supreme Court. Under the able Justice John Marshall, the Court took it upon itself to declare invalid Congressional resolutions which in its judgment violated the Constitution.

Strong popular movements in communities on the Atlantic seaboard brought manhood suffrage to a number of states during the first two decades of the nineteenth century. In Massachusetts, the victory was achieved despite Daniel Webster's dire warning that equal suffrage would lead either to assaults on wealth or to a reaction and to restraints on republican government. After the election of Andrew Jackson in 1830, white manhood suffrage was gradually accepted by practically all the states as an essential of democratic governments.[7] The extension of the franchise had the important effect of balancing the interests of various classes of property holders—the merchants of the Northeast, the slave-holding planters of the South, the middle-class farmers of the West.

Apart from the fact that it meant nothing to the Negroes, and little to the factory workers, the effect of the popular suffrage for the lower levels of the middle class was less evident than might have been

---

[6] Charles A. Beard, *The Rise of American Civilization* (New York, 1927), Vol. I, p. 334. The quotation is from *The Federalist*, No. 10.

[7] In Virginia until 1850, and North Carolina until 1856, the suffrage was restricted to landowners.

expected in the light of the importance usually attributed to the political factor taken alone. Farmers in the West continued to be bowed down by a burden of debt to the bankers in the East; the organization of labor and other efforts to improve the lot of the industrial worker was attended by strikes and violence. In the struggle between capital and labor after the Civil War, the Supreme Court, operating on assumptions of classic laissez-faire liberalism, was, as the late Harold Laski put it, "for all practical purposes, the agents of Big Business."[8] The wealth of the country increased marvelously with the expansion of industry, but the general equality of condition which had prevailed in the earlier days tended to be replaced by growing inequalities. In some parts of the country farmers were forced into tenantry and sharecropping; in the urban centers, immigrant workers were crowded into slums.

In the last decades of the nineteenth century and in the years before World War I, a union of farmers and organized labor led to the development of socially progressive movements. Laws were enacted to curb monopolies, to achieve a better distribution of wealth through graduated income taxes, to protect workers and safeguard the public from the excesses of competition and predatory business operations. The doctrine of laissez-faire was undergoing revision. Nevertheless, labor unrest continued, costly strikes attended by riots and by battles between workers and pickets, on the one hand, and employers' guards and state troopers, on the other.[9] Big business maintained the upper hand; Louis D. Brandeis, in testimony before Congress in 1915, pointed to "the contrast between political liberty and our industrial absolutism."

On the eve of the Great Depression in 1929, despite increased productivity and the advance of social legislation after the first world war, American society was marked by very great inequalities in income, by the insecurities of unemployment, by little government protection for the vicissitudes of illness and old age. The reforms of the New Deal, which brought about decisive improvements but did not resolve the basic problems of the free enterprise economy, were put through only in the face of a threatened breakdown of the capitalist system and the challenge of Soviet Russia which at the time made a strong appeal to a considerable number of intellectual liberals.

The view that liberalism has been an effective force in the "war

[8] Harold J. Laski, *The American Democracy: A Commentary and an Interpretation* (New York, 1948), p. 210.

[9] Samuel Yellen, *American Labor Struggles* (New York, 1936), xi-xvi.

against privilege, whether of birth, wealth or race" can least of all be supported in the case of the American Negro. The founders of the Republic sidestepped the issue of slavery as a concession to the South and in effect consented to its continuance. The famous Missouri Compromise of 1820 allowed the expansion of slavery into the southern part of the Louisiana Territory and retained the drastic laws for the return of fugitive slaves from the northern part. Despite its large concessions, the Missouri Compromise did not satisfy the Southern planters and was declared null and void in 1854 when Congress was dominated by them. The Supreme Court, under Chief Justice Taney, confirmed the congressional decision in 1856, in connection with the Dred Scott case, declared further that Congress could not constitutionally abolish slavery in any of the territories, any more than in any of the states.

It was the apprehension that the Missouri Compromise would be restored after the election of Abraham Lincoln that led to the secession of the Southern States. It was no part of the program of the Republican Party to abolish slavery throughout the country as a matter of principle. The Emancipation Proclamation was issued in the course of the war and freed the slaves only in territories which were still in arms against the federal authority. Subsequently, slavery was abolished by the Thirteenth Amendment (December 18, 1865) after the defeat of General Lee and the collapse of the Confederacy— the necessary votes for its ratification having been obtained by the exercise of military pressure on a number of the southern states.

According to the liberal view of Professor Schapiro: "The Negro now became a free man and a citizen"—although admittedly a "second class citizen" without a vote or civil rights, legally segregated in schools and other public places, and economically exploited.[10] In May 1954, the Supreme Court rescinded the earlier approval of segregated public schools under the "separate but equal principle."[11] But hailing the new decision as a "great vindication of the liberal principle of equality" appears to have been premature. In 1963, nine score and seven years after the Declaration of Independence, a century after the Emancipation Proclamation, almost a decade after the Supreme Court decision, the struggle for bare political equality in the South and for social equality in the North, was being carried on with increasing violence.

[10] J. Salwyn Schapiro, *Liberalism, Its Meaning and History,* An Anvil Original (New York, 1958), pp. 83, 86.
[11] *Plessy v. Ferguson,* 163 U.S. 537, 1896.

The record does not bear out the claim that continuous social progress under liberalist democracy has been made by peaceful means, by reliance on reason and the wide diffusion of knowledge, by mutual adjustment of interests and compromise. Even in its limited aristocratic form, liberalism as a political system was first established by revolutionary action. In England, despite favorable conditions, a strong sense of national unity and an empirical temper of mind, two centuries elapsed before the franchise was extended to the nonpropertied classes. In France, the cult of reason, the deep respect for individual independence, the devotion to the rights of man, did not avail to prevent revolution and dictatorship. A century elapsed after the revolution of 1789 before government on a popular basis was introduced and then only after a disastrous war. Moreover, parliamentary government has never been firmly established in France.

In the United States, the introduction of universal suffrage at a relatively early period resulted from the fact that a large proportion of the people were property holders. Nevertheless, the wealthy mercantile interests of the Northeast in combination with the Southern plantation owners retained dominant political control until the Civil War, when the hegemony passed into the hands of the captains of industry. Every important advance in the position of the wage worker was attended by strife—strikes, picketing, boycott, sabotage, mass protest, and demonstrations. Negro emancipation, whatever it amounted to, came as an incident of the Civil War. It was a by-product of the far reaching social and economic struggle by which the industrial capitalists of the North and the farmers in the West wrested the control of the national government from the planting aristocracy of the South.

Compromise, liberalism's cherished recipe for peaceful resolution of conflict, played but little part in the major instances of social change. Moreover, in so far as it may be said to have operated, it was not arrived at by rational negotiation and free give-and-take. The compromises were the result rather of the relative strength and endurance of the contending parties. Political compromise was generally at the expense of a third partner whose interests were neglected or sacrificed. The Reform Bill of 1832, cited as a transfer of power from one class to another through compromise, involved abandoning the principle of manhood suffrage requisite for the "happiness of the greatest number" in favor of the doctrine that "voting was a political *privilege* connected with property."[12] The famous Missouri

[12] J. Salwyn Schapiro, *Liberalism and the Challenge of Fascism* (New York, 1949), p. 121.

Compromise consisted of an agreement between the mercantile and the Southern plantation interests to keep slavery in force in exchange for tariff concessions.

Liberalism represented an attack against the special privileges of the aristocracy and not a movement designed to achieve a general equality of social condition. It was diffident toward the question of human equality, even opposed to equality when it came into conflict with the rights of property. In so far as it included an ethical humanitarian motivation, this may be ascribed to the influence of a secularized religious tradition, not to its own philosophical orientation. The transition to the social liberalism of the twentieth century in so far as this was at all influenced by political thought and not by the pressure of events, is to be attributed to the impact of socialism, not to any automatic evolution of the liberalist conception.

To point out the discrepancies between the ideology of liberalism and the actualities of the social and political development under its auspices does not imply that the liberalist ideas have not played a very important part in the progress achieved in the recent centuries. Nor does it imply that the aims of liberalism or even its methods have no significance for the future. But the distance between theory and achievement raises a number of fundamental questions—the relation of political forms to economic foundations, the place of force in the maintenance of the state, the limitations of reason in the resolution of serious conflict. More subtly and fundamentally, it challenges the liberalist conception of the nature of reason in relation to social organization. Underlying the liberalist reliance on discussion, negotiation, and compromise, there appears to be a conception of an abstract individual who is the unit of society and whose intelligent self-interest stands in a natural harmony with the welfare of the nation as a whole.

It was the gap between the promise of liberalism and its performance that led to the critique of its theoretical foundations formulated by Marx and Engels.

MARXISM AS A CRITIQUE OF LIBERALISM

The character of government of the U.S.S.R. and the shape of Soviet policy cannot be understood simply as an application of the ideas of Karl Marx any more than the nature of the contemporary American situation can be regarded as a direct growth out of Jeffersonian principles. In explaining the triumph of totalitarianism in Russia, it is undoubtedly necessary, as Professor Fainsod emphasizes, to take the historical background into consideration—the heritage of Czarist

125

autocracy and its secret police methods, the government obstruction of basic reform, the suppression of the relatively mild revolution of 1905, the subsequent emasculation of the Duma, the disillusionment of the idealistically-minded intelligentsia with the policy of gradualism.[13]

Underlying the failure to advance toward liberalism was a complex of economic problems: the poverty and the general backwardness of the peasants, the lag in the growth of industry, and the special conditions of its development. Industry played a role in the Russian economy during the nineteenth century, but it was largely dependent on government contracts and subject to bureaucratic control. The upper middle class failed to become a significant independent political force, able to challenge autocracy as it had in the first stages in the development of liberalism in Western Europe. At the same time, trade-unionism, the natural accompaniment of large-scale industrial development, was suppressed with the aid of the government police. Further, the dislocation of the first world war militated against a gradual transition to a liberalized industrial economic order which, despite the many handicaps, was nevertheless on its way. On top of all this, there was the well-founded fear of encirclement by external enemies, the memory of invasion from the past, the threat of intervention of the Western powers in the early years of the war, and the need of defense against possible German aggression. It should be evident that the failure of Alexander Kerensky to establish a social-democratic regime did not result merely as an accident of history.

A trend of thought has developed which plays down Marxist doctrines altogether as a factor in Soviet rule and present-day Communist policy. George Lichtheim, in his scholarly study, concludes that the impetus of the utopian and messianic ideas which inspired the Russian intelligentsia of the revolutionary period has now been spent and that Soviet society today "is simply another instance of modern planned and bureaucratized industrialism."[14] In accordance with this view, Marxism in Russia has become an official ideology by which the political elite attempt to bridge the gap between the original revolutionary faith and the planned and centralized society necessitated by any contemporary technological economy, whether capitalist or socialist. It is not the Soviet state, Lichtheim remarks, but the Marxist ideology itself which is destined "to wither away." Having lost its

---

[13] Merle Fainsod, *How Russia Is Ruled* (Cambridge, Mass., 1961), chap. I.
[14] George Lichtheim, *Marxism: A Historical and Critical Study* (New York, 1961), p. 399.

revolutionary function, Lichtheim believes, Marxism has suffered the fate of all academic philosophies—it has become "the repository of ideals and values not attained in actuality, and perhaps not capable of attainment." The major service of Marxism today is as a tool of historical analysis, as an instrument of anthropoligical and sociological understanding.

Another form of deflating Marxism comes from the side of the liberal as represented by the optimistic opinion of Chester Bowles.[15] On the basis of his travels in forty to fifty countries on four continents—accomplished in the course of a few months—he came to the conclusion that "Communism as an ideological force is ebbing." The pressure of events, Bowles believed, had disabused the pragmatically minded Soviet leaders of the Marxist-Leninist principles. It is not through ideological propaganda that the Soviet Union has gained its victories among the underdeveloped nations of the world, but through espousing the nationalist aspirations of peoples formerly under imperialist rule and by providing military equipment, economic aid, and other tangible services.

With all due respect to the valid elements in these critical interpretations, it would seem, nevertheless, that the demise of Marxism as a vital political idea, like the report of Mark Twain's death, has been "greatly exaggerated." No doubt some of the Marxist conceptions in their rigid ideological versions have become untenable, partly because they were one-sided to begin with—as all programmatic ideologies necessarily are—or because changes have taken place in the intellectual, political, and economic situation since they were formulated. But detailed and refined analysis of any political theory is likely to make us lose sight of the dynamic power of its inner motivating idea.

It would not be difficult to elaborate a deprecatory critique of the metaphysical concepts and the economic postulates underlying the views of Thomas Jefferson. His modern followers do not accept his deistic assumptions: the idea of self-evident truths concerning the purposes of the Creator, the belief in the divine endowment of inalienable rights, the appeal to the laws of nature as justifying the American people in assuming their equal status among the powers of the earth. The agrarian economy upon which he based his hopes for democracy can no longer serve as a major factor of influence in our contemporary social life. His plan of sending out the Negroes after

[15] Chester Bowles, "Is Communist Ideology Becoming Irrelevant?" *Foreign Affairs*, XL (July 1962).

their emancipation to separate colonies, supplying them with arms for self-protection, and setting them up as an independent people would hardly be regarded today as consistent with the principles of democracy.[16] Nevertheless, the ideas of the Declaration of Independence and the pronouncements on the toleration of error of political opinion remain powerfully moving forces in political thought.

The refutation of the metaphysical groundwork of Marxism or the denial of its special economic theories does not necessarily invalidate it for those who are seeking a program of radical social reconstruction. For Communist leaders, a rough grasp of basic Marxist ideas adapted to their own circumstances and purposes is sufficient. The acute technical analysis of Marxist doctrines does not vitiate the inner driving idea, as Friedrich Engels epitomized it at the grave of his lifelong friend: "the simple fact, previously hidden under ideological growths, that human beings must first of all eat, drink, find shelter, and clothe themselves before they can turn attention to politics, science, art, and religion."

Marxism may have lost its revolutionary force in Western Europe and even in Russia, but this does not mean that it cannot, in its broad outlines, serve as a basis for activist programs in countries still suffering under reactionary exploitive regimes whether of a feudal, paternal, or capitalist type. Whatever inconsistencies may have developed between its theory and practices, and whatever differences of interpretation of its doctrines have arisen among adherents, Marxism still represents a body of principles, attitudes, and practices of functional significance. It is not alone the material aid that the Soviet Union—and now China—supplies, but the combination of these tangibles with the concepts, the aims, and the strategies that communism symbolizes that makes effective appeal in situations where radical change is necessary.

Marxism cannot be written off as an obsolescent political philosophy. The communist philosophy developed by Karl Marx and presented to the world in collaboration with Friedrich Engels constitutes a comprehensive critical synthesis of mid-nineteenth century currents of thought. It utilizes the Hegelian dialectic as a framework but fills it with new content. Although it is marked by a materialistic and deterministic ontology derived from prevailing scientific conceptions of the nature of causation, it introduces a decisive factor of

16 Thomas Jefferson, "Notes on Virginia," in *The Life and Selected Writings of Thomas Jefferson*, Adrienne Koch & William Peden, eds. (New York, 1944), pp. 255-256.

human consciousness and will. At its core is a penetrating critique of the classical English political economy and its laissez-faire and individualistic implications.

Like every political philosophy, Marxism contains elements which are related to the conditions and conceptions of its day, but it also includes principles of wide applicability and of enduring significance. Recognized for what it is—an ideology and not an objective scientific world view as it claims to be—Marxism may be said to be a more sophisticated conception, less disingenuous than nineteenth century liberalism, which was likewise an ideology. In any case, to console ourselves by pointing up the inconsistencies and irrelevancies of Marxist ideology is to little purpose. It is more important to take note of what is still living in the Marxist conception.

Marxism embodies the deeply rooted, universal aspiration for a just social order based on a conception of essential human equality. This incorporates the heritage of secular socialism and reflects the early Christian ideal of equality and fraternity. Arnold J. Toynbee, noting that Marxism is a Western secular social philosophy, adds, "you might equally well call Marxism a Christian heresy, a leaf torn out of the book of Christianity and treated as if it were the whole gospel."[17] Erich Fromm has pointed up the humanist element in Marx's own thought—its concern with the liberation of man from the crippling effects of scarcity and from the sense of alienation that results from reducing man to a mere instrument of production.[18]

Although imbued with the ideas of equality and fraternity Marxism does not espouse egalitarianism as do other forms of socialism. But its utopian doctrine—from everyone according to his ability, to everyone according to his needs—leads to giving the basic common needs of all men for food, shelter, and clothing a prior claim on social organization. Marxist materialism thus involves an ethical principle, although it disavows the term "ethical" as smacking of an empty abstract moralism. Communism identifies itself with the exploited, the oppressed, the underprivileged. In the context of nineteenth-century capitalism, the Marxist doctrine supported the claims of the industrial proletariat, and looked to it as the agent of revolution that would bring the socialist society into being. But it is not inconsistent with the inner motivation of Marxist thought—as some critics seem to believe—to include the agricultural worker in the movement of emancipation and attempt to achieve a double revolution, as Lenin urged, through an alliance of the proletariat and the peasantry.

[17] Arnold J. Toynbee, *Civilization on Trial* (Oxford, 1948), p. 221.
[18] Erich Fromm, *Marx's Concept of Man* (New York, 1965), preface.

Liberalism and Marxism differ decisively in their conception of the relation of natural forces to social organization. In the background of liberalist thought there rested a pervasive assumption of the primacy of nature in human affairs. In its view, the position that the individual reached in society was due to his native capabilities. Moreover, the classical economist believed that there was a force in nature —"an invisible hand"—which made each individual's self-interested pursuit of his own good conducive to the welfare of society as a whole. In the Marxist conceptions, as originally formulated, there remained something of cosmic determinism, derived in part from Hegelian philosophy and in part from Newtonian science. But essentially, Marx's teaching led away from the primacy of nature to an emphasis on the part that man plays in shaping history. It views history in terms of man's struggle to control nature to serve his own basic needs. It centers attention on social conditions and processes; it holds that the inequalities among men are due to institutional arrangements, not primarily to natural differences.

It was the liberalist view with its laissez-faire conception, its dependence on the laws of nature, and a limited view of human nature as guided by pleasure and pain, that was deterministic at heart. Liberalism espoused the principle of equality of opportunity but at the same time compromised it by the insistence on the prior rights of property, and largely nullified it by the underlying assumption of "the iron law of wages." Classic liberalism allowed that capable, industrious, and thrifty individuals might rise above their station and join the honorable ranks of the propertied middle class. But simultaneously it insisted that natural economic laws prevented the working class as a whole from earning more than was necessary for bare subsistence and for perpetuation of the race without increase. The implication that economic success is largely due to the merit of the individual and that social inequality is the function of difference in natural capabilities still exercises a strong influence on conventional views in the United States.

Marxism, on the other hand, explicitly asserts that "man makes his own history," though he does not make it without regard to conditioning natural and social factors. The laws of social development must be understood, the historical situation must be taken into account. Men can create a new social order only when the historical situation is ripe for its emergence. Marxism—particularly in the form that Engels, under the influence of Darwinian evolutionary thought, shaped it—does retain a vestige of the idea that man cooperates with the inevitable when he directs his energies toward changing the world. But the total emphasis is social and activist: Marxism is a call for a radical reconstruction of the character of society. It maintains that the function of reason is not merely to understand the laws governing human behavior, but rather, as E. H. Carr says, "to reshape society and the individuals who compose it by conscious action."[19]

Determinism in Marxist thought refers primarily not to the idea of historical necessity—to the causal relation of prior conditions to subsequent events—but to the relation of the material basis of social organization, of its economic foundation, to the cultural and moral life of society. Marxism is thus an extension of the realistic conception exemplified by Aristotle, Harrington, and Madison, namely, that economics is the basis of politics. Marx went further, asserting that all cultural manifestations—the legal system as well as the political order, the religious conceptions and the moral conventions, in fact all social formations which involved thought—were conditioned by the character of the economic organization and the human relations it made necessary.

In this aspect, Marxism is an attack on German idealism. To Hegel, as Marx explained in the Preface to *Capital*, the "Idea" was the "demiurgos," the activating agent, of the real world, and the real world merely the external, the phenomenal form of the "Idea." Against this, Marx contended in an unusually extreme expression of his view, that "the ideal is nothing else than the material world re-reflected by the human mind, and translated into forms of thought." Engels later moderated this one-sided emphasis and explained that Marx and he never meant that the economic basis was the "sole active cause." Although the political, legal, philosophical, religious, literary, and artistic developments rested on an economic base, there was a "reciprocal interaction" among the various aspects with each other and with the economic factor. Reinhold Niebuhr, who believes that the Marxist materialistic and deterministic conception expresses a moral cynicism, admits that "stated in this reasonable form [the Engels interpretation], few economists or historians would dissent."[20]

Although the problem of a monistic or pluralistic conception of causation is involved, the major question at issue refers to the validity and potency of abstract ideals when these are unrelated to the character of the economic structure—to the human relations and the moral attitudes that are indispensable to the successful carrying out of any given system. The Marxist view explains why capitalism unavoidably makes a virtue of competition, encourages striving for

[19] Edward H. Carr, *What Is History?* (New York, 1963), p. 183.
[20] Reinhold Niebuhr, *Moral Man and Immoral Society* (New York, 1932).

success, places a premium on monetary values. It suggests why we cannot expect Christian values to be practiced in the sphere of capitalist economic activity and why moral admonition is not effective in the reform of business ethics. The Marxist analysis of the relation of moral ideals to material conditions is designed to support the view that the moral and cultural reconstruction of society requires a prior radical change in the basic economic organization of society through the transformation from capitalism to socialism. It was the union of an ethical aspiration of a just society with a realistic analysis of the economic foundations of society that gave, and still gives, Marxism great power as a political movement.

The hard core of the Marxist position was its critique of the classical political economy which provided theoretical support for the laissez-faire system. Karl Marx's subtle analysis has been subject to much controversy; competent economists have praised it and also condemned it; socialists have failed to understand it and have misinterpreted it. Some of the major difficulties are attributable to faulty assumptions taken over from the classical political economy, e.g., the "labor theory of value" assumed by Ricardo and too consistently driven to logical conclusion by Marx. Nevertheless, whatever its failings, Marx's economic analysis succeeded in undermining the belief of the classical nineteenth century view that the laws of capitalist production reflected deterministic natural laws.

The contention that exploitation of labor—which was, undeniably, a feature of the nineteenth-century factory system—is inherent in the free enterprise system is debatable; the hypothesis that it was accomplished through the indirect appropriation by the class of entrepreneurs of the "surplus value" created by the working class may, as Joseph S. Schumpeter concludes, "be dead and buried."[21] But even more "dead and buried" is the assumption that the wages of labor can never by nature's laws rise above the subsistence level. What is incontrovertible in the Marxist conception is that social organization responds to changes in the technological conditions and methods of production, and that it is subject to man's control and direction through legal and political means.

The most significant achievement of Marx's analysis was his prediction of a new stage in economic development as a result of the dynamic forces in industrial society, the application of science and invention, the substitution of machines for manual labor. He saw the new economic order as releasing great productive forces with the

21 Joseph A. Schumpeter, *Capitalism, Socialism, and Democracy* (New York, 1947), p. 25.

potential of eliminating the scarcity which lay at the root of exploitation and social conflict and of creating the abundance needed to realize the cultural possibilities of the human race. The new economic order, characterized by an extraordinarily high degree of specialization and the concomitant interdependence of the productive processes would demand large-scale planning and coordination within the nation and internationally.

Capitalism, which had brought the industrial order into being and had marvelously advanced it, Marx maintained, now obstructed its transformation into the socialized form necessary for its rational direction. The principles of competition, free-market, and laissez-faire which had operated well in the earlier stages of industrial society would turn into destructive forces—to the concentration of wealth and power, to impoverishment of the masses, to the accentuation of national rivalries, to destructive imperialist wars. The impending catastrophe could be forestalled and the era of socialized production ushered in only through revolutionary action; the dynamic energy for the revolution would by supplied by the proletariat, who were the worst victims of the crisis of capitalism.

VARIATIONS IN MARXIST DOCTRINE

The doctrine of the necessity of revolution and of subversive strategy was clearly outlined in the statements made by Marx and Engels during the period of 1848-1850, when the spirit of rebellion was still alive in France and Germany. However, in the second half of the century, the founders of communism tended to discourage direct actionism as premature. The revolutionary strategy was not repudiated in principle, but rather left in abeyance. In the latter part of his life, Marx expressed the view that under exceptional conditions where, as in England and the United States, the suffrage had been extended and trade-unionism well advanced, "the workers might secure their ends [of the conquest of political power] by peaceful means." More explicitly, Engels oriented his writings in the direction of an inevitable evolutionary—not revolutionary—realization of socialism. For all intents and purposes, Marxism, which assumed its character as an organized political movement toward the end of the nineteenth century, largely under German leadership, represented a social-democratic nonrevolutionary interpretation. The "orthodox" Marxism of Eduard Bernstein and the "revisionist" Marxism of Karl Kautsky both cooperated with the liberal movement for parliamentary rule, and promoted reform measures as a necessary step toward the transition to socialism.

In Russia, despite its special problems, the social democratic view was the prevailing one among Marxists before the revolution of 1905. Even Lenin, at the time, "agreed that the first order of business was to achieve a bourgeois-democratic revolution in Russia."[22] But the brutal suppression of the revolution and the frustration of hopes of genuine reform through the Duma led to the accentuation of extreme proposals. By 1917, on the eve of the debacle of the Czarist regime, Lenin—imbued with a knowledge of Russian realities—supported the extreme formulation of the Marxist revolutionary doctrine which became the foundation of Bolshevism.

There were two new elements in Lenin's restatement of Marxism. First, he included the peasantry along with the proletariat in the revolutionary struggle, thus widening its base. On the other hand, he discarded the idea implicit in the earlier Marxist conceptions that the revolution must wait for the awakening of the revolutionary consciousness of the people. He insisted that the revolution must be carried out from above by a disciplined organization of professional revolutionaries who would be prepared to use every means available—conspiracy, terror, and open force—in order to establish and to maintain the Communist regime.

The Leninist revision proved to be of the greatest significance for the future development of communism in two complementary directions, international and national. The concepts and strategies elaborated by Marx and Engels referred to a cosmopolitan world centered on Europe where industrial capitalism was fully developed. Lenin's concern with imperialism opened up a global perspective which included countries still essentially feudal and agricultural in their political economy. Implicit in it was the policy of aiding Communist revolutions initiated by indoctrinated native leaders in the backward countries of Asia and Africa. It foreshadowed the union of nationalism and communism which was to become a feature of revolutionary movements in a number of important instances. At the same time, Lenin's concentration on the problem of building socialism in Russia as a priority led to differences with Trotsky who placed the emphasis on the international scene and on the need of the overthrow of capitalism in the West.[23] Stalin made prominent the nationalist element in

[22] Fainsod, *op. cit.*, p. 35; Lichtheim, *op. cit.*, chap. VIII.

[23] This is not to say that Lenin differed with Trotsky about the international character of socialist society or that he looked with disfavor on subversive activities in capitalist countries. But he relied primarily on the internal breakdown of capitalism, on war between capitalist nations, and on nationalist movements to destroy capitalist imperialism.

Lenin's conception and propounded the doctrine of "socialism in one country," as Isaac Deutscher points out. Nevertheless, Stalin continued to hold "that the victory of socialism in Russia could not be considered secure as long as her capitalist environment threatened Russia with armed intervention."[24] In turn, on his part Khrushchev carried this line of development to a culmination in his explicit avowal of the principle of "coexistence."

Seen in historical perspective, Marxism was not really, as usually regarded, a rigid conception. In its contemporary manifestations, communism is clearly subject to a wide range of interpretations. In Western European countries the Communist parties are nonrevolutionary, and where they are allowed to operate, serve as a left wing within the parliamentary system. Communists press for social welfare measures, urge nationalization of major industries, advocate policies of coexistence and cooperation with the Soviet Bloc. In the underdeveloped countries where autocratic, oligarchic, or predatory personal dictatorships are in power, the revolutionary idea directs the activities of local Communist organizations. Even in these situations, positions vary from a general "communist-minded" orientation —primarily concerned with the betterment of the life of the oppressed masses of the people and the elimination of foreign domination of the economic life—to the acceptance of a definite official version of communism following the moderate Russian rather than the extreme Chinese pattern. Within the framework of the Communist movement, there is an increasing number of neutralist nations concerned in maintaining a certain independence in adjusting Marxist ideas to local conditions and to nationalist sentiment.

Furthermore, as is evident from the experience of the Soviet Union, once communism has been established and has to face the realities of economic development, the doctrines are moderated and aggressiveness restrained. When political control over the major economic agencies has been achieved, there is room within the Communist systems for ownership of private property and even for a measure of free enterprise. When Communist regimes feel secure, they may ease their repressive measures against freedom of thought and their censorship of the arts and literature. Despite the avowed atheism of the Marxist doctrine, Communist governments may tolerate religious activity when this is not opposed to their political and economic policies.

However, it is a mistake to think that because the Communist

---

[24] Isaac Deutscher, *Stalin, A Political Biography* (New York, 1949), p. 285.

ideology has lost its monolithic, doctrinaire character it can no longer serve as a directive of policy; its flexibility may be said to add to its effectiveness rather than to weaken it. In any case, in the under-developed countries where a revolutionary situation exists, the Marx-ist-Leninist conception still offers a definite pattern of ideas as a basis for action. Its main points may be summarized as follows:

(1) The primary, immediate purpose of communism is to raise the standard of living for the peasants and industrial workers who have been exploited in the past by feudalist and capitalist regimes. To provide for the basic needs of the lowest class in the population is, in the Communist view, the indispensable means for the advance of society as a whole. The improvement of the health, the material wel-fare, and the education of the masses of the people is the first con-sideration in the cultural and moral reconstruction of society through-out the world.

(2) This social reconstruction involves the creation of an industrial order so that the productive possibilities of modern science and tech-nology may be fully realized through rational planning and coordi-nation of the various aspects of the economy under central govern-ment direction. The reconstruction of the economic order—which implies public ownership of the major means of production—cannot be achieved without political control. The requisite political power has to be gained—except in rare situations—by revolutionary action.

(3) The revolution must be carried out by a trained, disciplined party organization imbued with Marxist-Leninist conceptions and directly or indirectly affiliated with the international Communist movement. For an indefinite period of time, until the Communist political and economic order is firmly established against internal subversion and foreign intervention, the dictatorship of the Commu-nist Party must be maintained. Education plays an indispensable role in the Communist program: in the training of the revolutionary van-guard, in the maintenance of the Communist state, in the promotion of its scientific endeavors, and in the propagation of its ideological conceptions.

(4) Representative institutions of a character compatible with the Communist purpose and form of organization are to be maintained. But the liberal parliamentary system of government with its plural parties reflecting divergent class and economic interests is explicitly rejected. Civil liberties are to be permitted to the extent that they do not threaten the foundations of the Communist state or the power of

the Communist Party, and are to be extended when the Communist political, economic order shall have been firmly established.

(5) Communism retains confidence in its ultimate victory through-out the world. This is not based on a blind faith in the automatic working of the historical process but on conviction of the validity of the Communist philosophy as a moral conception and as a political program. It relies on its appeal to the oppressed and underprivileged nations whose peoples constitute the majority of mankind and on the effectiveness of the centrally controlled and planned economic and educational development.

A major objective of the Communist foreign policies of the U.S.S.R. and of the Chinese People's Republic is to win over the economically backward countries of Asia, Africa, and South America through revolutionary action organized by native leaders with international Communist support. However, with the competition between Russia and China for leadership of the Communist world has come a sharp divergence in the interpretation of Marxist-Leninist doctrine.

Although the Soviet Union continues to support revolutionary activity where it regards this as practical and to its interest, it has relinquished the aim of leading a world revolution against capitalism. It has adopted a policy of coexistence as the better part of wisdom; it cooperates readily with neutralist countries, as in the case of India; it has given substantial aid to Egypt which bans the Communist Party. In the Russian view, the ultimate victory of communism will come without international war, as a result of communism's alleged effec-tiveness in the use of science and technology for the common good.

In marked contrast, the Chinese Communist view as formulated by Mao Tse-tung maintains that coexistence between socialism and capi-talism is impossible. It holds that the main struggle today is not be-tween the industrial proletariat and the bourgeoisie in each country but between socialism and imperialism, between the poor under-developed agricultural countries and the rich capitalist nations. Thus the Maoist doctrine goes beyond the Leninist position. Lenin had modified the Marx-Engels conception by including the peasants along with the industrial proletariat as agents of revolution; the Chinese Communist revision makes the peasants the major factor. As stated by Marshal Lin Piao, the Minister of Defense, in a pronouncement issued in the fall of 1965: "The country-side and the country-side alone can provide the revolutionary bases from which the revolu-tionaries can go forward to final victory."[25] Just as the Chinese Com-

[25] *The New York Times Magazine,* Sunday, Oct. 24, 1965.

munist revolution began in the hinterland and ended with the capture of the cities, so, it is argued, the world revolution must be initiated by guerilla warfare in the largely rural areas of the world, in Asia, Africa, and South America, and proceed to victory over the urbanized capitalist countries of North America and Western Europe.[26]

On the face of it, the grandiose strategy of mobilizing the peasants of the world for revolutionary action has as little substance as the original call, in the *Communist Manifesto,* to the proletarians of the world to unite. It is not clear how much of the Maoist statement is intended as a basis for an aggressive foreign policy, how much as a competitive bid against Soviet Russia for influence in the under-developed countries, how much a response to the escalation of the war in Vietnam. Some students of Chinese affairs believe that the extreme pronouncements in recent years were designed to cover up the weakened position of China in the Communist world and to mask a turn toward an isolationist position under the stress of serious internal problems.[27]

In total effect, the position of the Soviet Union, although avowedly Communist, is closer to that of the United States than to that of the Chinese People's Republic. It should be evident that international comity and the peace of the world in the ensuing period depends on a further development of cooperation between the United States and the Soviet Union.

BEYOND MARXISM AND LIBERALISM

Communism cannot be confuted by a denial of the metaphysical principles used by Marx as a framework for his conceptions, by correction of his critique of the capitalist economic theory, or by pointing out errors in his predictions. After discounting for all of its dis-

[26] A comprehensive study of the situation in China is presented by Franz Schurman, *Ideology and Organization in Communist China* (Berkeley and Los Angeles, 1966). An evaluation of the ideas of Mao Tse-tung is provided by Arthur A. Cohen, *The Communism of Mao Tse-tung* (Chicago, 1964).

[27] The attacks against outstanding personages in the Communist hierarchy during 1966 and the increase of disorders in early 1967 indicated that a critical factional struggle was going on between those who wished to follow the Russian pragmatic tendencies and the Maoist ideologists who laid the emphasis on revolutionary fervor and sacrifice. The anti-Western demonstrations by the Red Guards, under the slogan of the "great proletarian cultural revolution" were apparently encouraged by the government to strengthen popular support for the policies of Mao Tse-tung and to counteract the influence of prominent Communist leaders and local officials. For a recent analysis: Lucien W. Pye, "China in Context" and Mark Gain, "China Convulsed," *Foreign Affairs,* XLV (Jan. 1967).

qualifications, Marxism still constitutes a formidable body of concepts, aims, and strategies that are relevant to social realities in many parts of the world. Moreover, the achievements of the Soviet Union—the rapid industrialization and scientific advance, the elimination of unemployment, the extension of education, of health, and social services to all—have given substance to the Marxist claims. The same can be said of Communist China which, despite setbacks, is building up a modern society with unprecedented speed.

A high price has been paid for the successes of communism in Russia and China, in liquidations, forced labor, continued restriction of civil liberties. Perhaps some of the ruthlessness could have been avoided; as in all spheres of life, in peace and in war, as we reflect with the wisdom of hindsight, it always seems that things might have been done with less disorder and cruelty. But there is a serious question whether the vast revolutionary transition from reactionary regimes and backward conditions could have been achieved without resort to dictatorship. In Russia, the Leninist strategy was accepted only after more moderate policies had been frustrated. In China, the regime of Chiang Kai-shek did not touch—not to say, resolve—the basic problems. Germany, under the Weimar Republic, tried loyally to maintain a democratic regime according to all the rules, only to open the door to the nihilistic dictatorship of the Nazis which drew the world into the vortex of destruction of World War II.

Liberalism is not merely an attitude of mind, an assertion of the principle of individual freedom, or even the introduction of the democratic method of government. It includes all these elements in a complex integration of law and education, of social practices and habits of thought. Moreover, liberalism is not an abstract political theory: it finds its embodiment in a definite type of state with sovereign coercive powers. The liberal state cannot be created by fiat. It developed in the West, in the course of centuries, through the interaction of a heritage of ideas with forms of economic organization. In the major instances, in England, France, and in the United States, it was inaugurated by revolution supported by organized class interests.

Democracy cannot be artificially established in backward countries where poverty and illiteracy prevail merely by introducing universal suffrage and parliamentary methods. The first task is to raise the standard of living for the great mass of population, to improve health, to provide education. This is an enormous task requiring radical changes in property relations; it demands huge sums of capital, transformation of the character of the economy from an agricultural to

139

an industrial base. In the light of modern technology, it will require a high degree of socialization and centralized planning. In some instances, as notably in India, national history and religious attitudes have enabled leaders, influenced by Western culture as well as imbued with their own traditions, to direct social change without resort to violence. In cases where reactionary regimes have yielded only to revolution, the changes are likely to be drastic, carried out under dictatorships of one kind or another.

American policy has hitherto concentrated opposition against the Communist type of dictatorship. It has, in the interest of maintaining stable governments at all costs, aided dictatorships supported by military power even when these were designed to preserve a reactionary status quo. It is essential, as we face the pluralistic world order, that we recognize Communist regimes under native leadership as a legitimate type of government along with other types where democratic forces have failed to bring about necessary reforms. As Henry M. Wriston has pointed out, this is an "Age of Revolution" where drastic change of the political regime is necessary. We cannot impose on other people our own conceptions of how it is to be carried out. The leaders of victorious revolutions—achieved after life-long effort and through great sacrifice—do not take kindly to advice by outsiders, some of whom had aided and abetted their oppressors. Most of the revolutionary leaders, he remarks, "owe no thanks to armchair critics that they are now in power rather than in graves."[28]

It is necessary to disentangle the two strands in the East-West struggle—the ideological opposition with its philosophical, economic, and political underpinning on the one hand, and the struggle between the Western group of nations and the Communist blocs, on the other. Our primary concern is to protect the national security, to strengthen the Atlantic Community, to render aid to friendly nations. There are points at which the two aspects of the conflict merge: the democracies cannot look with equanimity at the increase in the number of Communist states. But the uncritical identification of the interests of Western democratic nations with absolute opposition to communism everywhere has been a catastrophic error. The intervention of the Allies at the beginning of the Bolshevist regime in support of reactionary counter-revolutionary adventurers set the pattern of distrust. The tacit support given by Britain to the build-up of Nazi Germany's military power was largely because of the belief that the

[28]Henry M. Wriston, "The Age of Revolution," *Foreign Affairs* XXXIX (July 1961), p. 540.

Hitler regime would act as a bulwark against Russia. In any case, whatever justification there may have been in the past for a wholesale anti-Communist policy has now disappeared. The differences in ideology and in national policy among Communist countries facilitates consideration of each Communist state on the basis of possibilities for cooperation.

Liberalism and Marxism were both responses to the expressions of nineteenth century intellectual conceptions in interaction with socioeconomic developments. Both of them reflected strains of thought and moral attitudes long active in Western tradition. At the same time, both were "ideologies," that is, one-sided partisan statements, mixtures of valid insights and special pleading. Marxism stressed the importance of satisfying the basic needs of all men as the condition of justice, freedom, and peace. It was right in the recognition of the part that the economic structure plays in social organization; it erred egregiously in the implication that once material needs were satisfied, justice, peace, and freedom would in due course result. In making the Bill of Rights the prerequisite to its system of government, liberalism retained more of the ethical insight and aspiration for freedom embedded in the religious and the political tradition of Europe. But it failed to recognize—rather, suppressed its awareness of the actuality—that its central emphasis on the rights of property qualified its assumption of equal rights before the law and seriously affected equality of opportunity. The proclamation of freedom sounds hollow when divorced from the principle of equality. And both freedom and equality lack a foundation when the basic needs of men are not decently met.

Moreover, liberalism underestimated the part that force necessarily plays in the organization of the state, whether democratic or authoritarian. Its pet fiction was that government in a liberal era was weak—a "passive policeman." It repressed the fact that the liberal state had itself come into being by revolutionary action, and ignored the degree to which force was built into its institutions. The separation of powers between the legislative and the judiciary, and between both and the executive, distributed responsibility between the various divisions of the government, but it did not signify the limitation of power—or its weakening. Franz Neumann has made a distinctive contribution in pointing out that: "the liberal state has always been as strong as the political and social situation and the interests of society demanded. It has conducted warfare and crushed strikes; with the help of strong navies it has protected its investments, with the help of the police it has restored 'peace and order'."[29] The liberal state exercised its power when it refrained from using it, as well as when it used it. In refusing to support the church's domination of the intellectual and religious life it made an indispensable contribution to the freedom of the mind and of conscience. But in refraining from interfering with the capitalist entrepreneur even when this meant the exploitation of the unprotected worker, it indirectly permitted a minority who were in possession of the means of production to exercise control over the lives of the masses of the population.

The heart of all government lies in its power to enforce its decisions. The state is distinguished from all other forms of organization by the legitimate power of "sovereignty," as H. J. Laski has defined it, "by possessing a coercive authority legally supreme over any group which is part of the society."[30] The slogan, "Reason versus Force" misstates the issue. In defining itself as a "government of laws and not of men," liberalism has accepted the support of the sovereignty of the state: mores, conventions, legislative enactments, become law only in so far as they can be enforced by the police power of the government.

John Dewey, who aims to substitute intelligence for coercion as the major means of social control, recognizes, nevertheless, "Force . . . is built into the procedures of the existing social system."[31] He points out that the political state is not the only agency endowed with coercive power in our society, that its power is pale in contrast to that exercised by organized property interests. What he does not make clear is that force is indispensable to any organized society and that when the state fails to exercise it, power falls to private agencies. The real antithesis is between the use of the state power in accordance with law to promote democratic ends—the protection of the person, the maintenance of civil liberties, and the promotion of the general welfare, on the one hand, and the use of the state power to deny the inalienable rights of the people or indirectly to protect the concealed power of private organizations in defiance of the public interest, on the other.

The neglect of the economic and power factors in political organization is connected with a third deficiency, namely, the idea that "the autonomy of the individual is the very keystone in liberalism." The

[29] Franz Neumann, *The Democratic and Authoritarian State* (Glencoe, Ill., 1957), p. 22.
[30] Harold J. Laski, *The State in Theory and Practice* (New York, 1935), p. 8.
[31] John Dewey, *Liberalism and Social Action* (New York, 1935), pp. 63-64.

142

concept, "the individual," has significance if viewed in its sociological and political context: current liberalism recognizes the social nature of the individual, but there still adheres to it something of John Stuart Mill's observation, "Men are not, when brought together, converted into another kind of substance." In a Pickwickian sense, this is true; however, as Edward H. Carr notes: "But the fallacy is to suppose that they existed, or had any kind of substance, before being 'brought together'. As soon as we are born, the world gets to work on us and transforms us from merely biological into social units."[32]

The individual is a social creature, not only in the sense that he is related to other individuals as progressive liberalism recognizes; he is ever a sociological, a communal person—a member of a family, of a profession, of a class, of a nation, perhaps of a church. Certainly in the realm of politics we act as members of regions, of parties, of vocational groupings—rarely as individuals pure and simple. Likewise, "freedom of the individual" must be described in terms of the concrete positive liberties and opportunities which society affords. To say, as does the liberal, that freedom consists of the right to do whatever one pleases as long as one does not injure another or does not violate the law, is essentially negative, and gives a false notion of the conditions and limits of freedom. The individual lives within a system of law which, at the same time, liberates and constrains him. The freedom of the individual depends not primarily on what the state *permits*, but in a more positive sense, on what the state *supports*.

In the movement "forward from liberalism," it will be necessary to clear our minds of the vestiges of laissez-faire that still cling to the doctrine of the "inevitability of gradualism." Social progress is not automatic; it requires conscious effort guided by principles and directed toward definitely formulated ends. Democratic ethics requires a harmony of means and ends, rejects the doctrine that the means justifies the ends. But the assumption that "democratic means" —universal suffrage, public discussion, widespread education— will by themselves suffice to bring about democratic ends is the prime ideological illusion of the liberal temper of mind. It leads to begging the question of the purposes of education, involves a misconception of the nature of the individual, implies an inadequate view of the function of the state.

The revision of liberalism necessitates focusing attention on the proximate aims of democracy in terms of specific freedoms, of racial equality, and of human welfare. It requires a realistic recognition of

[32] Carr, *op. cit.*, p. 36.

how both the ends and the methods of democracy are conditioned—facilitated or obstructed—by existing forms of economic organization and by the power structures permitted or promoted by the nature of the democratic state. It means viewing national policy in the international framework of contemporary society. In the following chapter, the critical issues in the domestic scene of civil liberties and racial equality will be discussed in the light of the suggested considerations.

The system of liberties that exists at any
time is always the system of restraints or
controls that exists at that time . . . For
the liberties that any individual actually
has depends upon the distribution of
powers or liberties that exists, and this
distribution is identical with actual social
arrangements, legal and political—and, at
the present time, economic, in a peculiarly
important way. JOHN DEWEY

5.

Democracy: Law, Civil Liberties, and Racial Equality

B EFORE entering upon the discussion of civil liberties and racial
equality, the subjects of this chapter, it is in order to state the
position assumed with reference to the political basis of the democratic society. The definition of democracy as "government by the
people" is likely to mislead; it tends to minimize the intrinsic relationship between the democratic form of government and its constitutional basis, and to obscure the ethical sanction supporting civil liberties and racial equality as inviolable ends. The position outlined below
is intended as an affirmation and clarification of a major concept in
liberalism, namely: that democracy represents "a government of laws
and not of men."

THE CONSTITUTIONAL BASIS OF DEMOCRACY

Democratic government is, first of all, constitutional government and
this carries with it three corollaries: (1) the prerequisite principle of
"inalienable," that is, of indefeasible rights which no government may
set aside; (2) a judiciary independent of the executive and the legislative which indirectly, through decisions in concrete cases, or indirectly, as in the United States through the Supreme Court, interprets and applies them; (3) a historically developed corpus of law
and body of principles in the light of which the inalienable or "natural" rights are interpreted and applied. It is the historically developed

body of law that gives the liberal-democratic constitution a link of continuity with the rational and ethical element in the Western political tradition.

In its meaning as "a government of laws and not of men," democracy implies a limitation by law on all arbitrary power, not only on the power of the executive, but also on the power of the legislature and of "the people" who elect the representatives and officers of government. The constitution defines the broad lines along which the limitations on arbitrary power are made. Actually, of course, the laws do not make themselves, they are made by men to fulfill the purposes of men. Will and judgment, special interests, and particular conditions unavoidably enter into legislative enactments, affect executive policy, and, no doubt, exercise an influence on judicial decisions. But the very nature of law as involving general principles as well as the acceptance of a constitutional basis places limits on legislative decisions and sets boundaries within which executive policies must be framed. It is going too far to say that "the constitutional legislator has only the one function of amending the constitution in accordance with procedures contained in the constitution."[1] The democratic legislator, drawing his authority from the people, may substantially modify old laws and add new laws. Nevertheless, he must be guided and controlled and may, at times, be vetoed, by the judges who are the custodians of the basic principles of the constitution.

The English principle of "parliamentary supremacy" was designed to curb the competence of the absolute monarch, not to transfer his autocratic powers to the legislature. In theory, the concept of "supremacy" has, at times, been interpreted to mean "that Parliament can do anything it desires."[2] But in practice it was assumed that it would act, not against, but in accord with the laws, precedents, and values embodied in the unwritten, but authoritative, English constitution. In the United States, the adoption of the Constitution and the creation of the Supreme Court to maintain and interpret it, make explicit the restriction on the legislative will.

In both the British and the American systems, legislators will naturally frame their proposals within the bounds of existing law, because they are members of the society for which they enact the laws, sharing a heritage of national culture and tradition. However

[1] Carl Joachim Friedrich, *The Philosophy of Law in Historical Perspective* (Chicago, 1958), p. 221.
[2] Franz Neumann, *The Democratic and the Authoritarian State* (Glencoe, Ill., 1957), p. 32.

closely they are concerned with local and class interests and however intent on immediate practical advantage, nevertheless some modicum of historical continuity, some infusion of general concepts, some regard for moral principles will affect legislation. But in addition, the legislator must reckon with the fact that his enactments will need to be interpreted and applied by the courts whose special function it is to maintain consistency, and hence continuity of development, with the historically developed body of principles and precedents.

Western law is the result of two thousand years of development. It represents an amalgam of custom, religious codes, edicts of princes, popular legislation, ordinances and rulings by governmental officials, judgments of the courts. In large part, it has been empirically developed and its purpose is practical—to achieve civil order, to protect the life and security of the person, to safeguard property arrangements, to define and thus limit the functions of the state. Moreover, since in the last analysis, law depends on power to enforce it, an irreducible element of "might makes right" remains in all enacted legislation. Nevertheless, a certain unity and a measure of equity has been achieved through juristic reasoning and through philosophic thought. Most significant is the rational-ethical principle which impinges on the Western legal tradition—the conception exemplified by Plato and Aristotle that genuine law—law that is "real"—must participate in the "Idea of Justice."[3]

A distinction is made in Western legal theory between the "positive law"—the body of statutes of a given society and a particular period— and a conceptual "higher law" based on reason and justice of universal applicability toward which the positive law should aspire. The Stoics formulated the conception in terms of "natural law," investing it with principles of equality and freedom as the birthright of all men— of barbarian as well as Greek, of slave and of master, of poor and rich —by virtue of their common possession of reason. Natural law meant that *lex* must aim to be in harmony with *ius;* it invested the concept of law with a universal-ethical spirit.

The Roman jurists merged the *ius naturale* with the *ius gentium*, the body of principles which seemed common to all peoples of the empire. Thus they contributed to the development of "the conception of a community greater than the state, to which all men belonged—a common civilization within which men were governed by common principles in relation to one another."[4] To the conception of natural

[3] Friedrich, *op. cit.,* chap. III, pp. 13-26.
[4] A. D. Lindsay, *The Modern Democratic State* (Oxford, 1947), p. 57.

law, Christian thought gave a divine sanction, at the same time conceiving it as the expression of God's love as well as of His reason and including compassion in the realm of justice. In the medieval period, *ius naturale* fusing with the *ius divinum* led to the conception of the supremacy of law to which the sovereign as well as the subject owed obedience. Natural law was not a body of prescriptions binding on the courts. It consisted, as Ernest Barker has noted, of a "spirit of 'humane interpretation' in the mind of the judge and the jurist—which may, and does affect the law which is actually enforced."[5]

Natural law theory has bequeathed invaluable principles to the liberal-democratic constitution. Among these are: the generality of the law, the quality of all men before the law, and, imponderable and yet profoundly significant, the idea that law must have regard for the reason and conscience of mankind. Prerequisite to these principles is the constitutionalist doctrine which "contains the demand for a restriction and limitation of sovereign power by a system of norms which are regarded as being above the positive laws of the state."[6] Ultimately derivative from natural law, is the liberal-democratic conception of the indefeasible Bill of Rights. Although it appears in the Amendments as an addition to the Articles, it is historically and logically prior to the Constitution itself. Whether it is a written one, protected by the Supreme Court as in the American structure of government, or unwritten as in the English system traditionally respected by Parliament and the courts, the liberal-democratic constitution is predicated on the principle of inalienable human rights: it is "to secure these rights that Government is instituted among men." These basic "natural" human rights may not be abrogated by the state power, either by the executive or the legislature, although they are subject to interpretation and to modification in application.

The doctrine of inalienable rights does not endow the individual with any prerogative to do as he pleases provided only that he does not infringe on the rights of others—a frequent but unsatisfactory formulation. There is a sphere of private relationships which the law neither helps nor hinders, but in the major instances the general idea of freedom must be translated into specific liberties so that they may be protected by law. The course of constitutional development has been to convert the vague concept of natural rights into definite rights guaranteed by coercive forces of the state, although as the

[5] Quoted by Walter Lippmann in *The Public Philosophy* (Boston, 1955), pp. 107-108.

[6] Neumann, *op. cit.*, p. 89.

150

Ninth Amendment declares, the enumeration of the Bill of Rights in the Amendments in the Constitution is not to be construed as denying "the other rights retained by the people."

The rights guaranteed by the Constitution may be divided into three categories as subject to different degrees of modification. First are the basic personal rights: of life, security of the person, of "due process of law," of immunity from "cruel and unusual punishment." The personal rights may be regarded as absolute, although here, too, limitations defined by the courts are unavoidable. A second group, to which the First Amendment addresses itself, is concerned with the major civil liberties: of religion, of the press and of speech, of assembly, and of criticism of government. These freedoms imply freedom of association as well as freedom of thought. In this sphere, there is a greater leeway for restriction than in the sphere of personal rights. The free exercise of these "societal rights" may be curtailed when generally-accepted moral conventions are violated—as in the case of the prohibition of polygamy—or when the safety of the state is involved, as in the "clear-and-present-danger" principle. However, the limitations are subject to the review by the judiciary and to the final decision of the Supreme Court. The third category consists of property rights, which besides affecting the exercise of the other rights, are indispensable for the conduct of the economy under the liberalist conceptions. The maintenance of the rights of property is basic to the democratic constitution, but in this realm there is room for great changes in the light of the vast transformation going on in the nature of the economic structure.

The content of the Bill of Rights is subject to interpretation by the courts and to amendment by the Congress. But the fundamental principles cannot be abolished by any branch of government, not even by the elected representatives of the people as a whole. It is sometimes held that the principle of "popular sovereignty" implies the right of the majority of the people to rescind the civil liberties and inalienable rights, just as they may make other changes in the laws. Since the people originally gave the Bill of Rights, so the argument runs, they may take them back. In the light of the development of Western political thought and of the history of the American Constitution, this is an untenable interpretation. As noted, the Bill of Rights preceded the Constitution and the Constitution was not ratified until the the Bill of Rights was included in the Amendments. As Professor Corwin points out, the Preamble says: "We the people of the United States . . . do ordain and establish," not *did* ordain and establish. It binds the present generation as well as the past. It indicates the source of the authority in the people, but at the same time serves as a self-limitation of the scope of the authority through the separation of powers and the Bill of Rights.[7]

Like the principle of parliamentary supremacy, the tenet of popular sovereignty came into being as a means of counteracting absolute monarchy. The introduction of the concept, "the people," is an essential of the democratic idea. It implies universal suffrage and emphasizes the importance of the active participation of all citizens in government. It signifies the need of consent to the major governmental policies either through elected representation or directly through referendum. It makes indispensable the public discussion of issues and the provision of education for all the people. But the liberal-democratic constitution does not give the people "sovereignty" in the sense of supreme and final power in the state; the people cannot abolish the separation of powers, nor deny the independence of the judiciary. To do so would transform democracy into totalitarianism, which in essence means the unconditioned concentration of power in the executive branch of the state. By the same token, it is necessary to reject the view that democracy means primarily "the rule of the majority," and that it implies the obligation to abide by the decision of the majority under all circumstances—even to the point of the abolition of the civil liberties.

It should first be noted that, in the democratic system, the right to decide by majority vote and to command obedience is limited to definite governmental functions within the general frame of the Constitution. Submission to the majority is not a wholesale principle, either legal or moral; rather it is a pragmatic device for electing officials and for deciding questions within accepted boundaries. As Franz Neumann notes, "A wrong cannot possibly become a right because the majority wills it so. Perhaps it thereby becomes a greater wrong."[8] The democratic state respects the right of civil disobedience in issues invested with moral quality and, when it is true to its ethic, will be lenient in punishment when the plea of conscience is sincere. Democracy is castrated in its vital part when it fails to protect the civil liberties, for the individual and for minorities, against the coercive force of the majority.

The defective character of the definition of democracy which equates it with the sovereign rule of the people and with the rule of the majority becomes evident when we consider the fact that the

[7] Edward S. Corwin, *The Constitution and What It Means Today* (Princeton, 1958), pp. 1-2.
[8] Neumann, *op. cit.*, p. 156.

deciding differential of votes may—and often does—constitute only a small proportion of the total population. Further, the voter is not an abstract number each standing for one autonomous individual. The citizen votes as resident of a locality through organized parties; his will is constrained and refracted by the necessary machinery of politics as well as influenced by his economic position and vocational affiliation, and perhaps also by membership in an ethnic or racial group. Moreover, the concept of "the people" is not identical with the body of voters; in a deeper sense, it signifies an ideal transcendental community enduring in time bound by cultural and spiritual ties. It is the latter meaning that Walter Lippmann has in mind in *The Public Philosophy* where he defines *The People*—writing the word in italics—as "a corporate nation," an entity which lives on though individuals may come and go. Democratic government requires not only the consent of the plurality of voters at a given time, but also the sanction of the invisible community—of predecessors and successors—united by tradition, by sentiment, and by law.[9]

Democracy represents a complex structure of ideas and of institutions, of imponderable ethical aspirations, of a historically evolved body of law, of empirically developed governmental processes. Essential to it are complementary interacting ideas: inalienable rights and popular sovereignty, the autonomy of the individual and the supremacy of law, the separation of powers and the unity of government. Each of these guiding ideas is indispensable; the antinomies represent not only checks and balances but elements of government that supplement one another. To eliminate any one of them would lead to a distortion of the liberal democratic system. Each principle of government must be viewed in context with the others in a moving equilibrium of interrelated functions. No single one of them provides a sufficient definition of the democratic process, no one of them has primacy or supremacy, no one of them possesses "sovereignty" in the proper sense of the word. Sovereignty—the right to use the coercive power of the state—belongs to the federal government alone and can be exercised only through the executive in accordance with the Constitution as amended by the legislature and as interpreted by the courts.

THE ALLEGED "MALADY OF THE DEMOCRATIC STATES"

One or another of the agencies and forces of government—the executive, the judiciary, the legislature, the public opinion of the people—

[9] Lippmann, "The Voters and the People," *op. cit.*, pp. 33-36.

may exercise greater or lesser influence at different periods with varying effects. From 1887 to 1937, the Supreme Court, its thinking strongly influenced by laissez-faire conceptions, protected business interests from government interference through censorship of national and state legislation. In more recent years, it has been a major factor in advancing the basic civil liberties and the cause of racial equality. In the earlier period, the representatives of the people exercised initiative in advancing the public interest. Today, in the light of the complexity of governmental problems in both domestic and foreign affairs, presidential leadership becomes ever more important in the initiation of legislation as well as in the exercise of executive power. Congress, reflecting local views, particular interests, and regional prejudices, tends to act as a brake on progressive social legislation and as a constraint on a unified national economic policy. Outworn election laws make it more representative of the rural community and of the small town than of the growing, less conventionally minded, urban population. Congress is bedeviled by the pressure of party politics, weighted toward conservatism by the seniority principle in the organization of the important committees, ham-strung by the privilege of the filibuster. The complexity of governmental problems, the control of political power by machines, the influence of organized lobbies, the high cost of promoting candidates—these concomitants of large-scale social organization have raised questions with reference to the effectiveness of mass participation in political decisions.

There are evidences, in recent years, of the growth of an elitist tendency among writers on politics which deprecates the influence of public opinion on government policy, particularly in the field of foreign affairs.[10] In *The Public Philosophy*, Walter Lippmann presents an extreme indictment: he attributes the crisis in the world situation since the end of the first world war to a devitalization of the governing power of the Western states. This "enfeeblement, verging on paralysis," he asserts is the result of the "democratic malady," i.e., the excessive influence of mass opinion on government policy. The Western democracies, he argues, suffer from a "derangement of powers," from the encroachment by elected assemblies on the sphere of the executive function of the state. Dominated by emotion, mass opinion, he alleges, has been intolerant of the calculated compromises essential to lasting settlements; the people have imposed a veto upon the informed and expedient judgments of responsible officials. In sum:

[10] J. William Fulbright and others, *The Elite and the Electorate*, Fund for the Republic (Santa Barbara, 1963).

"The Western democracies are in a declining power in human affairs ... due to a derangement of functions of their governments which disables them in coping with the mounting disorder."[11]

Sympathy with the attitudes that find expression in Mr. Lippmann's public philosophy—his regard for universals, for the imponderable values embodied in the Western tradition, for rationally developed law as the bond of civil society and as a basis for governmental policy—should not mislead us into accepting his analysis of what he calls "the malady of the democratic states." His wholesale indictment is subject to challenge on all of its major counts—the nature and causes of the contemporary disorder, the weakness of the democratic governments, the unexceptional wisdom of official judgments, and on the gravamen of his charge, the error of public opinion.

Public opinion is not an undifferentiated wave of spontaneous response. It includes the diverse views of the press, the calculated policies of organized business and labor, the ethically oriented conceptions of religious organizations. It has a left, a liberal, and a radical-right wing. On the whole, it tends toward a middle of the road position; these is no warrant for the assertion that it is, on the whole, averse to compromise. Nor can it be maintained that the positions of the allegedly well-informed experts and officials are generally unanimous, wholly dispassionate, uninfluenced by preconceived attitudes or assumptions. But apart from any detailed criticism, the entire thesis has little to support it: mass opinion has never been the major factor in the determination of the foreign policy decisions.

The policies of European governments have, notoriously, always been worked out within the confines of foreign offices and embodied in secret treaties of which the public knew little. In the United States, despite the greater powers of Congress in the declaration of war and in the ratification of treaties, the public at large has had little influence in the critical junctures. Our entry into the first world war, the imposition of a victorious peace on Germany, our acquiescence in the Allied intervention in Russia after the Bolshevist Revolution, the dropping of the bombs on Hiroshima and Nagasaki, the Korean War, our policy in South Vietnam, and not to be left out of account, the gauche invasion of Cuba at the Bay of Pigs in 1961—these fateful decisions were made by the Chief Executive, in consultation with the Cabinet, with the military establishment and the State Department, and in recent years with that new arm of government, the Central Intelligence Agency. The argument that the people are not qualified

[11] Lippmann, *op. cit.*, chaps. II, III, pp. 16-40.

to "administer the government," is a man built out of a very thin straw—since they never did, or could, under our Constitution.

That there was—as there should have been—an interaction between public opinion and government policy is, of course, true. To what degree public opinion was in accord with the government decisions before and after they were made, and whether it was beneficial or harmful, is a matter of historical analysis in each instance. But more than it influenced government, public opinion in the critical instances was directed by government itself. As Charles A. Beard has graphically described, vast propaganda was brought to bear at the time of the first world war on the people in the United States who had re-elected Woodrow Wilson on the slogan that he had "kept us out of war." Intellectuals and men of learning played a particularly important role in the organized pressure to promote the war fever. University professors, teachers in all ranks of the school system as well as journalists, magazine writers, and experts in advertising were mobilized in the huge effort of "selling the war to America." Those who were not convinced or silenced by the campaign of propaganda were brought to book by drastic espionage and sedition statutes.[12]

Likewise, during our prolonged embroilment in South Vietnam, government made its decisions in executive sessions. The public at large was informed—at times misinformed—after policies had been determined upon. The record of our increasing involvement was marked by secret arrangement, by disingenuous statements on our commitment to the "nation of South Vietnam," by ambiguous pronouncements about our willingness to negotiate "without preconditions." The rejection of Hanoi's offer to open peace talks, made to the Secretary General of the United Nations in 1964, was not revealed until a year later. During the summer of 1964, *The New York Times'* editorial on July 29 went so far as to say:"Until now the Government's negative—indeed repressive and distorted—news policies obscured both the purposes and policies of the war. The public was not only misinformed by Government statesmen but unpalatable facts were withheld and the truth subverted."

Despite the criticism of our Vietnam policy by eminent students of foreign policy, including Walter Lippmann, and the opposition of leading members of Congress, including Senators Wayne L. Morse and J. William Fulbright, chairman of the Foreign Relations Committee, despite the teach-ins in the colleges and demonstrations in the streets,

[12] Charles A. Beard and Mary R. Beard, *The Rise of American Civilization* (New York, 1927), vol. II, p. 640.

the Johnson administration steadily escalated the war to unprecedented proportions. The opinion polls, it is true, seemed to indicate a
balance of support for the President's line of action. It is hardly to be
expected that the public-at-large will openly oppose a determined
government position in time of war. But there was a strong undertone
of dissatisfaction; undoubtedly, public opinion would have welcomed
a more moderate course, if the government had provided the leadership.

The purpose here is not to disparage the part that the executive
branch of government plays in the formation of policy but to deny
the thesis that our failures have been caused by need of reckoning
with public opinion. Executive decision on foreign policy without
prior public discussion may be unavoidable; the mobilization of public
opinion in support is a necessity of democratic leadership. But there
is a vast difference between a genuine consideration of divergent opinion in the community, evaluating various views on their merits, and
the manipulation of public opinion in order to achieve a "consensus"
in conformity with policies predetermined in the State Department
and the Pentagon.

Public opinion is not always rational or wise; certainly it cannot be
decisive in the formulation of foreign policy. But it can act as a corrective of the specialized perspectives of the military and state department establishments. Moreover, when not distorted by propaganda,
it preserves a seed of man's impulse for peace and justice. With all his
emphasis on the importance of law and reason in the governance of
society, Lord Acton had a high appreciation of "the healing forces
that slept in the uncoerced consciences of the masses." No good purpose is served by diminishing the importance of public opinion; this
works only to protect inflexible policies and to conceal the real causes
of "the contemporary disorder." The task is to analyze the factors in
the formation and distortion of public opinion and to direct it toward
knowledgeable and humane policies. In this, education has a crucial
function—to counteract prejudice, provincialism, and partisan propaganda, and not least, to correct the one-sided influence of government
information agencies.

This excursus into the question of the part that "the rule of the
people" properly plays in the democratic process is incidental. The
entire construction which portrays Western power as in decline and
attributes its alleged weakness to defects in governmental procedures
is out of kilter. The Western democracies show no erosion of their
capacity to govern. They have met the vicious attacks of their enemies—of German autocracy, of fascist totalitarianism, and of Japanese

157

imperialism—with extraordinary vigor and with complete victory. They have held their own against the expansion of communism; wherever democracy had genuine roots, it has not been defeated nor supplanted. The West has played the leading part in the organization of the United Nations and in its subsequent development. The influence of the United States on world affairs is certainly greater than it was in the era before World War I.

In a relative sense, it is true, as Senator Fulbright has noted, "that the world-wide dominance of the Western countries has been lost."[13] If this refers to the passing of imperialism and to the checking of America's "manifest destiny," the loss of "dominance" is a good thing. In any case, the change of relative position is due to the rise of Asian and African nations rather than to the weakening of the Western countries. The reasons for the decline of Western influence in the world at large—in so far as this has actually taken place—are not those implied in the elitist analysis which ascribes it to defects of democracy. There are more tangible reasons—in part political and economic, in part social and moral.

The elementary conditions—social, economic, and educational—requisite for the successful operation of the liberal-democratic system are absent in most of the underdeveloped countries. This alone would preclude taking the Western economic-political systems as models, at least in the early stages of revolutionary change. The moral dilemma cuts deeper: the liberal-democratic order has fallen culpably short of the essentials of its promise. The ethical aspects of democracy have been too greatly compromised by a close alliance with industrial capitalism, by the identification of the Western role with the domination of the white race.

The "malady of the democratic states," to use Mr. Lippmann's phrase, is due to the gap between our public professions and the actualities of our life. The discrepancy between the proclamation of equality and the mores of inequality that persists in the chief West European countries has induced a schism in the soul; it has brought a sense of "bad faith" as we see ourselves, and created an image of disingenuousness as others see us. The controlling idea of the emerging era is the idea of equality—of the equal right of all for a decent satisfaction of basic needs, of equality in individual, national, and racial dignity, of equality as a prerequisite of true freedom. In the light of the revolutionary movement throughout the world, the principle of

[13] Fund for the Republic, "Is Government by the People Possible?" *op. cit.*, p. 4.

158

social inequality—as based on material wealth, on an assumption of white supremacy, on the implication of the inherent superiority of European man—has become indefensible and intolerable.

The ethical assumptions embodied in the Western tradition—the sacredness of human life, the inviolability of the person, the right to intellectual and spiritual freedom, the hope for the unification of mankind—must ultimately triumph throughout the world. Although as ideas they have been most clearly formulated in the course of European history, they represent universal imperishable human aspirations. In modern times, through the establishment of the liberal-democratic constitution, the West made a great step forward in implementing these principles—and for this it has justly earned a pre-eminent place in the social history of man. Whether the Western countries, and particularly the United States, will continue to be recognized as exemplifying the universal ideas of freedom and equality will depend on the degree to which these ideas are embodied in our laws and mores, and in our economic institutions. A necessary step in the maintenance of American influence is to abandon the claim to "primacy" and to "dominance," and accept that place among the nations of the earth to which our genuine contribution to the common task of advancing equality and freedom entitles us.

The complex nature of modern society with the great demands it makes on executive leadership and on the use of expert knowledge necessitates modifications in government procedures. But the deeper problems of democracy lie, not in the processes of government, but in the definition of its ethical and social aims. It lies not in the methodology taken in isolation of purposes, but in means directed to definite ends. Three major areas will be discussed in the following chapters in the endeavor to outline a democratic policy in the light of the urgencies and possibilities of contemporary life. These are: (1) civil liberties—particularly the question of freedom of political discussion and equality for the Negro; (2) the domestic economy—free enterprise and the welfare state; (3) international affairs—the building of a one-world order and the relation of the Western democracies to the Communist states. In the area of civil liberties, there is a basic consensus but considerable differences of view in application. In the area of economic organization and in the sphere of international affairs there is a wider range of valid differences in conception; in these areas it is essential to attempt to outline a defensible position.

DISSENT AND POSITIVE FREEDOM

The discussion of civil liberties by its official exponents still, for the most part, echoes the individualistic and anti-authoritarian attitudes of the modern libertarian mode of thought. "Freedom through dissent" continues to be a major theme as indicated in the 1961-1962 Report of the Civil Liberties Union. The introduction, written by the executive director, conveys the impression that "prescription of official ortho- doxy"—of which the converse is the "proscription of heresy"—repre- sents the major obstacle to the realization of freedom.[14]

Civil liberties, it is explained, are indivisible, dependent on the ex- tension of individual freedom. They are promoted primarily through unlimited inquiry and unrestricted debate by which, it is averred, our American heritage has taught us that truth is ever to be found. Ac- cordingly, the views we hate, as well as the principles we affirm, are to be permitted free public expression. The Report cites with satisfac- tion the decision of the New York Court of Apeals—which the Su- preme Court refused to review—forbidding municipal authorities to deny a forum to George Lincoln Rockwell's American Nazi doc- trines. This complete faith in the value of effectiveness of unrestricted public discussion is buttressed by citation of one of the time-honored dicta of Thomas Jefferson: "Truth is great and will prevail if left to herself."

So baldly stated with its eighteenth-century overtones, this over- simplified libertarian conception becomes largely ineffective, if not mostly irrelevant, in application to the real problems of freedom and civil liberties as we face them in the current situation. The view that liberty is indivisible neglects the need of defining in law the freedoms that are to be prohibited as well as those which are to be protected. It evades the question of the content and ends of freedom when it places the right to disseminate racial hatred on a par with the right of religious freedom. There may be practical reasons for allowing unrestricted expression of views subversive of all democratic and ethical principles, but giving Rockwell a platform for the propaga- tion of Nazism can hardly be regarded as a contribution to truth and freedom. In its implication that the suppression of freedom of thought derives from "official orthodoxy," it turns attention away from the part that public opinion and the courts play in the inhibition of dis- senting opinion. In its belief that the truth itself will make us free, it fails to consider that civil liberties do not implement themselves but require to be defended by the coercive forces of the state.

The difficulties spring from a too-general notion of the nature of

[14] John de J. Pemberton, Jr., "Freedom Through Dissent," *42nd Annual Re- port, July 1961-1962*, American Civil Liberties Union (New York, 1962), iv.

liberty as freedom from control. The libertarian view suffers from an overestimation of the possible range of individual autonomy, from inadequate consideration of the limitations on freedom inherent and essential in the organization of society at any given time. It neglects the conditions imposed by the complex of controlling forces that have come to be known as the "power-structure." John Dewey will scarcely be accused of underestimating the value of freedom or of the importance of inquiry and discussion in its maintenance and advance. But he recognized, and in his later years took pains to emphasize, that, "Liberty is not just an idea, an abstract principle. It is power, effective power to do specific things. There is no such a thing as liberty in general; liberty, so to speak, at large."

Freedom as effective power, Dewey points out, is always relative; the liberties enjoyed by individuals, groups, or classes must be seen in relation to those exercised by other individuals, groups, or classes. The increase of liberty, as effective power, for some may, and usually does, mean a loss for others. Liberty is never absolute, it always requires restraint at some point. He underscores in italics a conclusion which would not ordinarily be identified as Deweyan: "*The system of liberties that exists at any time is always the system of restraints or controls that exists at that time.*" With this goes the corollary that the problem of freedom is always a social, not an individual question: the liberties that any individual actually has is dependent on the actual social arrangements, legal and political—"and, in the present time, economic, in a peculiarly important way."[15]

The civil liberties protected by the Constitution do not represent a wholesale grant of freedom in general to the individual. The Bill of Rights, it is true, is rooted in a broad demand of humankind for freedom and equality, and is, in Western thought, supported by the theory of natural rights which no government may violate. But at any given time, the Bill of Rights consists of specific rights, such as freedom of worship, of speech and of the press, of peaceable assembly for the redress of grievances. The conversion of natural rights into civil liberties gives substance to freedom since the defined liberties will be protected by the sovereign power of the state; at the same time, definition implies restriction.

The freedoms protected by the state may be modified by legislative enactment or through judicial interpretation. They may be extended and new freedoms added; "freedom from want" may some

[15] John Dewey, "Liberty and Social Control." *The Social Frontier*, II, no. 2 (Nov. 1935), 41-42.

day become a constitutional right as well as a social desideratum. Liberty nevertheless involves setting bounds to conduct. Even the sphere of religion, which the democratic regime regards as a private domain, is not exempt from restriction. In the light of the state's responsibility to restrain freedom when it clashes with the public good, it would seem to be in accord with reason to prevent the dissemination of racial hatred, rather than to protect it, as libertarian thought urges in the name of freedom of speech.

Freedom cannot be achieved through dissent and discussion without regard to principles and ends. Responsible dissent from one conception implies affirmation of another view, discussion is fruitful when it is directed toward clarification of purposes and determination of the means necessary for accomplishment. The realization of liberty is a positive, many-sided task. It necessitates translating the general aspiration for freedom and equality into definite freedoms and equalities supported by social institutions and enforced by laws. Above all, it means establishing the economic conditions which make possible and facilitate freedom and equality. Despite Jefferson's noble sentiment, "truth"—in either the intellectual or the moral sense—can be achieved only by consciously directed thought and action; it never prevails of itself.

Even in the area of religious liberty, guaranteed by the Constitution, there remain unresolved juridical problems. Despite the general acceptance of the principle of the separation of church and state, an element of ambiguity persists in the interpretation of the "establishment of religion" clause of the First Amendment as in the question of government assistance to religious schools, the use of prayer in state functions, the right, as in the case of Jehovah's Witnesses, to refrain from the salute to the flag. Conventional social opinion often falls short of the spirit of tolerance reflected in the constitutional assumption of the equality of religions. Attitudes vary in different sections of the country with different groups in the population, depending also on the aspect of personal relations involved—whether in social life, in business or in politics. In centers where the population is heterogeneous, politicians prudently reckon with religious and ethnic background of candidates in calculating probability of success at the polls. It has become customary also, in national and state ceremonial functions, to give recognition to the three major denominations, Protestant, Catholic, and Jewish. The candidacy and election of John F. Kennedy to the Presidency in 1960, despite his outspoken allegiance to the Catholic faith, marked a significant change in the American tradition of confining the office of the Chief Executive to persons of Protestant background.

Nevertheless, discrimination against members of religious minorities remains an undeniable fact of life in the United States. Prejudice plays a part in business and in professional life as well as in personal affairs and social relations. Anti-Semitism, open and covert, vulgar and refined, persists, assuming vicious forms at times. On the extreme radical right, it is aggressively avowed and joined with anti-Negroism, anti-alienism, and anti-liberalism, generally in perverse, violent hatred. Anti-Catholicism, likewise, discloses an underlying social intolerance in some localities, and—compounded of the memory of past struggles against the Church and of apprehension of its present influence on legislation—also operates as an important factor in political life.

Discrimination against religious minorities is a complex psycho-social phenomenon that has little to do with theological or philosophical issues. Differences of ethnic and cultural background enter into the problem; the effort of old established groups of Protestant, "Anglo-Saxon" heritage to maintain their position of social dominance plays a major part in creating tensions. In view of the involvement of the problem of discrimination with economic stratification and the struggle for status, little can be expected from the preaching of tolerance. Common education in public schools, intercultural activities, and inter-faith projects undoubtedly have value in promoting understanding and cooperation. But the elimination of religious, as well as of racial prejudice, is unavoidably slow, dependent on many social factors.

Despite these qualifications, there has been great and continued advance in the area of religious freedom and of religious toleration. In marked contrast, freedom of discussion of political-economic conceptions has suffered retrogression during the last fifty years. Legal restrictions and social penalties virtually nullified Jefferson's famed pronouncement: "If there be any among us who would wish to dissolve this union or to change its republican form, let them stand undisturbed as monuments of the safety with which error of opinion may be tolerated where reason is left free to combat it." From the unpopular Sedition Act of 1798 which expired in 1801, until our entry into World War I, the liberal view, that radical speech unaccompanied by overt action was not to be prohibited, went unchallenged. The principle was reiterated by statesmen, praised by members of the judiciary, and supported by intellectual leaders in all phases of life. The right of free expression of dissident views and of public discussion of controversial political and economic issues was taught in

163

the schools not only as a matter of personal privilege but as an indispensable instrument of democratic government.

The process of deterioration began with the Espionage Acts of 1917 and 1918. During the first world war, the limitations placed on freedom of speech and of the press and the repressive political measures were ostensibly motivated by military considerations and by the purpose of counteracting pro-German sympathies and other attitudes thought likely to weaken the war effort. A barrage of propaganda and harassment was directed by government agencies against pacifists who were opposed to the war on religious and ethical grounds and also against socialists and others who emphasized the economic and imperialistic roots of war. The attacks against the opponents of the war merged with efforts to suppress radical conceptions. Commenting on the repressive measures of the government which he has described as rivaling the practices of the Czarist police, Charles A. Beard has written: "judging by its official reports, the main business of the Department [of Justice] was not the apprehension of people who gave aid and comfort to the Central Powers with whom the country was at war but rather the supervision of American citizens suspected of radical opinions about the perfection of perpetuity of the capitalist system of economy at home."[16]

With the success of the Russian Revolution, toward which in its earlier stages liberals as well as socialists were generally sympathetic, the repressive measures against radical political and economic conceptions were greatly intensified. State sedition laws, legislative investigation committees, raids on "reds"—a general term for socialists and other advocates of radical economic change—became the order of the day. The most serious statutory enactments were the criminal anarchist and the criminal syndicalist laws under which anyone could be persecuted for advocating, as well as for actually using, force to overthrow government or to promote change in the economic order. The California syndicalist statute made it a crime to teach or in any way aid the use of violence or terror "as a means of accomplishing a change in industrial ownership or control, or effectuating any political change." Advocacy of modification in the economic order in the direction of a greater degree of social control was likely, by the defenders of the status quo, to be tagged as "communist," as pro-Russian, and as disloyal.

The emergence of Stalinism, climaxed by the Moscow trials of 1936-1938, brought about a change in the climate of liberal opinion.

---

[16] Charles A. and Mary R. Beard, *op. cit.*, vol. II, p. 642.

The trusting attitude toward Russia and communism evaporated, and in some prominent instances was turned to embittered opposition. Membership in the Communist Party dwindled to negligible proportions. Nevertheless, suppressive measures continued, relaxed for a brief time during Russia's participation as an ally in the struggle against the fascist powers, but again aggravated in the aftermath of the cold war. The main targets were persons thought to be in influential positions—government officials, labor leaders, university professors, and teachers in the public schools.

The attack shifted from the state to the national level. The Smith Act of 1940 made it unlawful to advocate or teach, to publish or circulate materials, to organize any society or assembly with the intent of overthrowing any government of the United States. A provision of the Taft-Hartley Act of 1947 required officials of labor unions to sign noncommunist affidavits. The Internal Security and the Immigration Acts sponsored by Senator McCarran provided for the deportation of aliens alleged to be communists and Subversive Central Boards were set up to identify "Communist Action" and "Communist Front" organizations. Of national importance was the Feinberg Law of New York (1949) which required the dismissal of teachers who were members of the Communist Party or any other organizations considered subversive by the Board of Regents. Congressional Committees—the House Committee under Martin Dies and the Senate Committee under the late Joseph R. McCarthy—used their powers of investigation virtually to prosecute persons suspected of leftist tendencies.

Through these and similar measures—loyalty oaths, registration requirements, inquisitorial investigations, accusation of "guilt by association"—the long standing American liberal tradition, which tolerated, even encouraged, the expression of radical conceptions unaccompanied by overt acts of violence, was effectively brought to an end.

RADICAL THOUGHT AND THE SUPREME COURT[17]

The judiciary did not provide any effective hindrance to Congressional limitations on freedom of speech in cases which had radical political or economic implications. The Supreme Court regularly sustained the lower courts in convictions under state and national

[17] For an analysis of these and other cases mentioned, see Zachariah Chafee, Jr., *Free Speech in the United States* (Cambridge, Mass., 1948). Also, Max Lerner, *The Mind and Faith of Justice Holmes* (Boston, 1943), and Milton R. Konvitz, *Bill of Rights Reader* (Ithaca, N.Y., 1954).

repressive legislation. The "clear and present danger" doctrine, enunciated by Holmes and supported by Brandeis, though much praised by liberals, had little if any effect on the majority decisions. In the end it was exploited through strained interpretation to restrict, rather than to protect, freedom of speech and public discussion.

The clear and present danger test was first propounded by Justice Holmes in the *Schenk* case (1919), in an opinion upholding the conviction of the appellant for mailing circulars denouncing conscription to men eligible for the draft. Speaking for a unanimous Court, Holmes maintained that freedom of speech was not an absolute right: it could be restricted if the words used were "of such nature as to create a clear and present danger that they will bring about the substantive evils that Congress had a right to prevent." The defendants, he admitted, would have been within their constitutional rights in time of peace, but the nature of an act depends on the circumstances. Using a far-fetched analogy, he urged: "The most stringent protection of free speech would not protect a man in falsely shouting fire in a theatre and causing a panic."

In two other cases, during the same period, Justice Holmes disappointed the hope of liberals that the Espionage Acts would be invalidated by the Supreme Court. One case *(Frohwerk* v. *U.S.)* was against a German newspaper in which articles had appeared criticizing government policy on the purposes of the war and questioning the constitutionality of the draft. No evidence was adduced to indicate that any attempt had been made to obstruct the war through overt acts. Nevertheless the Court refused to reverse the conviction; Justice Holmes, delivering the opinion, held that it was "impossible to say" that the articles in question might not have had an inflammatory effect in the quarters where it was circulated. The other case concerned the famous trial of Eugene V. Debs, head of the Socialist Party who was convicted for a speech attacking the war program of the Administration. Expressing the view of the Court, Justice Holmes sustained the conviction which carried with it a ten-year sentence (Debs was pardoned by President Harding after serving more than two and a half years, but his citizenship was not restored). The staunchest of Holmes's admirers did not justify him in the Debs case.

It was only in dissenting opinions that Holmes in later cases reverted to the doctrine of clear and present danger. The most important of these was in connection with *Abrams* v. *U.S.* which came before the Supreme Court in the same year. A group of "socialistically minded" Russian Jews of immigrant background were convicted for violation of the Espionage Act of 1918 and received long sentences—Abrams and two associates as much as twenty years in addition to heavy fines. During August 1918, they had thrown leaflets from a loft on the East side in New York denouncing the sending of troops to Vladivostock as an act of intervention against the Russian Revolution and appealing to the munition workers of the United States to call a general strike to stop producing weapons to murder their brothers fighting for freedom in Russia.[18]

The case was important because of the severity of the punishment in comparison with the triviality of the offense and because the intention was to help Russia, not to interfere with the war against Germany. Holmes castigated the majority decision in no uncertain terms. He pointed out that the "silly leaflets" did not intend to impede the United States in the war against Germany, that by no stretch of reasoning could they be regarded as fraught with imminent danger, that if enough could be squeezed from them "to turn the color of litmus paper," only the most nominal punishment should have been imposed. He suggested that the defendants had been made to suffer not for what the indictment alleged but for the creed they avowed.

Professor Pritchett has described Holmes' dissenting opinion in the *Abrams* case, perhaps not without a touch of sarcasm, "as probably his most famous piece of rhetoric."[19] It was in this statement that Holmes made the oft-quoted declaration in behalf of free trade in ideas: "that the best test of truth is the power of the thought to get itself accepted in the competition of the market" and its counterpart, "we should be eternally vigilant against attempts to check the expression of opinions we loathe and believe to be fraught with death, unless they threaten immediate interference with the lawful and pressing purposes of the law that an immediate check is required to save the country." Justice Brandeis joined in the dissent, but Holmes's reasoning and eloquence failed to influence the other seven Justices. There were two other cases the following year *(Schaefer v. U.S. 1920; Pierce v. U.S. 1920)* in which Holmes and

[18] The intervention in Russia proved to be a fiasco from the military point of view, and politically an ill-advised adventure. George F. Kennan (*Russia and the West, under Lenin and Stalin,* [Boston, 1961], chap. II) believes that it was undertaken primarily under pressure from France and Britain for the purpose of reestablishing the Eastern front in the war against Germany. The Soviet Union has always regarded it as a counter-revolutionary action which undoubtedly it was, in effect, if not in deliberate intention .

[19] C. Hermann Pritchett, *Civil Liberties and the Vinson Court* (Chicago, 1954), p. 25.

167

Brandeis submitted dissenting opinions based on the clear-and-present-danger principle.

Another test of the efficacy of the clear-and-present-danger formula presented itself in 1925, in the case of *Gitlow* v. *U.S.* By a majority of seven to two, the Supreme Court sustained a conviction of the defendant and others for the publication of "a Left Wing Manifesto" calling for a general strike to promote "the mass struggle of the proletariat" against the "bourgeois parliamentary state." The conviction had been obtained in the lower courts under a New York Criminal Anarchy statute which had been enacted in 1902 after the assassination of President McKinley but which had remained a dead letter ever since.

Justice Sanford, speaking for the majority, argued that the clear-and-present-danger principle had been relevant in federal espionage cases as a means of deciding at what point words of incitement became unlawful acts. But in the New York statute, he maintained, the legislature had itself determined that certain words were dangerous. He applied the "bad tendency" and "remote possibility test," in accordance with which inciting words might be punished without waiting for the consequences in action. Using the conflagration analogy celebrated by Justice Holmes, he averred: "A single revolutionary spark may kindle a fire . . ." Justice Holmes, in the dissent in which Brandeis as usual joined him, "came up again with some fine prose," as Professor Pritchett puts it. He agreed that "Every idea is an incitement," but he did not think that the "redundant discourse" of the Left Wing Manifesto had any chance "of starting a present conflagration."

An important constructive by-product of the *Gitlow* case was the incidental recognition by the majority of the Court that the free speech protection of the First Amendment through the provisions of the Fourteenth also applied to the states. Until then the question had remained open; as late as 1922, Justice Pitney of the Supreme Court had maintained that "the Constitution of the United States imposes on the states no obligation to confer upon those within their jurisdiction . . . the right of free speech." The optimism aroused by this "Victory out of Defeat," as Chafee entitles his chapter on the *Gitlow* case, needs to be tempered in view of the fact that free speech under federal jurisdiction is, in the first instance, seriously qualified by the Supreme Court decisions in the cases under discussion.

A clarified and strengthened definition of the clear and present danger test was presented by Justice Louis D. Brandeis in the case of *Whitney* v. *California* which came before the Supreme Court in

1927. Miss Anita Whitney, a woman nearing sixty had attended a convention in Oakland of a newly organized "Labor Communist Party" in 1919. Several weeks later, she was arrested after giving a talk to club women in Oakland on the condition of the American Negro. She was brought to trial under the California Criminal Syndicalist Act and received a sentence of from one to fourteen years. At the convention, Miss Whitney had supported a moderate resolution which urged reliance on the ballot for achieving political power, and no evidence was produced during her trial that she had ever advocated any violation of law. Nevertheless, she was convicted for organizing and joining an association which the jury believed taught and advocated the use of terror in industrial disputes.

Justice Brandeis felt compelled, along with Justice Holmes, to sustain the conviction on technical grounds but he filed a concurring opinion on behalf of himself and Justice Holmes in which he disagreed strongly with the reasoning of the majority opinion. In restating the clear-and-present-danger test he placed emphasis on the *immediacy* of the danger. He declared, "no danger flowing from speech can be deemed clear and present unless the incidence of the evil apprehended is so imminent that it may befall before there is opportunity for full discussion. If there be time to expose through discussion the falsehood and fallacies . . . the remedy to be applied is more speech, not enforced silence. Only an emergency can justify repression." Despite the reenforced definition of the clear-and-present-danger principle, Miss Whitney went to prison. She was pardoned, after a few months, by the governor, who referred to Brandeis' argument in justifying his action. It may be that Justice Brandeis' statement affected Governor Young's decision. It remains a fact that it did not influence the Supreme Court itself.[20]

In the period before the cold war, the clear-and-present-danger doctrine did little or nothing to protect the freedom of public discussion but, at least, it was not used to support its repression. In the decade of the 1950s it was exploited in sustaining anti-Communist legislation.[21] The constitutionality of the Taft-Hartley provision

[20] In another case, on the same day, Justice Brandeis, speaking for a unanimous court, reversed the conviction of an I.W.W. organizer for lack of evidence to support the charge. Of this case, Chafee says: "In *Fish v. Kansas*, the Supreme Court for the first time made freedom of speech mean something" (*op. cit.*, p. 352). However, in a third case, *Burns v. U.S.*, the Court, Brandeis dissenting, sustained the conviction of an I.W.W. organizer on what amounted to guilt by association.

[21] For this period, see: Pritchett, *op. cit.*; also Milton R. Konvitz, *Bill of Rights Reader* (Ithaca, N.Y., 1954); Edwin S. Corwin, *op. cit.*

was upheld in 1950 *(American Communication Associates v. Douds)* by an evenly divided court with three justices not participating. In contrast to the test of the *immediacy* and *certainty* of the danger which Holmes and Brandeis had made the crux of the test, Justice Vinson maintained that the *extent* and *gravity* of the substantive evil was the main criterion of the "clear-and-present-danger" principle. This interpretation became an important factor of the Court's reasoning a year later when, in *Dennis v. U.S.*, it upheld by a vote of seven to two the conviction under the Smith Act of eleven leaders of the Communist Party. Again Justice Vinson argued that the probability of success was not the main issue: it was the conspiratorial nature of the Communist Party that made the promotion of its doctrines a clear and present danger. Justices Jackson and Frankfurter also placed stress on the conspiratorial theme although they did not accept Vinson's revision of the clear-and-present-danger test.

By this time, Justice Frankfurter, despite his admiration for Holmes and Brandeis, had given up the clear-and-present-danger doctrine because, as he thought, it had become an empty formula supporting "uncritical libertarian generalities." Evidently troubled by qualms of conscience, he delivered a long concurring opinion in which he elaborated on his reasons for affirming the judgment of the Court. In this and other cases, Professor Pritchett notes, Frankfurter was "concerned in showing why as a judge he has felt compelled to come to conclusions which as a citizen he would never support."[22] Justices Black and Douglas presented vigorous dissenting opinions attacking the Smith Act as a threat to free speech—"the glory of our system of government" which "should not be sacrificed on anything less than plain and objective proof of danger that the evil advocated is imminent."

The climax of infringement came with the breach of the walls of academic freedom. The New York State Feinberg Law was upheld *(Adler v. Board of Education*, 1951) with three justices—Frankfurter, Black, and Douglas—dissenting. Justice Frankfurter based his dissent on jurisdictional grounds; Justices Black and Douglas disagreed on the merits of the case, denouncing the majority decision as a virtual abrogation of academic freedom and as a threat to the democratic purpose of the American school system.

Justice Douglas' statement merits quoting at some length:

The present law proceeds on a principle repugnant to our society—guilt by association ... The very threat of such a procedure is certain to raise havoc with academic freedom. Youthful indiscretions, mis-

[22] Pritchett, *op. cit.*, p. 245.

taken causes, misguided enthusiasms—all long forgotten—become ghosts of a harrowing present. Any organization committed to a liberal cause, any group organized to revolt against an hysterical trend, any committee launched to sponsor an unpopular program becomes suspect.

The law inevitably turns the school system into a spying project. Regular loyalty reports on the teachers must be made out. The principals become detectives; the students, the parents, the community become informers . . . What happens under this law is typical in a police state. Teachers are kept under constant surveillance; their tasks are combed for signs of disloyalty; their utterances are watched for clues of dangerous thoughts.

A pall is cast over their classrooms. There can be no real academic freedom in that environment. Where suspicion fills the air and holds scholars in line for their jobs, there can be no exercise of the free intellect . . . A problem can no longer be pursued at its edges. Fear stalks the classroom. The teacher is no longer a stimulant to adventurous thinking. She becomes a pipe line for safe and sound information. A deadening dogma takes the place of free inquiry.

Yet it was the pursuit of truth which the First Amendment was designed to protect . . . A school system producing students trained as robots threatens to rob a generation of the versatility that has been our great distinction. The Framers knew the dangers of dogmatism; they also knew the strength that comes when the mind is free, when ideas may be pursued wherever they lead. We forget the teachings of the First Amendment when we sustain this law.

FREEDOM OF SPEECH—PRECIOUS AND PRECARIOUS GIFT

In summation: From the *Schenk* case in 1919 to the decision on the constitutionality of the Feinberg Law in 1952, the Supreme Court managed to withhold support from freedom of speech in cases of radical political belief or of advocacy of a basic change in the economic structure. By unanimous vote, by a majority opinion, or even as in one instance by the divided opinion of a "rump" court, the Justices sustained convictions by the lower courts and upheld the constitutionality of legislation directed against dissident political and economic thought even when this was not accompanied by detrimental overt action. In the important cases discussed, whatever the reason, whether of genuine belief of a grave danger to national security or to the stability of the social order, whether on the principle of judicial restraint in deference to the democratic process or in response to emotional popular opinion, whether for substantial reasons or on legal technicalities, the result was the same—the convictions were upheld.

The principle of clear and present danger had no force to upset a condemnation.[23] At best, it meant, as in the *Schenk* case when it was first expounded, only a possible danger which Congress had the right to prevent, not an actual danger as common sense might judge. In the end it came to mean the abridgement of the rights of persons in the public service suspected of holding views which legislators regarded as inimical. Clear and present danger came to mean possible, remote, unlikely danger. The minority views eloquently expressed by Holmes and Brandeis, by Black and Douglas, by Harlan F. Stone and Benjamin N. Cardoza, by Learned Hand and Roscoe Pound, reflect the Western tradition of reason and freedom at its best and can be defended on grounds of practical wisdom as well. We may have faith that the truths they express will rise again. But the course of development since World War I has demonstrated that these rational liberal views have not been accepted by the people as a whole, and that the courts will not or cannot protect freedom of speech in critical situations when the legislators supported by the coervice forces in the state oppose. As Franz Neumann says: "Power or 'necessity' or 'reason of state' cannot be effectively eliminated or restrained by constitutional law."[24]

It might be said that no loss to constructive economic and political policy was sustained by silencing the extreme, sometimes extravagant, views or by restricting the activities, sometimes erratic, of those whose convictions under espionage laws and the anti-Communist legislation were sustained by the Supreme Court. But the abridgement of public expression of divergent views and the infringement of academic freedom has extended far beyond the repression of radical labor agitation and the curtailment of Communist propaganda. The suppression of the libertarian view cast a pall on all critical public discussion outside the limits of conventional thought. It led to an attitude of disillusion and quietism among the intellectuals and promoted attitudes of conformity and passivism among the youth.[25]

There are many resources—libraries, some newspapers, periodicals—particularly in the larger cities which enable independent-minded

[23] Compare: Milton R. Konvitz, *Expanding Liberties* (New York, 1966), p. 117. "This Clear and Present Danger Doctrine, had had, up to the time of the trial of 1949 [the Dennis Case] a rather checkered career. It will suffice here to say that, with only rare exception the doctrine was used to support a denial of free speech; and no federal statute has even been invalidated under the test of the doctrine."

[24] Neumann, *op. cit.*, p. 175.

[25] During recent years, of course, with the struggle for equal rights for the Negro, on the one hand, and the escalation of the war in Vietnam, there has been a revival of the spirit of protest and a renewal of activism in the promotion

students and citizens to arrive at their own conclusions. The critical viewer or listener can find excellent panel discussions on television and radio. With the relaxation of the cold war, there was evidence of a freer attitude in the discussion of Russian affairs. But the mass communication agencies continued to be wary of expressing views which might seem to be "soft on communism." Conventional public opinion gives rightist views full opportunity for expression; racists, Jew-baiters, fascist-minded propagandists get off with moral admonition. Deviations on the left, though inspired by idealistic motivations, are severely discountenanced; those who hold them are subject to handicaps in obtaining positions, even if they are not, as in the period at the height of the cold war, penalized by years of imprisonment.

The extreme libertarian position which maintains that liberty implies an unrestricted individual right "to think as he pleases and to speak as he thinks"[26] is less harmful to democracy than the attitude of conformity that widely prevails. But stated so brashly with the emphasis on dissent, it has been a factor in aiding and abetting the repression of freedom of thought and expression. The indiscriminate glorification of the freedom of speech leads to a confusion between the license to preach racial hatred and the reasoned advocacy of a social policy designed to promote the national welfare. Undirected by ends, uncontrolled by principles, unrestricted by reasonable limitations, freedom of speech may become a force of negation, not a means of reconstruction. Unprotected by law, it is an incitement to repression. The broad libertarian principle of absolute free speech has been a delusion and a snare for the humanitarian idealist. As Ernst Freund, commenting on the *Debs* case wrote in 1919: "To know what you may do and what you may not do, and how far you may go in criticism, is the first condition of political liberty; to be permitted to agitate at your own peril, subject to a jury's guessing at motive, tendency and possible effect, makes the right of free speech a precarious gift."[27]

In concluding his treatise *Freedom of Speech in the United States,* Zachariah Chafee says: "Speech should be fruitful as well as free.

of social causes on the part of students and teachers, at least outside the classroom. The "new left" tendencies are marked by emotional defiance of "the establishment" rather than by the intellectual dissent characteristic of liberalism.

[26] T. V. Smith in *The Democratic Way of Life,* A Mentor Book (New York, 1951), p. 51.

[27] Ernst Freund, quoted by Zachariah Chafee in *Free Speech in the United States* (Cambridge, Mass., 1948), pp. 85-86.

Our experience introduces this qualification into the classical argument of Milton and John Stuart Mill, that only through open discussion is truth discovered and spread. In their simpler times, they thought it enough to remove legal obstacles like the censorship and sedition prosecutions. Mill assumed that if men were only left alone, their reasoning powers would eventually impel them to choose the best ideas and the wisest course of action. To us this policy is too exclusively negative."[28] Chafee's statement points in the right direction. But his conclusion still carries with it the liberal's primary dependence on method: "We must take affirmative steps to improve the methods by which discussion is carried on."

It has been the contention of the foregoing analysis that the real difficulty lies, not in the question of method, but in the question of *aims;* principles and ends are prior to method. Freedom of thought and of speech, as Justice Cardozo declared, is the "matrix, the indispensable condition, of nearly every other form of freedom . . . Neither liberty nor justice would exist if they were sacrificed." This can be true only if it means freedom to promote the civil liberties and the idea of equality that underlies them, not the freedom to undermine them.

A free-wheeling libertarian spirit was a distinguishing characteristic of American democracy. With its suppression during the last half-century has gone something of the *elan* that marked American life in its creative period. But the end of an illusion need not leave us in the perplexity of discouragement; it should bring us to the sobriety of understanding and the strengthening of resolution. There is much to be gained from the realization that limitation is inherent in the very nature of freedom as it moves from wish to actuality through its embodiment in law. There is wisdom in the courage to face the fact that freedom is likely to be restricted under stress of fear. To know how things are in the world saves us from the specious ease of self-deception and from the corroding evil of disingenuousness. The constructive result of the recognition of the weakness of the libertarian view which places all the emphasis on individual dissent is that it turns our attention to the positive tasks of freedom—to the need of focusing on the ends of freedom, of giving full consideration to the background of social conditions which hinder their fulfilment, and of devising the means that are effective in promoting its defined, clearly conceived purposes.

[28] Chafee, *op. cit.,* p. 559.

THE STRUGGLE FOR NEGRO EQUALITY[29]

The Supreme Court did less to protect freedom of speech in critical times than might have been expected in view of the central place it has in the American Creed. But the argument of *raison d'etat* may be brought forward in justification. The eloquent minority pronouncements in defense of freedom of speech on the part of great jurists provides some moral consolation for disappointed liberals. But in the matter of the civil and political rights of the Negro, the Supreme Court, as Professor Pritchett says, "has not until recently exhibited much concern over this lag in public morals or sought to use its great powers to reduce the gap between theory and practice. Rather, the Court's talents and powers have historically been devoted to rationalizing the gap and reconciling it with constitutional amendments."[30] The Plessy-Ferguson decision of 1896 which, on one side, defended, in theory at least, the right of the Negro to equality in state-supported facilities, at the same time gave judicial sanction to the system of legalized and enforced segregation. It was not until the period of the Roosevelt Court during the 1950s that a breach was made in the legally protected Southern code of segregation in transportation and education. But the removal of the legal barriers, important though this was as a prerequisite, had of itself no immediate or decisive effect.

It is true that during the previous half-century, considerable progress had been made in lessening discrimination, in broadening educational opportunities and in strengthening political influence. Even in the South, following industrial development, through the entry of the Negroes into business ventures, and as a result of better educational facilities, a degree of improvement had been achieved for an increasing number. In the North, more than a negligible proportion had attained equality of status with middle-class whites. Individuals had reached high positions in artistic, academic, and governmental spheres. However, despite the differences in the situation between the North and the South and the class distinctions within the Negro community, the generally inferior status characteristic of all sections of the country united the Negroes throughout the United States in the struggle for equality which assumed the character of a revolt in 1963.

A century after their "emancipation," the Negro people taken as a

[29] For a discussion of the many aspects of the Negro problem, see the two issues of *Daedalus*, "The Negro American," 94, no. 4 and 95, no. 1 (Fall 1965 and Winter 1966).

[30] Pritchett, *op. cit.*, p. 123.

whole—a "minority" of some twenty million native Americans—still constituted an underprivileged group, subject to economic discrimination and social prejudice, deprived of the measure of political power to which their numbers entitled them. Underlying the unequal status of Negroes in the North and in the West, as well as in the South, was their inferior economic position. Two-thirds of the Negro population, taking the country as a whole, suffered from sub-standard incomes; their incidence of unemployment was double that of whites. The low economic condition had a detrimental effect on every aspect of life— on health, on family life, on education.

The Negroes of the South were still largely disenfranchised. The decisions of the Supreme Court in reference to poll taxes and the conduct of primaries had been largely circumvented. The relatively small number who managed to run the gauntlet of literacy tests and other inventions could not exercise effective political influence. In the matter of desegregation in schools, on which liberals had placed great hopes, hardly more than token fulfillment had been accomplished in the course of the decade since the Supreme Court decision of May 1954. In the Deep South, in Arkansas, in Mississippi, in Alabama, and in Georgia, the modicum of progress was achieved only through the intervention of the federal government and the show of force against the state authorities. The efforts to equalize the rights of Negroes in the South were met by long drawn-out legal battles and other obstructive tactics. In critical instances, there was resort to extreme violence—bombings of homes and churches with incidental murders, assassination of Negro leaders, unbelievable police brutality against peaceful demonstrators with use of cattle prods and dogs, with tear gas and fire hose, mass jailings on trivial and trumped-up charges. The perpetrators were rarely apprehended and even more rarely punished. The white population as a whole passively acquiesced and reelected segregationists to high public office.

In the North, conditions were incomparably better with reference to voting rights and educational opportunities. Most important, the municipal and state governments carried out the federal laws and in some cases went beyond the national government in supporting measures designed to equalize the status of the Negro. But in a basic sense the Negro still was marked as separate and unequal. Discrimination in privately owned housing compounded by a low level of income made for *de facto* segregation in schools. Obstacles placed by a number of important trade unions in the way of admission to apprenticeship, and membership contributed to keeping Negroes in the ranks of unskilled labor. Exclusion from many hotels, restaurants, and

176

theaters constituted an offense to personal dignity. In recent years, the situation in the North has been aggravated to explosive dimensions by the influx from the South into the overcrowded city slums. There are still important differences in the nature of the Negro problem in the North and South, but more and more it has become an issue of national scope inextricably interrelated with the problems of poverty, slum conditions, narcotics, and delinquency associated with urban life throughout the United States.

Despite anti-discrimination legislation, the anti-poverty programs and the genuine advance in the economic and social positions of a growing number of individuals of the Negro race, the revolt begun in 1963 continued to spread in alarming proportions. The summer of 1964 brought riots in Chicago and New York; in 1965, the country was shocked by the destructive outbreak in the Watts suburb of Los Angeles; in the long hot summer of 1966, widespread disturbances, occurred in numerous cities and districts throughout the country, West as well as East, North as well as South.* The older responsible Negro leaders were apparently not always able to control the more extreme forms of protest. Serious differences with reference to policy and strategy emerged which threatened the united front of the Negro leadership.

In the face of disappointments and frustrations, the center of the organized movement for Negro equality and social betterment moved away from the legal emphasis maintained by the National Association for the Advancement of Colored People and the social-work approach of the National Urban League. The Ghandian nonviolent demonstrations of marches and meetings sponsored by the Southern Christian Leadership Conference led by Martin Luther King were supplemented by more aggressive but still nonretaliatory strategies of "freedom riders," "sit-ins," and similar methods encouraged and generally organized by the Congress of Racial Equality. In 1966, there emerged the philosophy of "black power," formulated by leaders of the Student Nonviolent Coordinating Committee and vigorously espoused by Stokely Carmichael. It called upon the Negroes "to cut themselves off from white people," to depend only on themselves, and to form their own economic institutions and political parties. Liberalism came in for attack as an extension of pater-

* During the summer of 1967, when the riots surpassed all previous outbreaks in extent and fury, a spirit of rebellion was in evidence which found expression in attacks on police and firemen. In a number of cities, as in Newark, the National Guard had to be called out; in Detroit, where arson, looting, and sniping continued for days, federal troops were brought in before order was restored.

177

nalism. There were positive elements in the appeal to self-reliance and self-help. But lacking a realistic economic program, the concept of "black power" with its emotional overtones of angry defiance represented a strategy of extremist activism rather than a constructive long-range social policy. Its rejection of white participation in leadership smacked of inverted racism. The ambiguity of the "black power" slogan allowed it to be interpreted as an appeal to violence.

The failure to achieve equality for the Negroes in the course of a century is distressing evidence of the inadequacy of the methodology of moderation and compromise, of education and persuasion in the resolution of major political and economic dilemmas. In his analysis of critical issues of American policy in 1960, Professor Clinton Rossiter, recognizing the gravity of the Negro problem, described it as "the oldest, most puzzling, the most distressing with which we have been faced or will ever be faced." But there was little of constructive value in his contrite declaration: "We must take it as a fact of history that we will have no peace in our minds nor self-esteem in our hearts until we have broadened the boundaries of American democracy to include the Negro . . ."[31] Such moralistic admonitions, unfortunately, have too often been the way by which the conservative salves his conscience while doing little to eliminate the admitted evils. Hardly more helpful is the solution proffered by the liberal-minded educators who believe that the removal of the disabilities can be achieved by preaching racial tolerance, by "sober discussion and information exchanges," and by "the problem-solving techniques" as advised by progressives. We should by now be disabused of the simple faith that, "When given facts and information, the American public can be counted on to support plans and actions which are good for the nation and the general welfare."[32]

Education, of course, has a part to play. But prejudice and discrimination are not merely attitudes of mind; they are complex psycho-sociological phenomena interlinked with economic struggle, with maintenance of social prestige, and with the protection of political power. A private owner completely devoid of prejudice may still be reluctant to rent to Negroes in fear of depreciating the value of his property. Trade unions place obstacles in the way of admitting Negroes because they wish to preserve the better jobs for their relatives and friends. White parents may object to rapid desegregation of

[31] *The New York Times*, June 13, 1960.
[32] Virgil A. Clift, Archibald W. Anderson, H. Gordon Hullfish, *Negro Education in America* (New York, 1962), p. 293.

schools because it might lead to a deterioration of the level of educational achievement. Overshadowing these substantial obstacles is the political problem. To allow the Negroes to vote in the South would lead to a revolutionary change in the constellation of the political forces in the United States. It would mean an end to the oligarchical rule and the introduction of an effective two-party system in the South. Ultimately, it would lead to a reduction of power of the South in Congress and to a diminution of its obstructive influence on progressive national policy in both the domestic field and in foreign affairs.

The Negroes are not a minority similar to the ethnic minorities of recent foreign extraction, who can in a relatively short period be assimilated and become a part of the white majority. To view the Negroes as an ethnic minority is to obscure the major issues. The Negroes are old Americans and their problems have deep roots in American political and economic history. The inferior status of the Negro traces to his original condition of slavery. The emancipation effected by Abraham Lincoln was more formal than substantial; the liberated slave had neither the land, the accumulated capital, nor the skills and experience requisite for achieving the genuine independence of middle-class status. The handicaps that affected small-scale farming in the South in an age of machinery and science, as Beard has pointed out, hindered the mass of Negroes, as well as the class of poor whites, from extricating themselves from their low condition.[33] Poverty, inadequate education, the economic status of the economy, as well as prejudice—indeed, far more than prejudice—have prevented the majority of Negroes from rising above the ranks of menial occupations, of servants of the well-to-do, of exploited sharecroppers. The burden of handicaps inherited from the era of servitude remains the hard core of the inferior status of the Negro.

It is because of the intricate involvement of the Negro problem with social, economic, and political factors that a many-sided attack is indispensable. Action projects—demonstrations, picketing, boycotts —have their part to play and can serve to ameliorate particular conditions and to exercise pressure for remedial legislation. The Civil Rights Bill of 1964 which gave legal support to the principle of equality for Negroes in voting, education, employment, and public accommodations supplemented by the Voting Rights Bill of 1965, the education

[33] Charles A. and Mary R. Beard, *op. cit.*, vol. I, pp. 710-717; vol. II, pp. 263-268. For the "unknown compromise" which ended the period of Reconstruction in the South, see E. Vann Woodward, *Reunion and Reaction* (Boston, 1951).

bills and the anti-poverty legislation—these measures, taken together constitute truly great historic steps forward. But despite the advance in legislation, the progress toward equality and toward integration will unavoidably be slow. The resistance to some aspects of the new measures, e.g., school desegregation and "open occupancy," in the North and West as well as in the South is a serious deterrent. However, insofar as such opposition is based on socio-psychological factors it is bound to be diminished in the course of time by the force of legislation and education and by the pressures of protest and demonstration. The real intractable difficulties lie in the objective economic situation.

A massive program of education and training will be necessary to offset the deprivations of generations and enable Negroes to take advantage of opportunities available. But even this, though it involves large sums, touches only the surface of the problem. The full measure of the huge task can be grasped only when we view the Negro situation in the light of the general problems that confront the American economy. The persistence of unemployment makes it impossible with the best of good will to quickly absorb the disproportionate number of Negroes necessary to achieve a fair balance with whites in the various occupations. The fact that housing is still largely in private hands prevents any early elimination of ghettos and the concomitant *de facto* segregation. The problem of equalizing the position of the Negro, as outstanding leaders—A. Philip Randolph, Bayard Rustin, and Martin Luther King—fully recognize, is interwoven with the problem of poverty and of raising the standard of living of low income groups generally. It demands the clearing of slums, the expansion of education and health facilities; it requires social services designed to help in psychological adjustment and in strengthening family life and responsibility.

The key responsibility for the equalization of the position of the Negro rests with the federal government in cooperation with the states and city governments. The participation of the Negro communities, through social organizations, political activities, and self-help endeavors is an important auxiliary factor. There would be a positive element in the "black power" proposals to establish Negro credit institutions and other cooperative endeavors if this part of its program were actually carried out. But the contribution of the Negro self-help projects to the solution of the vast economic problem could only be a drop in the bucket; its main affect would be symbolic and disciplinary. The cooperation of the Negro community is particularly important in the area of family life. The high rate of illegitimacy and of fatherless families among low-income Negro groups which the Moynihan Report[34] has brought into the focus of attention is, no doubt, traceable to economic factors. But there are cultural and psychological aspects which can best be dealt with by the Negro community itself.[35]

Because of the complex of disadvantages and disabilities, inherited from the past and inherent in underemployment, slum conditions, and inadequate education from which the larger part of the Negro people suffer, the Negro problem has special aspects and requires special measures. But in essence it is an acute case of the general social and economic illness which afflicts all sections of the population, white as well as Negro, the Northerner as well as the Southerner. It should be remembered that in absolute numbers—as against relative proportion—there are more whites than Negroes in the poverty class. The improvement in the position of the Negro is conditioned by the rate of progress in the solution of basic problems which face American civilization as a whole.

[34] U.S. Dept. of Labor, *The Negro Family* (Washington, D.C., 1965).

[35] In this connection, the sect of Black Muslims inspired by Elijah Mohammed may have elements of constructive force in the life of the Negroes. The demand for statehood emphasized by some of its members, is more expression of hatred for the "White Devil," than an actual practical aim. Looked at from within—with its slogan of "wake-up, clean-up, stand-up," with its puritanical moral code and its educational activities—it represents a movement of self-help, self-discipline, and self-defense. See " 'What Their Cry Means to Me'—A Negro's Own Evaluation" by Gordon Parks, *Life* LIV, no. 22 (May 31, 1963), 22-33.

CHAPTER SIX

THE WELFARE STATE IN AN INTERNATIONAL WORLD

Challenge to Affluence

Outlines of a Welfare Economy

The Nation-State in the International Order

Reconciliation with Coexistence

The Evolution of World Community

The world is moving away from the bipolar confrontation of East and West during the 40s and 50s towards a new international order marked by diversity, pluralism, variety, freedom and dissent . . . In great-power relations the key words are "coexistence" and "cooperation." And in small nations, life has to be lived on two levels: on the intimate level of national distinctiveness—and in the broader arena of intense international cooperation. In economic and social relationships the trend is no longer towards dogmatic extremes of exclusive private ownership or exclusive public control. Most of our societies are mixed societies in which private initiative and State planning exist together within a single economic framework. ABBA EBAN

6.

The Welfare State
In an International
World

CHALLENGE TO AFFLUENCE[1]

I am not worried by the fact that some people have too much. What
worries me is that many people do not have enough, even if they are
not in dire poverty. Furthermore, no society can be called classless
in the full sense of the word as long as there are still in it certain areas
of dire poverty, or to put it another way, as long as it does not
minister, free of charge, to the absolutely basic needs of human life.

JACQUES MARITAIN

GREAT economic progress has been made in the United States in
the last quarter of a century since the depression decade of
1929-1939. There has been an appreciable upgrading of incomes in
terms of real wages for a considerable portion of the population; the
highest average standard of living ever achieved anywhere in the
world has been attained. The federal and state governments have
assumed a degree of responsibility for stability and growth of the
economy and for advancing social security and welfare measures.
The costly World War II was fought and won without serious
restriction of consumption; after the war the demobilized army was

[1] The heading is taken from Gunnar Myrdal, *Challenge to Affluence*, Vintage
Books (New York, 1965).

185

quickly absorbed into productive occupations. Europe was aided through the Marshall Plan in getting to her economic feet. Under-developed countries throughout the world received assistance from the United States. Over and above the part played by government, there has been a generous outpouring of private contributions to many kinds of charitable and cultural institutions, both at home and abroad.

Despite these truly great accomplishments, a sense of uneasiness pervades economic and social thought in the United States. Favorable comparison with past achievements and with conditions in the less developed parts of the world will not satisfy. The American economy must be judged by its own standards and ideals, in reference to effec-tive operation and in relation to the democratic promise. Can it utilize the potentialities of the new technology and provide for con-tinuous growth? Can it fulfill the basic needs of all the people and progressively realize the requisite of equality of economic and of educational opportunity? Does it encourage a high level of art and culture and support the moral values of the Western tradition?

As a working machine, the American economy, though moving forward, is subject to stresses and strains. Measures introduced in the last quarter of a century provide safeguards against the recurrence of a catastrophic depression such as followed the stock market crash of October 1929. The supports of agriculture, social security and un-employment payments, pension funds and government insurance of savings bank deposits, would cushion the impact of a possible break-down of the free-market mechanism. The "business cycle," until recently the periodic illness of the free-enterprise system, has been brought under control to a large degree, although "corrective reces-sions" are still to be expected. Despite the important advances, the economic system continues to be faced by fundamental problems—by a hard core of unemployment, by inflationary pressures, by labor troubles.

Automation which should be a beneficent process has become a factor in causing unemployment among the unskilled members of the labor force. Inflation, slow but steady, takes back an appreciable part of the increases in wages and rests heavily on all who live on fixed incomes. Prolonged strikes in the major aspects of the economy interrupt the normal course of life and interfere with the orderly planning of production. They tend to be settled on the basis of the comparative strength of the contending parties rather than in the light of the national welfare and the public interest. With the power of organized labor now matched with that of corporate industry, the collective-bargaining process operates with increasing difficulty and, direct or indirect, government intervention has regularly become necessary for the settlement of major disputes. By means of fiscal measures and monetary policies as well as by extensive government expenditures—extraordinarily large military budgets, agricultural sub-sidies and social welfare payments, space explorations and research grants—we have managed to keep the free-enterprise system as a going concern continuously expanding in productivity. But the American economic structure lacks the character of a rationally-planned en-deavor concerned with the long-range peace-time needs of the nation as a whole.

On the moral debit side—with detrimental consequences for the efficient conduct of the economy as well—is the persistence of pov-erty and great inequalities in wealth. Only a few years ago, there was a widespread belief that, as a result of the New Deal social legislation and the general prosperity, mass poverty was no longer a serious problem in the United States. Now it is clear that an unduly large percentage of the population are still, to use Franklin D. Roosevelt's characterization, "ill-fed, ill-clad, ill-housed." Michael Harrington, in his notable study, concluded that about one-fourth of the population were poor in the sense they were denied "the minimum levels of health, housing, food, and education that our present state of scien-tific knowledge specifies as necessary for life as it is lived in the United States."[2]

During the years 1963-1965, official reports established the figure of $3,000 per annum for a family of four; the figure is now conven-tionally used to mark the poverty line of bare subsistence—poor diet, bad housing, inadequate clothing, little medical or dental care. It was estimated that about 35,000,000 Americans, roughly a fifth of the population, were living in poverty-stricken conditions at the time. These are average figures for the country as a whole. The proportion rises to one fourth if the nonwhites—Indians, Mexicans, Puerto Ricans, as well as Negroes—are separately considered. Since the ratio of chil-dren to adults is higher among the poor, the proportion of children growing up in "underprivileged" environments is larger than the general averages indicate. Taking the nation as a whole, it is esti-mated that one fourth of the children live in deprived conditions. The situation among nonwhites is much worse: nearly one half of the nonwhite children under fourteen are in poverty-stricken homes, the

[2] Michael Harrington, *The Other America: Poverty in the United States* (New York, 1962), Appendix, pp. 175-191; especially pp. 179, 182, 185, 191.

Negro component constituting as much as sixty per cent.[3] As Michael Harrington points out, in our day of increasing automation, poverty bears most heavily on the youth and "is tending to become hereditary."[4]

President Johnson's historic declaration of war against poverty in the State of the Union message of January 1964 has brought the condition of the deprived fifth of the nation into the focus of attention. In some quarters, there persists the impression that the remaining eighty per cent enjoy the blessings of prosperity. But the fact is that the family incomes of another fifth or more fall below the $6,000 regarded as necessary for the "modest but adequate" standard required for decent living. The families in this category can put little aside for insurance or unusual medical care and other emergencies; they cannot, generally, afford to let their children continue their education beyond the school-leaving age. The next higher two-fifths can be counted in the respectable middle-income group of moderate means. The upper-middle class and the rich make up the remaining fifth of the population. About fifteen per cent have the $10,000-$15,000 pre-tax income required in the cities and suburban areas to enjoy the opportunities and amenities that are usually associated with "the American way of life." The really wealthy who give the United States the appearance of an affluent society comprise about five per cent of the population. In addition to the disparities in annual income, there are great inequalities in the accumulated wealth and property.

There has been some reduction in the range of inequalities since the New Deal policies became effective a quarter of a century ago, although the impact of the change has not been evenly felt by the several groups. The upper crust of families have received the smallest relative increase, but they have made the greatest actual gain in terms of dollars. They are still "in the money" and a large disparity obtains between the highest and the next lower twenty per cent. The middle-income classes have made the largest relative improvement and now receive a somewhat higher proportion of the total income than they did before the second world war. The lowest fifth had shown no appreciable improvement in their relative position when the anti-poverty programs were initiated. Herman P. Miller of the Bureau of the Census, wrote in 1962: "Our 'social revolution' ended

[3] Daniel P. Moynihan, "Employment, Income, and the Negro Family," *Daedalus* (Fall, 1965), p. 760.

[4] Michael Harrington, *The Politics of Poverty*, League of Industrial Democracy (New York, 1965), p. 10.

nearly twenty years ago, yet important segments of the American public, many of them highly placed Government officials and prominent educators, think and act as if it were a continuing process."[5] In the same year, Harrington expressed the view that ". . . the poor have a worse relative position in American society than they did a decade ago. As technology has boomed their share in prosperity has decreased . . ."[6]

American society presents the profile of a class-structured system consisting—in W. Lloyd Warner's nomenclature—of "lowers," "middles" and "uppers," each in turn divided into lower and upper segments.[7] There is a degree of mobility which permits individuals to move from class to class, particularly within the middle and upper ranges. But "ordinarily, a person stays in the class in which he was born." In any case, although the individuals composing the class may change, the classes remain fairly fixed. Race, ethnic background, religious affiliation, type of occupation play a part, but income and wealth are the major factors determining the individual's social position. Although American thought has never been sympathetic to economic equalitarianism, great differences in wealth have been looked upon with suspicion, even with hostility, as calculated to create an upper class and as setting one section of the people apart from the common man. Another disturbing factor in the contemporary industrial America is the lack of a relationship between the money rewards derived from business operations and their contribution to the national welfare.

In defense of the American status system, it is sometimes urged that the complex nature of modern society necessarily brings with it, as W. Lloyd Warner says, "a series of hierarchies which organize power and prestige within the social structure." It is pointed out that, despite its equalitarian pronouncements, Soviet Russia was forced, after abolishing the Czarist aristocratic regime, to create new forms of rank through the party hierarchy, differential evaluation of occupations, and superior and inferior orders in the army and navy. But there are two points to note. First, there is a higher degree of social mobility and of equality of opportunity in the Russian system. Secondly, "there is a greater emphasis on rewarding the individual and his family with prestige for services rendered to society than in the

[5] Herman P. Miller, "Is the Income Gap Closed? 'No'," *The New York Times Magazine*, Nov. 11, 1962.

[6] *The Other America, op. cit.*, p. 185.

[7] W. Lloyd Warner, Robert J. Havighurst, and Martin Loeb, *Who Shall Be Educated* (New York, 1944), chap. II, and pp. 19, 144-145.

United States." In our own case, notoriously the greatest rewards are given for success in business and for those who serve business interests, as executives, salesman, advertisers.

The pivotal place that private business occupies in American civilization tends to raise money-making to the position of the dominating social motivation. It makes little difference, within the field of business, on what the money is made, whether on bobby-pins and brassieres or in the basic industries essential to national life. The "profit motive" pervades the field of entertainment and of the mass-communication agencies. Television programs have been all but monopolized by private interests; "commercials" wallow in the verbiage of half-truths; competent actors join the ranks of the smiling robots who promote the art of the "silent persuaders." Within the sphere of business the competition is fierce, the temptations to dishonesty are powerful. Ingenious devices for tax evasion, concocted and executed with the collaboration of lawyers and accountants, become accepted as the normal practice. Men high in public life, college teachers and writers, are drawn into the whirlpool of the easy virtue of commercial morality.

Although our system of economy has undergone important change since the days of laissez faire, the motivations of uncontrolled capitalism with its pervasive success drive and its tendency to rationalize expediency continue to distort the character of American culture. The mercenary attitudes do not necessarily pervade all aspects of life or affect the majority of the people. The image of the American as "materialistic" has a basis not in the character of the common man as individual in his personal relations, but rather in the impulsions of our system of economic organization.

The dilemmas of the private-profit system cannot be resolved by moral condemnation. One still finds conceptions in current literature which attribute the evils of contemporary life to individual motivations—to selfishness, to avarice, to "materialism." A high-minded American educator condemns the exponents of democracy who elevate "economic motives to the position of ultimate principles" along with the Communists who subscribe to the economic determination of history. There seems to be a confusion here between "economic motives" in the sense of the pursuit of wealth for its own sake and the meaning of the term "economics" as dealing with the need of food, shelter, and clothing and other essentials required for life. On the assumption that we are still living in a period of scarcity, counsels of abnegation, in the spirit of Christian Socialism, are advocated along with proposals for profit-sharing and partnership between owners and workers. No indication is given as to how the transfer of ownership of the major industries from its present directors and stockholders is to be effected, or how organized labor is to be persuaded to accept the responsibilities of management.

The moralistic approach misconceives the nature of the contemporary economic problem and neglects the relation of means to ends. The socio-economic predicament of our day does not arise from an inevitable scarcity but from inadequate exploitation of the potential plenty made possible by science and technology. Paradoxically, as Robert Theobald puts it, the question is, "Can we survive abundance?"[8] Moreover, any valid proposal for the reconstruction of the American economy, from the ethical viewpoint as well as from the angle of its operational effectiveness, must have the support of some defensible school of economic thought. It cannot be spun merely out of the humanitarian aspiration and utopian imagination. It must provide for increased production as well as for better distribution, for the fulfillment of tangible material demands as well as for the satisfaction of cultural needs. Superfluous to emphasize, it must be in line with democratic processes and values. The endeavor to eliminate the weaknesses and the evils of the contemporary economic situation cannot be confined to ameliorative *ad hoc* improvements. It must be guided by a nationally controlled policy designed to further the aim of the promotion of the general welfare.

OUTLINES OF A WELFARE ECONOMY

During the last quarter of a century, the outline of a reconstructed economy has been taking shape in the Western world under the concept of "The Welfare State." It has come into being as the result of the interplay between the social-ethical motivation of Western society and the necessities and the possibilities of contemporary technological economy. It is neither capitalist nor socialist in the doctrinaire formulation of these nineteenth century ideologies although it has elements of both—of the former, in the retention of "free-enterprise" as an indispensable component, and of the latter in its concern for the "underprivileged" classes of the nation.

The welfare principle implies the fullest realization of the person as citizen and as human being, and this means concern for the health, for the economic sufficiency and security of each individual as well as interest in his education, his social effectiveness, and his cultural

---

[8] Robert Theobald, *Free Men and Free Markets*, Anchor Books (Garden City, 1965), Prologue, pp. 1-16.

development. The outlook of the welfare state is national in the sense that it views the social and economic problems from the stand-point of the country as a whole and not from the angle of business, agriculture, or labor, or of any class or single sector of the country. While it views the economy from the perspective of the national interest, the welfare-state conception recognizes that every nation today, great or small, lives within the framework of regional systems and of international relations.

The welfare state implies a pluralistic form of economy which includes both privately and publicly-owned or publicly-directed enterprise. It retains private enterprise—individual, cooperative, and corporate ownership—but it does not rely on it exclusively. What distinguishes the welfare state is that it includes government-owned, subsidized, or directed enterprise and public-service authorities of various kinds. Moreover, private enterprise is no longer free in the laissez-faire sense; it is at many points regulated or influenced by government. The proportion of each form of economic organization will depend on numerous factors in each country—the historical background, the availability of accumulated private capital, the degree of achieved industrialization. The newly developing countries require greater amounts of public capital and national direction than the well-established countries of Western Europe. The democratic welfare state will favor the free-enterprise forms as far as this is compatible with the effective operation of the national economic system and the satisfaction of the basic needs of the people.

The emphasis on free enterprise as an important element of the welfare-state economy is derived from modern capitalism. But free enterprise and capitalism are by no means identical. The welfare state rejects the ideology of capitalism as usually propounded by its exponents. It denies the class-biased assumption which John C. Bennett notes is widely held by American industrialists, "that the general welfare of the nation is the by-product of the freedom and the profits of the business community."[9] It does not depend on the market system of supply and demand as the all-sufficient regulation of the economic process. It goes beyond the position of the modified interpretation of laissez faire which concedes that government may intervene on occasion to restrain the abuses of private economic power or to rectify the malfunctioning of the free market. The welfare state conception implies a positive policy; it places on government the

[9] John C. Bennett, *Christianity and Communism* (New York, 1949), p. 106.

major responsibility for the coordination and direction of the economy in the interest of the nation as a whole.

Moreover, the welfare-state concept, unlike the ideology of capitalism, does not rely mainly on the incentive of the profit motive and on the initiative of the individual entrepreneur in promoting economic growth and progress. Individual initiatives and incentives play a part in all economic systems, in socialist and communist as well as in capitalist forms. Moreover, the desire for excellence of performance and the scientist's concern with objective validity, may, given a society oriented toward the common good, be more effective than the profit motive in advancing the economy. But the main point is that today economic efficiency and growth depend mainly on impersonal factors, on large-scale organization, on the investment of great amounts of capital, on the rapid application of scientific discoveries and the power of government in the rational allocation of resources in men and materials. Under certain conditions, socialized productive systems nationally directed may prove more efficient than the loosely coordinated free capitalist type.

The desirability of maintaining free enterprise as an important component of the welfare state does not rest primarily on the superior efficiency of privately owned industry. Both privately controlled and socialized forms have their advantages and defects and different combinations would under varying circumstances be indicated if productive efficiency were the sole criterion.[10] The real justification for the retention of free enterprise, as generally recognized, is its indispensability for the maintenance of civil liberties and the support it gives to cultural diversity. Where all economic activity is in the hands of the state, and one's living depends on conformity to government views, there can be little personal freedom. In our own society, freedom to express independent views publicly is, to no small extent, dependent on security of position and income. More important, the differentials of income resulting from private enterprise make possible the independent research, the voluntary educational institutions, the freedom of the arts, and the maintenance of religious activities, all indispensable for the free society. However, an important proviso needs to be borne in mind—that the basic needs of all people are assured before allowing large surpluses of income for the few.

The application of the welfare principle to the American situation demands first and foremost a direct, comprehensive, unrelenting at-

[10] Jan Timbergen, *Shaping the World Economy*, The Twentieth Century Fund (New York, 1962), pp. 36-39.

tack on poverty. As President Johnson recognized in his historic declaration of January 1964, an "all-out war," a broad attack—economic, social, educational—must be made not only on the symptoms of poverty but also on its sources. Poverty in the United States has many causes and assumes a variety of forms. It is rarely the result of a lack of industry and thrift, as the well-to-do like complacently to believe. It may be traced to congenital deficiencies or to personal misfortune, to physical defects or mental retardation, to chronic illness or psychological disturbance, to illegitimate birth or to a broken home, to prolonged unemployment or to the death of the family's breadwinner. It may be the result of a poor economic or educational background. Poverty may affect whole communities, as in the Appalachian mountain region, in sections of the country that have declined as a result of the erosion of the soil or depletion of mines, of changes in industrial techniques. It may be the lot of special groups— of recent Puerto Rican immigrants, of sharecroppers and immigrant laborers, of Negroes in rural and city slums.

Next in line for public concern are the members of the low-income class who need occasional or continuing supplementation to their earnings to maintain that very modest style of life euphemistically called "the minimum comfort budget." This group would include the partially or periodically unemployed, families which have suffered catastrophic illness, and those who need special medical and psychiatric services. An important problem today has developed in the case of the elderly—among whom retired teachers and professors constitute a considerable number—whose pensions and other sources of income are inadequate in view of rising living costs in recent years. Over and above the efforts designed with particular reference to the poverty and low-income groups, the welfare concept implies tasks for government of benefit to the population as a whole—e.g., elimination of air pollution, construction of highways and parking places, setting aside of forest reservations and recreational sites.

Significant advances in the direction of a welfare society have been made during the last quarter century, through social security and unemployment insurance and minimum wage laws, through subsidies to agricultural and urban development, through social service and vocational retraining. But these developments represent minimal measures introduced piecemeal to meet emergency situations—the depression of the 1930s, the exigencies of World War II, and the fear of the growing scientific, industrial power of Soviet Russia. The anti-poverty programs and other social legislation of recent years evidence a better realization of the seriousness and complexity of the problem. The effective promotion of the welfare economy requires more—it demands a clearly-defined national policy and a high degree of coordination of the efforts of private, state, and municipal activity with a comprehensive federal program.

A society based on the welfare principle cannot be achieved as a by-product of the increase of the gross national product, by the Keynesian corrections in the swing of the business cycle, or by the use of fiscal and monetary measures alone, although these factors are essential. The program for the elimination of poverty must include soil restoration and the development of industries, aid in resettlement and occupational retraining. In the cities it requires slum clearance and extensive construction of low-income housing. It means setting up minimum standards of nutrition, medical care, housing and education, involves insuring employment opportunities and adequate unemployment payments, and offering various types of social service—advice in the management of family affairs, assistance in psychological adjustment. It requires adequate minimum-wage standards, supplementary payments to the elderly whose income is insufficient—in effect, some direct or indirect form of a modest guaranteed income above the poverty level.[11]

The shift to a welfare economy would bring difficult technical problems in its train—in the allocation of the resources of material and man power, in the management of credit and in the guidance of investment, in the forms of taxation, their incidence on various classes and sections of the country, on the division of revenues by federal, state, and municipal authorities. There is no legerdemain that can abolish the problems given by economics: as is evident from the experience of socialist as well as capitalist societies, every form of economic organization has common basic problems to meet in the use of resources and in the distribution of commodities.[12]

[11] See: Robert Theobald, *Free Men and Free Markets*, Anchor Books (New York, 1965) and *The Guaranteed Income*, edited by Robert Theobald (New York, 1965): also, Michael D. Reagan, "*Washington Should Pay Taxes to the Poor*." *The New York Times Magazine*, Sunday, Feb. 20, 1966.

A comprehensive plan to eliminate poverty, raise the standard of living for low-income groups and make significant progress toward the establishment of a welfare society is proposed by A. Philip Randolph in cooperation with social scientists, economists, and religious leaders under the title of "A Freedom Budget for All Americans." (A. Philip Randolph Institute. New York, Oct. 1966). The plan would require an enlarged public investment on the part of the federal, state, and local agencies, roughly estimated at ten billion dollars each year for the next ten years over and above current outlays.

[12] Paul A. Samuelson, *Economics, An Introductory Analysis* (New York, 1961), chap. II, pp. 16-36.

Huge and complex as the task of realization is, the concept of the welfare society is in no sense utopian: it is based on technological potentialities and on forces already at work in Western society. Far from violating "economic laws," it is a necessity if we are not to be choked by our abundance. Economists generally agree that we must utilize the reservoir of the unsatisfied needs of the lower-income groups in order to maintain our growing productive capacity. The additional one hundred billion dollars needed in the next decade is not beyond our means if the marvelous productive capacity of the American economy is fully and constructively mobilized. The annual expenditure on the war in Vietnam is considerably in excess of the amounts needed for a vigorous promotion of the welfare economy. The welfare society is realizable on objective grounds. Impediments arise out of ingrained habits of mind as well as from actual conflict of group interests.

Despite the concordance of the welfare concept with economic realities and with democratic values, steps toward its advance, have met, and still meet, with serious opposition. As in any social transition, some groups would gain and others might lose in relative income and status, although progress toward the welfare society would benefit the country as a whole. Perhaps the strongest opposition to the welfare society comes from the average middle-class citizen in the smaller cities and in rural districts. He feels the increase in taxes for welfare services immediately; the long-range benefits are music for the future. In the light of the age-long scarcity economy, payments from government sources to low-income families tend to arouse suspicions of a plan "to share the wealth." Still strongly rooted are the notions of the survival of the fittest and of the predestination of the elect that support the complacent belief that the poor are responsible for their low condition. The necessary augmentation of the functions and powers of the federal government meets the opposition on several sides—from business interests who object to government intervention, from states-rights defenders, from the upholders of the grassroots tradition. There are conservative economists of standing who lend support to the conventional views.

A favorite argument against strengthening government control and direction of the national economic effort is that it leads to the restriction of liberty—an argument epitomized in the title of Friedrich A. Hayek's *The Road to Serfdom*.[13] In its wholesale indictment of all

[13] (Chicago, 1944). A more balanced presentation of Hayek's position is given in *The Constitution of Liberty*, (Chicago, 1960). Hayek represents an attack

increase in state power, the argument is specious. Rational planning of the economy in democratic societies within the framework of a pluralistic economy is something far different from the monolithic centralized control of both the economic and the cultural life in totalitarian societies. There is no simple correlation between state power and individual liberties, as Franz Neumann points out: "It is historically impossible to maintain that government intervention of itself decreases the scope and effectiveness of the citizen's freedom ... A less interventionist Imperial Germany protected freedom far less effectively than a far more interventionist Weimar Republic..."[14] Whether increase of state power protects or restricts liberty depends on the purposes for which it intervenes and on the areas which it affects.

Welfare measures have gathered increasing support during the last three decades. The liberal wing of the Republican party has accepted major features of Franklin D. Roosevelt's New Deal, of Truman's Fair Deal, of Kennedy's New Frontier. President Johnson's proposals for "the Great Society"—advanced through legislation by the 89th Congress, through civil liberties provisions, education bills, and anti-poverty programs—consolidates and carries forward the previous gains. But important as these measures are, they represent piecemeal, ameliorative projects. The psychological and moral orientation essential for a consensus in favor of a long-range rationally planned welfare society has not as yet been achieved. That the United States will be able to meet its economic problems and maintain its high standard of living for the upper half of the population is hardly to be doubted. That some improvement for the lower half will be effected during the coming decade is also likely. However with both major parties internally divided and with reactionary forces still powerful in each, we can hardly look for more than slow, compromised progress. Perhaps the continuing racial disturbances may stimulate more effective action.

Advance toward equalization of the status of the Negro depends on the elimination of poverty and on the improvement of the lot of low-income families. The liquidation of the war in Vietnam will require stepped-up economic growth if a recession accompanied by

against socialism and a defense of classical liberalism which he believes is adaptable to the new economic and social situation. He is opposed to extensive interference with the market mechanism by government, and to the power of labor unions. But there are aspects of the welfare state which he would accept. (See pp. 253-266; and the "Postscript: Why I Am Not a Conservative," pp. 397-409.)

[14] Franz Neumann, *The Democratic and Authoritarian State*, Herbert Marcuse, ed., (Glencoe, Ill., 1957), pp. 177-178.

increased unemployment is to be avoided. The achievement of an entente with the Soviet Bloc will make possible a substantial reduction in the military budget. These urgencies and possibilities may perhaps lead to a decisive turning of the corner toward a planned and unified welfare program. It is evident, moreover, that advance toward a welfare society in the United States depends on developments in the world-at-large as well as on the solution of domestic problems.

THE NATION-STATE IN THE INTERNATIONAL ORDER

We are already, in all actuality, living in a one-world realm in which the events in one part of the globe have their repercussion on distant lands and the political, economic, and social policies of one of the great nations has its effect on all nations. And we are no doubt entering upon a new epoch in history in which the age-long vision of the unity of mankind will receive its embodiment in an effective world-wide political order necessary to achieve peace and a measure of justice among men. However, the experience of the last two-score years has impressed upon us the enormous difficulties that stand in the way of an early consummation of the ideal of world community and of a secure world order.

At the end of World War I, when the League of Nations was in the process of being established, hope ran high that the *terra firma* of international organization was in the offing. Although sobered by the events of World War II, the founders of the United Nations had reason to believe that the wider participation of peoples, and particularly the inclusion of the United States and the Soviet Union, would result in the elimination of major international conflict. But the emergence of the cold war and the expansion of nuclear weapons and long-range missiles again betrayed our optimism and engendered a deepening mood of disillusionment. The mitigation of antagonism between the United States and the Soviet Union during recent years has given some relief to tension. But the strains placed on the United Nations by unrest in Asia, Africa, and Latin America, by the anomalous position of Communist China, by the prolonged involvement of the United States in the Vietnam war—situations which are crucially affected by the residual legacy of the "two-world" ideology—permit us to cling to our faith in ultimate victory only in a mood of grave apprehension.

If we are to avoid the futility of defeatism, we must divest ourselves of the simplistic conceptions and the utopian programs that have, in the past, led to false expectations. The advocacy of internationalism has been marked by a superficial rationalism and moralism: it has denounced the inhumanity of war, demonstrated its unprofitableness to victor and vanquished, urged that world government is a necessity in the light of the growing interdependence of nations. In educational literature, the obstacles to international understanding has largely been attributed to cultural and religious differences; the main problem, it is implied, lies in the area of enlightenment and persuasion—in spreading knowledge about the lives and problems of other peoples, in strengthening the will to cooperate, in "furthering democratic processes."

In the rationalistic-moralistic approach, recognition is, at times, given to the material factors—the destitution of hunger and economic inequality—underlying causes of war. These evils, apparently, are also regarded as amenable to the influence of education and moral suasion—through the elimination of illiteracy, the use of scientific knowledge, the appeal for an equitable distribution of wealth among the nations. In some instances, the major cause for war is diagnosed as the result of materialistic motives—to the unlimited desire for money, fame, or power. Mortimer J. Adler, who, just before the end of World War II, instructed us on "how to think about war and peace," believed that the obstacles to peace "can be overcome only by changing the wants of men and nations."[15]

Education, intercultural communication, the creation of a psychological attitude against war as an instrument of national policy—have, of course, a part to play in any program for international organization and the promotion of world peace. But the rationalistic-moralistic approach tends to draw attention away from the exigent economic and political difficulties involved in any serious attempt to mitigate world conflict. In three aspects of the problem, the positions generally taken by the idealistic proponents of world peace actually tend to weaken effective promotion of international organization. First is the antagonism generally expressed against the principle of national sovereignty and self-determination. With this is connected the failure to understand the part that coercive force necessarily plays in the support of law and of any political organization. The third is the belief that the economic problems of the world can be resolved by admonitions to the richer nations to share their wealth with the poorer.

During the period of the first and second world wars there was a general tendency among liberals to believe that as Kenneth W. Thompson notes, "everything international was good, and everything

15 *How to Think About War and Peace* (New York, 1944), p. 234.

national was bad."[16] Internationalism was identified with universal values, with love of mankind, with the pursuit of peace. Nationalism implied divisiveness, bred misunderstanding, incited chauvinism which was the cause of war. Undoubtedly the principle of nationality can be perverted and abused just as the principle of individuality can be distorted into an egotistical individualism. But, apart from the fact that nations cannot be abolished by fiat, the principle of nationality has been a major factor in the development of civilization. Modern nationalism arose as a liberating and unifying movement and still functions as a constructive force. It freed trade from the barriers of provincial toll gates and facilitated movement over a large territory. It served to throw off the secular chains of the feudal barons and to emancipate man from the cultural domination of the clergy. Today, nationalism plays the major part in Asia and Africa in emancipating peoples from European colonial domination and in fusing tribal and sectional divisions into viable political and economic unity. It is at work in India in breaking down the caste system and in resisting the aggression of Communist China. The sense of national consciousness enabled Yugoslavia to avoid complete submission to Russia; its independent action initiated the movement toward diversity and moderation in communist practice. The principle of nationality has been the major factor in preventing the consolidation of a monolithic Communist bloc that could possibly dominate the globe. Provided that nationalism is contained within an international framework, it serves as a positive, as well as an inescapable, factor in world organization. The principle of national self-determination as embodied in the Charter of the United Nations, is an indispensable condition of democratic freedom, the chief safeguard against imperialism.

The discussion of the problem of national sovereignty suffers from an ambiguity that results from merging two distinct components of the nation-state conception. The term "nation," taken by itself, refers to the historically developed community, united by a common language and heritage of literature, marked by common customs and ideals, bound by a sense of identity and a consciousness of mutual interests. The term "sovereignty" is an attribute of statehood, not of nationality. The state represents the organ of society which exercises the coercive power necessary to enforce the law, to maintain internal security, and to provide the basis for the economic structure. The tendency to confuse nation with state results from the fact that the

[16] Kenneth W. Thompson, *Political Realism and the Crisis of World Politics* (Princeton, 1960), p. 18.

nation has been the basic mode of social organization in modern times in Western Europe. But other forms exist. One nationality may be divided in a number of states, as in ancient Greece and in the Arab Middle East today. Or one state may include many nationalities, as in the Roman Empire and in the Union of Soviet Socialist Republics.

Wars are not caused by national cultural differences, although national feeling may be aroused and exploited in their pursuit. Wars are fought between states which may be city-states, nation-states, coalitions of states, or empires. Although systems of values may be involved, essentially, wars are fought, as Plato said long ago, for material reasons, in defense of or the expansion of the economic power of a state or in the interest of the controlling political group within the state. Today the danger of a large-scale devastating war does not come from the imperialistic rivalries of powerful nation-states of Europe, as was the case in the first and second world wars. It arises from the conflict of interests of great blocs of nations, the Western Alliance, the Soviet Union and its satellites, and the vast Chinese People's Republic.

Whether conceived of as cultural communities or as states exercising political and economic powers, nations cannot be wished out of existence. Nor would it be in the interest of world community to abolish them if this could be done. The weakening of the sovereignty of independent nation-states would, in the present stage of world development, lead either to social disorder or to subordination to a more powerful national or regional state. The development of international authority with sovereign powers can only come gradually by strengthening alliances among nation-states and through the formation of regional blocs of nations. For an extended period of time in the foreseeable future, peace depends on the creation of a balance of power among the various great blocs, and the creation of a coalition strong enough to prevent any single power group from initiating large-scale war.

The ultimate unification of the world order will require the acceptance of common minimal essentials in political ideals and the establishment of a body of law in harmony with them. Before this will be effectuated there must be a leveling off in the vast differences of the standard of life between the Western nations and the underdeveloped areas in Asia, Africa, and Latin America. But even in the future, the purpose of international organization is not to destroy national and regional cultural diversities, but rather to allow them to develop freely in the light of their unique cultural heritage and their special conditions of life.

RECONCILIATION WITH COEXISTENCE

In recent years, the ardent humanitarian view which deprecates national sovereignty and rests all hope for international order and peace on moral and educational influences has given way to the strategy of "political realism." In this view, the analysis of the actual forces at work in international relations is made the basis of foreign policy. Its central thesis is that "power" as an organized coercive force is an indispensable, an ineluctable, factor in all social organization. It abandons the view that power is always and necessarily pernicious which finds expression in Lord Acton's oft-repeated epigram: "All power corrupts and absolute power corrupts absolutely." Power has a constructive function in assuring social order, in giving effect to law, in righting wrongs committed against the weak. Reinhold Niebuhr, outstanding Protestant theologian, has given strong support to this turning away from traditional Christian moralism as well as from the liberalist Wilsonian idealism. As Kenneth W. Thompson summarizes Niebuhr's view: "He found in the fateful concession that ethics makes to politics that coercion is a necessary instrument of social cohesion, whether it be coercion in Gandhi's protests of nonviolence in his march to the sea . . . or coercion in the violence of management and labor at war in the first decades of this century. Moreover, he found that power is never checked by the voluntary action of those possessing it, but only by raising a countervailing power against it.[17]

Political realism discountenances clothing nationalistic aims in idealistic terms, e.g., "making the world safe for democracy," fulfilling the obligations of "the White Man's Burden," "liberating the oppressed peoples." It rejects the cynical interpretation of *Realpolitik* which makes might the criterion of right. It affirms the Western regard for universal law, and recognizes that the achievement of a world community is an essential for world peace. But it maintains that in international politics where collective security and enforceable law are in the embryonic stage, where the sense of identity with the human community is not built into the "moral infrastructure"—partial advance, mutual adjustments, and expedient arrangements are the only methods available. Blueprints based on abstract ethical principles and wholesale utopian programs can lead only to disillusionment.

In application to American foreign policy, political realism makes the national interest the core of concern while recognizing at the same time that we live in an age of developing international order. It

[17] *Ibid.*, pp. 24-25.

rejects the view that unilateral disarmament can itself prevent war, but it works for the reduction of armaments and for the abandonment of the use of thermonuclear energy for war purposes. Relying on adequate safeguards for the protection of national security, political realism supports participation in the United Nations and whenever feasible would utilize its instrumentalities. But it would not neglect any opportunity for arriving at mutually advantageous arrangements between nations wherever possible. It relies mainly on the balance-of-power conception as a main instrument for preserving peace and would make full use of diplomacy as a means of avoiding irritations and arriving at workable compromises.

As George F. Kennan, one of the chief exponents of the doctrine has phrased it, "we must be gardeners and not mechanics in our approach to world affairs. We must come to think of the development of international life as an organic and not a mechanical process. We must realize that we did not create the forces by which this process operates."[18] This empirical approach has led the advocates of political realisms to move from the policy of "containment"—the prevention of the expansion of communism—to the more constructive strategy of promoting the rapprochement with Russia and other Communist countries. Its influence is discernible in the steps during the last half-dozen years to improve relations and to cooperate for specific purposes with the Soviet Union and its satellites in Eastern Europe, e.g., the encouragement of cultural exchanges and tourism, the reduction of restrictions on trade. A most significant development is the nuclear-test-ban treaty of 1963 and the continuing negotiations for halting the spread of nuclear weapons. The policy of political realism reached a high point in its evolution in President Johnson's explicit pronouncement in October 1966: "Our task is to achieve a conciliation with the East, a shift from the narrow concept of co-existence to the broader vision of peaceful engagement."

In the concern with concrete issues and actual situations, with relating available means to proximate ends, and in its de-emphasis on military force while it recognizes the importance of power, political realism represents a constructive approach to foreign affairs. It holds out greater promise for advancing the cause of peace than the ambitious idealistic programs put forward in the optimistic days of the Wilsonian era. Nevertheless, as usually presented, political liberalism is a doctrine of limited scope. It represents a strategy based on the

[18] George F. Kennan, *Realities of American Foreign Policy* (Princeton, 1954), p. 93.

existing state of affairs for "keeping a world intact" rather than a long-range political policy that reckons with the deeper forces at work in the contemporary world. Its purpose is to maintain the dominant position of the United States and the West European powers, rather than to press energetically forward toward an international order.

Focusing attention on practicality and power, political realism is subject to the danger of regressing to opportunism and expediency—to condemn intervention in the affairs of other nations not because of dubious moral validity, but only when it is likely to fail. It shies away from formulating a long-range policy on the basis of democratic essentials which would bar cooperation with reactionary powers. Lacking a deliberate, unremitting determination to promote actively the conditions and the measures essential for the development of a secure world community, foreign policy loses the dynamic necessary to extricate the situation from its present unstable and precarious condition. Another weakness lies in its inadequate consideration of the economic basis of politics. Although it recognizes that poverty and misery underlie the unrest in the underdeveloped countries and realizes the need of social reform conjoined with economic assistance, it tends, like liberalism generally, to underestimate the revolutionary potential generated by the backward conditions.

Writings on foreign policy and on international organization are replete with references to "the unhappy circumstances—the misery, the oppression, the injustice—within which great masses of human beings live out their lives."[19] It is recognized that the enormous disparity in living standards throughout the world is a major underlying cause of instability and unrest—that in this "lies the peril of universal destruction which casts its shadow over the hard-won achievements of the human race." But with all this, we shrink from acknowledging the revolutionary implications of these conditions; we try to persuade ourselves that nonpolitical measures—financial aid, technical assistance, administrative reform, training in skills, popular education, perhaps birth control—will suffice to raise the standards of living steadily to approximate those which have been achieved in the West.

We refuse to face the fact that in many, if not in most, instances substantial improvement can be gained only by a radical transformation in the social and economic organization which cannot be achieved without a prior basic change in political control. As Robert L. Heil-

[19] Commission to Study the Organization of Peace, *Strengthening the United Nations* (New York, 1957), p. 11.

broner points out in his discussion of the struggle in the under-developed countries to escape from poverty and misery: *"Economic development is not primarily an economic but a political and social process."*[20] Inherent in the drastic social change is the displacement of former rulers and a reorganization of the class structure. Such shifts of power can rarely be accomplished by democratic methods and are seldom likely to result in the early introduction of democratic forms.

The establishment of republican government in Western Europe was the result of a long historical process in which ideas interacted with material conditions. The principles propounded by Locke and Rousseau rested on a background of legal, philosophic, and religious conceptions. At the heart of the Western tradition lay restraints on autocratic rule supported by the concept of the rational natural law and the medieval division of powers between king and clergy. More-over, the condition of the European serf was never as abject as that of the worker of the soil in the backward countries of Asia and feudal rule was never as oppressive as oriental monarchism. Nevertheless, the republican regimes in West Europe were brought about by revolu-tionary action, were made possible by the rise of a new commercial and manufacturing class. Finally, it needs to be borne in mind that the capital needed for the development of the economic basis of industrial society in the European countries was obtained at the expense of a low standard of life for the peasant and the factory worker and through exploitation of the labor of great masses of men in Asia and Africa through the colonial system.

If their standards of living are to be substantially improved, the underdeveloped countries of the world must, in a generation or two, pass from social systems that have remained static for a thousand years or more to the highly developed technological form, supported by advanced scientific agriculture, characteristic of the West. This de-mands a destruction of landlordism and the introduction of a new form of land ownership. It requires huge funds for capital investment in industry and agriculture, only a small part of which can be derived through loans from foreign sources. The major part, including sums needed for repayment of loans, must be derived internally by keeping consumption down to necessities and setting aside a large part of the national product for investment.

The conduct of a modern economy in newly developing countries involves a high degree of centralized planning and administration for the coordination of industry and agriculture; it means government

[20] *The Great Ascent* (New York, 1963), p. 24.

provision of health and educational services. It is in the realm of possibility, given favorable combination of attitudes and able leadership, that the needed radical social, political, and economic transformation could be achieved gradually with due regard to the maintenance of democratic processes and of civil liberties, as India is trying to do. But it should not be surprising that the totalitarian road should be chosen—either in its nationalist form under the personal dictatorships supported by the army or in the more extreme, but better grounded theoretically, form of communism.

Communism with its Marxist underpinning offers a rationally defensible program as leaders in countries subject to despotism or deprivation might see it. Despite the violence attending the application of Marxism, it still retains an element of idealism in the eyes of its advocates; it provides a plausible theoretical basis and a moral justification for revolutionary action. To Marxist theory, Leninism adds a revolutionary praxis—a system of organization, of party discipline, and of trained leadership. But what is decisive is "that communism has a *functional* attractiveness to the underdeveloped lands."[21] Gaining political control, it attacks the economic problem with the single-minded purpose of eliminating poverty and providing for the satisfaction of the basic needs of the people.

The success of the Soviet Union provides evidence of the potentialities of the Communist economic system for speeding up development. Likewise, mainland China, despite difficulties it has encountered in the attempt to industrialize too rapidly, has succeeded in transforming its backward economic system; it has grown much faster than India whose population explosion to a large extent neutralizes its slow growth. Both great Communist countries are in a position to help the underdeveloped countries where, uniting with nationalism, it gives added impetus to revolutionary struggle. In the light of the differences that have developed among the Communist powers, the acceptance of aid from Russia or China by smaller nations does not necessarily lead to blind subordination to any particular version of Marxist ideology.

Communism, in any of its contemporary interpretations, brings with it the suppression of freedoms enjoyed by the middle and upper classes under previous regimes. But since parliamentary rule has seldom been effective in the underdeveloped countries and the masses have never enjoyed political liberty, the absence of these prerequisites of democracy can hardly be felt. On the other hand, Communist

---

[21] *Ibid.*, p. 160.

victory brings immediate benefits in release from arbitrary exactions by oppressive and despotic rulers. Wherever communism establishes itself, land reforms are quickly instituted, employment for all becomes available, the health and education of the masses are vigorously promoted.

In striking contrast to the clearly defined and explicitly stated ends and means of communism and the forceful determination in the execution of its program, democracy—of which the United States is the avowed protagonist—presents an ambiguous image to the underdeveloped countries. The proclamations—of freedom, of national self-determination, of concern for the common man, of human equality—enunciated by American leaders, have been heard around the world. But our actual way of life is too far from our professions to inspire confidence. Our affluence and the uses to which we put it—our concentration on the pursuit of wealth, the persistence of extreme poverty, the low status of the Negro—create a psychological sense of distance between ourselves and the peoples of the underdeveloped countries. Although the form of our economy has been greatly modified in the last half-century, we still remain the outstanding exponent of competitive capitalism in our own eyes as well as in the eyes of the world. And "capitalism" carries with it, in the underdeveloped countries of Asia and Africa as well as in Latin America, connotations of "exploitation, imperialism, and abuse."[22]

Emancipation from the condition of poverty, disease, and illiteracy under which the masses of the people live in the underdeveloped countries requires radical economic reconstruction directed by political regimes devoted to this purpose. In some countries it may be possible through adequate and timely aid to enable the more moderate political forces to introduce democratic procedures and preserve basic freedoms while creating the new economic forms, improving living standards, providing general education, and training in skills. But we must recognize that in many instances in Asia, Africa, and South America the necessary social transformation cannot be accomplished without revolutionary action—either through military *coups d'etat* or organized party action.

The social-political systems resulting may be communist, national-socialist, or mixed systems which retain features of democracy in varying degrees. In each case, the type of regime set up will depend on a combination of factors—on military and financial aid from other

[22] George C. Lodge, "Revolution in Latin America," *Foreign Affairs*, XLIV, (Jan. 1966), 188.

countries as well as on internal conditions and personal leadership. But all these factors operate in the context of historical and cultural backgrounds and of geographical location and ethnic affiliation. In the long run, political and social systems cannot be imposed or controlled from without. The political character of a regime will unavoidably be taken into consideration in the shaping of America's foreign policy. But this is warranted, as political realism maintains, only when vital national interests are tangibly affected, not simply on a priori ideological grounds. In the light of recent developments, it is fallacious to assume that the Communist pattern of social revolution and economic reconstruction is an absolute evil, *semper, ubique, ac omnibus*.

It is necessary to reconcile ourselves to a policy of coexistence with the Communist states, not only because they have become too strong in military and industrial power for us to defeat, but in recognition of the fact that the Communist type of revolution and economic organization, however alien to us in spirit and repugnant in its methodology, is not illegitimate in the light of the backward conditions and repressive regimes in which many of the underdeveloped countries find themselves. This is not to say that communism was or is "inevitable" in any situation. But the concatenation of events, the existence of bad conditions, the weakness of liberal forces within the country, the failure of democratic nations to support the necessary social changes in the past, may make communism an acceptable alternative to a continuance of age-old misery and oppression by feudal and patronal systems. Moreover, Communist regimes vary and their totalitarian features are likely to be moderated when they become established, economic conditions improve, and the threat of foreign intervention decreases.

In his *Realities of American Foreign Policy*,[23] published over a decade ago, George F. Kennan suggested that we must transcend the outlook of "bipolarity" which based foreign policy mainly on the East-West confrontation, and, instead, view the world situation in the light of the rise of the neutral or uncommitted "in-between" nations. In view of the important variations of ideology and of practice that have developed among them, we can extend the same principle to the Communist-type states. We need not take the position that those who are not wholly with us are against us. Today in the total outlook and in international policy, the Soviet Union stands with the Western powers against Communist China under the Maoist regime.

[23] *Op. cit.*, p. 100.

Since the end of the Stalin era, the breaks in the Iron Curtain have grown steadily wider through the increase of trade, through cultural exchanges, and the freer movement of tourists. The further easing of trade and travel restrictions, the establishment of direct air service from New York to Moscow, and other cooperative projects initiated in the fall of 1966, joined with President Johnson's avowal of "peaceful engagement" indicate that we have moved from the position of coexistence *faute de mieux* to the threshold of rapprochment. On its part, in response to the American advances, the Soviet Union, through Leonid I. Brezhnev, defying Chinese criticism, vigorously defended Russia's cooperation with the Western governments in the interest of peace and international security. A realization of a genuine entente awaits the liquidation of the Vietnam war. Relations with Communist China, now in possession of nuclear power must also be normalized in the predictable future.

The doctrine of political realism has served an important purpose in moving American policy away from ideological anti-Communism toward pragmatic judgments based on the degree of cooperation warranted in each case. It has been concerned mainly with United States foreign policy and with diplomatic activities designed to prevent war. More is needed as a basis for a valid political philosophy of international relations. It is necessary to fit the policy of political realism into the frame of a conception of an international order which, distant as may be its full realization, must nevertheless be the goal of persevering effort. The summary of the essential lines of development which follows will at the same time serve as a review of major ideas presented above.

THE EVOLUTION OF WORLD COMMUNITY

The achievement of a secure world order requires the simultaneous development of three phases of social life: the ethical, the political, and the economic. These are not to be conceived as disparate elements that must be combined, but rather as different aspects of social existence which are interrelated and interact with each other. They need to be separated in discussion to indicate the lines of action necessary and possible in the movement toward world community.

The Ethical Foundation

Parallel to the effort of strengthening the United Nations and of reducing the disparity of living standards in various parts of the world, it is necessary to work toward an ethical consensus as the basis of the legal structure and the political organization of the world community of the future. The concept "community" is meaningless without a bond of common ideals and moral values. The ethical principle implies an affirmation of belief in the unique value of each person and in the unity of mankind. This commitment is in harmony with the democratic moral conception but it is necessary to give a new emphasis to the definition of democracy differing from the nineteenth century individualistic interpretation which still persists in many liberalist statements.

It is essential to reintroduce into democratic political theory as paramount with the idea of liberty, the idea of human equality which is inherent in the Western religious tradition and which found explicit expression in the American and French Declarations of the eighteenth century. In view of the widespread tendency to identify democracy only with freedom, it is important in every statement of its meaning to join the word "eqality" with the word "liberty." The principle of equality, both in the religious tradition and in the secular doctrine, does not imply that all men have equal capacities or that they are entitled to equal rewards. These interpretations of the meaning of equality are put forward by opponents and not by its friends. What we derive from the religious tradition is the sentiment that, without reference to his capacities, each person is of infinite worth, no matter of what race or nationality, of what class or social condition.

Translated into secular terms, the religious principle signifies that every child is worth developing to the fullest of his abilities whether he is crippled or whole, retarded or gifted. In the declarations of the eighteenth century, it implies that there should be no discrimination against any man or woman on the grounds of race, religion, or condition of poverty. In terms of contemporary needs and possibilities, the principle of equality requires that society must assume responsibility for ensuring for all of its members the material essentials necessary to achieve "freedom from want" without which the equality of rights and equality of opportunity become deceptive pretensions.

A second area of affirmation and of revision relates to the sphere of "human rights and fundamental freedoms." In this, the model is provided by the Universal Declaration of Human Rights adopted in principle by the United Nations at the third session of the General Assembly in September 1948. Its Preamble recognizes "the inherent dignity and the equal and inalienable rights of all members of the human group as the foundation of freedom, justice and peace in the world."

Its thirty articles include the classic civil and political rights of the modern liberal state as developed in the English, American, and French constitutions: *the personal rights:* the security of the person, equality before the law, public trial, ownership of property, freedom of movement; *the social and spiritual rights:* the right of freedom of association, of religious belief, of expression of deviating opinion. To these fundamentals have been added the following notable require- ments: *nationality rights:* the right of every person to a nationality including the right to change it; *the right to marry and establish a family:* without any limitation as to race, nationality or religion; *educational rights:* the right to free education at least in the elementary stages, and the prior right of parents to choose the kind of education for their children. Finally are the *economic rights:* protection against unemployment, free choice of employment, the standard of living adequate for health and well-being.

The Declaration was approved by a large majority of the members of the General Assembly. There were no opposing votes but states in the Soviet orbit abstained. The approval of the Declaration indi- cated that there is a broad consensus, as Dr. Charles Malik rapporteur of the Commission on Human Rights expressed it, "on our inherent rights as human beings." However, the Declaration has no legal binding force. Before it can become effective it must be embodied in international covenants and in the laws of each country. The degree of acceptance as a guide to policy depends on the social attitudes, the economic conditions, and the structure of government in each case. In defense of the Soviet Union's abstention, Andrei Y. Vishinsky, Deputy Foreign Minister of the U.S.S.R. pointed out realistically that, "the rights of human beings cannot be considered outside the prerogatives of government." It is in point to note that the United States—which participated actively in the work of the Com- mission on Human Rights of which Mrs. Franklin D. Roosevelt was chairman—has not yet ratified it.

The United Nations Declaration avoided any reference to the principles of government, conceiving human rights in terms of social and personal relations. It is obvious, however, that the democratic thesis of participation in government by the people, besides being indispensable for assuring the basic human rights, is itself a moral demand. In its modern embodiment, democracy implies universal suffrage in the election of the legislators and of the chief officials of the state. In addition to universal suffrage, the minimum essentials of democratic government include civil liberties and an independent judiciary. These essentials established, there is room for variation in the relation of the legislative and the executive powers of the state. In the context of the complexities of contemporary social organization, the executive branches of government in consultation with advisory bodies of scientists and other experts must bear the major responsibility for formulation and direction of policy. But as A. D. Lindsay concludes: "A modern democratic state is only possible if it can combine appreciation of skill, knowledge and expertness with a reverence for the common humanity of everyday people."[24]

Strengthening the United Nations[25]

The United Nations has demonstrated its ability to survive despite the great changes in the world situation since it was created in 1945 and the strains it has been subjected to by the division of the world into the Western and Eastern blocs. It has served as a great forum for discussion of critical international issues and as a meeting place for statesmen from all over the world. It has provided a resort for quiet negotiation as well as a platform for public utterances addressed to the conscience of mankind. Something has been accomplished in each of its concerns—in the protection of human rights, in technical assistance programs and information functions, in the extension of credit and of financial aid through its associated monetary agencies.

In limited situations, the United Nations has made effective contributions to the maintenance of peace, as in the Arab-Israeli armistice of 1948, the Korean War, the attack on the Suez Canal in 1956, and in helping to stabilize the situations in the Congo and in Cyprus. It played a dramatic role during the Cuban crisis of 1962 and arranged the partly successful cease-fire and withdrawal of troops in the India-Pakistan dispute during 1965. However, by all accounts, the United Nations has fallen far short of expectation as an instrument for the preservation of peace for which, as the Preamble of the Charter declares, the United Nations was primarily founded. Its weakness results from defects in its structure and from the attitudes of its chief members; both these factors are in turn reflections of the underlying politico-economic situation in the world.

24 Lindsay, *The Modern Democratic State* (New York, 1947), p. 262.
25 Commission to Study the Organization of Peace, *Strengthening the United Nations* (New York, 1957), Part I; Clark M. Eichelberger, *UN: The First Twenty Years* (New York, 1965), chap. VIII.

The powers of the Security Council, charged with the primary responsibility for international peace and security were severely restricted at the outset. As a result of the collaboration of the United States and the Soviet Union, the privilege of the veto was granted to the five permanent members: the United States, the U.S.S.R., the United Kingdom, France, and Nationalist China. Thus the Security Council, for the most part, is prevented from taking coercive action whenever the interests of the Great Powers are involved, indirectly as well as directly. The General Assembly may recommend peace-keeping measures, but the Charter did not grant it any powers of implementation. The "Uniting for Peace Resolution" adopted at the time of the Korean War somewhat enlarged its authority: the General Assembly gained the right to mobilize forces in order to prevent aggression or other breaches of the peace when the Security Council takes no action. However, its competence is narrowly limited by the necessity of obtaining the cooperation of the disputants. Its resolutions have been flouted when these did not suit one of the parties concerned, as in the case of Egypt's refusal to allow Israel the use of the Suez Canal, India's aggressive takeover of Goa, and South Africa's obstinate policy of apartheid.

The Middle East crisis of June 1967 which eventuated in a third Arab-Israeli war sharply illustrated the weakness of the United Nations—and its all but complete impotence—in face of the failure of the Great Powers to agree on a common policy. The provocative Arab actions—the removal, at Nasser's behest, of the United Nations peace-keeping force from the Gaza Strip and the Sinai Peninsula coupled with the closing of the Gulf of Aqaba to Israeli shipping, the massing of Egyptian troops and tanks on Israel's border accompanied by threats to annihilate Israel in which the surrounding Arab states joined—obviously created imminent danger of an outbreak of war. The Security Council was called into an emergency session on the initiative of Western nations. But the Soviet Union, championing the Arab cause, led its satellites in tactics of delay with the purpose of preventing United Nations intervention. It was only after the war was in progress and the Arab armies were facing disaster that the Soviet-Arab bloc consented to a cease-fire, unconditioned by a condemnation of Israel. Something of the United Nations usefulness and prestige was salvaged through the appointment of a United Nations commission to supervise the cease-fire and the acceptance of this arrangement by Israel as well as by the Arabs.

In view of the attitudes and circumstances attending the discussion in the Security Council and subsequently in the General Assembly, it

213

was fortunate that the United Nations had so little power at this juncture of events. The positions taken by the member-states—with a minority of notable exceptions—were dictated solely by national interests and political considerations, with little regard for the promotion of peace efforts. The representative of the Soviet Union knew no bounds in his vituperative accusations against Israel and in his brash defense of the Arab States. India, which in former years had maintained a position of nonalignment, now appeared to be completely subservient to the Soviet-Arab line. France—having failed in its proposal for a four-power agreement (to include besides itself, the U.S.S.R., the United States, and Great Britain) to end the crisis— remained on the side lines, playing an ambiguous role. Underlying Russia's intransigence and France's coolness was opposition to any extension of United States power in world affairs. Great Britain, which would have been ready to join the United States in a common policy, was too dependent on Arab oil and on revenues derived from concessions in Arab lands to allow it to take firm action. The position of the United States looked toward a rational long-range solution of the conflict between the Arab States and Israel—liquidation of the problem of the Arab refugees, recognition of the State of Israel by the Arabs, the end of belligerency, the opening of the Suez Canal and the Gulf of Aqaba to Israeli shipping, the reduction of the arms race in the Middle East. But its influence on international policy was compromised by its unrelenting pursuit of the Vietnam war.

Of the four Great Powers, the Soviet Union has shown the least interest in expanding the functions and increasing the strength of the United Nations. It has used the veto power extensively not only in self-protection but also, without regard to the merit of the issues, in support of other countries, e.g., India and the Arab States, when this suited its political purposes. France, in earlier days a foremost advocate of world community has, in recent years, following deGaulle's nationalist bias, been more concerned with opposing intervention in matters which it deemed to be within the domestic jurisdiction of a state than in promoting international organization. Great Britain's attitude has generally been constructive, but, it too, had its reservations when the discussions affected relations with its former dependencies.

The United States has done more for the development of the United Nations than any other single Power. On the other hand, as Clark M. Eichelberger makes clear in his last report,[26] it has also

---

[26] UN: The First Twenty Years (New York, 1965), pp. 169-170.

214

played a negative role. Its opposition to the admission of Communist China has been a major handicap in the development of the United Nations as a truly international body. It went beyond the United Nations' mandate in crossing the 38th parallel in the Korean war and by-passed it in applying the Eisenhower Doctrine to the Middle East. It has disregarded United Nation's public opinion in the drastic escalation of the war in Vietnam.

The purpose here is not to allocate blame among the various Powers but to point up the perplexities that arise in the complex interaction of interests and conditions, of means and ends. The difficulties that confront the United Nations have been compounded by the extraordinary changes that have taken place in the last score of years. In his report a decade ago, Dr. Eichelberger pointed out four critical developments: the breakup of the "five-power system" on which the Security Council was based; the advent of the atomic age; the passing of colonialism; the "revolt against misery."[27] With the retention of China's seat by the National Government of Taiwan, the Security Council has become altogether unrepresentative of the actual distribution of power in the world. The perfection of long-range ballistic missiles, the multiplication of sputniks and satellites, the further developments in nuclear fission, have enormously complicated the problems of armament control and reduced the possibility of collective security to the vanishing point. The end of colonialism has brought into being a host of new nations, an Afro-Asian bloc of great potential influence. The struggle against misery, i.e., poverty, disease, and illiteracy, has taken on the character of a political and revolutionary movement.

The further development of the United Nations requires changes in its composition and organization. As declared by the Commission to study the Organization of Peace more than a decade ago, adherence to the principle of universal representation requires that the admission of China—which includes a quarter of the population of the world—cannot be indefinitely postponed. Some improvement in the representative character of the Security Council was achieved in 1966 by the addition of four nonpermanent members, giving more favorable recognition to the Latin American and Afro-Asian countries. But the veto power has remained in the hands of the original five Great Powers, and the difficulties that the Council faces will probably be aggravated should Communist China replace Taiwan. Two complementary changes in the constitution of the United

[27] *UN: The First Ten Years* (New York, 1955), chap. I.

Nations are necessary: increasing the powers of the General Assembly for effective peace-keeping among the smaller nations and restricting the veto power of the permanent members to major threats of conflict involving the use of large-scale force.

The problem of enlarging the power of the General Assembly is made more complex by the increase of new and small nations. At the inception of the United Nations, there were 51 member states with the representation of Europe and the Western hemisphere in the majority. When the twenty-first session convened, in September 1966, there were 117 members and several were to be added during the session. Moreover, almost two-thirds came from the Afro-Asian countries and another fifth from Latin America. Thus, more than three-fourths of the members of the General Assembly represent underdeveloped or developing countries who have great needs—and often large demands—but little financial ability to contribute or to accept responsibilities. However, as Charles M. Yost has pointed out, the problem is not as serious as might appear. In the first place, the Asians, Africans, and Latin Americans do not necessarily vote as a bloc: they tend to unite only on issues related to decolonization and to human rights of subject peoples. Furthermore, the General Assembly cannot compel acceptance of its recommendations and unreasonable demands are checked by the fact that the countries of the West supply on a voluntary basis the greater part of the funds for peace-keeping operations.[28]

Finally, there is the crucial question of financing. In 1964-1965, the United Nations was brought to the point of insolvency by the refusal of a number of nations, led by the Soviet Union and France, to pay assessments for peace-keeping operations decided upon by the General Assembly. The Soviet Union maintained that such appropriations must be voted by the Security Council. The United States made an attempt to invoke Article 19 of the Charter which provides that any member in arrears for two years shall have no vote in the General Assembly. The attempt was unrealistic since the exclusion of the Soviet Union and France would have reduced the United Nations to impotence. The issue was settled, for the time being, by a proposal to accept "voluntary contributions," as a means of keeping the United Nations alive. The United States, agreeing to this face-saving device, has asserted its own right, following the example of the Soviet Union and France to refuse to pay assessments which it has not approved.

[28] Charles M. Yost, "The United Nations, Crisis of Confidence and Will," *Foreign Affairs*, XLV (Oct. 1966), 37.

This solution still leaves the basic problem of financial support unresolved. In his last report, Dr. Eichelberger emphasizes the need of developing independent sources of income.

In conclusion, although the United Nations has come to stay and already is an indispensable factor in international relations, there is a sober recognition that it cannot regulate or greatly influence the development of armaments in the immediate future. All that the United Nations can undertake is the maintenance of a relatively small police force which, together with voluntary contingents, would be of value in promotion of peaceful settlements in lesser conflicts; e.g., supervising cease-fire and withdrawals, patrolling armistice lines, providing temporary occupation of disputed areas. Moreover, all such efforts in the interest of pacific settlements must be subject to the consent of the state or states directly affected. In the main, the United Nations must continue to rely on moral influences and on the resources of peaceful adjustment by consent, and if these measures fail, by deprivation of economic and other benefits derived from membership in the United Nations system. But it is evident that such deterrents can be effective only in minor cases.

The Growth of International Economy

Recent proposals for international organization reflect a more realistic attitude than that which prevailed two-score years ago when the United Nations was established. There is a better understanding that "all the problems of social existence are interrelated"; there is a recognition of the importance of "the breaking down of the world's polarized structure." Nevertheless, there is still a tendency to gloss over the pervasive economic factor that underlies the political divisions in the world.

The primary prerequisite of a genuine international order is the elimination of poverty within each nation, and the provision of the basic needs in food, shelter, and clothing, in health and education, for every member of society. Seen in the global perspective, this implies the reduction of the vast disparity in the standards of living, in social conditions, and in educational opportunities, between the highly industrialized nations in Western Europe and in North America, on the one hand, and the backward and underdeveloped countries in Asia, Africa, and South America, on the other. The necessary upgrading of the level of life involves the transformation of the economic system from one based on peasant cultivation and handicraft manufacture to large-scale, scientifically directed, technological production in agriculture and industry. The effective execution of the radical change of the economic structure demands very great amounts of capital. It requires a planned development program and an adequate degree of centralized political control.

Assistance in the form of financial aid, technical advice, and trained personnel from Western countries can play an important part in the amelioration of conditions in the underdeveloped parts of the world. But its potential effect on the economic development of the backward countries may easily be exaggerated. The Western countries are not prepared to set aside large sums for foreign aid or to disregard political affiliations. Apart from these considerations, no nation, or for that matter, no single bloc of nations, is rich enough to provide anything but a minor proportion of the investment funds needed for the reconstruction of the economic systems of the underdeveloped countries.

The comprehensive transformation of the economic and social system in the backward and underdeveloped nations can be achieved only through the efforts of the countries themselves. Whether the radical change will be accomplished gradually through democratic procedures or through revolutionary action accompanied by violence will depend on conditions in each situation and on the conceptions of the national leaders who rise to positions of power. Where well-entrenched reactionary and exploitive regimes have been in power and major reform has been blocked for long periods of time, the new social order can be brought into being only through radical change in political organization and in the class structure. For a period of time, some form of authoritarian rule will be maintained, of the personal dictatorship, the military-national, or of the totalitarian Communist type. This will be necessary not only to prevent counter-revolutionary efforts, but also for the purpose of effectuating the planned developmental program.

Whether achieved through gradual process of change, or by revolutionary action, the emerging economic systems will lean toward socialism even if they do not assume an extreme Communist pattern. As political exigencies diminish, with the suppression of counter-revolutionary forces and the elimination of the fear of foreign intervention, the economic forms will probably gravitate toward mixed systems in which some private ownership and enterprise as well as state-controlled and directed operations will be included. As Jan Timbergen points out, "The present Western economies are themselves a mixture between pure nineteenth century capitalism and socialism. Both systems will continue to learn from experience, and from each other, and will continue to change."[29] We must expect a pluralistic world economy—mixed systems ranging from the welfare society with a major emphasis on free enterprise to socialist types where state ownership and control predominate. Each country will in due course work out the optimum combination in accord with its own conceptions and conditions.

Despite the many difficulties, international economic bonds are continuously being developed. The change in the American attitude from the rigid position of extending aid to underdeveloped nations only for the purpose of combating communism to the more flexible strategy which includes assistance to unaligned countries, and even to Communist satellites when this serves our purpose, is a great step forward. The unaligned and the deviationist Marxist countries play an exceptionally important role in advancing the international order. In serving as junctions of economic exchange they act as bridges between the two worlds of capitalism and communism. The most important factor in forging the links of international union is the expansion of trade which crosses the boundaries of the ideological front. It is through an empirical, developmental approach that an international economy is to be attained rather than by basing socio-economic policy directly "on the interests of the world at large." In the next period of development we must rely on the broadening of the national interest instead of depending mainly on perfecting the financial and coordinating agencies of the United Nations. The empirical and national approach should be regarded as a means of strengthening the United Nations, not as a substitute for its activities.

The analysis in this chapter is in accord with the view that international development is an organic growth and depends on an interplay of forces—of ideas and attitudes, of the growth of law, of the perfection of institutional organization. But the main intent of the argument has been, without diminishing the importance of the other aspects, to point up the significance of the economic factor as interlinked with all of them. The purpose has been to press the thesis that endeavor must be directed to the improvement of the material basis of social life if any decisive progress is to be made in the national life, in racial relations, and international organization. One may reject the Marxist doctrine of economic *determinism*, but it would be sheer obscurantism to neglect the fact of economic *conditioning*. It is cor-

[29] Jan Timbergen, *op. cit.*, p. 39.

rect to say that progress in the development of world community is dependent on the "breaking down of the world's bipolarized structure." But it is necessary to realize that the bipolarized structure is itself an expression of the underlying economic disparity between the different parts of the world, and that raising the standard of life in the underdeveloped countries will generally necessitate major changes in the political and social structure.

Implied is the assumption, also, that the international order, whether in the ethical meaning or as organizational concept, cannot be imposed from above. International cooperation must grow from within, must rest on national organization and on regional blocs. It cannot depend on the dominant influence of the West; it must be the product of the interests and activities of many nations. For an indefinite period, the maintenance and strengthening of the United Nations will depend on the cooperation of states of widely different ideological, economic and political systems. To what extent the United States will contribute to the development of the international order will depend on its own course of action. Its wealth and power and its heritage of democratic ideals are assets for leadership. But there are also handicaps in the survival of poverty despite our boast of affluence, and in the persistence of racial discrimination despite our affirmation that all men are created equal.

A specious moralism afflicts us which prevents us from seeing ourselves as others see us. We suffer from a schism in the soul, from an ambivalence between the probity of Puritan ethics and the shrewd practicality of the Yankee trader, from a conflict between our belief in the worth of Everyman and the Calvinist conviction of the predestined election of the successful. Our agrarian background has left a streak of provincialism in our outlook. And there remains the burden of the original sin of slavery, the stain of which we have not yet been able to wash away. Some measure of progress we shall, no doubt, make during the next generation in developing an international outlook. But perhaps it is meet that we drop any claim to leadership; it will suffice if we fulfill the obligations of partnership in the task of building the world community.

PART THREE

CONCLUSIONS AND RECONSIDERATIONS IN EDUCATION

CHAPTER SEVEN

REVIEW AND COMMENT

The Reorientation of Liberalism

Reason, Science, and Ethics

The Moral, the Ideal, the Community

Democratic Principles and Social Program

In philosophy, the fact, the theory, the
alternatives and the ideal, are weighed
together. Its gifts are insight and foresight,
and a sense of the worth of life, in short,
that sense of importance which nerves all
civilized effort. ALFRED NORTH WHITEHEAD

7.

Review and Comment

THE REORIENTATION OF LIBERALISM

IN THE preceding chapters, the discussion was carried on in the light of historical reference and in relation to sustaining and opposing views. This method of presentation illustrates the thesis that new ideas arise out of existing ideas and can be properly understood only in contrast with views which they subject to criticism and aim to displace. It has the advantage, also, of allowing the reader to follow the line of argument and to judge better the validity of any conclusions offered. Although the positions taken by the author have been indicated, the endeavor has been to formulate a pattern of beliefs seen to be emerging rather than to express an individual opinion. The resumé, to which this chapter is devoted, will serve to sharpen the statement of position and to add the accent of personal interpretation and evaluation.

The point of departure is the philosophy of liberalism in the broad sense of the compound of beliefs and attitudes, metaphysical notions and social conceptions, which operated as guiding ideas of progressive thought in Western Europe and in the United States during the period of world history now passing. At the core of the conception expounded in this book there remains an affirmation of distinctive principles advanced by liberalism, e.g., reliance on constitutional government, insistence on intellectual and religious freedom as prerequisites, and, more generally, concern with this-worldly human happiness. The policies proposed may be taken as an extension and application of the social-liberalism characteristic of the half-century before World War II to the needs and conditions of the new era in world civilization now emerging. However, there are differences in some basic assumptions as well as in perspective and in mood. A major reorientation in outlook and a reformulation of the liberalist pattern of beliefs has become necessary.

The revision requires a consideration of the new findings in the various spheres of knowledge. The change from Newtonian to relativity concepts in the field of physics has modified our views of causation and of scientific explanation, even though the new outlook does not imply, as some think, any radical transformation in our conception of the nature of the universe as a whole nor provide any additional insights into human nature. More significant for the understanding of man and of his discontent under the pressures of civilization are the revelations of psychoanalytic theory as to the extent that subconscious tensions and compulsions influence our judgments and actions and affect our ability to adjust ourselves to institutional life under existing conditions. Sociological analysis makes clear how inextricably the individual is bound up with class affiliation, with racial or ethnic origin, and with group attachments generally. Divested of its one-sided ideological extremism, the Marxian thesis of the relation of the mode of economic organization to political structure and to moral conceptions and practice is indispensable for an understanding of the revolutionary character of the vast transition taking place in the world today. Transcending all these influences, arising from the changes in scientific and social knowledge, has been the experience of the terrifying events associated with the two world wars. Gone forever is the liberalist optimistic faith in the natural rationality of man and in the cosmic inevitability of evolutionary progress.

A general difference in stance underlying the present exposition from the liberalist posture arises from the radically altered character of the era we live in. Liberalism reflecting an age of protest—against arbitrary government, religious dogmatism, and intellectual absolutism—embraced a metaphysics of change and process. It decried the unchanging as "static," it suspected all presuppositions as harboring "a priori absolutes," it discountenanced the formulation of definite aims as likely to lead into a blind alley of "fixed ends." Along with a feeling of impatience with "external control," it exhibited an impulse for emancipation from the "burdens of the past." At heart, liberalism retained a high regard for the fundamental values of the

Western civilization, for the concepts of reason and law, of freedom and equality. Its criticisms were directed against the institutions of the immediate past rather than against the classic ideas of the European philosophic and religious tradition. It aimed to free the ethical essentials and spiritual insights from the encrustations of dogma, from mechanical ritualisms, and meaningless verbalisms. In a period of gradual transition, when the foundations of Western civilization were still firm despite important changes in the superstructure, liberalism took for granted the continuity of Western civilization and worked for its advance.

The situation today reflects a deeper crisis in Western life. Anxiety and disillusion have infected the thought of the intellectual class and invaded the precincts of academic philosophy. To a lack of faith in the traditional religions has been added doubt as to the value of reason. Existentialism retreats from rational inquiry, seeks salvation in egocentric subjectivity; philosophic analysis, challenging from the opposite side, reduces reason to a narrow logic and to technical discourse about language. Both deny to philosophy its function of the rational guidance of life, and in both, in existentialism and in the analytic philosophy, there is a turning away from concern with democratic political principles. In the face of these symptoms of the disintegration of the Western ethic, a more positive and constructive orientation than liberalism provided has become imperative. We must become aware of the moral and political principles on which we stand and define the goals to which we are prepared to commit ourselves.

The reconstruction of the liberalist position requires a broad historical perspective. It implies a recognition of values and ideas better appreciated in the medieval era, e.g., the reality of universals, the understanding that ends determine means, the dependence of the inner spiritual life on the existence of a community of belief. It means devotion to the twofold ethical ideal of justice-and-compassion which Christianity inherited from Judaism, but which the churches as well as society at large have honored more in the breach than in the observance. It involves constant recourse to the concepts rooted in the thought of Athens and Rome—of reason and of law, and of the close relation of the ethical and the political. In confronting the problems of the international order in the making, it is necessary to build on the broad foundation of Western civilization seen in terms of its historical development as it adapts its insights to changing conditions and to new knowledge. In this there is no sentimental nostalgia for the past as such. The orientation is toward the future—the future is as much a part of history as is the past.

227

In the important sense, history is not a record of a past that is gone; it represents the remembrance of events and ideas that our own generation regards as of significance for the present and the future. History adds a dimension to our existence, it gives us perspective, it cultivates breadth of vision, it identifies us with man's continuous struggle for justice and freedom, for dignity and understanding. The progress of man has been halting, marked by retrogression as well as by advance. Nevertheless, history testifies that as a whole we move forward; it sustains the hope that man may someday become master of his destiny. History teaches us, as Bertrand Russell has remarked, "to think in long stretches of time, and not to be reduced to despair by the badness of the present."[1]

The resumé will be presented in three sections. The first, "Reason, Science, and Ethics," will make explicit underlying assumptions concerning the nature of rational thought and review the conception outlined in Chapter Two above of the realm of science and its limited relation to ethics. The second, under the heading, "The Moral, the Ideal, and the Community," summarizes the observations made on the moral-ethical problem and on the relation of authentic personality to the inner acceptance of a pattern of ideals, on the one hand, and to community loyalty, on the other. The third is entitled, "Democratic Principles and Social Program." It formulates a definition of democracy as an ethical-political philosophy and applies it to contemporary problems in the domestic and in the international situations. Reference to educational issues, on which more extended comments is offered in the concluding chapters, will be borne in mind.

REASON, SCIENCE, AND ETHICS

"Metaphysical"[2] Observations: Thought, History, and Philosophy

Thought is protean: it may appear as a stream of consciousness, as intuitive grasp, imaginative speculation, contemplation of the universe, and as mystic communion. All of these forms have significance —may contribute to the enrichment of experience and the under-

---

[1] *The Philosophy of Bertrand Russell*, Paul Arthur Schilpp, ed. (Evanston, 1944), pp. 17ff.

[2] Following a clue suggested by R. G. Collingwood in his *Essay on Metaphysics* (Oxford, 1940), I here use the term "metaphysical" in a wholly non-ontological sense as a descriptive statement of the "absolute presuppositions . . . made by this or that person or group of persons, on this or that occasion or group of occasions, in the course of this or that piece of thinking."

standing of life, may enter into the complex processes of scientific and of moral judgment. But thought as reason deliberately pursued has had a special role in Western culture in a two-fold sense—in leading to the advance of understanding for its own sake, on the one hand, and to the achievement of control over life's affairs, on the other. Thinking has served both as a means of satisfying man's propensity to wonder and as an instrument for resolving problems of knowledge and of conduct. In the development of science and of ethics, both aspects of thought, the one we may call theoretical and aesthetic, the other, functional and practical, have interplayed for mutual advancement.

Pragmatism has made a contribution in pointing up the indispensable part that operational procedures and practical applications play in clarifying and verifying theory. What is misleading in some of its versions, is the implication that the end of all thought is action and that all knowledge must have an immediate practical use. Thought as instrumental, it should be emphasized, functions to advance scientific theory as well as to serve practical wisdom. And the need to understand ourselves and the world, to evaluate and appreciate, is as deep a human impulse as is the need to improve our conduct and to better the conditions of life. A major weakness in the instrumentalist interpretation of pragmatism is its tendency to neglect the definition of principles and to avoid the formulation of the ends of thought.

Thought in its active sense, as a means of arriving at valid judgments in the sphere of knowledge or of morals, involves definite presuppositions and definite ends; the presuppositions and the ends are intimately interrelated. All reasoning demands a postulation of major premises; agreement on conclusions can be reached only if there is a prior acceptance of the premises. Experimental inquiry becomes possible only on the basis of warranted assumptions with reference to which problems may be formulated and hypotheses of explanation may be suggested. Ethical action, likewise, must be grounded in convictions and commitments.

There is a difference in the way we validate scientific generalizations, on the one hand, and ethical principles, on the other, but both necessitate making assumptions and entertaining purposes. The judgment by an individual of a particular case always implies criteria of judgment embodied in presuppositions and ends. These may be so generally taken for granted or so deeply embedded in consciousness that one is not aware of them. The fruitlessness of many a discussion results from differences in the inarticulated fundamental assumptions or in unacknowledged purposes rather than from faults in the process

229

of thinking and the chain of argument. In scientific research and teaching, and especially in the discussion of ethical questions and social problems, the first essential is to make clear what principles and what purposes are involved.

In the highest developments as well as in their primitive stages, beliefs and evaluations have arisen out of the interplay of man's experience with his speculative explorations. At the heart of human thought as differentiated from animal intelligence is man's power of imagination—the power to overcome egocentricity and to transcend immediate, concrete experience: to see ourselves as others see us and to see others as ourselves, to conceive an ideal of perfection despite the actual unsatisfactory existence. The most important aspect of the imagination is its power to formulate abstract general principles as a basis for science and morals, for art and political life and to envision new possibilities and future worlds to come. Generalization and conceptualization do not result directly from unmediated examination of individual instances or through collation of individual experiences. Applied to the history of human thought there is significance in the notion that: "In the beginning was the *logos*." Historically as well as logically, theory is prior as well as prerequisite to explanations that may be called scientific, the ideal is prior and prerequisite to a truly ethical way of life. Reason has not developed by moving from observation to thought, but the other way round—by chastening the imagination though reference to experience, by pruning the exuberant, by restraining the fantastic.

The basic principles that lie at the foundation of the contemporary sciences and of current systems of morals have developed historically and are the products of slow growth. Present knowledge is based on prior knowledge; new theories arise out of modification of old theories in the light of added knowledge, of new experiences, and of novel ways of looking at things. Every new idea is a criticism of an old idea and a proposal for a new formulation; every new conception can be understood only in the light of the conception it opposes and supersedes. This does not mean that ideas evolve out of inner logical force; experience enters, and the changed idea may be, in pattern or in substance, quite different from the traditional. But it can be understood only in historical context, not as a metaphysical concept floating in a sea of pure being. The historical nature of knowledge and theory is concealed in science because the new science absorbs the old in its body. The pursuit of modern science and its practical application does not require a study of ancient works of science. But even in the sphere of science, creative work in theory and philosophy involves the study of the growth of scientific ideas. In the field of ethics and politics, in philosophy and education, a knowledge of the history of thought is an essential.

This emphasis on the history of ideas is an aspect of the conception that meanings are contextual, that ideas can be understood only in relation to their frames of reference. The context of any conception includes the language in which it is expressed, and this itself would give it a definite, regional cultural, character. All historical ideas of importance have a significance beyond their own time and place, but to discern what is of mere local interest and what is of enduring value requires knowing what their meaning was in the social and cultural context where they originated. Another aspect of the contextual or "relational" character of ideas is illustrated by the heuristic principle of "polarity"—the idea that philosophic terms involve their opposites and that rational comprehension requires a deliberate consideration of general concepts in relation to their contrarieties. Unity implies diversity, the particular must be seen in the light of a general or universal frame of reference; process involves structure, change can be observed and measured only in the background of the enduring.

All systems of philosophy which interpret natural phenomena or historical developments monistically represent ideologies, i.e., arguments in defense of one view as against another or strategies to promote this or that cause. Such one-sided programmatic interpretations may be justifiable in practice as correcting equally one-sided policies. The metaphysics of change and process adopted by liberalism was calculated to counteract institutional inertia supported by an ontology of unchanging truth. The Marxian materialist interpretation was a reaction against the Hegelian purely ideaistic conception of historical development. A synthesis of opposites tends to provide a more balanced and a more comprehensive conception. It does not imply a mechanical compromise, nor does it necessarily lead to the Aristotelian golden mean; it may lean toward one side or another in a given situation. But a consistent regard for the principle of polarity is a safeguard against forcing all reality into a single dogmatic mold, on the one hand, and against merging all phenomena in a cloud of amorphous "being," on the other.

Philosophy has both a critical and constructive function. It aims to mediate between opposing concepts, to reconcile the various spheres of understanding, the scientific and the religious, the ethical and the political. It strives to achieve unity of knowledge, to bring the actual closer to the ideal. Philosophy begins with criticism of accepted assumptions and conventional ends when these no longer harmonize with advancing knowledge or with an ethical conception. But its function is not fulfilled by analysis and criticism of existing views and policies. Its work must go on until it has reformulated principles, until it has achieved a higher degree of consistency in thought, until it has offered a proposal that satisfies better a cherished ideal. A mature philosophy will realize that aporias always remain, that perfect consistency can never be attained, that in life the actual ever falls short of the ideal. This knowledge should lead to strengthening philosophic endeavor and not to its discouragement or abandonment.

The word philosophy when used in its broadest sense connotes a Weltanschauung, a philosophy of life. In this meaning philosophy includes an ethical conception, an envisaged ideal of human relations correlated with a pattern of personal and social behavior. Of necessity this implies an organized community life, framed in a cultural setting and expressed in institutional forms. A philosophy of life may be religious, with the church occupying the position of the major communal organ as Christianity served in former times and still does for some of its adherents today. It may be centrally rational, as in the Stoic and Epicurean schools of thought which in Athens constituted fraternal orders with characteristic codes of conduct. Today the major philosophies of life carry a political imprint, as illustrated by democracy and communism, by fascism and nationalism. An individual philosophy of life may include elements from all of these forms, the religious, the rational, the political. But all significant philosophies of life involve an ethical conception, a community attachment, and some political implication.

When fully expounded, a philosophy of life will reveal a metaphysical reference, in the sense of some assumption of man's relation to nature, to the cosmos, to the totality of things. The metaphysical conception may serve as background, it may add depth and breadth, may suffuse the ethical conception with radiant spirit. A metaphysical principle may be used to justify or support a system of values, but it is never the basis of it. A philosophy of life arises out of man's many-sided nature and conflicting experience, in which his urge to survive and to reproduce and his need of living in communities interact and struggle with his imaginative idealizing propensity.

When the word philosophy is used in connection with some special area of knowledge, e.g., science, law, politics, religion, it likewise has the function of criticizing fundamental assumptions and of constructing better warranted and more comprehensive principles. Philosophy also has the function of making clear relations among the several areas of knowledge. But even less than in the formulation of a philosophy of life does this imply imposing a preconceived metaphysical "first cause and ordering principle" without regard to the nature of each field of knowledge. Each broad sphere of knowledge, mathematics, the natural sciences, the social studies, ethics and religion, art and literature, is in a sense, autonomous, has its own distinctive principles. No sphere has authority over the other, although an understanding of principles underlying one may be helpful in the inquiry of related fields of knowledge. Physics may be necessary for the understanding of chemistry, both may be invaluable for the understanding of biology and psychology. But the "higher" order can never be explained merely in terms of the "lower."

The concept "the unity of knowledge" is a directive of philosophic inquiry, not a statement describing fact. There is no unitary or monistic principle, no "scientific method" applicable to all fields of knowledge without regard to the content of knowledge. To engage in the philosophic study of law, politics, or religion, one must have competent knowledge of the fields in question. The philosophy of education deals with education considered in its broadest relations, in the framework of a system of values and of a definite form of social organization; it is not the application of an abstract metaphysical—ontological or epistemological—conception to the educational problem. What is said here about law, politics, and education applies with particular force to the realm of the natural sciences.

The Realm of Science

The elevation of science in modern times to the position of supreme authority in the fields of knowledge and of ethics was an aspect of the revolt against the domination of the church over the intellectual and moral life. The dethronement of "religion" brought with it the installation of the rival sovereign regime of "science." The remarkable achievements of the natural sciences lent plausibility to the belief that the new mode of achieving knowledge as well as the new knowledge itself was applicable to, and significant for, all phases of human understanding. Moreover, as is indicated in our use of the word "natural" to mean the "essential quality of things," the new faith drew support from a deeply rooted presupposition in Western thought—the presupposition that experienced phenomena reflect an underlying reality in the universe. The high esteem in which the natural sciences are held is in line of continuity with Platonic and Aristotelian thought and with the Stoic identification of nature with reason. It retains something of the notion that the source of truth and

233

of goodness lies outside man—resides in an order of nature by which the entire universe is governed.

In a view still widely entertained, the belief that nature is the source for the understanding of the life of man is narrowed to mean that physics, described as "the most authoritative of the sciences," offers a clue for a "synthesis of scientific and philosophical thought."[3] But physics is not a study of nature as a whole; it is a study of certain aspects of the inorganic part of nature: "the science of the properties and interrelations of matter and energy"—as the Oxford dictionary has it—or the application of mathematical concepts to the problem of interrelations of motion, space, and time as revealed in experience, the definition which Einstein in one place suggests.[4] Nor do the natural sciences in combination provide us with a knowledge of the universe as a whole. It is essential to scientific investigation that it be directed to definite limited areas of phenomena. To warrant the designation "science" an area of study must possess a body of organized knowledge, a set of established principles, approved procedures of investigation, special terminology with clear and accurate meanings. Science implies a community of trained personnel—research workers, teachers, commentators, and philosophers. Every science has its leaders whose authority is recognized and respected. The members of the scientific community, in its various sections, are the custodians of the accumulated heritage of knowledge in their special fields and at the same time serve as frontiersmen in the extension and enrichment of that heritage.

Roughly, the sciences may be divided into three types, each with its different modes of procedure as well as different subject matters. Mathematics stands on one side, the exemplar of a "pure" and precise science: it consists of a study of existing and possible patterns of abstract relations; its propositions are not necessarily relevant to the actual world, although they are wondrously applicable to it. On the other side lie the social studies which deal with the various aspects of group behavior. The social studies involve value-judgments as well as descriptive and explanatory functions; since there is little agreement on principles, their claim to be called sciences is questionable. In between are the large groups of natural sciences, which include, on the one hand, the "static," descriptive sciences, e.g., geology, zoology, botany, and, on the other, the "dynamic" sciences concerned with

[3] F. L. Kunz, "The Reality of the Non-Material" in *Main Currents in Modern Thought*, vol. 20, no. 2 (Dec. 1963).

[4] Albert Einstein, *Out of My Later Years* (New York, 1950), p. 41.

explanation, e.g., physics, chemistry, and biology. Psychology, in a certain sense, the most complex of all the sciences, is a mixture of biological, social, and ideational elements. It is marked by a diversity of approaches and as yet by a lack of a consensus on basic principles.

The diversity of the sciences and their dependence on specific bodies of knowledge should caution against the view that "scientific method is essentially the same in all the sciences."[5] The modes of procedure and the knowledge developed in one area may be helpful, even prerequisite, for related areas. But effective work or research in any field cannot be separated from a knowledge of the subject matter, of the methods of operation, and of the presuppositions and problems of the particular field of consideration. One cannot train a biologist by teaching him mathematics, even though he may use quantitative methods of study elaborated by mathematicians in his work. Notoriously the special knowledge of the scientist or training in scientific method is of little, if any, help in common-sense judgments or in the determination of social policy. The views of Alexis Carrel on the spiritual life have as much or as little value as those of Mary Baker Eddy. Albert Einstein's pacifist opinions on international organization, whatever their merit, carry no greater authority than Frank Buchman's proposals on moral rearmament.

Not convincing is the Deweyan view that there is "a common logical pattern in scientific and moral knowing."[6] Some analogy can be drawn between scientific and moral inquiries: both require making assumptions, formulation of principles, a clear idea of the purpose of the inquiry. But no refined philosophical analysis can abolish the common-sense distinction between the "is" and the "ought"—between the descriptive and explanatory purposes of study characteristic of the sciences and the normative function of ethics which demands a commitment to a freely-willed line of action. In the natural sciences, conclusions can be verified by objective tests which the individual scientist cannot avoid accepting. But ethical and moral principles, however wide the measure of agreement, remain social opinions, rationally defensible perhaps, but lacking the sanction of verifiable truth.

We can with a degree of reasonableness argue that certain values and behaviors lead to happiness. We can point to the lives of the saints, recall the prophets' vision of justice, we can quote the words of statesmen who assert that all men are created equal. We can reflect

[5] Theodore M. Greene and others, *Liberal Education Re-examined* (New York, 1943), p. 51.

[6] *The Philosophy of John Dewey*, Paul Arthur Schilpp, ed. (Evanston, 1939), p. 578.

on the teaching of the philosopher who tells us that the unexamined life is not worth living, we can appeal as the Stoics did to the common view of mankind. However, all these efforts of persuasion represent testimony, not proof. Whether the testimony is convincing depends, to a large extent, on the person who is addressed. In the final analysis, the individual cannot avoid taking the responsibility of making a choice.

The belief that scientific method is the same for all types of investigation, joined with the idea that it represents the high road to truth, has tended to divert attention from the part that ends and values play in the field of inquiry. This tendency is compounded by the confusion of objectivity with neutrality. The scientist is objective in that he does not allow his prejudices, his likes or dislikes, to influence his conclusions. But he is not neutral in the sense that he has no purpose in making his investigations or that he must be indifferent to the practical implications of his conclusions. During a particular investigation the scientist may be concerned only with the solution of a theoretical problem, but this does not mean that he must refrain from indicating what effect his findings, if applied, are likely to have. The confusion of neutrality with objectivity has been particularly deleterious in the social studies. Description and classification have their place in the social studies—in economics, politics, in history and sociology—as well as in the natural sciences. But it is imperceptive, if not disingenuous, to omit reference to underlying value systems and to avoid pointing out the moral consequences of alternative forms of social organization.

It is only when the moral ends have been decided upon that science can render assistance. The knowledge that science provides can lead to modifications in conventional moral regulations. But science, conceived either as method or as knowledge-content cannot of itself produce a moral or an ethical system. The great advances in morality —the abolition of slavery, the recognition of the equality of the races, the emancipation of women, the elimination of child labor, the emergence of democracy as a moral as well as a governmental concept— have not resulted from the progress of scientific thought or the use of scientific method. In these great steps forward, economic and political factors have operated; science has been indirectly involved in making possible conditions which permitted a more generous fulfillment of human needs and aspirations. But behind the material factors there has been also a moral impulse—not only a demand for justice on the part of those deprived, but a recognition of the rightness of the demand, supported by religion and philosophy. Insofar as a basis can be discerned common to ethics and science, it is to be sought not in the achievements or the methodology of the sciences, but in the root of both of them, namely, man's unique power of creating ideas and ideals and of embodying them in the practical actions of life.

THE MORAL, THE IDEAL, THE COMMUNITY

The Moral and the Ethical

The moral-ethical concept cannot be reduced to prudential wisdom, to the calculus of pleasure and pain, or to the critical evaluation of wants. The difficulties in views which define the moral and the ethical in terms of the evaluation of satisfactions are not met by adding that the judgment of the individual must be made in the light of consequences, with full regard for others and in concern for social welfare. The discussion of the moral problem in terms of the satisfaction of wants is, in the first instance, misleading and evades the issues.

Moral choice is not of the order of preference in food or dress, or even in the more serious sense of the choice of a vocation. It refers to situations of conflict which affect the personality deeply or which are likely to disturb existing social arrangements—in sex relations, economic affairs, in the organization of the state. The moral choice is not between the fulfillment of one satisfaction or another, but as common sense well understands, between what one *wants* to do and what in the judgment of society or of oneself one *ought* to do. No subtle psychological analysis, no philosophical sophistication should obscure the fact that moral choice involves a conflict between desires and impulses on the one hand, and duties and obligations, on the other. A moral choice involves a conception of right and wrong; it cannot be made apart from a body of principles, and a commitment to a pattern of values.

Values are not objectives that can be secured by direct pursuit. They are qualities that inhere in life-activities to which we are impelled by instinctive drives and human aspirations. It is the *way* we fulfill the basic life-functions and realize our cultural and spiritual needs—in making a living, rearing a family, carrying on social relations generally, organizing political and religious institutions—that marks our actions as moral or immoral, ethical or unethical. The moral and the ethical begin in the urge to live: "Behold I have put before you life and the good, death and evil, and ye shall choose life." In the ancient Hebraic view, the good life included enjoyment of the fruit of the land, the blessing of the abundance of corn, wine, and oil. But it meant also and essentially love of God and of fellow men, obedience

237

to the law, pursuit of righteousness, aspiration for the peace of the spirit.

The moral-ethical problem arises from man's "predicament" in a sense quite different from that assumed in the existentialist philosophy. The primary anxieties of men are not the "ontic" apprehension of death and "meaninglessness"; the worries that men normally experience are connected with the ongoing activities of life, with problems of health, sex relations, economic affairs, with success and failure, achievement and frustration. However, there is a sense in which mankind as a race is faced by a predicament; namely, the predicament of having to live simultaneously on three gradients, on the biological, the sociological, and the ideational levels. The biological basis is prerequisite to both the social and the ideal forms of human behavior and aspiration, and there is a reciprocal interplay among the three levels. But there is no preordained harmony either between the biological and the sociological or between the social and the ideal. Rather, there is a subsistent conflict that can rarely be completely resolved; insofar as any degree of adjustment is possible, this involves restraint and sacrifice. The moral-ethical struggle is not a struggle between "the individual" and "society," but a struggle within the individual and within society to bring about some accord among the three phases of human existence and achieve a bio-social-ideal integration.

A distinction has to be made between the moral and the ethical. Morals and ethics overlap but they represent two different aspects of man's nature. The former arises out of man's character as a social, an institutionalized, a political animal; the moral problems relate to conflicts between man's primary biological drives and the restraints which are associated with his need of living in organized communities. Morality requires regulation by custom and law; its basic purpose is to keep society operating as a going concern. The ethical, on the other hand, derives from man's imaginative power, from his tendency to idealize, to envision perfection, to extend his selfhood in identification with humanity as a whole. Ethics is concerned with the quality of life; its aspiration is towards the spiritual, it sees the good as a form of beauty to be prized for its own sake. Both the moral and the ethical demand control and discipline of biological impulses; the ethical may also involve a struggle with the moral—with the conventionally approved and the established positive law. The ethical problem arises from the fact that—as St. Augustine following Seneca and Marcus Aurelius recognized—man is a citizen of two cities, the city of his birth and "the City of God."

238

The moral, as well as the ethical, implies the assent of the conscience and the reason of the individual person. The observance of the law for fear of punishment and the uncritical acceptance of convention do not merit the attribute "moral." Obedience to custom and law acquires moral quality only when it is done as a matter of principle in recognition of its justice and its service to the general welfare. Nevertheless, what is moral is determined by the common good and not what gives satisfaction to the individual considered as an independent self. In the sphere of the ethical there is a larger measure of freedom for the expression of the unique personality. But as in the moral sphere, choice does not mean arbitrary decision: the freedom that the ethical life gives is the result of the conscious adoption of a pattern of values in place of those conventionally approved. Usually, the ethical conception supports the existing social morality but goes beyond it; sometimes it will actually oppose it, in the name of the ideal conception. In both the ethical and the moral sphere, the judgment of the individual is exercised within a framework of a social system as well as of a consciously held pattern of values.

The argument is directed against individualistic antinomian views and subjective anti-rationalist conceptions that fail to give consideration to the part that law and ordered thought play in the control and guidance of the personal and social life—and, above all, in the maintenance and advance of genuine freedom. The evils attendant on the operation of law cannot be remedied by outcries against legalism; bad laws need to be replaced by good laws. The critique of a narrow rationalism should lead to a richer conception of reason that gives scope to speculative philosophy, appreciates the insights of religion, and values the understandings revealed in literature. The concept of the "inner-directed" life is meaningless, worse than outer-directed conformity, if it is not inspired by a consciously held ethical conception. The existentialist lament about the alienated condition of man in collectivist society may offer psychological relief to a disillusioned intellectual class. But withdrawal from the communal life can only weaken the cause of justice and liberty. Nor is the courageous involvement in the battle of the hour, as Sartre suggests, sufficient. The achievement of an order of peace and of freedom is a many-sided, a long-time task that requires a formulation of a positive conception of the nature of the good life and of the political institutions necessary for its furtherance.

The humanization of life, on the moral level, means discipline of impulse, fulfillment of obligation, assumption of responsibility for the unforeseen consequences of our actions. It requires a transference

239

from ego-centricity, not only in the sense of a consideration of others; it means an identification of the self with the good of the community as a whole. At the ethical level, morality implies an inner acceptance by the individual of a code of values to direct conduct. The unprincipled and undirected life is no more worth living for man than is the unexamined life which Socrates condemned. Within the framework of our obligations, every joy that can be gathered from life, every delight than can be savored, is to be accounted a blessing. But in the end, happiness cannot be attained by a multiplication of satisfactions, by a fulfillment of disparate wants. Happiness in the sense of *eudaimonia*, of the "good life of the spirit," can be attained only in the service of the ideal to which we aspire, by devotion to the cause we have chosen, by loyalty to the community of which we are a part.

The Institutions of Community and the Unique Person

All associative life involves moral factors—regulations to be observed and obligations to be met. Of special significance for the development of the ethical personality are the forms of social organization to which the term "community" properly applies. One joins a voluntary organization such as a trade union, a professional association, or a social club for a specific purpose; one may leave it without any great emotional disturbance when interest has been lost or a benefit no longer derived. The genuine community, e.g., the family, the nation, the religious grouping, involves a sense of psychological attachment and personal identification; it implies, in some respects, a common destiny and it inspires a loyalty. The community is united by common bonds of practical interests, on the one hand, and by common beliefs and aspirations, on the other.

The moral-ethical problem is never a matter of the accommodation of an abstract individual to another abstract individual, or the adjustment of an individual to society at large. The grave moral and ethical problems arise in the contexts of the various spheres of community life and have reference to conflicts between needs and values. Every community faces the problem of preserving its organization, on the one hand, and of maintaining its ideal aims, on the other. Each individual has the double problem of reconciling his interests with those of other members of his community and also of remaining true to the values which the community represents. It is in the struggle of individuals and communities to reconcile needs, loyalties, and ideals that consistency and integrity of character are tested. The moral-ethical problem is particularly acute today, because the principles and the material bonds that link the pivotal institutions of family, nation, and religion have been greatly weakened.

In former times, the nation, the family, the church, supported each other and were unified in the life of the village and the small town. The conditions and forces of contemporary life—enormous urban centers, heterogeneous character of the population, the ease of anonymity, social mobility, education in large public schools, mass communication media—have tended to reduce the sense of attachment and have combined to diminish the moral and cultural influences of the pivotal communities. The loosening effects of the sociological forces have been abetted by the cosmopolitan, individualistic views of a free-wheeling intellectual class for whom nonconformity is itself a virtue. A major factor in the neurotic anxieties of our time lies in the lack of roots in a community life as well as in the absence of a systematic, controlling system of values. A primary problem in the development of moral personality is to strengthen the sense of attachment to the communities of family, of nation, and of the religious associations and to involve the individual in the responsibilities and the ideals which these pivotal institutions of Western civilization represent.

Despite the narrowing of the scope of its activities, the family still remains the one institution on which the economic, cultural, and spiritual forces all converge; it has the potentiality of integrating the various aspects of life as they impinge on the individual. At the same time, the life of the home affords a measure of control over the environmental pressures, allows a certain freedom in the style of living and in aesthetic expression, provides protection from the intrusion of vulgarities, and serves as a haven of refuge from the coercive distractions of the collectivist life. The family organization induces a regard for the ethics of mutual obligation; in a more positive sense, it impels toward the giving and receiving of love in its most enduring and deepest meaning. Family life fulfills itself in the rearing of children and in helping them in their adjustment to life until they can stand on their own feet. The family is a mutual-aid society in miniature, providing material and moral support in times of need; it offers the sustaining solace of a common sorrow in the hour of bereavement.

These positive fulfillments of family life represent possibilities. The plenitude of opportunities for satisfaction and happiness are paralleled by the probabilities of disappointment and vexation of the spirit. The frustrations and failures may be caused, in part, by the infirmities of our biological nature never designed to function within the confines of a monogamous institution. They may have their roots in psycho-

241

logical maladjustment during childhood. They may in part be due to the poverty of condition and the misery it may entail. "The rebirth of the family," to use Lewis Mumford's phrase, as a center of life, as an agency for personal development and for the enhancement of social life, demands a many-sided effort—a commitment to a pattern of values by parents and material support on the part of the community. It necessitates for the population as a whole, adequate provision for social security and medical care and ample assistance for catastrophic cases of illness and for the upbringing of defective children. It requires the elimination of degrading poverty and of slum conditions, the provision of social services and psychiatric help when necessary. In the light of the changed conditions under which men and women live in contemporary times and the institution of coeducation at the high school and college level, it is necessary to face the problem of a reformulation and reestablishment of a socially-approved code in sex relations conducive to the stability and integrity of family life.

Like the family, the nation represents a community of destiny with which the fate of the individual is interlinked. Although we are moving in the direction of a greater degree of international cooperation, the nation remains the basis of social and political organization throughout the world. The term "nation" has two distinct meanings: that of a social-cultural entity and that of a sovereign state, the agency of coercive force. In the American situation, nationality and statehood coincide. As a social unit we are dependent on it for our language, for our heritage of literature, and for our education, with all that these integral components of culture imply for our ideas and values, for our political conceptions and our philosophy of democracy. As a state, we are dependent on the national organization for security, for economic organization, for enforcement of the law, for the protection of our liberties.

As in all community affiliations, the national attachment is replete with moral conflict. The citizen owes a double allegiance to the nation, the duty to defend the state to assure its survival and to advance its interests, on the one hand, and a loyalty to the democratic ideals for which the Republic stands, on the other. As a cultural community, America is a historical and regional expression of Western civilization; in its involvement in international affairs, it is a part of the emerging world order. The ethics of citizenship demands a reconciliation of the individual's group attachments to local community, to class, and to religious denomination with his allegiance to the nation as a whole. At the same time, it means transforming patriotic devotion into loyalty to the universal principles and the international vision which America symbolizes.

The family and the nation are existential institutions indispensable for the maintenance of civilized life. To all intents and purposes they are imposed upon us; the only questions are what possibilities and what responsibilities they imply. The religious association stands in a different category: though still generally a phase of the family and cultural heritage, the religious affiliation today is essentially voluntary. Moreover, in the eyes of the humanist, the traditional churches, still the dominant form of religious association, stand as defendants before the bar of reason and justice. Of all the social institutions, it might be said, the churches have been least consistent in the realization of their high professions. Claiming the possession of ultimate truth, they have tolerated gross superstitions; preaching love and charity, they have fed the fires of fanatical hatreds. Inquisitions, suppression of thought, support of princes against the people, stain the pages of the history of Christianity. The part that Christian doctrine has played in the instigation of anti-Semitism cannot be left out of the accounting. The compromising position taken by the Catholic Church in the confrontation of fascism and Naziism illustrates the quandaries and expediencies to which religious as well as secular leaders fall prey in the struggle to preserve the power of their organizations.

It was a day of defeat from the spiritual point of view when the Christian Church, in order to become a world power, accepted the partnership of "the murderous egoist Constantine," who was "driven without cease by ambition and lust for power," as Jacob Burckhart had characterized him.[7] It would have been far better from the ethical as well as the intellectual point of view, if Christianity, no longer persecuted, had been satisfied, renouncing the claim to supreme truth, to assume the status of a purely religious community alongside of the philosophic fraternities and enlightened tolerant monotheisms that flourished in the Hellenistic-Roman Empire. The prerequisites of all genuine religion is that it be free from any scintilla of coercion—that it rely on the persuasiveness of its teachings, that it draw its adherents with bonds of understanding, that it attract to its rituals by the spiritual emotions they inspire. It is only in the complete and unqualified separation of church and state that the religious associations can maintain their integrity and perform their true work.

Under the democratic regime—provided that all vestiges of the use

[7] Jacob Burckhardt, *The Age of Constantine the Great*, Moses Hadas, trans., Pantheon Books (New York, 1949), pp. 291ff.

of the coercive forces of the state to enforce religion are eliminated—the religious associations, the traditional churches and synagogues and the new forms of religious expression have invaluable functions to perform as communal, educational, and spiritual organizations. They support the institution of the family, minister to it in the critical episodes of birth, marriage, and death. They symbolize kindness, encourage charity and good works; their music and rituals compose the spirit. They provide a bond of attachment to a wider community than the family and nation and enlarge the consciousness to include all men. They sustain the hope for an era of peace and good will. As Lewis Mumford says, "they keep alive through all the tribulations and frustrations of living, those ideal points of reference without which human life becomes savage, degraded, and brutish."[8] The religious associations give a divine sanction to that which is distinctively humane and nourish man's sense of communion with a transcendent cosmic order.

The pivotal communities of family, nationality, and religious association supplement one another, but at the same time stand in relation of tension to each other. Each type of community institution must relate its interests and functions to the other; each individual, likewise, must achieve some reconciliation between his family responsibilities and his obligation to the nation as a whole, between his duties as a citizen and his loyalty to the universal, ethical, spiritual principles embodied in his religious commitment. It is in the struggle to achieve some measure of accord, some viable adjustment between private needs and interests, communal obligations, and envisioned ideals, that the individual comes to realize the necessities, the potentialities, and the limitations of the human condition and achieves a moral, rational, and mature personality.

Within the bounds of the institutional and communal life each individual remains unique, a distinctive integration of the biological, social, and ideational factors. In each flows a private stream of consciousness; each individual is signalized by a particular combination of traits, each has his special modes of enjoyment, interests, and hobbies; each is identified by characteristic manners, by nuances of expression, by a style of living. The individual is not a mere passive recipient of the forces that impinge upon him; he is a reagent who interacts with his environment, an organism which to some extent selects its own stimuli and refracts the energies which pass through him. Living within the interlocking frames of social organization

[8] Lewis Mumford, *Faith For Living* (New York, 1940), p. 166.

244

and of a system of values, he remains unique but not alienated; he may withdraw for periods of time from active involvement in affairs and still not be isolated from the life of the community.

Freedom of the individual does not consist of freedom from social control or of the absence of commitment to a definite system of beliefs. Positive freedom involves expression of natural impulses and vital needs through institutionalized forms; it means the right to establish associations and maintain communities; it signifies conscious choice of a pattern of values by which to live. The achievement of liberty does not entail the weakening of government, but the use of the power of the state to promote the conditions of life and to protect the freedoms necessary for human existence. This brings us to the problem of the interplay of ethics and politics, to the implications of democracy for social welfare, to the issues involved in our relation to Communist and socialist states and in the promotion of world community.

DEMOCRATIC PRINCIPLES AND SOCIAL PROGRAM

The problem of ethics cannot be divorced from the problems of the political organization of society. The human relations, the pervasive motivations, and the conventional practices in any society are conditioned by the associations and institutions, by the economic structure and the legal system which the state supports. Moreover, the state itself, through the principles upon which it is founded, constitutes a moral agency as well as an instrument of power.

Western political philosophy has given consideration to the dual function of the state: it has recognized the necessity of a coercive authority for defense, for maintaining internal order, for enforcement of the law, for protection of the economic system. At the same time, it reveals a concern that the state and the law it enforces should be based on a conception of justice. Though the opinions of the right ordering of the state vary greatly, the relation of ethics to politics has been a major issue in Western political theory. In the classical conceptions of Plato and Aristotle, in the Christian medieval views of St. Augustine and St. Thomas, in the modern philosophies of Locke and Rousseau, of John Stuart Mill and of Karl Marx, the central problem of political theory, it may be said, is to find a *modus vivendi* between the function of the state in maintaining the security and material welfare of the citizens, on the one hand, and its purpose of achieving justice, protecting freedom, and promoting the cultural and spiritual aspirations of men, on the other.

245

In the present exposition, "democracy" is taken to signify the pattern of values and the structure of government which distinguishes Western civilization in its modern, most highly developed form. Democracy is compatible—always within limits—with different metaphysical orientations and religious conceptions, with diverse national cultures and individual styles of life. But it cannot be confined to a process of government, to an attitude of mind, to a moral relativism. Democracy in the sense here used is a positive ethical conception correlated with a definite system of government. Its roots lie in the classical Mediterranean civilization to which Judea, Athens, and Rome made the seminal contributions. Its meanings have been enriched from time to time, and its principles more consistently embodied from age to age in social and governmental institutions. Today, as we are emerging from the period of liberalism, new applications of the enduring principles are necessary.

The summary which follows represents an attempt to formulate the principles and goals of a social and political program already in the process of development within the framework of a democratic philosophy. It includes: (a) a statement on democracy as an ethical-political conception; (b) comment on necessary changes in government procedures; (c) discussion of the economic factors involved in the advance toward a welfare society; (d) consideration of the problem of creating an international order.

Some of the propositions set forth, particularly with reference to the democratic, ethical, and governmental principles, are rather in the nature of "a vindication of the obvious." But the divergence of opinion on foundation principles makes clarification and reaffirmation desirable. The application of the principles to the current social situation, to the Negro problem, to the economic sphere, and to international affairs may properly be regarded as controversial. But in these matters, too, there is a growing liberal consensus supported by professional opinion in the several areas. In some instances, the programs proposed, e.g., in the anti-discrimination and the anti-poverty measures, have in the last few years become matters of determined federal policy. The greatest differences of opinion perhaps would be in reference to the strong emphasis on the economic basis of social organization and particularly on the importance of achieving a rapprochment with the Communist states. But in these matters too, the positions proposed are defensible in the light of current events and of contemporary developments in American foreign policy.

Ethical-Political Foundations

At the heart of the democratic ethic is a belief in the worth of human life, in the possibility of achieving a good life for man on this earth, of man's becoming master of his own fate, of realizing the rational, moral, and spiritual promise inherent in his nature. Man is the theme—man individual and man universal. Democracy affirms the inestimable value of each unique individual, on the one hand, and of the unity of all mankind, on the other. A corollary is the belief in the essential equality of all men and women, regardless of class, of nationality, or of race.

These ideas and sentiments have found expression in religious, philosophic, and legal conceptions. They are reflected in the Judeo-Christian teachings of the brotherhood of man and of the equality of all men before God. They have been expressed in the Stoic conception of the dignity of all men regardless of race or class condition, of their equality of rights in a cosmopolitan world order. They have found exemplification in the Roman doctrine of a rational natural law as model for the positive legislation of the state. Democracy attempts to actualize these attitudes and ideas and to embody them in social and political organization.

A great advance toward democracy was made during modern times in the formulation of the principle of "natural rights"—of inalienable, indefeasible rights—as basic to the liberal conception of government. In the American system, the inalienable rights are implied in the body of the Constitution and explicitly provided for in the Bill of Rights contained in the original Amendments. The rights guaranteed by the Constitution as interpreted by the courts fall into three categories: (a) the protection of life and security of property and personal privacy; (b) the safeguarding of freedom of thought and belief, of the press, of the right of assembly, and of criticism of the government; (c) the maintenance of the right of voluntary associations for religious, charitable, and educational purposes, and for promotion of economic interests.

Rights, whether "inalienable" or created by legislative action, can never be absolute. They must be defined by law: limitations must be set to prevent one right defeating other rights, to safeguard social order and advance the general welfare. Particular applications of the inalienable rights are subject to change by legislative action and to modification by judicial rulings: property rights may be curtailed, the freedom of the press may, in some respects, be restricted in crisis or in wartime. But the Bill of Rights as a group of principles cannot be rescinded or any of its major categories abrogated by the democratic process; so to maintain is a sheer self-contradiction. To abolish the Bill of Rights or to seriously infringe on it would mean a revolutionary subversion of the Constitution.

At the same time, every period of great social transformation necessitates substantial changes in the interpretation, in emphasis, and in application of the basic constitutional rights. During the rise and establishment of the modern liberal state, from the seventeenth to the twentieth centuries, the emphasis was on freedom for the individual. Freedom was thought of as freedom from the restriction of arbitrary government and from intellectual domination by organized religion. The demand for equality represented a middle-class attack against aristocratic privilege. Today, the problem of implementing and advancing the Bill of Rights has shifted to new ground.

The struggle for freedom of thought centers on political-economic issues, not primarily on the conflict between religion and science. The emergence of a large-scale collectivist society makes the right to form voluntary associations, to maintain the integrity of the family and the religious community, of particular significance in supporting the liberty of the person. The economic struggle is concerned not with the promotion of middle-class interests against a landed aristocracy, but with securing the general welfare of all the people, and particularly with raising the standard of living for the poverty-stricken and low-income groups. The most urgent, most critical, most complex and difficult issue is the implementation of the Bill of Rights for the Negro—the elimination of racial discrimination and the emancipation from economic deprivation.

Governmental Instrumentalities

The democratic state is an organ within society that defends, maintains, and facilitates the ongoing life activities of the nation, protects the rights, and serves the needs of individuals, associations, and communities. This implies a pluralistic society, tolerant of diversities, allowing scope to minorities, depending on a balance of forces and on an adjustment of special interests, not on the domination of any one group or class in society. To fulfill its purposes, American government rests on the constitutional provisions which, besides the foundation principle of inalienable rights, include the separation of powers and the division of responsibilitites between federal and state jurisdictions.

The powers and relative influence of the three branches of government—the legislative, the executive, and the judiciary—may need to be modified with changing conditions, but the division of authority is an essential principle of the Constitution. However wide its powers, the executive is always subject to the legislature; despite any theoretical claim to supremacy, the legislature is always subject to the courts. The states, in accordance with the Tenth Amendment, enjoy powers not delegated to Congress; by the same token they cannot contravene laws enacted by the national legislature or defy decisions handed down by the Supreme Court.

Participation of the whole people in government is a *sine qua non* of the democratic polity. This implies universal adult suffrage and a high regard for public opinion. But like the other factors in government the functions and powers of "the people" are limited by the Constitution. "Majority rule" is confined to particular spheres of decision: it is restricted by the powers assigned to the three branches of government; it is conditioned by the rights of minorities; it has no final authority over the inalienable rights of the individual. As historically developed, the democratic process includes supplementary instrumentalities of government: the two, or more, party system, one of which acts as "a loyal opposition" to the administration in power; the right of the Supreme Court to declare legislation "unconstitutional." Auxiliary to these are the well-established rights of picketing and of other forms of demonstration that have grown out of the constitutional right of peaceable assembly for the redress of grievances. Finally, democratic government lives in an atmosphere of public opinion sustained by freedom of communication and discussion.

Despite the vast social changes that have taken place since its inception, the democratic constitutional system remains a remarkably effective system of government. It has secured stability, allowed adjustment to change, maintained continuity of development, survived the exigencies of economic crises and of war. In the light of the contemporary situation, the further advance of democracy requires a more consistent application of professed principles as well as a modification of a number of conventional conceptions and processes.

In the former category is, first, the removal of the electoral devices in the southern states which have practically nullified the Negroes' right to vote or deprived them of their fair representation in government. A less crucial, but, nevertheless, an important reform is the reapportionment of representation in Congress and in the state legislatures to accord with population changes in recent years. This is necessary not only in fairness to individuals, but also to offset the undue and unwarranted influences of conservative rural and small-town communities. In both these matters, legislation and court rulings have already prepared the ground. An issue of importance, less widely recognized, is the seniority principle in the appointment of the chairmen of Senate committees, which has given the South a strategic position in hindering and delaying progressive legislation.

The over-arching change lies in the increase of the part that the federal government must play in the control and direction of the national life. A new emphasis has to be placed on the purposes set forth in the Preamble to the Constitution: "To form a more Perfect Union" and "Promote the General Welfare." The large-scale interrelated character of the national life and its dependence on global affairs make necessary an increase in powers and a widening of the functions of the federal government along three lines: regulation, coordination, and direction of the economy to maintain its stability and to stimulate its growth; the protection of civil liberties and the enforcement of anti-discrimination legislation; responsibility for the health and education of the nation and for a decent general standard of living.

The increase of the responsibilities of the federal government unavoidably brings with it an augmentation of the power of the executive branch. It enhances the part of presidential leadership in domestic legislation as well as in the conduct of foreign policy. The extension of the role of federal power, it should be clear, is in the interest of securing the freedom of the individual as well as ensuring the welfare of the nation as a whole. The enlargement of the powers of the national government restricts the scope of "reserved" states rights. But federal aid does not replace the responsibilities of the state and local authorities; it supplements and stimulates them. The increase of federal intervention in the economic sector signifies an abandonment of laissez faire. But it is predicated on the preservation of private enterprise in industry and agriculture and on the protection of labor's right to bargain collectively as major principles of the economic organization, as long as these several interests are consistent with the national welfare.

The complexity of social and political issues and the necessity of the enlargement of the executive power have raised the question of the part that "the people" can play in democratic government. Although constitutional democracy by which the United States is governed has never in fact been based on popular sovereignty, the folk idea, that democratic government is government "of the people, by the people, and for the people" has occupied an indispensable place in the democratic process. Besides leading to an extension of the suffrage to all, it has made for a high regard for public opinion, for the intangible—"a fine thin smoke," Carl Sandburg called it—but an absolutely necessary element in democratic government.

In the light of the growth of the executive power of the national government, regard for public opinion becomes increasingly significant. The concept "public opinion" has a double implication: it necessitates bringing proposed policies into the open forum of discussion and it forms a climate of opinion—a core of views from which policies may diverge toward the right or toward the left. Today, it represents a complex and unstable mixture of local and traditional prejudices, of common-sense wisdom, of enlightened and sophisticated opinion. It is subject to many influences and pressures, of newspapers, television and radio, of propaganda for vested interests. It is greatly affected by government information activities which in defense of its policies may distort as well as restrict the news.

Public opinion cannot make or formulate governmental policy, but it always conditions it, can obstruct or facilitate it. In the light of the vast social transition of contemporary life, it is essential not only to enlighten it but to attempt to guide it toward positive, intellectually defensible policies. This implies a serious responsibility for the press, for the mass communication agencies, and particularly for the educational institutions.

Economic Organization and the Welfare State

The advance of the democratic ends of equality of opportunity for the individual and of the promotion of the general welfare is conditioned by the character of the economic organization in two senses—its efficiency and its justice. Plans based only on moral considerations, without regard to the problems of productive efficiency, e.g., sharing of wealth, Christian socialist plans, reliance on good-will and cooperation—deflect attention from the real difficulties that need to be solved. Programs for economic reform must take contemporary economic theory into consideration. Whatever view one follows—whether the careful technical analysis of Arthur F. Burns, the Keynesian theme of Alvin H. Hansen, the liberal synthesis of Paul H. Samuelson, the free-wheeling ideas of John K. Galbraith, the socialist views of Paul M. Sweezy—there are fundamental economic principles that must be taken into account. Proposals must grow out of existing forms of economic enterprise and must be achievable by democratic means.

Democratic society implies a mixed economic system in which the

251

relative proportion of private, corporate, public and government-directed enterprises will be determined by reference to the national welfare in the light of technological developments. A pluralistic economy with a wide scope for private enterprise and private property is an essential for the maintenance of democratic society. It is a safeguard against encroachments by the state on individual freedoms and makes possible the maintenance of associations for cultural and religious purposes. Nevertheless, the complex interdependent character of contemporary economic organization demands control, direction, and planning on the part of the federal government. The task of government includes three interrelated aspects: (a) maintaining the economy in working order and planning its growth; (b) promotion of social welfare; (c) raising sub-standard incomes and eliminating poverty.

In the light of our marvelous productive capability, improvement of the condition of the poor is not only possible but could be a great stimulus to the growth of the economy as a whole and to further improvement of the average standard of living for the generality of the population. A consistent application of the Judeo-Christian ethic, a genuine devotion to the democratic social idea of a general equality of condition, an intelligent, dynamic promotion of the welfare economy combine to demand the provision of a minimally adequate annual income for every individual and every family.[9] The aim is to assure every person, well-born or handicapped, useful or expendable, the victim of misfortune or of the individual's own errors—without regard to any "means test" whatsoever—the minimum necessary to maintain a decent life and to afford equality of opportunity of development for the children.

The elimination of poverty implies an integrated approach on a wide front—economic assistance, medical and social services, provision of educational facilities of the right kind. In rural districts, it means restoration of eroded areas, the development of hydroelectric power, the stimulation of new industries. In the cities, slum clearance and the provision of low-rent housing are the keys to deliverance from misery and degradation. The effort must be directed toward rehabilitation of the family as a whole, and not mainly toward alleviation of the lot of individuals. Different tasks are involved with refer-

[9] Such a program which might have been regarded as utopian only a few years ago has been recommended by the National Commission on Technology, Automation, and Economic Progress (appointed by President Johnson) in its report delivered December 1965.

252

ence to various groups—sharecroppers, migrant workers, unemployed miners in depleted areas, recent immigrants. As always, the Negroes represent a problem of special concern.

Particular concern for the Negro section of the population does not mean giving preference in filling positions to individuals who happen to be black at the expense of individuals who happen to be white. Leaving aside the moral and democratic issues involved, such preferential treatment would do less than scratch the surface of the problem. Particular concern means a comprehensive attack on the inferior social position of the Negro: it implies adequate provision of low-cost housing, extension and adaptation of educational and training facilities, the creation of new job opportunities. It implies special social services designed to strengthen family life, encourage birth control, reduce illegitimacy. It involves enlisting the cooperation of Negro leadership in developing self-help organizations within the Negro community. Raising the level of Negro life is prerequisite for the normalization of American life as a whole; it is correctly seen as a more acute case of the general problem of social reconstruction and family rehabilitation of underprivileged groups.

The International Order

The establishment of an effective international order, supported by a system of collective security is a long-range, many-sided task. It involves the expansion of trade, the furtherance of cultural exchange, an educational program designed to promote international understanding. It requires support of the United Nations, acceptance of the Universal Declaration of Human Rights as a guide to policy, the elaboration of a code of international law. But prerequisite to a realization of international organization and a world community is the reduction of the gross disparity in the standard of living among the nations of the world.

Underlying national rivalries and the conflict between the Western groups and the Communist blocs which hamstring the work of the United Nations are life struggles for existence—for sheer survival as well as for domination, for emancipation from destitution and disease as well as for preserving the position of cultural superiority already achieved. The world struggle and the contest between political ideologies are inextricably related to the divergences of economic and cultural development that have, on the one hand, produced the industrialized and scientific societies of the West with their relatively high standards of living, and on the other, left a large part of the world poverty-stricken, dependent on a relatively primitive agriculture under the control of feudal, paternal, or tribal governments.

The United States and other industrialized nations of the West can make some contribution toward raising the standard of living of the backward and underdeveloped countries through bilateral arrangements and through the agencies of the United Nations. They can provide financial aid, render technical assistance, offer counsel and give training in the areas of health and education. But in the final analysis, any serious improvement in many, perhaps most, instances necessitates radical social and political changes which can be carried out only by the countries themselves in the light of conditions in each case under the direction of native leaders.

In some cases, the movement will be toward democratic institutions; in others, revolutionary change will result in adaptations of socialist and Communist types of polity. The emerging era will be characterized by a diversity of social, political, and economic systems, ranging from the Western type based on a democratic constitution and a mixed economic system to the largely centralized and predominantly state-controlled socialist and Communist forms. The United Nations can be developed only on the assumption of such a diversified participating membership.

Recognition of the legitimacy of diverse forms of political-economic organization is of the first importance in advancing international understanding in the ensuing period of development. We may endeavor to forestall radical political change and through financial and technical assistance try to make possible gradual social evolution along democratic lines. But to attempt to suppress revolutionary movements by force with the support of military dictatorships, besides being a violation of democratic principles, is more likely to prove futile in the long run.

It is only after the exigent material needs of mankind shall have been minimally fulfilled, only when the equality of all men regardless of race shall have been universally recognized, only when every nation shall have won its independence from colonial domination and from exploitive internal rule—only then can we hope that a democratic international order and world peace established on firm foundations will come into being.

All that is said above is predicated on the assumption that the purpose of international organization is not to do away with individual nations—either in the cultural or political sense—but to enable each nation to develop freely within the perspective of an international outlook and the framework of international law. The United Nations is properly conceived as a federation of nationalities and not as a cosmopolitan organization of individuals. The establishment of international order will require all states, whether composed of a single nationality or of a group of nationalities, to submit to limitations of their jurisdictional authority in defined areas, but for any state to yield its sovereign power wholesale would simply mean to subordinate itself to some other state.

Whether a world-state possessing absolute sovereignty with power to enforce its collective will on all regional states is at all desirable is, at the present time, an academic question. A world-state, if ever it comes, is a matter of the distant future. To base politics on the assumption that we are about to become citizens of the world without a sense of allegiance to the nations of which we are a part, and to propose that the control of schools be placed in the hands of the world-state[10] distracts attention from the actual problems in the organization of social life and of education that must be met in the advance toward internationalism.

In the two chapters which follow, the educational situation will be discussed in the light of the lines of thought indicated in the foregoing review. In chapter eight, the broader questions of educational philosophy and social policy will be taken up. The concluding chapter will deal with pedagogical and curricular issues in the current controversy concerning the purpose and function of the school.

[10] As Alexander Meiklejohn counselled: see *Education Between Two Worlds* (New York, 1942), chap. XXI.

RECONSIDERATIONS IN EDUCATIONAL POLICY

Educational Philosophy and Democratic Policy

Indoctrination and Academic Freedom

The Public, the Private, and the Religious School

The Competence and Limitations of School Education

The reconstruction of philosophy,
of education, and of social ideals
and methods thus goes hand in
hand. JOHN DEWEY

8.

Reconsiderations in Educational Policy

A LINE OF continuity can be traced from modern educational thought and practice to the classical system which took shape in Graeco-Roman times. But every period in European history has stamped its character on the prevailing educational conceptions and on the content and method of school work. The outline of the Western educational pattern—with its concern for the development of body and mind, its interest in moral training and aesthetic appreciation, its recognition of the relation of education to the political community—is clearly indicated in Athenian philosophy of the classic period. The Hellenistic era witnessed the establishment of the formal school curriculum with its core studies of language and literature. During the Middle Ages, education declined, but the schema of the Graeco-Roman course of studies was preserved in an attenuated form through the seven liberal arts within the frame of a Christian outlook. The Renaissance restored the classical conception of "the education of the whole man" in an enriched humanistic version, but without the communal and political element which had played so central a part in the Athenian educational theory. The Protestant Reformation and the French Revolution each had its impact on the content and method of the school. The educational developments of the nineteenth century reflect the triumphs of science, the influence of the industrial order, the rise of nationalism and democracy.

Every period of social change has been accompanied by educational controversy. The sharp differences that mark the current discussion are, clearly enough, related to the vast transformation taking place in science, social thought, and in world organization. The issues cover a wide range of questions, political as well as intellectual, philosophic as well as pedagogic. In some cases, the social reference is implicit rather than avowed, as in the perennial question, already broached by Aristotle, whether education should be general and liberal, pursued for its own sake, or functional and practical, related to social needs and to vocational and professional training. In other instances, the political concern is dominant, as in the several aspects of the communist issue—the competition with the U.S.S.R. in technology and weaponry, the rivalry for influence over the underdeveloped countries, the challenge of communism as a political ideology and philosophy of life. Within the field of professional education, much of the discussion relates to the learning process, to intellectual discipline and critical thinking, to character development and growth of personality. These are, in part, psychological questions, but more often than not the views asserted are conditioned by social and political as well as by philosophical preconceptions. Positions differ with reference to the meaning of democracy and its relation to education.

In the discussion of the educational issues, the lines of thought developed in the preceding chapter will be borne in mind, e.g., the relation of science to critical thinking and to moral judgment; the dependence of the moral personality on a consciously held pattern of values and on community attachment; the definition of democracy as an ethical conception interrelated with a political system. In view of the complexity of the problems, the discussion can hardly be more than a series of comments on the main issues. In any case, it is not the purpose to offer a new conception unrelated to current proposals and to the existing school organization. The intention is rather to explore the main areas of controversy and to suggest defensible positions. The American educational system is the product of a long historical development and embodies significant educational concepts. It is essential that continuity be preserved. The purpose of a reconsideration of educational principles is not to emancipate from the past but to make secure the values which have found expression in Western civilization in its democratic interpretation and to apply them more consistently in the light of contemporary views on the nature of personality and of the social and political character of the emerging era.

In the present chapter, the discussion will center around issues in the philosophy of education: the nature of educational philosophy;

the conflict of views on the implications of democracy for school policy; the problems of indoctrination and academic freedom; the place of the private school and the religious school in the American system; the special province and function of school education. In the next chapter, issues in the educative process within the school's domain will be taken up. The topics discussed include: the eclipse of progressive education; liberal education—false claims and genuine values; and the need for revision in the field of educational philosophy.

EDUCATIONAL PHILOSOPHY AND DEMOCRATIC POLICY

Metaphysics and Social Philosophy

An educational policy cannot be derived deductively from a stated metaphysical position—from naturalism, rationalism, or intuitionism, from realism, idealism, or pragmatism. This is not to say that metaphysics has no significance for education. Certain metaphysical positions accord better with given educational philosophies than do others. Scientific and sociological views lean toward neo-realism, progressive education has a root in idealism, the Deweyan exposition is associated with experimentalism, Catholic education is generally based on scholastic realism. A full exposition of any educational position would require an explication of the underlying conception of man's relation to nature or the cosmos, and of the assumed theory of knowledge. But there is no simple, direct connection between stated ontological or epistemological views and the educational consequences supposedly derived from them, as is frequently asserted in textbook treatments of educational philosophies. The metaphysical orientation may lend a certain emphasis to an educational program and surround it with a moral and spiritual aura. Often it serves as a defense of an educational policy—as an intellectual buttress rather than as a foundation.

One difficulty is that each metaphysical position has a variety of interpretations and its import can be understood only in the context of the views on ethics and politics of a particular philosopher. There are great differences between the realism of Aristotle and that of Thomas Aquinas, and between these views and that of modern neo-realism. The pragmatism of Charles S. Peirce carries the realistic imprint; William James's philosophy is predominantly idealistic, even subjectivistic; Dewey's experimentalism is, in part, realistic in accepting "things and events for what they are independently of thought" and idealistic in holding that the mind has power to change the world. The analysis of the metaphysical premises may help in penetrating into the secret places of the philosopher's heart and reveal the sub-

261

stratum of belief on which the structure of reason is erected. It may add breadth and insight. But it may also lead into a maze of ontological and epistemological subtleties that have no reference to the actual problems of education. The greatest defect of the metaphysical approach to education is that it diverts attention from the biological and social matrix of human behavior. It tends to conceal or to neglect the unavoidably political connections of educational philosophies.

An educational conception is an aspect of a philosophy of life, not of "philosophy" in the technical academic sense. At the heart of every philosophy of life is an ethical conception—an envisaged ideal of human relations leading out to a pattern of behavior. An ethical conception is always universal in outlook applying to man as man without regard to race or condition. But it is always framed within a particular cultural setting which gives it unique character. It implies relations among human beings as persons, but always within an institutional structure of organized community life, religious, philosophical, or political. A philosophy of life may include elements from all of these forms. But it must always have three aspects—a pattern of values, an affiliation with an organized community life, some conception, negative or positive, of the relation of the individual to the state. A philosophy designed to give unity and direction to educational endeavor cannot be derived from a theory of being, a theory of knowledge, or even from an abstract theory of values. Education always rests on a social philosophy, on ethical and political foundations.

Another consideration must be borne in mind. The philosophy of education deals with education, just as the philosophy of science deals with science. The issues discussed must be seen, in the first instance, in the context of the process of education itself. This means that the child and youth cannot be considered merely as the passive objects to whom a preconceived system is to be mechanically applied. The democratic ethical-political conception underlying the present exposition requires a central regard for pupil and student as developing persons who are ends in themselves. Education has three sides: a growing individual, a definite community, a pattern of ideals and values. The educational discussion must keep these three aspects constantly in mind. The task of the philosophy of education, then, is not to be conceived as a deductive application of an ethical-political system to educational problems, but the other way around. It is to be conceived as a discussion of major issues in education in the light of a proposed set of ethical and political principles.

The concept of "democracy" is generally assumed to be an essential element, if not the very basis of American educational policy. It satisfies admirably, this writer believes, the ethical-political criterion set forth as the prerequisite of any educational philosophy. However, there is a wide divergence of view among educators as to the meaning of democracy and as to the scope of its relevance in application to major educational issues. In the face of this lack of consensus, the term "democracy" has become largely ineffectual as a directive of educational policy. A brief comment on various positions will serve to focus attention on important issues in dispute.

Conflicting Views of Democracy

A conservative view which confines the definition of democracy to a system of government is represented in the sociological and institutional approach of the late Henry C. Morrison. He maintains with the emphasis of italics: *"Democracy means the participation of the folk or people in the conduct of Government and nothing else."*[1] He rejects the notion that democracy is a term of approval for anything in social organization that one may happen to like. He does not believe that everyone has a natural right to elect those by whom he is governed—for instance, that prisoners in a penitentiary should have the right to choose their wardens. Although he regards the electoral principle as essential, he seems to be diffident about universal suffrage: he implies that only "the competent and responsible" have a natural right to vote. He is by no means convinced that the "Voice of the People" is the "Voice of God"; he remarks drily, "At least it has never been revealed that it is, so far as I know." Democracy is valuable in the measure that it fulfills the ends of civil government—securing domestic tranquility, maintaining the common defense, guaranteeing civil liberties. If it does not succeed in achieving these ends, some other system is to be preferred. He does not, however, indicate what the alternative system might be.

This is a restricted conception but it recognizes the purposive character of democratic government and maintains the foundation principle of civil liberties. Very different in the approach and conclusion is a recent exposition of *Democratic Educational Theory* by Professor Ernest E. Bayles, who defines democracy in terms of a "process of governance" only.[2] He rejects the idea that democracy implies definite social ends. Although he avows strong sympathy with the

[1] Henry C. Morrison, *The Curriculum of the Common School* (Chicago, 1940), pp. 320-322.
[2] Ernest E. Bayles, *Democratic Educational Theory* (New York, 1960), pp. 147-165.

pragmatist line of thought as expressed in the writings of John Dewey and Boyd H. Bode, he regards as misleading their tendency to describe democracy broadly as "a way of life" rather than as purely a form of government. He proposes that democracy be defined as: "*equality of opportunity to participate in making group decisions and equality of obligation to abide by them*." He identifies democracy with absolute popular sovereignty, with the rule of the majority. To the minority he allows the right of protest and of continued advocacy of their views with the purpose of winning converts and becoming the majority.

Professor Bayles frankly recognizes that his position stands at variance with the principle of inalienable rights. But he considers this principle, "on which our nation supposedly was founded," an outworn seventeenth-century political doctrine which was never the basis for legislative enactment and is altogether outmoded today! Professor Bayles admits that "it is not easy at first to see how it could be democratic for a majority to hold a group disenfranchised because of their color or sex."[3] But he maintains that "this is exactly what one must accept" as a consequence of the principle of sovereignty. Even the cherished doctrine of the freedom of the press goes by the board: since it was enacted by the people, "it may democratically be modified or rescinded just as readily as it was originally established."[4] And unflinchingly facing up to the *sequitur* of his logic, Professor Bayles concludes that "we might democratically decide to eliminate democracy entirely is exactly what the definition means."

This *reductio ad absurdum* is accomplished by pressing hard two propositions: that democracy means the *absolute* sovereignty of the people and that it is a *process* of government wholly unrelated to the *ends* of government. Throughout Professor Bayles's discussion of democracy runs the idea: " . . . if a people is to be sovereign, then whatever decisions it makes must stand (until changed by it) regardless whether they are good or bad, or indifferent."[5] Applying to education, his two-fold principle of the supremacy of process and the sovereignty of the people, Professor Bayles attacks the view that the teacher and the school are justified in taking a definite position on controversial issues to support programs based on "a frame of reference" even when this is in accord with democratic principles and purposes. He believes "Advocacy is doubtless justified in democratic

---

[3] *Ibid.*, p. 162. [4] *Ibid.*, p. 168. [5] *Ibid.*, p. 257.

264

politics, but not in democratic education." He would have the teacher maintain strict neutrality in all controversial issues.

The idea of the supremacy of process aligns Professor Bayles, in one aspect of their teaching, with the pragmatist school of educational thought as delineated by John L. Childs in *American Pragmatism in Education*.[6] However, in total configuration, these pragmatist outlooks represent quite a different orientation. All the views described— which include those of John Dewey, William H. Kilpatrick, Boyd H. Bode, George S. Counts, and his own—acknowledge a commitment to democracy as a broad social principle implying ends as well as means, purposes as well as method. It is the emphasis on the social aspects of education that distinguishes them. Underlying their conceptions is a liberal-democratic policy of social change. But the devotion to the experimentalist doctrines of "the supremacy of method," "continuous inquiry," "no fixed ends," has led to a certain diffidence in making explicit what democracy means in terms of definite goals. The assertion, "On democracy we take our stand," affords no firm ground on which to maintain a position or from which one may advance, if no clear statement is proposed as to the content and substance of the democratic idea. The analysis of the interdependence and continuity of ends and means, a favorite theme in the experimentalist exposition, does not lead to the determination of the means necessary and appropriate for realizing concrete ends; it dissolves ends into processes so thoroughly that they become invisible.

Moreover, in most expositions of experimentalism, the emphasis is on the negative implications of critical intelligence—on depreciating the significance of tradition and convention rather than on focusing thought on the constructive tasks necessary for social reform. Professor Childs quotes the founder of pragmatism to the effect that: "The scientific spirit requires a man to be at all times ready to dump the whole carload of his beliefs the moment his experience is against them."[7] The other indispensable side of Charles S. Peirce's conception, namely, that the purpose of inquiry is to establish clear and stable beliefs, although sometimes mentioned, is, in practice, generally neglected in experimentalist educational theory. The pragmatist view as expressed by Professor Childs assumes that democracy "has its own standards, ideals and values." But when we come to examine what the standards are, we find a reiteration of the old slogans; e.g., "the

[6] (New York, 1956).   [7] *Ibid.*, p. 48.

reality of change," "the challenge of all forms of absolutism," "to prepare the rising generation to think for themselves."

During the "crisis decade" of the 1930s, a number of leaders in the progressive and experimentalist wings of educational thought called for the participation of the teaching profession in the reconstruction of the social order. Harold Rugg introduced his *Culture and Education in America* by a chapter entitled: "The Problem: Social Reconstruction through Educational Reconstruction."[8] George S. Counts urged the abandonment of the traditional policy of "philosophic neutrality" in education.[9] William H. Kilpatrick proposed that students be encouraged to envisage a defensible social program and that teachers should be made conscious of the part they could play in promoting desirable social changes.[10] John Dewey, writing in collaboration with John L. Childs, agreed that: "Education must itself assume an increasing responsibility for participation in projecting ideas of social change and taking part in their execution in order to be educative."[11] Despite the programmatic implications of the "reconstructionist" proposals, the experimentalists in the main, continued to rely on the methodology of critical intelligence and cooperative endeavor. There remained a reluctance to state what democracy implies in terms of specific criteria and clear social aims.

The need of a consensus on social policy as a basis for education has received recognition in a conception expounded under the title, *The Improvement of Practical Intelligence*.[12] The authors regard American education as defective because it has placed all the emphasis on studies which deal with things as they are—with factual knowledge, descriptive sciences, technical efficiency—and neglected the normative disciplines which direct attention to things as they ought to be

---

[8] Harold Rugg, *Culture and Education in America* (New York, 1931), chap. I.

[9] George S. Counts, *The American Road to Culture* (New York, 1930), pp. 173-194.

[10] William H. Kilpatrick, *Education and the Social Crisis* (New York, 1932), pp. 60ff.

[11] "The Underlying Philosophy of Education," in *The Educational Frontier*, William H. Kilpatrick, ed. (New York, 1933), p. 319.

[12] R. Bruce Raup in collaboration with George E. Axtelle, Kenneth D. Benne, and B. Othanel Smith (New York, 1950). Each of the members of the group has made independent contributions in the application of the general conception. Professor William O. Stanley has developed a line of thought sympathetic to the "practical intelligence" conception in *Educational and Social Integration*, (New York, 1953). Professor Raup has restated and elaborated his position in "The Community Criteria in Judgmental Practice" in *Studies in Philosophy and Education*, I, no. 1 (Sept. 1960).

if a democratic way of life is to be realized. In line with this distinction, they propose a two-method conception of judgment as against the Deweyan experimentalist view of a unitary method for scientific and moral inquiry.

The essential aspect of the proposal is embodied in the concept of "the uncoerced community of persuasion." This has two sides. It points to the indispensability of a "communion of belief, feeling, purpose and direction" as a basis for responsible judgments on the part of the individual. The second aspect is the contention that, in the light of the breakdown of community orientation in contemporary life, the central task of education ought to be directed toward "the reconstruction of common persuasions as the basis of common actions." To avoid doctrinaire solutions and ideological rigidity, educational values and social objectives must be worked out through discussions and continuously subjected to revision. Decisions for action should be taken in the light of underlying traditions of the people and in the perspective of long-range purposes.

The conception of "practical intelligence" represents a constructive departure from the neutralist attitude of the individual-centered type of progressive education. In its urging ethical commitment, its recognition of the need of a substratum of common beliefs, its emphasis on decision-making and on participation in social action, it includes elements that are indispensable for any sound educational theory. The distinction between judgment in science and judgment in morals is to the point. It has significant implications for subject-matter organization and curriculum construction. However, "the practical intelligence" proposal fails to state the ethical assumptions and to suggest the social policies that might serve as directives of the educational program.

Like the experimentalists, the exponents of the "community of persuasion" represent a socially progressive group who are committed to the principles of racial equality and civil liberties, favor economic planning and the welfare state, support the movement toward international organization. But like the experimentalists also, they refrain from explicit enunciation of their beliefs and their ideas of institutional change. No framework of ethical principles is set forth: the "community of consent" apparently is the final determinant of decisions and policies. The difficulties of the conception are compounded by vagueness in the definition of the community whose beliefs are to be taken as a basis. Is it the local community, is it "we the people of the United States," is it the transcendental "community of mankind"? Is the reconstructed "community of persuasion" to be worked out by teachers and students, by the educational profession as a whole, by the public at large?

In his forthright version of "reconstructionism," Professor Theodore Brameld presented a more definite proposal.[13] In his view, the vast transformation in technology, the developing democratic idea of equality, the growth of international interdependence, demands a radical change in the social order. He supports the idea of a "planned society" and urges that educational agencies unite with political forces in bringing about the needed reconstruction of the economic system. He suggests the concept of "defensible partiality," the right and the obligation of the teacher to take a stand on controversial issues when commitment to a definite position is warranted after discussion of alternatives. He advocates "group consensus" as the method of reaching dependable conclusions. However, he has not clearly formulated the assumptions of his socio-economic policy and the failure to state a position on major issues has left his conception ambiguous, after all. His use of the word "blueprint" as the basis for the planned society has opened his conception to misunderstanding.[14]

As long as there remains such a wide divergence of views with reference to the implications of democracy on the part of its avowed exponents we can hardly hope that educational philosophy will offer the needed guidance for school policy. Any program proposed must be in accord with the substratum of value-beliefs of the American community considered as a developing corporate entity. But before we can expect to achieve a public consensus, the educators must themselves come to some agreement on social fundamentals. If democracy is to serve significantly as the underlying philosophy of American education, its meaning must be defined in terms of principles and goals, its implications for major issues in social policy must be indicated. As in parliamentary debate, a definite proposal must be made if discussion is to be fruitful and result in conclusion.

Democracy and Social Policy

The outline of "democratic principles and social program" presented in the previous chapter is proposed as a framework for educa-

[13] Theodore Brameld, *Ends and Means in Education: A Midcentury Appraisal* (New York, 1950).

[14] In the revised version of *Ends and Means*, entitled *Education for the Emerging Era* (New York, 1961) Professor Brameld lays less emphasis on the term "reconstructionism." Nevertheless, he reaffirms the main theses of the earlier work.

tional policy. It is conceived as comprising a group of "controlling ideas" to direct the formation of attitudes and, particularly, to guide the organization of the social studies curriculum. The following restatement points up aspects of special significance in the light of the current discussion.

Ethical-Political Fundamentals:

Democracy is not a method of government only: it is an ethical concept correlated with a constitutionally-based political system. The cornerstone of the ethical-political democratic structure is the principle of "inalienable rights" as broadly defined in the Bill of Rights embodied in the Constitution.

The Bill of Rights may be modified—expanded or restricted in certain respects in the course of application—by amendment or by judicial interpretation. But in its major categories, it cannot be abolished by the government in power, by the legislature, or even by "the people."

In the light of the contemporary situation, it is necessary to emphasize particularly: the principle of racial equality, the legitimacy of voluntary organization for educational purposes, the right of the criticism of government policies and of nonviolent demonstration for the redress of grievances.

Government Instrumentalities:

Participation of the people in government is an essential of the democratic political system. But the functions of the people are limited by the powers assigned to the executive and legislative branches of government. "Majority rule" does not imply the absolute "sovereignty of the people"; it is conditioned by the Bill of Rights as interpreted by law.

Although the relative competences of the several branches of government are subject to modification in practice, the separation of powers and the independence of the judiciary remain indispensable principles of the democratic constitution.

In the light of the interdependent character of contemporary social life, the principles of democracy require the enlargement of the scope of the federal government in the economic area, in the protection of civil liberties, and in the promotion of health, education, and general welfare.

Economic Aspects and Social Welfare:

The implementation of the ethical-political principles of democracy is conditioned by economic factors and by the type of economic organization supported by the state. A mixed economy of public and

269

private enterprise is necessary for promoting the national welfare, to guard against encroachment on individual freedom, and to make possible the maintenance of voluntary associations.

The major responsibility for control and direction of the economic system must rest on the federal government. Its functions include two major aspects: (1) the coordination of the economic effort and the stimulation of its growth; (2) the assurance of an adequate system of health, education, and social services.

The eradication of poverty and the improvement of the standard of life for low-income groups is the crucial task. This demands a many-sided effort in health and social services, in education and vocational training, in provision of employment opportunities, in slum clearance and urban renewal. The effort must be directed toward a rehabilitation and normalization of family life.

The attack on poverty is an integral part of the battle for the equalization of the status of the Negroes and other underprivileged ethnic groups. The elimination of discriminatory practices is, of course, indispensable. But at bottom, the inferior status of the underprivileged groups is rooted in deprivation.

The International Order:

The establishment of an effective international government by a system of collective security is a long-range, many-sided task. Support of the United Nations, promotion of its Universal Declaration of Human Rights, elaboration of a code of international law, are factors to be developed. But prerequisite to realization of an international order is the reduction of the gross disparity in the standard of living among the nations of the world.

The more affluent nations of the West can make fruitful contributions toward raising the standard of living in the economically backward countries. They can provide financial aid, render technical assistance, offer advice in health and educational problems. However, in most instances, any decisive improvement necessitates drastic social and political changes which can be carried through only by national leaders.

The type of political and economic organization adopted by the nations emerging from the backward conditions and exploitive rule will include democratic welfare-states, national-socialist and communistic regimes. The recognition of the legitimacy of diverse forms of political-economic organization is of the first importance in advancing international peace in the ensuing period of development.

Our faith in the ultimate victory of democracy, when the basic material needs of men shall have been fulfilled, rests on its rationality and its concordance with human aspirations.

INDOCTRINATION AND ACADEMIC FREEDOM

The foregoing assumptions are submitted as defensible in the light of democratic principles and current trends of thought. They are definite enough to provide guidance and broad enough to permit flexibility in the strategy of implementation. If these principles and proposed policies are not acceptable, the contention is that educational philosophy must propose other assumptions on the main areas under discussion. The burden of the argument is that the educator, as a teacher in the classroom and as a member of the educational profession, must have a defensible position on the meaning of democracy. He must understand its significance as a pattern of values and as a system of government; he must have a considered judgment of its import for the main lines of social policy today. What is denied is the desirability, even the morality, of "philosophic neutrality" in education.

The denial of the position of educational neutralism raises the issues of indoctrination and of academic freedom. The former has to do with the relationship of the teacher to his students; the latter is concerned with the relationship of a member of a profession to the official authorities of the community that supports the schools. Correlated with this is the right of the teacher to engage in political activities outside the school and to participate in social-action programs. Some clarification of these issues is in order.

In progressivist educational conceptions, which make critical thinking a major objective, any expression of a definite position on the part of the teacher is deprecated as indoctrination, as "imposition from above." Meticulous exponents of the view question whether the teacher is justified in trying to induce favorable attitudes towards the values of which they themselves are warm advocates, e.g., tolerance of diverse opinions and the encouragement of intellectual curiosity. They are apprehensive lest in the attempt to affect attitudes, teachers "may come close to the kind of indoctrination found in totalitarian nations."[15] The development of attitudes, it is held, ought to be a matter of "the individual conscience." This view, which equates positive teaching of generally accepted democratic values with the coercive practices of fascism and communism, moves, it would seem, in that dark night of perception in which all cows are black. It represents an abdication of the primary responsibility of the school in transmitting knowledge and in nurturing ideals.

In its literal meaning of instruction, indoctrination has a necessary

[15] Paul L. Dressel and Lewis B. Mayhew, *General Education, Exploration in Evaluation,* American Council on Education (Washington, 1954), p. 240.

and legitimate function in imparting the warranted knowledge in any area of study and in inculcating the principles on which the democratic society is founded. The question of indoctrination in the reprehensible sense arises only in controversial issues when one side is presented and other conceptions and proposals are suppressed, inadequately discussed, or, as is too often the case, treated in deprecatory fashion. Indoctrination of the objectional kind may be present when the underlying assumptions are not brought to light and the objectives only vaguely indicated, as in the exhortations to build "a better society." It may result from enthusiastic advocacy of a humanitarian cause without regard to the actual problems of achievement. Critical thinking as applied to social questions means the evaluation of concrete measures in relation to stated puposes.

Explicit avowal of position is conducive to clarity and cogency of discussion. It challenges thought and evokes the expression of opposing or alternative proposals. It is essential for intellectual integrity. The impediment to good teaching in the social studies today does not lie in the undue influence of teachers on their students. It arises out of the pressures from the public relations which deter from straightforward, open-minded treatment of controversial issues and invite the calculations of expediency on the part of teachers and students.

The teacher is not always called upon to express an opinion. When there is a wide range of agreement, no serious problem arises, and there are points of policy on which no warranted conclusions can be drawn. The best thing to do in some cases is to present the views of equally competent authorities. But there are crucial occasions when a failure to take a stand is tantamount to a culpable evasion of the issue. The aims and content of the teaching is not to be confused with the method of teaching. The latter should depend on various factors: the level of the instruction, the preparation of the students, the size of the classes, the time allowed, the character of the issues.

At the appropriate age, student participation in the learning process—through discussion groups, projects, committee reports, term papers—should be encouraged as valuable auxiliaries to formal instruction. But it is to be borne in mind that discussions praised as the "coordinated thinking of the cooperative group" may lead to psychological manipulation by the teacher. When a statement of position gives consideration to data, when conclusions are supported by evidence and alternative views carefully analyzed, formal presentation in the lecture hall or classroom may challenge thought more effectively and involve far less indoctrination of the undesirable kind than the exchange of off-the-cuff opinions by unprepared students. Discussion

272

itself cannot produce warranted judgments on social issues; the student as well as the instructor must have knowledge and be capable of defending his conclusions by evidence.

The academic freedom of the teacher reflects the twofold function of the school as custodian of advanced knowledge and of the community's heritage of ideal values. As an agency of society, the school necessarily ministers to the needs and serves the purposes of the existing community. But it should not merely mirror prevailing conceptions and customary practice. The function of the school is to raise the level of knowledge, to promote excellent achievement, to establish standards of conduct, and to enhance the quality of life. Essential to the school's purpose is the nurturing of the ideals which leaders of thought proclaim but which are compromised in the existing social life. Although the school is always subject to a particular community, the cultural heritage it transmits and the values it upholds represent a wider community than that which supports it. The school's purpose is to broaden the sense of community, to see the local community in the frame of the national community as a whole, and to view the national community in the perspective of the regional civilization and the world community.

The principle of academic freedom confers no right on the teacher to conduct propaganda for a private conviction even when it is motivated by the claims of conscience. Advocacy of social reform in an emotional manner is not a function of the school. The work of the school implies the use of knowledge and of critical intelligence in the promotion of ethical ends. Academic freedom is not identical with freedom of speech in the market place which has no restrictions as long as it causes no public disturbance and poses no clear and present danger to the nation. Academic freedom is not a civil right protected by the Constitution. What is termed "acedemic freedom" should be called "academic responsibility." It is akin to the autonomy enjoyed by the professions of law and medicine. It means intellectual integrity in service of the common good: the duty of the teacher to follow the argument based on competent knowledge wherever it leads, despite interference on the part of any outside body—the church, the state, or even the opinion of the majority.

The teacher is warranted in maintaining a position which deviates from either the official or the popular view when he supports a program in line with professional opinion, when he promotes the national welfare as against class and local interests, when he is guided by an ethical principle despite the pressures of social expediency. Even before antidiscrimination measures became the law of the land, the

273

teacher was under a moral obligation to advocate equality for the Negro. Before the federal government turned the searchlight on the evils of poverty, the teacher would have been right in urging the principle of "a general equality of condition," which Alexis de Tocqueville in his classic study declared to be the pivotal factor in the development of American democracy. Despite the opposition by chauvinistic groups who may, in certain districts, dominate the local Board of Education, the school would be properly exercising academic responsibility when it emphasized the dependence of the state of the nation on the state of the world and urged support of the United Nations. It is a corollary of the position presented in the foregoing chapters that the educator would be warranted, in accord with political realism, to promote rapprochment with Communist states wherever practicable.

The school should be ahead of conventional public opinion in social policy but its proposals must be related to the existing institutional structure. Education should face the future but it is concerned with the next generation, not with the prophetic end of days. The positions taken by the teacher may represent a minority view but they must have some support in responsible community opinion—in proposals made by leaders in special fields, by professional associations, by social welfare organizations. The advocacy of social programs which are drawn from the recesses of an individual's conscience or which merely reiterate the slogans of a party cannot be defended on the basis of the right of academic freedom.

What is said above about the responsibilities of academic freedom as implying competent knowledge and an intellectual approach in the discussion of controversial issues refers to the role of the teacher in the classroom and in the lecture hall when he acts in his professional capacity. In extramural activities, the teacher plays the part of citizen, and the broader principles of free speech and of civil liberties should apply to him as to all other citizens. Activities which further civil liberties and other social causes do not need the defense of academic freedom; they are justifiable on the basis of their merits and supported by the constitutional guarantees of free speech and the right of peaceable assembly. It goes without saying that modes of demonstration and proprieties of expression ought to be such as comport with membership in the academic fraternity. What applies to the professors should apply equally to the students. When regulations of the university are violated or its reputation affected, judgment and disciplinary action should be in the hands of the faculty and not of the administrative authorities who are likely to be under the pressure of outside political forces.

The lack of discrimination between academic freedom and freedom of thought, speech, and action in the public forum was gravely evident during the period of the "cold war," when professors and teachers were harassed and hounded for engaging in activities—for participation in peace meetings and opposition to the use of the hydrogen bomb, for indicating sympathy for Russia as well as for suspected membership in the Communist Party. Several different questions got entangled in the melée of argument. May a professor expound communism when he believes in it sincerely? Is it legitimate to teach *about* Marxism?—sympathetically or deliberately to counteract it? Should a teacher be automatically dismissed for membership in the Communist Party?

One view supported by eminent representatives of the academic world maintained "that to deny a sincere Communist opportunity to expound views held by millions of human beings is as wrong as to deny a sincere Democrat the same right."[16] The justification is hardly cogent: sincerity and mass following are not sufficient criteria for teaching anything in a school; the analogy of democracy with communism is out of balance. Democracy is not merely one of a number of opinions which a teacher is free to accept or to reject. It is the principle on which our political, social, and educational institutions are erected. Within its framework there is a wide latitude for differences of interpretation and of strategy in application; nevertheless it involves a commitment to a definite system of beliefs with which the major principles of communism are incompatible. The school has as great a responsibility for positive teaching of democratic principles as it has for nurturing loyalty to the American state.

The analysis which justifies the teaching of Marxism as a "heresy" comes nearer the mark. But it concedes too much. A heresy implies a deviation on points of doctrine within a framework of belief basically accepted; the heresy is in the interest of defending the essentials of a belief as against conventional formulations. There are aspects of the thought of Karl Marx that are compatible with democracy. But as a whole, Marxism as a political philosophy turns its back on the fundamentals of democracy: on inalienable rights, the parliamentary system, the division of powers. It is not a heretical form of democracy but an alternative, opposing system.

[16] Howard Mumford Jones, ed., *Primer of Intellectual Freedom* (Cambridge, Mass., 1949), xiii.

275

In the period of ferment after World War II, James B. Conant wrote: "The first requirement for maintaining a healthy attitude in our universities in these days is to get the discussion of modern Marxism out into the open."[17] However, to start out with the purpose of studying it "in order to defeat it" is likely to lead to a misconception of the task. The question of acceptance or rejection is not the issue: in the premises, communism as a political doctrine is antagonistic to the Western democratic system. Communism should be studied objectively in its several aspects, e.g., as a philosophy of historical development, as an economic theory, as a revolutionary doctrine. It is important to take cognizance of its criticism of capitalism and of liberalism and to analyze why—although it is repugnant to our own philosophy of life and conception of government—it has become a moving force for change in many parts of the world. It needs to be studied in light of its several interpretations and of the modifications it has undergone in the course of implementation under varying conditions.

The question of affiliation with Communist organizations is no longer a critical issue. Disillusion with the course of events in the U.S.S.R. under Stalin reduced communist sympathizers to a negligible remnant. With the passing of McCarthyism, loyalty oaths became, for the most part, dead letters, although they remained as offensive, demeaning rituals. Belatedly, in January 1967, the Supreme Court voided the New York Feinberg Law and other statutes directed against alleged Communist Party membership. The decision defended the right of the state to bar subversives from employment as public teachers or as civil servants, but it held that the existing legislation—because of the vague, sweeping, "blunderbuss" character—constituted an infringement of fundamental rights as well as a threat to academic freedom. In particular, it ruled that membership in the Communist Party was ground for dismissal only when there was proof that the accused subscribed to unlawful methods and intended to use them.

There is some consolation in the explicit denial of the "guilt-by-association" principle. But the Supreme Court decision has come after irreparable harm has been done. Hundreds of teachers have been unjustly dismissed or forced "to terminate their services" for alleged membership in the Communist Party or for refusal to inform on others. Condemnation by insinuation has imposed a burden of restraint and repression that still bears heavily on freedom of teaching

[17] James B. Conant, *Education in a Divided World* (Cambridge, Mass., 1948), p. 174.

in the United States. The "guilt-by-association" accustation has left a residue of "bad faith" and an odor of disingenuousness. There may have been a few "conspirators" among the active members of the Communist Party. But most of those who followed the "communist line"—in any case a tiny minority—naively believed that communism was an advanced form of social democracy. They were guilty not of disloyalty but of ignorance.

The failure to give adequate and objective consideration to the study of communism has been a serious deficiency in American education. Today the critical study of Marxism and communism is more important than ever. It is necessary to recognize that the conjuncture of events in backward countries may make some form of communism the likely, perhaps the unavoidable, alternative to a continuance of the status quo of exploitation and suppression. A critical understanding of communism in its diverse manifestations should disabuse us of the illusion that we ought to suppress it in all instances throughout the world or that we can do so effectively in alliance with military dictatorships. While safeguarding our own security and assisting the advance toward democracy, with financial aid, technical assistance, and educational endeavors, we should, at the same time, aim to promote cooperation with Communist nations for mutual benefit and in the interests of world peace. Informed opinion on foreign affairs has favored such a policy for more than a decade; in recent years, our government has explicitly accepted it as far as it applies to Eastern Europe. It is essential that education play a part in the liquidation of what remains of "the crusade against communism" which still acts as a drag on the normalization of international relations and, indirectly but seriously, hampers social progress on the domestic front.

THE PUBLIC, THE PRIVATE, AND THE RELIGIOUS SCHOOL

The Significance of the Private School

There are developments in the contemporary situation which warrant a modification in the American liberal's attitude of diffidence toward private schools and of unfriendly toleration of parochial schools. An important factor is the realization of the significance of identification with a community symbolizing a distinctive system of values. The problem is affected by the growth of metropolitan cities; as a result, the public schools in many places have lost their character as representative of village, small town, or neighborhood communities. The church-state issue which dominated the educational discussion in the nineteenth century is still important. But it is no longer the overriding question, in part because the sharpness of sectarian conflict has been blunted, in part because it has been overshadowed by social and political problems. The questions of desegregation, of the impact of poverty on education, of the achievement of international comity, cut across denominational lines. The problem of national unity and of the implications of democracy have to be seen in a new perspective.

On the main principle there is no disagreement: the free public school system open to all who wish to attend without regard to race, religion, or economic condition is an essential of a democratic society. The maintenance and further development of the public school system has economic and administrative, as well as educational aspects. It requires the elimination of segregation by race and by poverty; it involves the upgrading of rural schools; it means the equalization of opportunities for higher education. It demands a great increase of federal support for education and a large measure of direction, coordination, and planning by the Department of Health, Education and Welfare in Washington. Moreover, the unification of the public school system requires the elaboration of a national policy on basic educational issues.

In the folklore of educational liberalism, the public schools are idealistically described as the creation of the American people and controlled by them through their government.[18] They are portrayed as devoted to freedom and to the promotion of democratic values. The fact is that the schools are controlled by local boards of education juridically responsible to the individual states. It is obvious that local control does not necessarily lead to freedom of inquiry or to equality of opportunity or to the elimination of racial discrimination. Some of the Catholic schools of the South have been more liberal in the matter of desegregation than the state schools. In many instances throughout the country the restriction placed on the freedom of discussion in political questions is due to popular influence. The persistence of denominational religious teaching in public schools is also generally due to the support of the lay community as well as to the pressure of church officials.

The "secularist" conception which would make scientific method, freedom of thought, and humanist democratic values the basis of public education is not, as claimed, in all actuality the expression of

[18] R. Freeman Butts, "Public Funds for Parochial Schools? No." *Teachers College Record*, LXII (Oct. 1960).

the views of the American people taken as a whole.[19] It represents rather, a high-minded interpretation of American civilization by an intellectual group who constitute a minority. Even among the educators who affirm democracy as a directing principle there are, as noted above, serious divergencies which prevent the formulation of a consensus to serve as foundation for the American school system. In the light of the many differences in conditions, outlooks, and stages of development, it is inevitable that the schools supported by the individual states, subject as they are to local control, should represent compromises, restraints, and reservations in the discussion of both political and religious issues. Some schools may have reached a large degree of freedom of political discussion and may have eliminated formal religious teaching and practices. But even this does not mean that they are actuated by a positive philosophy of moral and spiritual values.

It is essential to work for a better embodiment of democratic educational principles in the American public schools. However, before we can hope for such a realization, democracy must have a wider acceptance among the people at large in its ethical as well as in its political meaning and in its embodiment in the principle of "a general equality of condition." In the light of the actualities, it is necessary to recognize the legitimacy and the value of the nonstate schools as supplementary to the public schools. The humanist as well as the religionist needs the private school for a consistent and integrated education. Private schools can, of course, be worse than the public schools, but, if conducted by universities, special educational organizations, or humanist societies, they have also the possibility of being better, not only from the pedagogical but from the democratic point of view as well.

The Public School and Religion

The further development of the public schools requires the elimination of all vestiges of the teaching of formal religious views. In the past, the retention of broad religious concepts and elements of worship were not felt to be sectarian in communities which were predominantly Protestant. The Christian religious tradition was part of the cultural background. Unitarians and Deists as well as doctrinarily-minded members of the church could subscribe to the conventional

[19] John L. Childs, "The Spiritual Values of the Secular Public School," in *The Public Schools and Spiritual Values*, John S. Brubacher, ed. (New York, 1944), pp. 58-80.

GOOD STUFF!

formulations. Even "atheists" (whose quarrel with the theists was often, as Samuel Butler wrote in his Note Book, "whether God should be called God or shall have some other name") recognized the moral elements in the traditional religious teachings. Today, with the growth of urban centers whose populations reflect diversities of cultural background as well as divergences of belief, the watered-down non-denominational prayers which supposedly represent a common denominator of religious belief can hardly be of genuine significance.

Today the vestiges of religious teaching and of worship that remain in the public schools may no longer be cause for sectarian divisiveness. But religious practice in school may induce a sense of alienation on the part of those who do not inwardly share the conventional beliefs or for whom the language in which the religious ideas are expressed does not inspire any religious feeling. For the orthodox members of a religious group, the neutral prayer is no prayer at all. Conscientious humanists do not wish to render lip service to phraseology which does not reflect their personal convictions. Moreover, religious practice connotes the affirmation of an allegiance to a community as well as an assertion of belief. The problem does not lie only in the literal meaning of the words of a prayer which may be inoffensive, but in the associations which it arouses and the sense of community which it supports or weakens.

When religious worship does not attest to a community of shared values nor betokens "a service of the heart," it becomes a negative element in character development. For those whose families practice no religious observance at home, a worship in the public school is likely to be a matter of outer conformity, if not of hypocrisy. Further, the emphasis on prayer as the essence of religion tends to divert the focus of attention from its ethical aspect. The worst feature is the use of the state to support religion. The sincere religionist as well as the humanist has reason to demand the elimination of religious worship and religious teaching from the public schools.

There is a growing recognition on the part of American educators that the exclusion of religious teaching from the public schools requires some compensatory consideration of religion in the educational program. The Educational Policy Commission of the N.E.A., though opposed to any and all forms of religious teaching in public schools, has taken the position that: "the public school can teach objectively *about* religion without advocating or teaching any religious creed."[20]

[20] *Moral and Spiritual Values in the Public Schools*, Educational Policies Commission of the National Education Association (Washington, 1951), p. 77.

It argues that the controversial nature of religious beliefs should not bar teaching about religion any more than difference of views need lead to the exclusion of the study of economic and social issues in public schools. However, the analogy limps: economics and politics claim no transcendental sanction and are subject to critical inquiry. A study of religion in the same way that we study social questions would reveal the errors and evils as well as its contribution to the ethical life. It might result in a rejection of the religion in which the student was born or in skepticism toward all the traditional religious faiths. A study of the part that religion plays in cultural development would undoubtedly be valuable; it would serve to counteract the negative attitude suggested by the apotheosis of science as the sole source of wisdom. But this is quite different from what is intended by the inclusion of religious teaching and worship in the public schools.

The nature of the problem of the relation of the public school to religion is not disclosed when religion is conceived as concerned primarily with furnishing a sanction for generally accepted moral values, e.g., respect for personality, sympathy and brotherhood, toleration of differences, and devotion to freedom, which the Educational Policy Commission enumerates. In the context of the educational discussion, the term "religion" does not imply general abstract values but commitment to a definite, integrated, institutionalized pattern of beliefs and attitudes, and a system of worship and ritual practice. Further— and without this an essential element is missing—the beliefs, the attitudes, and the forms of worship and ritual practice are aspects of the life of families which are identified with communities, bound to some extent, at least, by ethnic ties as well as by membership in historically-developed churches or religious groups.

Religious education of genuine character is concerned not only—in some instances not primarily—with the inculcation of special doctrines but with nurturing loyalty to a family tradition and to a historical community which is the custodian of a cultural heritage. The function of a religious education is to transmit the inheritance of the religious community which includes a particular literature and unique music, a patrimony of symbols and concepts, a treasury of insights and of rituals which minister to psychological adjustment and to spiritual understanding. A primary function of religious education is to maintain the stability and the integrity of family life—to support its virtues of patience and charity, of compassion and mutual responsibility which family life necessitates. The moral and spiritual values of religious education are nurtured by leading to involvement in, and

281

identification with, the religious community more than by direct teaching of doctrine and creed.

Seen in the community context, there is a greater degree of validity in the "release-time" program introduced in the last score of years. In accordance with this plan, children whose parents so wish are allowed to leave school an hour or two earlier on one day a week so that they may receive religious instruction under the chosen denominational auspices. The sanction of the plan by the Supreme Court (in the Zorach case of 1952) indicated a modified interpretation of the "wall of separation" principle which had generally been conceived by liberal educators as meaning avoidance of cooperation with religious bodies in the educational endeavor.

Justice William O. Douglas, who delivered the majority opinion, confirmed a previous decision enunciated in the McCollum case (1952) to the effect that no religious instruction could be given on the public premises. But with reference to religious education outside of the public schools he declared: "When the state encourages religious instruction or cooperates with religious authorities by adjusting the schedule of public events to sectarian needs, it follows the best of our tradition." The decision was in harmony with the opinion of the Supreme Court in the famous Oregon case (1925) which unanimously confirmed the right of parents to send their children to parochial schools on the ground that: "the child is not the mere creature of the state; those who nurture him and direct his destiny have the right, coupled with the high duty to recognize and prepare him for additional obligations."

The Religious All-Day School

The release-time program has significance in giving recognition to the validity of cooperation between the school authorities and religious communities. However, it cannot be regarded as an adequate solution for those who are committed to a definitive religious philosophy of life. The dualism between the education of the public school and the religious outlook and the community affiliation of the child's family still remains a serious problem. The issue is not merely a question of the constitutional right of the parent to choose the religious school, a right that has been fully confirmed by the Supreme Court in the Oregon case. An educational question is involved. As the Court stated: "the fundamental theory of liberty upon which all governments in this union repose excludes any general power of the State to standardize its children by forcing them to accept instruction from public teachers only." The maintenance of nonstate schools is not only a right of parents, it is a necessity for the preservation of democratic society. Of all the important differences between the totalitarian and the democratic societies, the freedom to conduct educational as well as religious institutions is the most significant. It is an indispensable aspect of the denial of the supremacy of the state in cultural and spiritual matters.

This discussion is intended to suggest a broadening of the concept "public school" to include nonprofit educational institutions conducted by organizations which fulfill the state requirements as outlined by the Supreme Court decision in the Oregon case. These conditions include the right of the state to regulate and inspect all schools, to set minimum standards in physical facilities and in curriculum, to ensure adequate instruction in subjects prerequisite to good citizenship and "that nothing be taught which is manifestly inimicable to the public welfare." It is imperative that the state public school remain the major type and that the effort of American educators be directed toward an ever better realization of the democratic values. But it is desirable to encourage—rather than deprecate as liberals have hitherto done—the development of schools consciously devoted to a clear philosophy of life of both the humanist and the religionist type.

Such a pluralistic conception of the public school system should lead to an enrichment and deepening of the American culture as well as to a better integrated education for the individual. It should also lead to greater national unity with reference to social fundamentals. With the lessening of the conflict on doctrinal issues and with the greater emphasis on the communal significance of the religious groupings, there is for the humanist, the neutral public school, and the school affiliated with a religious community the opportunity of building a common foundation on the basis of the principles of democracy. We cannot unite on the basis of metaphysics or of religious doctrine, but we can work hand in hand for the defense of civil liberties, for the absolute elimination of racial inequalities, for an eradication of poverty, for the promotion of international organization, and the creation of an order of lasting peace.[21]

---

[21] The complex question of financial aid to church-affiliated schools is beyond the purview of the present statement but a brief comment may be added to indicate the general position implied.

The tenor of the argument leads to a favorable consideration of the extension of auxiliary services that can be brought under the "child benefit" theory, e.g., bus transportation, free state-approved text books, scholarships for further study in secular institutions. Shared-time plans and education centers as proposed in

THE COMPETENCE AND LIMITATIONS OF SCHOOL EDUCATION

The discussion of the educational problem is bedeviled by a failure to distinguish between the broad meaning of the word "education," as inclusive of all the social and cultural influences that are brought to bear on the growing individual on the one hand, and the part that the school plays or possibly could play in the development of knowledge and character and mind and morals on the other. There are general ideas and common principles in any given society that should govern the work of the school as well as the activities of the home and of the political life. But much writing on education suffers from vagueness, even from irrelevance, because of the failure to bear in mind the distinctive—and, at the same time, the necessarily limited—competence of the school. This lack of discrimination, moreover, is compounded when broad definitions are proposed without regard to the grade of the school, whether elementary, secondary or university, and within each category to the needs of different groups of students.

Education and the School

In its inclusive sense, education refers to any influence which produces a more or less permanent change in the knowledge or abilities, in the disposition or mental attitudes, in the understanding or the conduct of any person—child, youth, or adult. The profoundest educational effects are achieved incidentally in the course of just living. Since we grow up in a definite social environment, our casual as well as our habitual experiences are inlaid with cultural ingredients, with elements of knowledge, with forms of behavior, with notions of right and wrong. Our activities are structured by the regularities of family and professional life, and by the necessities of the economic organi-

recent legislation are constructive in that they bring parochial and public-school children into contact with each other.

On the other hand, the theory of "multiple establishment"—in accordance with which financial aid could be given to church-affiliated schools for general support provided only that all denominations share equally—should be rejected as undesirable as well as inconsistent with the basic principles of the separation of church and state.

The "wall of separation" concept could be liberally interpreted to allow assistance to church-affiliated schools for instruction in neutral subjects, e.g., the three R's and the natural sciences, provided secular standards and state supervision could be assured. But the time has not yet come for such a radical change of policy. The doctrines, the rituals, and attitudes that generally attend the teaching in church-affiliated schools still give them a predominently sectarian character.

zation; they are infused with community purposes and conditioned by the restraints of law. The predominance of rural and urban background, the character of the mores and folk ways, the style of housing and the modes of transportation all have their formative influences. Newspapers and periodical literature, television and radio, the kind of recreation and entertainment, are powerful molders of opinion, attitudes, and tastes. It is because these many factors are continuously at work, that educational theory must be concerned with the sociological background of the school, with the nature of the institutional structure, and with the economic and political forces that condition and direct the life of society.

The influences are so diverse and complex that no single institution or group of sociological factors can be accounted as having a decisive educational effect on the individual. Nevertheless, it may be said that the home plays the major role, since it is through the family that the social and moral influences are brought to bear on the child and youth during the formative years. Its influences are exerted over long periods in the life of the individual; the relations among its members are intimate, involving moral problems and mutual responsibilities. The family affects the destiny of the person: social status, racial descent, sometimes ethnic background, condition the neighborhood where the child grows up. The family decides the religious affiliation if any and determines the type of schooling and the probable career. The strengthening and enhancement of family life is the main lever for raising the general standard of cultural and of personal morality. Its influence, whether for good or evil, depends on the support that it receives from the social environment and from the community at large.

The educational processes accompanying institutional life are very effective, but conditioned as they are by numerous factors their quality is mixed. They keep society operating as a going concern on a conventional level rather than contributing to its improvement. The family, charged with bringing up the young and often supported by a religious association, has a more direct educational function, particularly in personality development. Nevertheless, the educational responsibility is a by-product of the marital relation; the measure in which the family can fulfill its educational responsibilities will depend on the character and ability of the parents and will be conditioned by economic factors and social status.

In contrast with all the other institutional agencies, the school is distinctive in that it is set up deliberately for the purposes of education. It comes into being when the family cannot adequately fulfill the tasks of the transmission of the cultural heritage and of training for a vocation. Broadly speaking, the school has the function of insuring the acquisition of the skills and the knowledge, of the understanding and the values, that would not be adequately secured through the incidental and institutional experiences of everyday life. Moreover, the school is always the creation of a community—of like-minded families, of a religious association, or, as most often in contemporary times, of a political body.

The school's function is in the realm of the normative and the ideal —its purpose is to raise standards of achievement, to promote excellence, to enrich the mind, to broaden the consciousness. The first schools in Western civilization were for novitiates and apprentices— for the training of priests, scribes, and artisans. This, the vocational and professional aspect of education, remains, obviously, an indispensable aspect of deliberate training in the contemporary world which is wholly dependent on specialized workers of various grades in many fields. More generally recognized is the part that the school plays in the transmission and enhancement of the social heritage—in leading the young to acquire the basic language and mathematical skills, in imparting knowledge of literature and art, the sciences, and the social studies.

Another and distinct area of school concern relates to the broadening of the social consciousness. This includes the cultivation of the beliefs, the aims, and the aspirations that the individual must have in common with others in order to become a true member of the community. Although the school is always a creation of a definite society, the heritage of ideas and ideals represent a wider community than the one that supports it. In its pursuit of both knowledge and values, the work of the school is pervaded by universals. Enlarging the community sense implies identification with the human community in the dimension of time as well as of space. It means viewing the national life within the frame of an international order. It also signifies seeing the present in a dynamic historical perspective, in the light of its relation to the past, on the one hand, and of its relation to the emerging era, on the other.

The Scope and Competence of the School

To what extent the school can accomplish its purposes in raising cultural standards, bringing social practice in line with professed ideals, and broadening the sense of identity with the human community, will depend on many factors. In some measure, this will be determined by the aim and the curriculum of the school itself, by the training and the attitudes of the teaching personnel. But, to a far greater degree, what the school can do will be conditioned by the level of culture in the community at large, by the prevailing economic and political conceptions and conditions, by the social background of the school population. There is a reciprocal action between school and society, no doubt, but the influences emanating from existing society—the conventional beliefs, the sociological structure, the actual conditions—are immeasurably great as compared with the effect that the school can have on the nature of society or on the character of the individual.

On individuals, the effect of school education may be incalculably great—affording economic opportunities, raising social status, opening up new worlds for activity and new vistas of understanding. But the measure of its influence can be judged only in relation to the many-sided social conditions and forces. The formation of individual personality is affected by native tendencies interacting with structured institutions; it is conditioned by entrenched habits and internalized value-judgments; it may be subject to emotional disturbances and poorly adjusted behavioral patterns. The widespread need of psychotherapy by high school students and college graduates is indicative of the inadequacy of the rational and verbal types of learning characteristic of school work as far as personality development is concerned. Seen from the social standpoint, the education of the school is indispensable for the conservation of the social heritage and the preservation of community life. But its influence is stronger when it supports the existing society than when it attempts to promote progressive trends. The school cannot of itself "build a new social order," although it can retard or facilitate social reform.

These comments do not imply that the school should abandon its role in moral development and social betterment. On the contrary, the intention is to emphasize the importance of conscious effort directed toward these ends. Recognition of the limitations of formal education points to the need of *defining* as well as of *affirming* values and ends. It strengthens the view that the educator ought to take a stand on controversial issues when this is warranted by an ethical aim supported by relevant knowledge. What is denied is that school education—however indispensable and significant, whether conceived of as transmission of the cultural heritage, as cultivation of the intellectual virtues, or even as the Deweyan "institution of intelligent action"—can by itself be a primary factor in character development or in social reconstruction.

We must divest ourselves of the illusion that we can counteract the disintegrating effect of modern technological organization by "more and better education," or that we can avoid world chaos and catastrophe, as the late Alexander Meiklejohn believed, "only as we succeed in devising better learning and better teaching."[22] Such statements, motivated by liberal humanitarian sentiment, are intended to strengthen the role of the school in promoting the good society. But they are likely to issue in utopian proposals and to neglect the realistic consideration of the concrete economic and social reforms necessary for the improvement of the life of the community and prerequisite to the effective operation of the schools.

What the school needs to do as well as what it can do will depend on the character of the society that maintains it—on the level of its cultural development and on the nature of its political organization. There are common elements in all civilizations in a similar stage of evolution, and Western education inherits a body of literature and a fund of ideas of universal significance. But it does not follow that "education should be everywhere the same," and that local variations are merely administrative adjustment of details.[23] Such wholesale assertions detract from the valid part of Robert M. Hutchins' thesis that a core of general education is essential for all, that continuity with the past is to be preserved, that the classics should have a central place in the course of studies. It is true that biologically man has a common nature, but we live in time and place. However broad its purpose and universal its outlook, the school has a regional location, is heir to a definite form of cultural life and national tradition, can exist only under the protection of a firm political constitution. These particularities are not applications of abstract "universal truths." They are of the very stuff of social and cultural life and must be taken into account in the initial formulation of the educational principles.

The scope and functions of the school are unavoidably modified and enlarged as civilization grows more complex. In contemporary society, extraordinary burdens are placed upon the school. The great increase in scientific knowledge and techniques makes a large degree of specialization inevitable. The diminution of the influence of family life makes it necessary, especially for a considerable part of the population in the large cities, for the school to assume custodial functions

[22] Alexander Meiklejohn, *Education Between Two Worlds* (New York, 1942), p. ix.

[23] Robert M. Hutchins, *The Higher Learning in America* (New Haven, 1936), p. 66.

and to be concerned with psychological guidance. Conditioning all problems is the principle of universal education and along with this the need of preparation for citizenship in a democratic society. In the face of the actualities that confront us, it does not solve anything to insist, as Hutchins does, "that the heart of any course of study designed for the whole people will be, if education is rightly understood, the same at any time, in any place, under any political, social or economic conditions." There is a vast difference between maintaining that education for all must have a *common* foundation—must be based on a common body of knowledge and a common heritage of values—and saying that it should be the *same* for all at all times.

The Common Curriculum

Education must be viewed as a national problem; it must be related to the diverse needs of children and youth, as persons and as future citizens, as human beings who will have to earn a living and make a life for themselves within the framework of American society. Simultaneously, it must be seen in the perspective of the national community, of the task of maintaining the institutional and political structure and of advancing its welfare. Education has a primary function to perform in transmitting "the arts and sciences and the moral attitudes which make up the fabric of civilization," as Henry C. Morrison has said.[24] This includes the contribution of the present generation as well as the heritage of the past. It has no less a duty of preparing the young to understand the needs and problems of the emerging era and to participate in its development.

Despite much conflict in current educational theory, there is in practice a large measure of agreement among American educators with reference to the major areas of the course of study on the elementary level. All programs include the thorough teaching of the "fundamental processes," of reading, writing, and arithmetic. American history and English literature, nature study and science, have long been a part of the standard curricula. Social studies in some form, as preparation for citizenship and as a means of understanding contemporary life, have been widely introduced in the better schools. There is a general recognition of the value of extra-curricular activities, of the need of recreational facilities, of the importance of conserving physical and mental health. There are serious differences of opinion with reference to methods of teaching, to subject-matter content, to

[24] Morrison, *op. cit.*, p. 1.

ideas and attitudes. The divergent approaches of the "progressive" and the "essentialist" which will be discussed in the next chapter have important implications for school policy. But it is well to bear in mind that the differences need to be viewed in the light of the basic agreements.

In the secondary school and college, there are wider differences of view exemplified sharply in the conflict between those who follow the "education-for-life-adjustment" thesis and those who uphold the concept of liberal education for its own sake. Both views agree on the importance of general education for all, but the conception of its nature greatly differs: the most important difference of view revolves around the question of the place of vocational and professional education at the secondary and early college level. The divergent positions represent variations in philosophic and social outlooks, in conceptions of the learning process and of psychological development. But they also reflect selective interest in different bodies of the school clientele. The advocates of "education-for-life-adjustment" have in mind, first of all, the students for whom high school is terminal education; the defenders of liberal education are concerned with those who are preparing to go to college and with the higher learning in college and the university.

We cannot hope with the seventeenth century pansophist John Amos Comenius, "to teach all things to all men." The individual child or youth, his potentialities and limitations, must at some stage in the educational career be taken into account. At the elementary level it is still possible to consider most children as falling into a fairly homogeneous group. Attention to individual differences need not greatly affect the general course of study. However, even at the earlier stages, the gifted and the retarded, the latter particularly, require special consideration not only with reference to the quantity and rapidity of learning but from the viewpoint of their whole education in the broader sense of personal and social adjustment. At the secondary level, economic and social background, as well as native abilities, affect the length of the educational career and the choice of a vocation or profession. It is not possible to develop an educational program on the basis of child nature and needs apart from the cultural heritage and the social system in which he lives. But, on the other hand, it is even less defensible to seek it in a metaphysical realm of being and truth without regard to the economic and political character of the society in which the child or youth lives and without regard to their potentialities and probable social destiny.

Every valid educational theory has three interrelated areas of reference. The first is the accumulated body of culture—the fund of skills and knowledge which the community possesses and the heritage of the values and ideals which it affirms. A permanent problem of the school, as Paul Monroe wrote in concluding his classic *History of Education*, "is to transmit to each succeeding generation the elements of culture and institutional life that have been found to be of value in the past, with that additional increment of culture which the existing generation has succeeded in working out for itself . . ."[25] A second indispensable aspect is present-day society, as a political and economic structure. This implies a concern with contemporary social problems in the domestic life and in international affairs with a view to maintaining and advancing the democratic social order in the light of the national ideal and of the emerging international order. The third element is the individual child, youth, college student—who must be considered not only in the capacity of a learner of the school subject material, but as a potential member of society and as a personality developing in his own right. These three points of reference—the cultural heritage, the social-political structure, the individual as a person—will be kept in mind in the discussion of the educational issues in the next chapter.

[25] Paul Monroe, *A Text Book in the History of Education* (New York, 1912), p. 758.

Since past and future are part of the same time-span, interest in the past and interest in the future are interconnected . . . Good historians, I suspect, whether they think about it or not, have the future in their bones. Besides the question: Why? the historian also asks the question: Whither? EDWARD HALLETT CARR

9.

Controversial
Educational Issues

I**N THIS** concluding chapter, comment will be made on a number of
outstanding issues of the educative process from the perspective
of the foregoing analysis. The following have been selected for discussion as having a general public, as well as a professional, interest:
(1) the critique of progressive education; (2) intellect, intelligence
and the ability to think; (3) liberal education: false claims and
humanist values. A final section will discuss the need of reorientation
in the teaching of the philosophy of education.

Decline of Leadership

For a period of a half century before World War II, the Progressive
movement occupied a position of leadership in American educational thought. It was espoused by outstanding educators, acclaimed
by social reformers, received enthusiastically by liberals. It reached
a height of influence during the 1920s before the onset of the depression at the end of the decade. In recent years, its popularity as an
educational idea has sharply declined. Progressive education was
attacked for a variety of reasons—pedagogical and philosophical,
social and political. It was blamed for the poor work of the American
schools generally, for the laxity of discipline and morals, for radical
political tendencies. Not a little of the criticism consisted of virulent
diatribes by lay organizations against caricatured versions of pro-

gressivist educational conceptions and practices. But some of the objections emanated from informed professional circles and reflected valid differences of opinion on psychological issues and on educational values.

During the decade of the 1930s, the professional criticism of Progressive education became crystallized in a number of counter positions: essentialism, perennialism, and reconstructionism. The positions are sometimes referred to as educational philosophies or theories. Perhaps these designations are too ambitious. The views might more properly be called "ideologies": they represent programmatic formulations rather than full-dress presentations which give balanced consideration to the various aspects of the educational process. Moreover, there are important differences within each category and the views crisscross and overlap in some aspects. Nevertheless, the three points of view represent distinct perspectives. A brief delineation of each one indicates major issues in the present-day discussion of education and provides an introduction to an evaluation of the progressivist position.

The essentialists generally reflect the views of schoolmen concerned with elementary and secondary education. They represent a conservationist orientation: although they recognize the necessity of gradual evolutionary social change, they emphasize the "transmission of the cultural heritage" and the "reproduction of the social type" as the main function of the school. Commending the pedagogical contributions made by Progressive education, they nevertheless regard the newer educational methods unsatisfactory substitutes for the "systematic and sequential learning" necessary for the mastery of the organized subject-matter of the schools. A particular complaint is directed against the increased emphasis on the social studies at the expense of the classical and mathematical studies. Although essentialists agree that training for citizenship and the consideration of controversial issues are necessary elements in the education for democracy, they do not favor extensive discussion of social problems; they decry using the schools as a means of promoting ambitious plans for social reform. William C. Bagley, an outstanding leader who coined the term "essentialism," directed the severest attack against the Progressivist's loose use of the word "freedom," which he believed engendered a disrespect for tradition and authority, stimulated a crude individualism and "enthroned a glorified hedonism."[1]

---

[1] For a summary of William C. Bagley's views, and for references, see my *Education Faces the Future* (New York, 1943), pp. 186-192.

The essentialist point of view is culturally and sociologically oriented. A more extreme and less knowledgeable criticism of Progressive education came from academic circles concerned with the upper levels of education, the secondary schools and the liberal arts colleges. This view, aptly termed "perennialism" by Professor Brameld, carries a rationalist scholastic signature. It places the "permanent studies"—mathematics and the classics—at the center of the curriculum. In the perennialist expositions, Progressive education is generally represented in its poorest forms as the extreme example of the retreat from learning which, it is alleged, is widely characteristic of American schools. Progressive education is often confused with "education-for-life-adjustment" to which this view is likewise opposed. Regarding the "cultivation of the intellect" as its primary purpose, the perennialist condemns adaptation to social needs as an educational aim. He would minimize or eliminate vocational and professional training from the high school and college program of studies as not consistent with genuine education "rightly understood."

Philosophically, the perennialist is opposed to pragmatism, which he believes is responsible for the "four cults" of modernism—skepticism, presentism, scientism, anti-intellectualism. He favors those forms of traditional philosophy which extol universal principles, emphasize the common element of human nature, and assert that truth is unchangeable. Although the perennialist agrees with the Deweyan concern for the cultivation of the ability to think, his conception of reason as pure intellect sets him worlds apart from the experimentalist who conceives of mind in terms of "intelligent action." Needless to say, the perennialist rejects the central idea of progressivism, namely, that education should be based on individual experience. In general, he evinces little interest in child psychology and pedagogy. Viewing the educational scene from the high and wide perspective of universal, unchangeable truths, the perennialist loses sight, apparently, of the fact that education has to do with unique individuals, with growing children and developing youth.

Contrasted with the essentialist and perennialist position was the newly developed "reconstructionist" tendency which advocated the active participation of the school and of the educational profession in furthering economic and social reform.[2] The proponents of the

[2] In my *Preface to an Educational Philosophy* (New York, 1940) I used the term "reconstructionist" (p. 32) to characterize the point of view put forward by members of the Dewey school of thought and others in *The Educational Frontier*, edited by W. H. Kilpatrick (New York, 1933) and in the *Social Frontier*, a publication sponsored by the John Dewey Society. I took the word "recon-

297

reconstructionist conception were largely drawn from the ranks of progressive education, especially in its Deweyan socially-oriented manifestation. Although sympathetic to the newer pedagogical conceptions, they were critical of the exclusively child-centered emphasis of the prevailing progressivist tendency, of its lack of direction, and of its neutralist social policy. Taking their stand on the indispensability of inquiry and discussion directed toward contemporary affairs, they nevertheless deviated from the nonindoctrination thesis to the extent of pointing up the need of a democratic frame of reference, of basic assumptions and of social goals toward which to aim. Although diffident toward formulation of specific objectives of social reform, it was evident that the reconstructionists were thinking in terms of social planning, of furthering a gradualist evolution toward a welfare state, and of promoting international organization. Despite occasional exuberant expression, e.g., the challenging, "Dare the school build a new social order?" and the ambitious, "blueprint for the future," the actual proposals were moderate, consistently in accord with a democratic outlook. Nevertheless, the reconstructionists were suspected of "leftist" leanings. With the onset of the cold war and the spread of "McCarthyism" the development of the reconstructionist effort was checked. It had, moreover, caused inner divisions and became a factor in weakening Progressive education as an organized movement.

The Character of Progressive Education

The charges leveled against Progressive education as responsible for the allegedly poor work of the public schools and the laxity of discipline in American society have little justification. Progressive education has been used as a scapegoat for general social deficiencies—for lack of adequate support and for over-crowded classes; and for the many difficulties in large urban communities resulting from the heterogeneity of the school population and from deprived cultural and economic conditions. There have, no doubt, been misapplication of such clichés as "teach the child and not the subject," "real life experiences," "activity for further activity," that have been detrimental. The newer pedagogical devices of "project," "unit-of-

struction" from Dewey's statement in *Democracy and Education*, (p. 386) "The reconstruction of philosophy, of education, and of social ideals and methods, thus go (*sic*) hand in hand." A comparison of my "reconstructionist" position—if so it may be called—with other versions is presented by V. T. Thayer, in *Formative Ideas in American Education* (New York, 1965), pp. 323-328.

work," "core curriculum," involve complex procedures and require special conditions for their effective operation—small classes, additional equipment, and particularly more broadly-educated teachers. The introduction of the newer educational concepts in the average public school in the large cities may have led in some instances to poorer results than could be achieved by the more limited formal types of curriculum organization. There are, of course, plenty of bad examples of the conventional types of school work.

Where the conditions are appropriate, there is reason to believe that the Progressive pedagogical conceptions have much to add to the traditional educational practices. One important study has indicated that the graduates of schools using the newer educational procedures do as well and better in the fundamental language and mathematical skills and in the academic subjects generally as those who attend equally good schools using the more formal methods.[3] In addition, they reveal a richer experience in the arts and in music, reflect a broader understanding of the sciences, evince a stronger interest in public affairs. And they tend to exhibit a greater independence of thought. No equally comprehensive study has been made which challenges these conclusions. Moreover, the fact is that private schools and schools in suburban areas which command adequate financial support have incorporated progressivist educational ideas in curriculum construction and in the methodology of teaching. The enormous improvement in American education during the last half century cannot be attributed exclusively to progressivism. But it has undoubtedly been a major factor, as knowledgeable critics agree, in the advances that have been made.

Progressive education includes the main features, characteristic of all modern education: emphasis on the study of literature as against acquisition of book-learning, enrichment of the curriculum to include music and art, concern with the all-round cultivation of the personality of the individual, physical and emotional as well as intellectual. To these elements derived from Renaissance humanism, the modern curriculum has added science and the social studies during the last century. Another aspect of modern educational thought, both essentialist and progressivist, is a concern with psychology and pedagogy, with the problem of child growth and youth development. In the United States, modern education has emphasized the common school as a prerequisite of democracy and as a means of affording each individual an equal opportunity to develop his capacities to the full. This

[3] Wilfred M. Aiken, *The Story of the Eight-Year Study* (New York, 1942).

299

has had the result of conceiving of high school as continuous with the elementary school, as "education for all American youth."

In one sense, Progressive education was an emphatic—perhaps a one-sided—expression of the fruitful modern educational tendencies. But this is not the essence of the matter, and the analogy with other forms of modern education fails to reveal its distinctive inner character. As Lawrence A. Cremin has pointed out: "Actually, progressive education began as part of a vast humanitarian effort to apply the promise of American life . . . to the puzzling new urban-industrial civilization that came into being during the latter half of the nineteenth century. The word *progressive* provides the clue to what it really was: the educational phase of American Progressivism writ large."[4] In its distinctive character, the Progressive education movement was an aspect of the nineteenth century liberal-democratic protest against staticism and formalism, against authoritarianism, and also against "rugged individualism." At its heart, lay a great respect for the learner as a developing person.

The End of an Era

Progressive education embodied a rich historical experience. It retained a deposit from the village community life in early New England—a respect for the concerns of the common man, a recognition of the need and the fruitfulness of manual work, a high evaluation of cooperation, a faith in practical intelligence. It was imbued with the spirit of the open frontier, with the impulse toward informality and nonconformity, and with a belief that the future would be better than the past. It absorbed some of the naturalistic transcendentalism of New England humanism. It represented a reaction against the harsh competitiveness and the predatory acquisition of the advancing industrialist capitalism. Echoes from Emerson, from Thoreau, from Walt Whitman, are audible in its teachings. With the influence arising out of the American experience, there mingled an impingement of German idealism which conceived of education in terms of self-realization. Pervading the progressive educational movement, furthermore, was a humanist distillation of the Christian faith in the child—of the attitude which expressed itself in Biblical phrases: "And a little child shall lead them" and "Suffer little children to come unto me, for theirs is the Kingdom of Heaven." In Dewey's early writings, this idealistic religious theme is evident: in concluding *The Child and Curriculum*, he wrote, "The case is of Child."

---

[4] *The Transformation of the School* (New York, 1961), vii.

The condemnation of Progressive education on the part of the laity and of sections of the educational profession is not based on studies of what actually goes on in schools following progressivist conceptions. Nor is it founded on careful reading of the philosophic writings that support progressive educational theory. Its source lies rather in the impression of the social attitudes and the philosophic tendencies which progressive education is supposed to foster. Some of the disapprobation is due to superficial presentation on the part of devotees as well as to misunderstanding or distortion on the part of critics. But a core of opposition comes from genuine disagreement with the moral sentiments and humanitarian attitudes which Progressive education symbolizes.

There were from the beginning contrasting elements in the formation of the American character. Alongside of the tolerance represented by Jefferson was the heritage of a narrow Calvinism. From the first, as Vernon Louis Parrington has shown, there was an interweaving of the idealism of the Puritan with the shrewd practicalism of the Yankee trader. Although American social progressivism, with its emphasis on moral and intellectual freedom, its sympathetic attitude toward childhood and its broad humanitarian impulse, was a genuine expression of American life, it was always a minority movement. We tend to overestimate the degree to which it was shared by the American public at large, either in the rural communities or in the small towns throughout the country.

With the steady encroachment of industrial capitalism upon the family-based agrarian economy during the nineteenth century, the pristine virtues of cooperation, independence of mind, and idealistic spirit gave way to the mores of competition, conformity, and a secularist practicalism. Although the old ideals remained to influence social thought and education, in fact individual success and mechanical efficiency became "controlling ideas," as George S. Counts has pointed out.[5]

Today, with the expansion of the age of technology and under the threat of totalitarian forces, the pressures for social conformity and mechanical efficiency are more powerful than ever before. The need is for men who can attend automated machinery, for well-trained technicians and research workers, and for experts in the theoretical and applied sciences. It is not surprising that in our mechanized society Progressive education, with its emphasis on the personality as

[5] George S. Counts, *The American Road to Culture* (New York, 1930), pp. 3-10.

a whole and with its sentiment of goodwill to all men, should not appeal to the engineers concerned with surpassing the Russians in atomic competition and in the conquest of space. Less understandable is the attack from the defenders of liberal education, from whom there might have been expected an appreciation of the humane elements of progressive education.

Progressive educational theory was undergoing reform in the period before the second world war as a result of criticism from within its own ranks. Its loss of popularity in the last score of years was not the result of its imperfections, whatever these may have been. Its decline reflects a change in the climate of opinion: it is an aspect of the contemporary retreat from social liberalism which was in the ascendant in the earlier part of the twentieth century. It is not Progressive education that has failed; rather it is our civilization that has failed Progressive education, as it has dampened our hopes in the promise of American life.

The Revision of Progressive Education

Positive appreciation of the contribution of Progressive education to the practice and the spirit of the school does not imply that it represented a well-balanced educational theory. As new crusading movements tend to do, Progressive educational thought, in its popular presentations at least, emphasized what it was against—blind submission to authority, harsh discipline, verbal learning, routinized habits. In *Experience and Education*, published toward the end of the decade of the 1930s, Dewey criticized Progressive education for developing its principles negatively rather than positively. He pointed out that the abandonment of traditional conceptions of authority, of discipline, and of curriculum organization provides no solutions; it merely presents us with difficult problems of constructive reformulation. He joined with critics of Progressive education in affirming the necessity of direction on the part of adults, of parents and of teachers, and in recognizing that concern with the present and the future demands a respect for the contribution of the past. However, the continued insistence that the educational program must be based on a philosophy of experience in the sense of the actual "life experience of an individual," and the one-sided devotion to the experimentalist "method of intelligence" as applicable to all areas of thought opens the moderated Deweyan position to criticisms not unlike those which may properly be leveled against the progressivist tendencies generally. The following summary of comments applies in some respects to the carefully elaborated experimentalist version of Progressive education as well as to the earlier, romantic, child-centered types.

Some General Considerations

Like all modern liberal educational conceptions, Progressive education overestimates the part that the school acting on the individual can play in the development of the person and in the improvement of the social order. With all its seeming emphasis on the social dimension, it retains an individual-centered psychological orientation. It seems to believe that by changing the mind of the individual we can directly effect changes in society. Thus it draws attention away from the positive part that institutions play in character formation and in the realization of selfhood. Moreover, it tends to an underestimation of the difficulties attending social reform which always involves political and economic factors.

Progressive education lays all the stress on process, on method, on continuous change, and neglects the equally important aspects of form, of aims, of stability. The concepts, "education as growth" and "the reconstruction of experience" have important meanings in specific contexts. But Dewey's broad assertion—that "the educational process has no end beyond itself; it is its own end"—is too vague an idea to be of much service in the work of the school. It becomes misleading when it is used, as by some progressives, to turn attention away from the content of teaching, as when it is said that the aims of education "are lines of growth, not subject-matter to be mastered." Growth of the personality is a *by-product* or *result* of many activities and experiences of the individual; it is not a single aim or group of aims that can be directly achieved.

The experimentalist view with its biological analogies conceives of growth in terms of interaction between the individual and the social environment. This is an advance over the concept of "self-realization" drawn from German idealism which suggests a purely inner development. But in the usual interpretation, the failure to make clear that the social environment is institutionally structured tends to leave out of account that all adaptation requires a conforming to existing conditions as well as a degree of freedom in individual adjustment. Personal development implies the imposition of restraint and the acceptance of discipline. In final analysis, the element of "external control" cannot be eliminated from the human situation. If the authority of persons is rejected, some other form of authority— of the law, of a rational conception, of a commitment to a pattern of values—must be accepted. If we are to contend against the status quo

303

of the existing institutional structure, we must have an internalized system of ideals to support and direct us.

Pedagogical Observations

Progressive education deprecated the traditional subject-matter organization. It advocated relating the acquisition of knowledge to the interests and experiences of the learner and to the needs and problems of present-day society. This conception of building the school curriculum around immediate concerns, despite its value, is likely to lead to superficiality and looseness. It is necessary in all but the lowest grades of the elementary school to reassert the centrality of the organized subject-matter curriculum in school work. The particular form of organization and the method of presentation will vary with different groups of students. The newer pedagogical conceptions have value within the subject-matter organization and as auxiliary methods of teaching. But the school work must nevertheless be based on a definite curriculum of subject-matter, of clear objectives, and planned activities.

This means that the content of education is prior to the methodology of education. The character of the methods of teaching is important not only from the point of view of their efficiency: it has significant side-effects from the point of view of future learning and of attitudes. It is from the standpoint of method that interests, needs, and experiences must be taken into consideration. Nevertheless, what we want to teach, what knowledge is to be imparted, what aims are to be achieved, what ideals are to be encouraged, must serve as the directives.

The development of the will and the ability "to think for oneself" was a primary objective of Progressive education, particularly emphasized by the exponents of experimentalism. Paradoxically, it is in reference to the problem of effective thinking that educational progressivism is most open to question. It is qualified by an undercurrent of belief that emancipation from reliance on tradition and "external authority" would of itself result in critical independent thinking. Although the experimentalist concept of the nature of the thinking process is superior to the faculty psychology which lies at the basis of the concept of "cultivation of the intellect," it is, itself, too broad a conception to be of much significance in making valid judgments.

INTELLECT, INTELLIGENCE, AND ABILITY TO THINK

That the school has a special function in developing rational attitudes, in training the mind, in developing the ability to think, is an essential idea in the Western educational tradition. The several types of educational theory—the essentialist and the progressivist, the perennialist and the reconstructionist—all acclaim the cultivation of the ability to think as a major purpose of the school. However, the rub is that there is no agreement in current discussion as to what constitutes effective thinking and how it is to be promoted. What the experimentalist calls scientific intelligence, the scholastic-minded perennialist condemns as anti-intellectualism.

There is still among some of the exponents of liberal education vestiges of the doctrine of "formal discipline," the idea that the mind's power can be greatly increased by the study of certain subjects which demand exact reasoning. There are variations as to the number of subjects which are supposed to have superior efficacy in mental training. Robert M. Hutchins follows a time-honored view when he asserted that: "Correctness in thinking may be more directly and impressively taught through mathematics than in any other way."[6] He implies, moreover, that the correctness in thinking derived from mathematical study is significant "as a means to practical wisdom" as well as essential for theoretical knowledge. A broader point of view includes the natural sciences along with mathematics and the social studies on the assumption that: "The crucial fact is that man's basic mental processes are essentially the same, whatever the specific matter upon which they are focused."[7] Arthur Bestor, who maintains that, "Liberal education is training in thinking," holds that the unity of the intellectual life requires the ability "to command several, not merely one, of the distinctive ways of thinking that are central in the modern world."[8] However, he believes that the truly distinctive ways of thinking are limited in number, and that there is a hierarchy of importance among them.

Common sense is rightly skeptical of the idea that academic study makes a man proficient in the practical wisdom required in the many-sided affairs of private and public life. Psychological investigation supports common sense and goes further: there is a general agreement that the "transfer of training" from one field of study to another is dependent on the presence of "identical elements," of common factors or similar aspects in the different situations. Furthermore, what

[6] Robert M. Hutchins, *The Higher Learning in America* (New Haven, 1936), p. 84.

[7] Theodore M. Greene and others, *Liberal Education Reexamined* (New York, 1943), p. 48.

[8] Arthur Bestor, *Educational Wastelands* (Urbana, 1953), p. 162.

305

is meant by the terms "common," "similar," or "identical" is relative to the context; even a small difference in the situation may vitiate the transfer or make it negative. Concentrated training in one area may develop tendencies which are quite inappropriate for others. Discernment of underlying principles may increase the amount of transfer in related areas; habits of work developed in the course of study of one subject may undoubtedly be generally useful.

Nevertheless, the conclusion of common sense and of psychological investigation is that the power of thinking in any area as well as the knowledge of the area depends on the study of, and experience with, that particular area, be it mathematics, the natural sciences, the social studies, or the humanities. Creative work in any scientific field requires a rich knowledge of related fields of knowledge; this, too, indicates the weakness of the disciplinary concept which ascribes to any one science, or to any group of sciences, unique potency in the development of the general ability to think. It should be obvious that the ability to think effectively is dependent on a thorough knowledge of the facts and of the principles in the area of concern.

The experimentalist concept of "critical intelligence" rejects the faculty psychology which lies at the basis of the doctrine of formal discipline. It follows modern educational psychology in denying the existence of separate potentialities in the mind, specialized to reason, to remember, to observe, and to judge—each of which can be trained by practice as a muscle can be developed by exercise. There are no general mental powers that can operate in a vacuum without regard to particular subject matters. As Dewey forcefully puts it: "There is no such thing as an ability to see or hear or remember in general; there is only the ability to see or hear or remember *something*."[9] And certainly there is no power to think in general. All types of judgment —intellectual, aesthetic, moral—represent complex processes of selective and coordinated response to definite situations.

Dewey agrees with the advocates of a broad liberal education that specialized training is likely to be narrowing. If training in the ability to think, in the sense of making judgments, is to have a general effect, it must cover a variety of fields. Above all, it should concern itself with grasping meanings and relationships. Here enters the characteristic Deweyan theme, that understanding—grasping relationships—implies discerning the social connections of subjects of study. He anticipates the current interest in relating the sciences to the humanities and to the social studies. He declares: "Isolation of subject

9 John Dewey, *Democracy and Education* (New York, 1916), p. 76.

matter from a social context is the chief obstruction in current practice to securing a general training of the mind. Literature, art, religion, when thus disassociated, are just as narrowing as the technical things which the professional upholders of general education strenuously oppose."[10]

Insofar as the "method of intelligence" defines thinking in terms of problem-solving, it has the potential merit of focusing attention on vital issues in social life. If constructively carried out in its intended empirical spirit, it could be utilized to bring relevant knowledge to bear in the formulation of policies designed to realize clearly-conceived democratic ends. Unfortunately, in much of educational literature, the concept of "critical intelligence" has been used as a stick by which to beat "traditionalism" and "authoritarianism." It has been employed, as in some progressivist conceptions, to minimize the significance of organized subject-matter, to deprecate adherence to definite moral principles, and to overestimate the part that the individual plays in the making of rational judgments.

In recent years, there has been an effort to counteract the one-sided emphasis. It is recognized that "hypotheses for future action must take careful account of past experience." It is conceded that scientific method sanctions many of the traditional moral and pedagogical canons. The idea of consensus arising out of the interchange of opinion is stressed. The conventional school, it is said, is liable to criticism not because it is based on organized subject-matter, but because it fails to relate knowledge to present-day problems. But these qualifications do not affect the faith in critical intelligence as the center of emphasis in the educative process and as the major instrument of human progress. The negative bias toward the traditional and the stable persists; teachers are advised to stress the contingent, changing nature of reality. The need of structure in social organization and in the formation of personality are left out of account. "The democratic faith," it is said, "is simply faith in intelligence; it does not attach itself to any particular form or organization."[11] The experimentalist method loses its character as an instrument of analysis of specific problems; it becomes a panacea for all the world's troubles.

There is no royal road to the ability to think, no supreme method equally applicable to all the sciences, no single mode of understanding appropriate alike for the natural sciences and the social studies, for

[10] *Ibid.*, p. 79.
[11] Robert E. Mason, *Educational Ideals in American Society* (Boston, 1960), p. 232.

the arts and for morals. Both conceptions, the one that identifies mind with intellect and the other which conceives it as a process of intelligent action, flagrantly oversimplify what is involved in the ability to think effectively. Hence they grossly exaggerate what the school can do to cultivate it. The ability to think cannot be separated from the subject-matter of thought. It depends on an abundance of relevant knowledge, on the correctness of the assumptions made, on the clarity with which the ends of the act of thinking are envisaged. The school is effective in developing the ability to think in the sciences and in the professions of medicine, law, and engineering because of the availability in these areas of bodies of dependable knowledge, agreement on basic principles, definite purposes to be achieved, and awareness of the sort of problems that may be encountered and of the possible solutions. Even in these areas, where much is known, the school can only make a beginning in imparting knowledge and in technical training. To achieve an adequate degree of proficiency, either in the theoretical sciences or in the professions, requires years of study and of practice.

We are accustomed to regard the ability to think effectively as the result of a process that goes on in the individual's mind, a natural ability raised to a higher coefficient by the training it has received. There are, of course, variations in the ability to think which are caused by differences in mental capacities and their development through education. But, in a sense, rationality exists not in the individual mind but in the organization of knowledge, in the assumptions and logical relations embodied in patterns of thought, in the techniques and instrumentalities used in dealing with any problem, theoretical and practical.

However gifted, the research worker would not discover anything of significance if he had not mastered his field of study—its knowledge, principles, methodologies. His knowledge would be of little avail if there were no laboratories and other facilities for experimentation, if there were no communities of scientists with whom he could discuss his conceptions and who would force him to verify his conclusions by accepted methods of proof and testing. The mere existence of scientific instrumentalities, of institutional facilities, of a body of knowledge and of a corps of workers, does not guarantee their effective use. Thinking requires the intervention of an individual mind, to interpret, to exercise judgment, to suggest solutions in concrete cases. But without agreement on assumptions, without organized knowledge, without the discipline of logic, there could be thinking only in the sense of musings, of metaphysical speculation, of communion with the Absolute, but not in the sense of effective rational thought or of intelligent action.

Likewise, whether we use the term reason or intelligence, thinking in the moral sphere is not merely a matter of applying mental processes. One cannot "draw out" virtues from the inner nature of man any more than one can spin scientific truth out of one's head. The use of "intelligence in action" is also a meaningless phrase without a clear definition of ends, knowledgeable proposals for solutions, a reckoning with the problems of implementation. The application of thought to ethics requires the prior acceptance of some communally-approved assumptions and some agreed-upon solutions derived from man's heritage of experience. It implies commitment to a system of values; but the commendation of the importance of values-in-general leads nowhere.

It is essential to state the ends we wish to promote not in terms of "final values" only, but in terms of concrete proximate aims. The emphasis on "ultimate ends" is too often a way of evading the necessity of dealing with the immediate actual problems of life. And finally—this is indispensable to the whole matter—the ethical conception must be seen in terms of, and have reference to, a system of social, economic, and political organization. There is always the necessity of adapting principles to particular situations; the individual has a range of freedom in choice of style of life within the given pattern of values and forms of social organization. Where traditionally-sanctioned mores and practices become unsuitable in the light of reason, it is necessary to establish new conceptions and institutions communally-accepted. But purely individual morality is as impossible as an individually-conceived science.

Bearing in mind the complex nature of the ethical problem, its psychological conditioning, its involvement in sociological organization, it should be obvious that the school can do little to improve morals or reform society through the cultivation of reason in the abstract either through fostering intellectual virtue or through stimulation of critical intelligence. Neither method produces a clear pattern of values adequately related to the formation of personality or to social organization. Where the school stands for a definite conception of life and supports a code of conduct, it can, working together with other social forces, have a significant enhancing effect. Even so, the possible influence of school education has to be estimated in the light of the beliefs and practices in the family, the usages in business life, the conventions of social life, and the character of public opinion.

When the school adopts the neutralist policy of a "value-free education" and avoids taking a position on controversial issues, one can hardly expect that it should have any positive influence at all on the moral and social life. No doubt, the inspiration of a teacher, the insight gained in the course of instruction in the humanities, the knowledge and attitudes developed in the social studies, may have significant influence on sensitive students in individual instances. But in view of the diverse pressures in contemporary life, the disorientations resulting from emotional stress, the widely conflicting conceptions, American education today, particularly in our mammoth high schools and multi-universities—when not offset by a heritage of beliefs and values derived from a stable family life or from an attachment to a religious community—is more likely to have a disintegrating effect than to lead to a rational personal philosophy or to contribute to an enlighted social policy.

In the face of the harassing dilemmas in personal adjustment and in social organization, the confident reliance on formal discipline and the optimistic appeal to critical intelligence seem inadequate to the point of irrelevance. These methodological advices provide no guide to the perplexed, offer no help to the emotionally disturbed, give no counsel to direct social policy. They turn attention away from the tasks of dealing realistically with the actual problems that beset us. In their generality and vagueness they weaken rather than strengthen our ability to think effectively.

LIBERAL EDUCATION: FALSE CLAIMS AND ENDURING VALUES

The current discussion of secondary and college education reflects changes that have taken place during the last half-century in science and society as well as in conceptions of the nature of mind and moral discipline. The great increase in high school and college attendance has led to diversity in the character of student bodies, in the range of abilities, interests, and probable future careers. The extraordinary expansion of scientific theory and its technological applications has made a very high degree of specialization unavoidable. The revolutionary character of the economic and political changes demands giving the social studies an indispensable place in the curriculum of general education.

Under the impact of the new conditions and ideas, the concept of "liberal education" is undergoing modification in a number of directions. It has given up its former opposition to scientific and social studies as aspects of a humanistic education. It is losing its exclusive emphasis on the classical languages and mathematics as well as aban-

doning its major reliance on faculty psychology and formal discipline. In the more balanced programs there is recognition of the need
of adapting the courses of study to different groups of students, of the
importance of a measure of specialization, of the value of vocational
and professional education for the national good as well as for the
success of the individual. Above all, in response to the democratic
tendency at work in American higher education, liberal education is
emancipating itself from the conception which regarded it as education for the cultural refinement of a privileged class of gentlemen
who, as Algo D. Henderson has described them, "do not deign to
soil their hands with productive activity or disturb their minds with
vexatious contemporary problems."[12]

A central pattern may be discerned in current proposals.[13] There
is a general agreement that the course of studies in academic secondary
schools and at the college level should be devoted primarily to a program of general education comprising three major areas: the humanities, mathematics and the natural sciences, history and the social
studies. The curriculum in the humanities includes the study of the
English language as a means of communication and clarity of expression, general literature and the arts, and some foreign language requirement. Emphasis is laid on the need of a unifying principle, on
counteracting departmental isolationism, and of relating the several
areas of study to each other. All proposals stress the value of "reason,"
in some form or another—the cultivation of the intellect, the development of the power to think, or the nurture of critical intelligence.
With this goes the theme of responsible freedom of thought as the
indispensable precondition of "the education of free men." Integral
to conceptions which use the term "liberal education" is the belief
that Western civilization rests on a foundation of common ideas and
values which have their roots in the experience of Athens, Rome, and
Judea, and that it is a primary consideration in all social and cultural
endeavors to preserve continuity with the past.

Stated in these broad terms, the conception of liberal education is
in accord with the views expressed in the foregoing chapters. However, the wide range of differences in philosophical orientation, in

[12] Algo D. Henderson, *Vitalizing Liberal Education* (New York, 1944), p. 2.
[13] The discussion in the following books is also of interest: *General Education
in School and College*, A Committee Report by members of the faculties of
Andover, Exeter, Lawrenceville, Harvard, Princeton and Yale (Cambridge,
Mass., 1952); *General Education, an Account and Appraisal*, Lewis B. Mayhew,
ed. (New York, 1960); the recent comprehensive study of Columbia College
by Daniel Bell, *The Reforming of General Education* (New York, 1966).

theories of mind, and in social attitudes revealed in the different proposals, makes the apparent consensus deceptive and precludes unqualified agreement. On the one side is the insistence, as by Dr. Hutchins, that education should be conceived as "the cultivation of the intellect" and be "the same at any time, in any place, under any political, social, or economic conditions." Quite different in spirit is the humanist view presented by Jacques Maritain, who has a high regard for the classics and for the enduring values of European civilization but who sees Western culture in terms of a historical development, lays emphasis on the aesthetic as well as the rational aspects of man's psyche, and recognizes the close relation between education and social concerns.[14] At one extreme is the assumption that good thinking follows mathematical and syllogistic models; on the other end is the experimentalist conception that conceives thinking in terms of an active process of problem-solving. One approach is retrospective, celebrating the superiority of the contribution of the past; the other faces the present and looks toward the future.

Liberal Education and Life Adjustment

The balance of emphasis among those who are most insistent on the retention of the term "liberal education," as against the noncommittal "general education," is in the conservative direction. Although the several proposals imply a belief in democracy in some sense, a bias toward dependence on an intellectual élite for leadership rather than faith in the contribution of the common man to the social good, seems to predominate. There adheres, particularly to the conceptions that make the cultivation of the intellect the primary purpose, more than a vestige of the idea that higher education should be the privilege of the selected few. Along with this goes a negative attitude toward the functional aspects of education—toward vocational and professional training. To the caricature of progressive education as "regressive education" is joined a condemnation of "life-adjustment education" as a "parody of education."[15]

There is an element common to progressive education and the life-adjustment conception. In both, the child and youth undergoing the educational process and the society in which he lives are matters of paramount concern. But, taken as a whole, these two views represent contrasting educational philosophies: progressive education makes the growth of personality the underlying motivation; "life-adjust-

[14] Jacques Maritain, *Education at the Crossroads* (New Haven, 1943).
[15] Arthur Bestor, *op. cit.*, chaps. 4, 5, and 6.

312

ment," on the other hand, makes adaptation to social needs the predominant consideration. As noted above, progressive education traces to Swiss and German educators, to Pestalozzi and Froebel, who were imbued by a humanitarian and idealistic outlook. Education for life-adjustment is utilitarian and empirical and has its origin in Herbert Spencer's "education for complete living."

Spencer's famous *Essay on Education* (1859) was an attack on the classical education of the English Public School, which in his day was still largely confined to the study of Latin, Greek, and mathematics. He castigated it as a mere decorative embellishment for the aristocratic upper class, as devoid of significance for the happiness of the individual or for the good of society. Instead, he proposed that the sciences—physics, chemistry, biology—be made the basis of a broad educational program designed as a "preparation for life." In his "education for complete living," he included five areas: education for health of body and mind, for intelligent parenthood, for a productive vocation, for citizenship in a republican society, and for cultivated use of leisure time.

The influential *Cardinal Principles of Secondary Education*, formulated by a commission of the National Education Association and published by the Bureau of Education in Washington (1918), followed the same broad pattern of functional education, with added emphasis on the "fundamental processes" (the three R's) and on the formation of democratic ethical character. The recent "life-adjustment-education" proposals, put forward by a widely representative conference of American educators in cooperation with the United States Commissioner of Education—which has aroused the ire of the proponents of intellectualism—represent an elaboration of the earlier programs.[16] It directs itself primarily to the needs of the high school student who does not intend to go to college; it gives attention to the problem of psychological adjustment as well as to vocational guidance, and to the issues facing democratic society in times of cultural and economic change.

Some of the objectives proposed in life-adjustment programs which have been subjected to criticism by Professor Bestor, such as "acquiring the ability to study and help solve economic, social and political problems," are, no doubt, over-ambitious. Others may appear to the scholar as trivial, e.g., "improving one's personal appearance." But caricature of oddities culled from detailed programs should not ob-

[16] U. S. Office of Education, *Vitalizing Secondary Education* (Washington, 1951).

313

scure the valid aspects of the education-for-life-adjustment concept. Concern with contemporary issues has a legitimate place in any balanced educational program; attention to health or even to personal appearance, in the case of adolescents, are legitimate aspects of the school's responsibility. For many high school students, psychological guidance and vocational orientation may be of decisive importance. The life-adjustment principle is crucial in the education of the underprivileged, the retarded, the emotionally disturbed, and, not infrequently, in the case of the intellectually gifted. A common basis of general education for all American youth is essential, but in the complex conditions of modern life, a consideration of the special needs of various groups is indispensable. A degree of differentiation between the education of those who are preparing to go on to college and of those for whom high school is terminal education is unavoidable if justice is to be done to both groups. The education of neither group should be subordinated to the other.

The life-adjustment concept cannot be left out of account even at the college level, where the idea of a liberal education may be accepted as the guiding principle. College life under modern conditions presents a serious emotional hazard. There is increasing recognition of the need of psychological guidance and for many, some form of therapy to help students to resolve their personal problems as well as to enable them to do effective work. Moreover, it is necessary to face the fact that college education includes, for most students, an element of pre-professional training. The really difficult problem at the college level lies in the correlation of the Liberal Arts course with the arduous demands made for a professional career—in medicine, engineering, research in science—in terms of prerequisite specialized studies.

The enemies of a liberal education are not the teachers colleges with their alleged concentration of pedagogy nor does the opposition derive from the supposed anti-intellectual tendencies of pragmatism. The main obstruction comes from the scientific departments of the universities who are forced in the direction of acute specialization by powerful factors—the complex character of scientific and technological knowledge, the pressures of competitive economic systems, the compulsion to keep pace with rival nations. The problem of relating general to professional education has never been easy; it has become enormously difficult as a result of the complexity of civilization and the democratic purpose of making liberal studies more than a cultural adornment of a leisured upper class. The quandaries of liberal education cannot be resolved by derisive quips against education-for-life-adjustment or by diatribes against pragmatism.

Proposals which feature the title "liberal education" generally neglect consideration of the needs of the larger part of the American youth. They are oriented toward the interests and abilities of those who are destined for academic and professional careers. To this defect, as seen from the democratic point of view and from the perspective of a national plan of education, the scholastic versions which make intellectual cultivation the main purpose add another intrinsic deficiency. Apart from the falsity of the claim to secure general mental discipline through the study of mathematics and logic, they violate the very spirit of liberal education through their elevation of the intellectual virtues above all else. The heart of liberal education is humanism—not intellectualism. The cultivation of reason is an essential element in all forms of humanism, classical and Renaissance, but it always emphasizes the human being as a whole, and conceives of the mind in its diverse aspects, not in terms of an intellectual apparatus.

Liberal Education and Humanism

The character of humanism has undergone periodic change from the time of its origin in Athens, when Greek thought turned from its primary concern with cosmic speculation to the search for "the true nature of man." As represented by the sophists who contributed greatly to its advance, humanism had several facets. It was anthropocentric: it constituted a philosophy of culture anti-theological in tendency. Moreover, it was pervaded by the idea that "ethics and politics taken together are one of the essential qualities of true paideia," of a genuine cultural education.[17]

Although classical humanism conceived of culture in universal terms as applicable to all men, and though it regarded education as a means of personal development, it saw the individual as inseparably a member of a community. As H. I. Marrou points out: "This is the true humanism—this emphasis on the social aspect of culture, on the danger inherent in any activity that tends to be self-enclosed and aloof from the ordinary intercourse of daily life."[18] As an educational conception, it had its beginnings among those sophists who, like Protagoras, opposed the narrow, technical, over-specialized training of the *rhetor* and who maintained that the education of the professional pleader in the courts and of the leader in political life should be broad-

[17] Werner Jaeger, *Paideia: the Ideals of Greek Culture* (New York, 1939), I, p. 297.

[18] H. I. Marrou, *A History of Education in Antiquity* (New York, 1956), p. 223.

ly cultural, should include history and literature, philosophy and poetry. Although classical humanism generally valued mathematics as an element in its program of studies, it represented, as Marrou emphasizes, "a literary as opposed to a scientific humanism."

With Isocrates, the pattern of liberal education in its humanist connotation took definite shape. There was a political element in the background of his outlook. Isocrates represented the "enlightened aristocracy" of the time which recognized, though with some reluctance, the necessity of a reconciliation with democracy. In foreign affairs he was a staunch advocate of Panhellenic unity as a means of opposing the advance of "barbarian" Persian forces. There was a universal element in his conception of Greek culture; although he was not free from the general belief that the superiority of Hellenic civilization had a racial basis, it was the common culture, not common kinship, that made a man a Greek. He maintained: "The people we call Greeks are those who have the same culture as ours, not the same blood."[19]

In his program of studies, in which he includes some mathematics as exercising and sharpening the mind, he moved in the humanist direction of a literary and aesthetic emphasis. In the teaching of rhetoric, Isocrates stressed both content and style. In consonance with Greek philosophy, he placed *logos*, as idea and as word, at the heart of his educational conception: it is "the Word that turns man into a Man." Thus, in Isocrates' view, language becomes a source of moral influence as well as a means of persuasion in the courts of law and in public life. However, in the Hellenistic world the social and political aspects of classical humanism gradually wither away. As R. R. Bolgar notes, "with the Alexandrians the connection between literature and life came to an end. Literature stopped being the artistic expression of contemporary culture and became instead an instrument of education."[20] Liberal education assumed the form of an education of the upper classes of society, for cultivated leisure, for good taste in art and literature, for the enhancement of inner experience.

The humanism of the Greek classical period found the distinctive nature of man in his need for political organization and in his power of reasoning. But *philanthropia*, man's love for man, was not characteristic of it. Christian humanism, in theory at least, added the element of humaneness; its central motivation was charity toward men conjoined with the adoration of God; it was imbued with sympathy for

[19] *Ibid.*, p. 87.
[20] R. R. Bolgar, *The Classical Heritage* (Cambridge, 1954), p. 20.

the lowly and compassion for suffering. These sentiments entered into the synthesis of Christian virtue and Graeco-Roman thought that emerged in the Middle Ages—and no doubt touched the lives of common men as well as of the saints. But in practice, the doctrinal and ritual aspects of the Church overshadowed its ethical teaching. In some senses, there was regression as well as advance: intellectual dogmatism and religious persecution replaced the rational and tolerant attitude of pagan humanism. The concept of liberal education as the broad education of the free and autonomous individual was submerged; the schools, few in number, were agencies for the education of the monks, clerics and officials of government. What remained of the seven liberal arts was a mere skeleton of the broad curriculum of science and literature of ancient Greece. The course of study was narrow, confined mainly to the learning of Latin through its grammar. Philosophy was subordinated to the service of theology; logic became a tool for subtle disputation rather than an instrument for advancing knowledge and promoting clear thinking.

Renaissance humanism represented a reaction against the confinements and constraints of the medieval world, against scholastic pedantry, against ecclesiastical authority in the intellectual domain, against the other-worldly metaphysical orientation. It expressed itself in diverse ways in the different parts of Europe. In Italy, it was associated with the revival of letters, with devotion to classical Latin style; it encouraged imaginative exploration in thought and stimulated naturalism in art. In the Northern countries, it took the form of a return to the Scriptures as a basis of moral teaching and a reliance on reason and learning as a support of ethics. In the countries where nationalism had emerged as a political and cultural force, humanism encouraged the "education of the gentleman," not only in the connotation of the cultural refinement but in the sense of the education of the active man of affairs. Renaissance in education represented a return to the classical conception of a rounded education—for physical, moral and mental development, for participation in public life, and for social improvement, as well as for the enhancement of the cultural life of the individual. Although it turned to the past for enlightenment, in reality the Renaissance looked forward toward the future as is evidenced by the many utopias of the period.

In every age, humanism has signified a concern with what is distinctive in man's nature in its many-sided manifestations. It has aimed for excellence and for breadth. It has struggled against tendencies to reduce education to technical knowledge, to formal study, or, it should be emphasized, to mental discipline. In its creative periods it

317

has been concerned with man's moral aspirations and aesthetic sensitivities, not as isolated from social life but as expressed in human action and in community organization. In the revitalization of liberal education, it is necessary to make use of its key concepts as these have marked its course in the several stages of its development—its aesthetic as well as its rationalist interest, its political as well as its personal aspect, its broad universal and humane concerns, its orientation toward an ideal future as well as its sense of continuity with the past.

The Revitalization of Liberal Education

The reestablishment of liberal education means retaining the central position of the humanities in a broad course which includes the natural sciences and social studies. The humanities include history when it is studied as "philosophy teaching by example"; it should embrace the study of philosophy in the broad sense of Weltanschauung. History as the chronicle of events unrelated to humane interests, and philosophy as logical analysis, may have auxiliary import, but such neutral studies are not to be considered as parts of a liberal education.

At the core of the humanities, which should include some experience in the arts and music, lies the study of literature in its diverse expression in poetry and drama, in philosophic, political, and religious writings. Literature gives voice to the heart as well as to the mind of man. In literature, as the Harvard Report tells us, "a division into the intellectual and aesthetic components is for analysis only... the whole mind is at work in literature."[21] In the deeper sense, literature has a moral purpose, though we should bear in mind that "the ethical results of literature are not to be seen as obedience to a body of precepts, but come in quickened imagination, heightened delight, and clearer perspective." Literature makes of the beauty of the moment a joy forever, but it also reveals man's anxieties and his sorrows, records his frustrations as well as his triumphs of the spirit, his experience of despair as well as his enduring hope.

The field of literature should include the creative works of many nations of Asia as well as of Europe. But each regional civilization is characterized by its distinctive productions. For us, the Western classics have a special significance. These are the books which should be read and reread throughout our lives.[22] The classics date from

[21] Harvard Committee, *General Education in a Free Society* (Cambridge, Mass., 1945), p. 111.
[22] Important works in science have their place in courses in the history of

many periods: the Scriptures, the Greek and Roman authors, the English and American masterpieces. They reflect the unique individuality of each creative mind. Nevertheless, they are rooted in a community of experience, express a unity of mind and a common heritage of thought. They provide "a common body of tradition—to accept, to revolt against, either way to work from," and thus serve as "our primary protection against ethical ignorance." The classics express the *ethos*, the inner character, the lasting insights of the Western community; they are a resource of common understanding within the Western community, and since they reflect basic responses to the human condition, they serve also as a link of universal communication.

The revitalization of liberal education signifies identification with purposes and interests of mankind as a whole—not in the sense of an exaltation of an abstract "humanity," but in the sense of a genuine feeling of common destiny with the actual community of mankind in its international dimensions. This signifies, also, identification with the national community of which one is a member viewed in the framework of the Western community as a whole. It means viewing the Western community in the light of a struggle of all men to lift themselves out of the morass of primitivism and of poverty toward a humane life of material sufficiency and of high civilization.

Literature and classics, history, continuity with Western tradition —these several essential elements comprise only one side of a genuine humanism. The other side has to do with the social and the humane. Here, too, we may follow Jacques Maritain, who, speaking in the language of religious faith, says: "A true humanism which has a real and effective respect for human dignity and for the rights of personality, I see directed toward a socio-temporal realization of the evangelical concern for humanity which ought not exist only in the spiritual order but to become incarnate.[23] In the contemporary world, the union of humanism with democracy requires the abandonment of the philosophy of neutralism in social questions. A true liberal education today would be socially and politically liberal as well as humanistic. It would lay emphasis on the study of contemporary civilization, not in a descriptive sense merely, but from the point of view of ad-

science, but including them among "the great books" distorts the spirit of the humanities. In our selection of the masterpieces of literature we should be guided by Jacques Maritain, who chooses those "which feed the mind with the sense and knowledge of natural virtues, of honor and pity, of the dignity of man and of the spirit, the greatness of human destiny, the entanglement of good and evil, the *caritas humani generis.*" *op. cit.*, pp. 68-69.

[23] Jacques Maritain, *True Humanism* (New York, 1938), xvi-xvii.

vancing a just social order in tangible terms. It would join in the movement to abolish racial discrimination, to eliminate poverty, and to diminish gross economic inequality. It would endeavor not only to promote international mind and understanding; it would also work to reduce the enormous disparity in the standard of living throughout the world; and it would work to promote the political ties leading to international organization.

IN CONCLUSION: PHILOSOPHY, HISTORY, AND EDUCATION

There is a growing recognition, it is said, of the importance of the philosophy of education. But there is little agreement among the professors as to what is meant by "philosophy" or by "education."

On the one hand, there is the time-honored view that conceives the philosophy of education in terms of the application of metaphysical positions, e.g., scholasticism, idealism, pragmatism, to educational practice. On the other, is the treatment which begins with current educational conceptions—essentialism, progressivism, perennialism, reconstructionism—and lays little stress on "ultimate reality." Akin to this approach is the view that educational philosophy implies a critical consideration of actual problems in curriculum and method in the light of the sciences of human behavior, of a theory of values, and of the nature of the society in which the school operates. Some writers are concerned primarily with helping the students to engage in systematic discussion of educational problems and to build a personal philosophy of education for themselves. Others regard the achievement of a consensus among educators on pivotal issues as of critical importance today. But then again, there is the position which maintains that the main business of philosophy—including the philosophy of education—is not so much to give answers as to raise questions.

Finally, there are the newcomers, philosophical analysis and existentialism, which have entered the precincts of educational philosophy from opposite sides. The former is concerned primarily with the analysis of general educational concepts and disavows any intention to yield a practical program for the guidance of the schools. The exponents of existentialism claim more, but its contribution to the school, to its theory or its practices, is not apparent.

Philosophy of Education versus Educational Philosophy

A survey of the diverse conceptions, such as presented in John S. Brubacher's comprehensive treatise,[24] has value in illustrating the

[24] John S. Brubacher, *Modern Philosophies of Education* (New York, 1962).

many-sidedness of the educational problem. A comparative analysis of the various approaches could be used to stimulate thinking. Each of the modes of approach to the philosophy of education has some merit and an able instructor can develop understanding and insights, whatever approach he favors. However, this will be due to his general knowledge of educational conceptions and his experience with the practice of education, rather than to the philosophy of education as an organized discipline. Much that is presented under the formal title, "philosophy of education," has no perceptible relation to the problems of school work. The most serious defect is that it tends at times to deflect attention from the social, political, and economic context of the educational enterprise.

The title "philosophy of education" is likely to mislead in its implication that much is to be gained by a direct application of ontological positions or of an all-sufficient "philosophic method" to the educational situation. The term "educational philosophy" is preferable in that it focuses attention on educational issues in the first instance. The subject of discourse, after all, is education—not philosophy. Education is an art in which theory and practice are ever related. The approach from current educational conceptions is likely to be more productive from the point of view of theory as well as practice than the approach from philosophy in the academic, professionalized sense. It could be used as a point of departure for a broader discussion, relating to educational issues, and to social, psychological, and intellectual principles. It could lead on to the analysis of the metaphysical assumptions.

Insofar as philosophy can serve as a frame of reference for an educational program, it is in its connotation of a Weltanschauung, or a "philosophy of life." In its full exposition, a philosophy of life will reveal a belief about the nature of the cosmos and man's place in it. But at the center of any authentic philosophy of life is an ethical conception in which three points of reference are essential: man's relation to his fellow man, the relation of men and women to each other, the relation of man's "true self" to the various selves that contend within him. A philosophy of life represents a pattern of values—not as an abstract cognitional system; it reflects experience as embodied in organized community life. It may be religious in its sanctions, as are Catholicism and Judaism; it may be intellectually grounded, as were Stoicism and Epicureanism; it may be dominated by a political idea, as are democracy and communism. Despite the significant differences in outlook, these several conceptions constitute social philosophies requiring appropriate institutional arrangements within a definite

321

political order. A philosophy of life is a system of beliefs coordinated with a way of life: it has two indispensable aspects—a pattern of ideals and a community which avows it.

As method, philosophy implies analysis and criticism. But philosophic analysis cannot be satisfied with scrutiny of terms and concepts. Philosophy is concerned with ideas and not merely with terms; with conceptions, not with concepts only. Philosophy as inquiry means analysis and criticism of the premises and purposes underlying a given area of knowledge or practice. It signifies relating one area of knowledge to another, it implies not only the search for, but also the establishment of, a unifying principle.

In the field of education, likewise, philosophic inquiry requires making underlying assumptions explicit and subjecting them to evaluation in the light of a consciously held philosophy of life. Thus, the purpose of philosophic inquiry in the field of education is normative, not merely analytic; it asks questions in order to find answers. Philosophic inquiry begins with analysis and criticism but it should eventuate in proposals for solutions of the problems discussed. The solutions need not be represented as perfect or everlasting, but they should satisfy the ideal criteria better than existing theory or practice. The philosophic analysis may merely reinstate old solutions, giving them a rational basis. But philosophic inquiry may result in modified or new solutions; educational philosophy may have a reconstructive as well as a normative function.

In expositions influenced by experimentalist and progressivist doctrines, the revisions of educational theory and practice indicated by philosophical criticism are regarded as necessary primarily because of new developments that have taken place in science and society. A metaphysics of change dominates the discussion. Educational philosophy must, of course, give consideration to the need of adjusting the curriculum to intellectual and social changes. But there are two other aspects of the philosophic outlook that are more significant.

Philosophy connotes breadth of vision as well as rational criticism. It should broaden perspective, endeavor to see the particular in the frame of the universal and the enduring. But more, philosophy finds its consummation in the envisagement of an ideal that may serve as a criterion of judgment as to which changes to promote and which to counteract. The need of reconstruction of educational theory and practice does not primarily arise in the necessity of absorbing new scientific knowledge into the curriculum, of adapting to new technologies, or of reckoning with new forms of social organization. It arises from the continuous struggle of men to bring the actualities of life closer to the enduring and growing humane ideal. In essence, this is a struggle between an ethical vision and the existing social and political organization.

The Revision of the Philosophy of Education

A revision of the philosophy of education as a subject of study is in order. First, the focus of attention should be shifted from concern with metaphysics and philosophic method to consideration of major issues facing the school at various levels. Not all educational problems necessarily involve philosophical principles. How best to teach reading, whether mathematics trains the mind, whether effective teaching of some subjects can be achieved through the mass communication media—these questions are, in a measure, amenable to solution by common-sense judgment and scientific investigation. However, even such questions may assume philosophic import when they influence the development of the learner as a person and directly or indirectly impinge on social policy. Although the educational philosopher must take account of scientific findings, his function is not fulfilled in bringing knowledge to bear on the educational issues. Philosophy comes into play when ethical and social implications are involved: it is concerned with such problems as the development of the personality as a whole, the relation of the individual to society, the function of the school in maintaining and advancing the social order, the place of the church and the state in the control and direction of the educational process.

The revision calls for a transfer from metaphysics to social philosophy as the foundation of educational philosophy. Educational philosophy cannot profit much from a discussion of "the nature of man" in general; it must deal with human nature as it affects, and is affected by, social organization. It will not get far by the search for eternal cosmic truth; the framework of evaluation must be a conception of a good society. *To epitomize the thesis sharply: it is necessary to base educational philosophy on politics—not on metaphysics.* This idea follows classic Greek thought in its recognition of the close connection between ethics and the form of the state. It embodies the principle enunciated by Aristotle—that political science is "the most authoritative or architectonic" with reference to ethics and that the nature of the constitution determines the character of the educational system. It reflects the view of Plato's *Republic* in which a conception of an ideal state is made the framework of an educational plan. It follows the suggestion—advanced by Ernst Cassirer's interpretation of Plato's insight—that we cannot reform philosophy itself unless we begin by reforming the state: "That is the only way if we wish to reform the ethical life of man. To find the right political order is the first and most urgent problem."

The political order includes the body of law as well as the established processes of government, the economic structure as well as the sociological organization. The institutional arrangements, protected and encouraged by the state, are the true educators: they mold the beliefs and practices, exert the most powerful influence on the character of the individual and on the quality of life in the community at large. The political order, moreover, determines the conditions under which the school does its work, and, in final analysis, sets limits to what it may or may not do. On the philosopher of education rests the responsibility to participate along with the social scientist and the statesman in defining the nature of the good society. His special obligation is to indicate how the school—through the organization of the curriculum, through the cultivation of attitudes, through the activities of the teaching profession as an organized body—can serve to promote the realization of the envisaged social ideal.

The assumption is that democracy is "the right political order": it represents an ethical conception as well as a political system. It is the philosophical principle that provides the premises and the ends of the national educational endeavor. American experience and thought have greatly contributed to transforming it from a governmental process to a broad social philosophy pervaded by an ethical outlook. The word "democracy" carries with it echoes of the Declaration of Independence, of the struggle for freedom from oppressive foreign rule, and of the right of all men to life, liberty, and happiness. It embodies the principles derived from the modern European revolt against absolute monarchy: the foundation of the state on parliamentary constitutional government, the separation of powers and the independence of the judiciary, the subordination of the state power to civil society. Its inspirating ethical ideas—the unique worth of each person and the unity of mankind, the essential equality of all men regardless of race or social condition, the foundation of government on law supported by reason and at the same time responsible to the people—have their roots in ancient Judea, Greece, and Rome. Democracy is the contemporary expression of the moral and political tradition of Western civilization. It is regional in its historical development, but it is universal in its significance.

As an ethical-political philosophy, democracy is compatible with diverse metaphysical orientations. We may not be able to—nor do we need to—reach agreement on the question of the nature of Being. But it is essential that we achieve a consensus on the meaning of democracy. A task of educational philosophy is to define the foundation principles of the democratic social order and to relate them to the educational situation. In doing this, it will be necessary to take a stand on major issues in controversy. The position of noninvolvement in political questions or of complete neutrality in controversial issues encourages a spirit of evasion and equivocation. It makes for an attitude of distrust on the part of students toward the educational establishment, and diminishes the moral influence of the school in the community.

A revision of the philosophy of education has an importance beyond its effect in giving the individual teacher or educational administrator a broader understanding of the educational process, or in improving the curriculum and methods of the school. Education, using the word to include the public activities of the teaching profession as well as the work of the teacher in the classroom, cannot of itself greatly effect changes in the social order. But it can, supporting liberal trends of thought and working along with other agencies— social welfare organizations, religious associations, political bodies— make a contribution toward the advancement of the common good. Education always exercises some influence, positive or negative; when it fails to work for social advance it becomes an agency of cultural lag.

Philosophy and Teacher Training

In the education of the teacher, "philosophy of education" should be conceived in the broadest terms as the study of educational ideas in relation to social forces and intellectual trends, to ethical outlooks and political organization. In this meaning, a knowledge of the history of education and a survey of contemporary issues in education are essential; they are invaluable in themselves and prerequisite to the study of the philosophy of education in the more specific sense.

The history of education is too narrowly defined when it is regarded as a faithful description of "what has happened in the past in respect to education." It should be thought of, rather, in terms of Lord Bolingbroke's characterization of history as "philosophy teaching by example." The study of the history of education disabuses of the fallacy that ideas can fruitfully be considered "on their own terms apart from their historical connections." The great ideas of the Western tradition have enduring significance; the history of education reveals the continuity of development as well as change. But the meaning and the import of ideas cannot be divorced from cultural and social context of the time and place of their origin. Their significance for the present cannot be grasped except in terms of possible application to our own situation.

The history of education should include an account of the leading educational ideas and of the school systems of each period. Two complementary modes of treatment are desirable: (1) a study of the educational conceptions of the philosophers and educators who have contributed to the body of Western educational thought; (2) an analysis of the relation of the prevalent educational ideas and practices of each period to the intellectual currents and social organization of the time. An important aspect of inquiry is to learn to what degree, if at all, the conceptions advanced by philosophers and educators influenced practice in their own day or in subsequent generations. Likewise, it is important to ascertain to what degree the school reflected social change or suffered from cultural lag.

The study of the educational ideas of leaders of thought is especially valuable in that it relates the educational conceptions of each thinker to his total outlook. Among the contributors to educational thought are philosophers, religious leaders, and statesmen as well as educators in the professional sense. They include the great figures—Plato, Aristotle, Rousseau, Locke, John Dewey—who occupy a central position in the history of political and social thought and whose educational conceptions are an integral aspect of their general philosophy. Supplementary to these are the many thinkers who have expressed themselves incidentally on some phase of the educational problem: Cicero and Seneca, Augustine and Aquinas, Kant and Fichte, Luther, Calvin, and Loyola. Herbert Spencer, Robert Owen, and Karl Marx are important as representing contrasting responses to the industrial revolution. On the American scene, Benjamin Franklin and Thomas Jefferson have a place in the history of education as well as in political thought. Not less significant from the philosophic point of view are educators who have contributed to educational thought as well as to school practice: Isocrates and Quintilian in ancient times; Vittorino da Feltre and Aeneas Sylvius in the Renaissance, Pestalozzi, Herbart, and Froebel, the founders of modern pedagogy; Horace Mann, William T. Harris, and Francis W. Parker, who shaped American educational thought in the nineteenth century.

In all the instances, whether dealing with the philosophers, the religious leaders, or with the educators who have made contributions to school practice, it is of the essence to relate their educational ideas to their general philosophies of life and social outlook. Likewise in the study of the systems of school practice of the curriculum, methods of teaching and conceptions of discipline, it is necessary to trace the relations to prevalent intellectual attitudes and religious beliefs, on the one hand, and to the sociological structure and to the political and economic organization, on the other. The school is never merely a reflection of social, economic, and political conditions. But it cannot be adequately understood without taking into consideration the material factors underlying cultural formations. Related to the social organization is the question of the character of the school population. Is the education of the school concerned mainly with the training of special groups—a priestly caste, professional personnel, an intellectual elite, or a leisured upper class? Or is it designed for the education of all the people and conceived in terms of the national welfare as a whole?

Paramount in importance with the history of educational ideas is the study of the contemporary situation in two aspects: (1) the consideration of the major educational conceptions and of the conflict of opinion in American educational thought; (2) a survey of comparative educational systems throughout the world. In the category of the present, we may include the earlier part of this century, particularly the last fifty years since World War I. For this period John Dewey is far and away the outstanding figure, equally important as philosopher, social thinker, and educator. An understanding of his position is as necessary for those who oppose his views—or think they do—as for those who support them. The opinions of Bertrand Russell and of Alfred North Whitehead on educational matters are of interest as the views of eminent men, although their educational conceptions are not closely related to their metaphysical positions. The views of Jacques Maritain are more directly connected with his humanistic Catholic outlook. The sharp criticisms made by Robert M. Hutchins and the constructive proposals of James B. Conant are significant from the philosophical point of view as well as from the angle of school practice. Among the professors of education of the recent period, who have expounded definite conceptions and left an impress on current educational thought, the following readily come to mind: on the essentialist side, Herbert C. Morrison, William C. Bagley, Edward L. Thorndike; on the progressivist side, Boyd H. Bode, William H. Kilpatrick, Harold Rugg, and, happily still with us, John L. Childs and George S. Counts.

In the light of the international character of contemporary society and of the struggle of rival political ideologies, the study of comparative educational systems assumes critical importance. Today comparative education includes the study of the national systems of the democratic countries of the West, the organization of education in

Communist states, and the educational problems of the underdeveloped countries. The analysis of educational conceptions and problems in foreign lands is an exceptionally good way of understanding the social and political situation in each case. At the same time it can contribute to an evaluation of the strengths and weaknesses of the American educational system. Perhaps it is not superfluous to add that the school organizations in the totalitarian countries need to be studied for their deficiencies from the democratic point of view as well as their alleged effectiveness in the training of scientists and technicians.[25] The educational problems of the underdeveloped countries in Asia and Africa and in South America whose political organization is undergoing a transition deserve particular attention. In these areas, American educational ideas, duly related to actual social and political conditions in each case, could have a significant and constructive part to play.

Courses in the history of education and in contemporary educational issues could have great value for the liberal arts program. Such courses should be required for prospective teachers. Supplementary studies in educational thought should be offered on a graduate level. However, the title "philosophy of education" leaves too much room for vague and irrelevant discussion; in any case, it is desirable to indicate the content of courses, e.g., "contemporary philosophies and their impact on education," "trends in modern literature and their implications for education," "religious systems and education." For most students, basing the course in educational philosophy primarily on a survey of metaphysical conceptions, is of dubious value. Analysis of formal ontological positions in the light of their social and cultural contexts as well as their educational implications should be included in the preparation of those who intend to teach courses in the philosophy of education.

For the teacher of the history and the philosophy of education, the study of political theory and of contemporary social conceptions should occupy a central position. Western philosophy is in part an effort to mediate between reason and religion. But at the same time it has been preeminently concerned with the interplay between ethics and politics. The great figures in philosophy, Plato and Aristotle, Augustine and Aquinas, Locke and Rousseau, Hegel, Marx, and John Stuart Mill, can be properly understood only when their conceptions of the relation of man to the state are brought into focus. And politics

[25] As featured by Vice-Admiral H. G. Rickover in *Education and Freedom* (New York, 1959).

cannot be understood except in relation to economics. The teacher of the philosophy of education requires a very broad cultural preparation in general literature, in philosophic and religious thought, on the one hand, and in the behavioral and anthropological sciences, on the other. But his education would be lacking in a fundamental if it did not include a knowledge of political-economic theory.

Historical Continuity and the Future

The foregoing outline for the study of educational philosophy reflects a dual perspective which in current parlance may be called, on the one side, "essentialist," and on the other, "reconstructionist." These two points of view are generally described as standing in opposition. However, thinking of "the future as history," of the emerging era in a line of continuity with the past, we may regard the two contrasting positions as polar concepts, each representing a point of paramount consideration in the formulation of an integrated school policy.

The essentialist position implies a conservationist but not necessarily, a conservative orientation. It represents an indispensable element in every educational program. Just because we live in an era of great transition when the traditional values and the institutional structures which support them are subject to the stress of radical change, it is imperative to reiterate the theme of "education as the transmission of the cultural heritage." This component of the educational process accords with that aspect of Dewey's thought—unfortunately too much neglected by both adherents and critics—beautifully expressed in the concluding passage of *A Common Faith*: "The things in civilization which we most prize are not of ourselves. They exist by grace of the doings and sufferings of the continuous human community of which we are a link. Ours is the responsibility of conserving, transmitting, rectifying, and expanding the heritage of values we have received that those who come after us may receive it more solid and secure, more widely accessible and more generously shared than we have received it."[26]

However, in the current educational discussion essentialism is usually associated with a conservative temper of mind. Its plea for a mastery of "the exact and exacting" disciplines of the traditional curriculum is likely to be accompanied by a deprecatory opinion of the social studies on the ground that they have not achieved the degree of precision of the natural sciences. Essentialism tends to defend a policy of neutralism in controversial issues even when democratic

[26] John Dewey, *A Common Faith* (New Haven, 1934), p. 87.

principles demand taking a position. The perennialist variant of essentialism, postulating a metaphysics of unchanging principles, betrays a nostalgia for worlds gone by. It contrasts "the colossal triumph" of the classic and the medieval civilization with "the latest nostrums in economics, politics . . . and education."[27] It turns eyes away from the slaveries and servilities, from the mass ignorance and widespread superstitions of the pre-modern eras. It diminishes the value of recent achievements in the realms of thought, in democratic political organization, and in general social welfare.

The heritage of the past, like the culture of the present, is a rough mixture of good and evil, of truth and error. A function of philosophic criticism is to distinguish what is living idea and what is dead hypothesis, to differentiate what is enduring principle and what is temporal embodiment. The task is to clarify and to formulate anew the perennial conceptions of worth, indicating their bearing on major contemporary issues, applying them in the light of economic possibilities and the developing world order. In the critical analysis of the heritage and in the formulation of educational policy, reconstructionism has a crucial part to play. It serves as an antidote to a static society and to uncritical idealization of the past. In a more positive sense, its future-centered idealistic orientation gives dynamic direction to the educational purpose.

Reconstruction retains a kernel of faith and of will which, as Friedrich Paulsen maintained, lies at the heart of "every philosophy that strives to be a philosophy in the old sense, a conception of the world and of life . . ." As he notes, philosophy is centrally concerned with knowledge. Nevertheless, the ultimate object of all philosophy is to bring meaning into things; in the last analysis, "this meaning is not a matter of knowledge, but of volition and of faith." In Plato's "idea of the good," in Augustine's "faith precedes reason," in Hegel's world-process growing in rationality, in Comte's positivism—indeed, underlying the materialistic philosophy of Marx—there is an aspiration for a better form of life. "So everywhere a man's ideal of the future is the fixed point from which his interpretation of history proceeds. It determines the most significant points of the past, and through these points the curve is plotted which describes the course of history."[28]

The ideal of the future has been conceived in spiritual, other-world terms. It has expressed itself in utopian visions unrelated to actual

[27] Hutchins, *op. cit.*, pp. 80-81.

[28] Friedrich Paulsen, *Introduction to Philosophy* (New York, 1896), pp. 313-318.

conditions or emerging possibilities. To uphold the idea-concepts of justice and equality, of freedom and law, of compassion and human welfare as points of reference for thought is an indispensable prerequisite of rational-moral endeavor. But to be satisfied with affirming them, wholesale and in the abstract, leaves them impotent to move actualities forward in the direction of the ideal. Maintained in their absolutist form they may at times be destructive of the existent, though imperfect, good.

With all the emphasis that has been laid in the foregoing chapters on the need for clear formulation of ideas, it is necessary to bear in mind the experimentalist conception of the interaction of thought with experience, of the interplay of the ideal with the actual. The reconstructionist component in the present exposition of educational policy remains within the framework of Dewey's thesis: "The reconstruction of philosophy, of education, and of social ideals and methods, goes hand in hand." Without the cooperation of economic and political forces, the school cannot greatly influence the character of the social order. But the major question is not whether it can or cannot, or in what measure it can do so. The first question is whether the school ought to exert thought and effort in that direction. The real question is one of clarity and consistency in the definition of the principles of democracy, and of moral integrity in the active pursuit of its ends.

Selected Bibliography

(This bibliography lists only the references used in the preparation of the text.)

I. PHILOSOPHY, SCIENCE, ETHICS

AYER, A. J. *Language, Truth and Logic*. London: Victor Gollancz, 1950.

BARKER, ERNEST. *The Politics of Aristotle*. Oxford: Clarendon Press, 1946.

BARRETT, WILLIAM. *Irrational Man: A Study in Existential Philosophy*. New York: Doubleday, Anchor Books, 1962.

BUCHLER, JUSTUS (ed.). *The Philosophy of Pierce: Selected Writings*. New York: Harcourt, Brace & Co., 1940.

BURTT, E. A. *Metaphysical Foundations of Modern Physical Science*. New York: Harcourt, Brace & Co., 1925.

BUTTERFIELD, HERBERT. *The Origins of Modern Science*. London: G. Bell & Sons, 1951.

CASSIRER, ERNST. *An Essay on Man*. New Haven: Yale University Press, 1944.

———. *The Problem of Knowledge*. New Haven: Yale University Press, 1950.

———. *The Myth of the State*. New York: Doubleday, Anchor Books, 1955.

———. *The Question of Jean Jacques Rousseau*. Translated, edited, and with an Introduction and Notes by PETER GAY. New York: Columbia University Press, 1954.

COHEN, MORRIS R. *Reason and Nature*. New York: Harcourt, Brace & Co., 1931.

COLE, STEWART G. (ed.) *This Is My Faith: The Convictions of Representative Americans Today*. New York: Harper & Brothers, 1956.

COLLINGWOOD, R. G. *An Essay on Metaphysics*. Oxford: Clarendon Press, 1940.

CONANT, JAMES B. *On Understanding Science*. New York: New American Library, A Mentor Book, 1951.

DANTZIG, TOBIAS. *Number: The Language of Science*. New York: The Macmillan Co., 1930.

DEWEY, JOHN. *Human Nature and Conduct*. New York: Henry Holt & Co., 1922.

————. *The Quest for Certainty*. New York: Minton, Blach & Co., 1929.

————, and JAMES H. TUFTS. *Ethics*. Revised. New York: Henry Holt & Co., 1936.

EINSTEIN, ALBERT. *Out of My Later Years*. New York: Philosophical Library. 1950.

HARRINGTON, MICHAEL. *The Other America: Poverty in the United States*. New York: The Macmillan Co., 1962.

————. *The Politics of Poverty*. New York: League of Industrial Democrats, 1965.

HEINEMANN, F. H. *Existentialism and the Modern Predicament*. New York: Harper & Brothers, 1953.

HEISENBERG, WERNER. *Physics and Philosophy*. New York: Harper & Brothers, 1958.

HIMMELFARB, GERTRUDE (ed.). *Lord Acton, Essays on Freedom and Power*. Glencoe, Ill.: The Free Press, 1948.

INFIELD, LEOPOLD. *Albert Einstein: His Work and Its Influence on Our World*. New York: Charles Scribner's Sons, 1956.

JAEGER, WERNER. *Aristotle*. Oxford: Clarendon Press, 1934.

JAMES, WILLIAM. *The Will To Believe*. New York: Longmans, Green & Co., 1917.

JASPERS, KARL. *Way To Wisdom*. New Haven: Yale University Press, 1951.

KALLEN, HORACE M. *The Book of Job as a Greek Tragedy*. New York: Hill & Wang, Inc., 1959.

KUHN, THOMAS S. *The Structure of Scientific Revolutions*. Chicago: University of Chicago, Phoenix Books, 1962.

KIERKEGAARD, SÖREN. *The Last Years 1853-1855*, ed. RONALD GREGOR SMITH. New York: Harper & Row, 1965.

McKEON, RICHARD. *Thought, Action, and Passion*. Chicago: University of Chicago Press, 1954.

MUMFORD, LEWIS. *Faith for Living*. New York: Harcourt, Brace & Co., 1940.

NAGEL, ERNEST. *The Structure of Science*. New York: Harcourt, Brace & World, Inc., 1961.

NIEBUHR, REINHOLD. *The Nature and Destiny of Man*. New York: Charles Scribner's Sons, 1943.

OPPENHEIMER, J. ROBERT. *Science and the Common Understanding*. New York: Simon & Schuster, 1953.

PAULSEN, FRIEDRICH. *Introduction to Philosophy*. New York: Henry Holt & Co., 1896.

PERRY, RALPH BARTON. *Puritanism and Democracy*. New York: Vanguard Press, 1944.

RUSSELL, BERTRAND. *A History of Western Philosophy*. New York: Simon & Schuster, 1945.

SANTAYANA, GEORGE. *The Realm of Truth*. New York: Charles Scribner's Sons, 1938.

————. *Three Philosophical Poets*. New York: Doubleday, Anchor Books, 1953.

SARTRE, JEAN-PAUL. *Being and Nothingness*. New York: Philosophical Library, 1956.

SCHILPP, PAUL ARTHUR. (ed.). *The Philosophy of John Dewey*. Evanston: Northwestern University Press, 1939.

————. *The Philosophy of Alfred North Whitehead*. Evanston: Northwestern University Press, 1941.

————. *The Philosophy of Bertrand Russell.* Evanston: Northwestern University Press, 1944.

TILLICH, PAUL. *The Courge to Be*. New Haven: Yale University Press, 1952.

TOULMIN, STEPHEN. *The Philosophy of Science*. New York: Harper & Row, Torchbooks, 1960.

TSANOFF, RADOSLAV A. *Ethics*. New York: Harper & Brothers, 1947.

WINDELBAND, W. *A History of Philosophy*. New York: The MacMillan Co., 1919.

WELDON, T. D. *States and Morals*. New York: McGraw-Hill Book Co., 1947.

ZELLER, EDWARD. *Outlines of the History of Greek Philosophy*. New York: Harcourt, Brace, & Co., 1931.

II. SOCIAL THOUGHT, POLITICS, ECONOMICS

American Academy of Arts and Sciences. "The Negro American." *Daedalus*. Fall 1965; Winter, 1966. Issued as vol. 94, no. 4; vol. 95, no. 1 of the proceedings.

BEARD, CHARLES A. AND MARY R. *The Rise of American Civilization*. New York: The Macmillan Co., 1927.

BURCKHARDT, JACOB. *The Age of Constantine the Great*. Translated by MOSES HADAS. New York: Pantheon Books, 1949.

BENNETT, JOHN COLEMAN. *Christianity and Communism Today*. New York: Association Press, 1960.

CHAFEE, ZACHARIAH, JR. *Free Speech in the United States*. Cambridge: Harvard University Press, 1948.

Commission to Study the Organization of Peace. *Strengthening the United Nations*. New York: Harper & Brothers, 1957.

COHEN, ARTHUR A. *The Communism of Mao Tse-tung*. Chicago: University of Chicago Press, Phoenix Books, 1964.

CORWIN, EDWARD S. *The Constitution and What It Means Today*. Princeton: Princeton University Press, 1958.

CRANKSHAW, EDWARD. *Krushchev: A Career*. New York: The Viking Press, Inc., 1966.

DEWEY, JOHN. *Liberalism and Social Action*. New York: G. P. Putnam's Sons, 1935.

EICHELBERGER, CLARK M. *U.N. The First Ten Years*. New York: Harper & Brothers, 1955.

————. *U.N. The First Twenty Years*. New York: Harper & Row, 1965.

FAINSOD, MERLE. *How Russia Is Ruled*. Cambridge: Harvard University Press, 1961.

FRIEDERICH, CARL JOACHIM. *The Philosophy of Law in Historical Perspective*. Chicago: University of Chicago Press, 1958.

GALBRAITH, JOHN KENNETH. *The Affluent Society*. Boston: Houghton,Mifflin Co., 1958.

HAYEK, FRIEDRICH A. *The Constitution of Liberty*. Chicago: University of Chicago Press, 1960.

HEILBRONER, ROBERT L. *The Great Ascent*. New York: Harper & Row, 1963.

KENNAN, GEORGE F. *Realities of American Foreign Policy*. Princeton: Princeton University Press, 1954.

————. *Russia and the West under Lenin and Stalin*. Boston: Little, Brown & Co., 1961.

KONVITZ, MILTON R. *Bill of Rights Reader*. Ithaca: Cornell University Press, 1954.

————. *Expanding Liberties*. New York: The Viking Press, Inc., 1966.

LASKI, HAROLD J. *The American Democracy: A Commentary and an Interpretation*. New York: The Viking Press, 1948.

————. *The State in Theory and Practice*. New York: The Viking Press, Inc., 1935.

LERNER, MAX. *The Mind and Faith of Justice Holmes*. Boston: Little, Brown & Co., 1943.

LICHTHEIM, GEORGE. *Marxism: A Historical and Critical Study*. New York: Frederick A. Praeger, 1961.

LINDSAY, A. D. *The Modern Democratic State*. New York: Oxford University Press, 1947.

LIPPMANN, WALTER. *The Public Philosophy*. Boston: Little, Brown & Co., 1955.

MEHRING, FRANZ. *Karl Marx: The Story of His Life*. New York: Covici Friede, 1935.

JONES, HOWARD MUMFORD. (ed.). *Primer of Intellectual Freedom*. Cambridge: Harvard University Press, 1949.

MYRDAL, GUNNAR. *Challenge to Affluence*. New York: Pantheon Books, 1963.

————. *Value in Social Theory*. Edited with an Introduction by PAUL STREETEN, New York: Harper & Bros., 1958.

NEUMANN, FRANZ. *The Democratic and Authoritarian State*. Glencoe, Ill.: The Free Press, 1957.

NIEBUHR, REINHOLD. *Moral Man and Immoral Society*. New York: Charles Scribner's Sons, 1932.

NORTH, ROBERT CARVER. *Chinese Communism*. New York: McGraw-Hill Book Co., 1966.

PRITCHETT, C. HERMANN. *Civil Liberties and the Vinson Court*. Chicago: University of Chicago Press, 1954.

The Rockefeller Panel Reports. *Prospect for America*. New York: Doubleday & Co., Inc., 1961.

SABINE, GEORGE H. *A History of Political Theory*. New York: Henry Holt & Co., 1937.

SAMUELSON, PAUL A. *Economics: An Introductory Analysis*. New York: McGraw-Hill Book Co., Inc., 1961.

SCHAPIRO, J. SALWYN. *Liberalism, Its Meaning and History*. Princeton: D. Van Nostrand Co., Inc., Anvil Originals, 1958.

————. *Liberalism and the Challenge of Fascism*. New York: McGraw-Hill Book Co., Inc., 1949.

SCHUMPETER, JOSEPH A. *Capitalism, Socialism and Democracy*. New York: Harper & Brothers, 1947.

SCHURMAN, FRANZ. *Ideology and Organization in Communist China*. Berkeley and Los Angeles: University of California Press, 1966.

SMITH, T. V. *The Democratic Way of Life*. New York: New American Library, Mentor Books, 1951.

THEOBALD, ROBERT. *Free Men and Free Markets*. New York: Doubleday, Anchor Books, 1965.

THOMPSON, KENNETH W. *Political Realism and the Crisis of World Politics*. Princeton: Princeton University Press, 1960.

TIMBERGEN, JAN. *Shaping the World Economy*. New York: The Twentieth Century Fund, 1962.

TOYNBEE, ARNOLD J. *Civilization on Trial*. New York: Oxford University Press, 1948.

WOODWARD, E. VANN. *Reunion and Reaction*. Boston: Little Brown and Co., 1951.

YELLEN, SAMUEL. *American Labor Struggles*. New York: Harcourt, Brace & Co., 1936.

III. EDUCATION

AIKEN, WILFRED M. *The Story of the Eight-Year Study*. New York: Harper & Brothers, 1942.

American Historical Association. *Conclusion and Recommendation of the Commission in the Social Studies*. New York: Charles Scribner's Sons, 1934.

BAYLES, ERNEST E. *Democratic Educational Theory*. New York: Harper & Brothers, 1960.

BELL, DANIEL. *The Reforming of General Education*. New York: Columbia University Press, 1966.

BERKSON, I. B. *The Ideal and the Community*. New York: Harper & Brothers, 1958.

————. *Education Faces the Future*. New York: Harper & Brothers, 1943.

————. *Preface to an Educational Philosophy*. New York: Columbia University Press, 1940.

BESTOR, ARTHUR. *Educational Wastelands*. Urbana: University of Illinois, 1953.

BODE, BOYD HENRY. *Progressive Education at the Crossroads*. New York: Newson, 1938.

BOLGAR, R. R. *The Classical Heritage*. New York: Cambridge University Press, 1954.

BRAMELD, THEODORE. *Ends and Means in Education*. New York: Harper and Brothers, 1950.

————. *Philosophies of Education in Cultural Perspective*. New York: Dryden Press, 1955.

————. *Toward a Reconstructed Philosophy of Education*. New York: Holt, Rinehart & Winston, Inc., 1956.

BREED, FREDERICK S. *Education and the New Realism*. New York: The Macmillan Co., 1939.

BROUDY, HARRY S. *Building a Philosophy of Education*. Englewood Cliffs: Prentice-Hall, 1954.

BRUBACHER, JOHN S. *Modern Philosophies of Education*. New York: McGraw-Hill Book Co., 1962.

————. (ed.) *The Public Schools and Spiritual Values*. New York: Harper & Bros., 1944.

BUTLER, J. DONALD. *Four Philosophies and Their Practice in Education and Religion*. New York: Harper & Brothers, 1957.

CHILDS, JOHN L. *American Pragmatism and Education*. New York: Henry Holt & Co., 1956.

————. *Education and the Philosophy of Experimentalism*. With a Foreword by WM. H. KILPATRICK. New York: The Century Co., 1931.

CLIFT, VIRGIL A., ARCHIBALD W. ANDERSON, H. GORDON HULLFISH. *Negro Education in America*. New York: Harper & Brothers, 1962.

CONANT, JAMES B. *Education in a Divided World*. New York: Harper & Brothers, 1943.

————. *The American High School Today*. New York: McGraw-Hill Book Co., 1959.

COUNTS, GEORGE S. *The American Road to Culture*. New York: John Day, 1930.

————. *Education and American Civilization*. New York: Teachers College, Columbia University, 1952.

CREMIN, LAWRENCE A. *The Transformation of the School*. New York: Alfred A. Knopf, 1961.

DEWEY, JOHN. *Democracy and Education*. New York: The Macmillan Co., 1916.

————. *Experience and Education*. New York: The Macmillan Co., 1938.

DRESSEL, PAUL L. AND LEWIS B. MAYHEW. *General Education: Explorations in Evaluation*. Washington: American Council on Education, 1954.

Educational Policies Commission. *Moral and Spiritual Values in the Public School*. Washington: National Education Association, 1951.

GREENE, THEODORE M. and others. *Liberal Education Re-examined*. New York: Harper & Brothers, 1943.

Harvard Committee. *General Education in a Free Society*. Cambridge: Harvard University Press, 1945.

HENDERSON, ALGO D. *Vitalizing Liberal Education*. New York: Harper & Brothers, 1944.

HUTCHINS, ROBERT M. *The Higher Learning in America*. New Haven: Yale University Press, 1936.

————. *The Conflict in Education*. New York: Harper & Brothers, 1953.

————. *Education for Freedom*. Baton Rouge: Louisiana State University Press, 1944.

JAEGER, WERNER. *Paideia: The Ideals of Greek Culture*. New York: Oxford University Press, 1939.

KILPATRICK, WILLIAM H. *Education and the Social Crisis*. New York: Liveright Publishing Corp., 1932.

————. *Philosophy of Education*. New York: The Macmillan Co., 1951

————. (ed.). *The Educational Frontier*. New York: D. Appleton-Century Company, 1933.

KIMBALL SOLON T. AND JAMES E. McCLELLAN. *Education and the New America*. New York: Random House, 1962.

LEE, GORDON C. *Education and Democratic Ideals*. New York: Harcourt, Brace & World, 1965.

KNELLER, GEORGE F. *Introduction to the Philosophy of Education*. Los Angeles: University of California Press, 1964.

————. *Existentialism and Education*. New York: Philosophical Library, 1958.

MARITAIN, JACQUES. *Education at the Crossroads*. New Haven: Yale University Press, 1943.

MARROU, H. I. *A History of Education in Antiquity*. New York: Sheed & Ward, 1956.

MASON, ROBERT E. *Educational Ideals in American Society*. Boston: Allyn & Bacon, 1960.

MAYHEW, LEWIS B. (ed.). *General Education: An Account and An Appraisal*. New York: Harper & Brothers, 1960.

MEIKLEJOHN, ALEXANDER. *Education Between Two Worlds*. New York: Harper & Brothers, 1942.

MONROE, PAUL. *A Text Book in the History of Education*. New York: The Macmillan Co., 1912.

MORRIS, VAN CLEVE. *Philosophy and the American School*. Boston: Houghton Mifflin Co., 1961.

————. *Existentialism and Education*. New York: Harper & Row, 1966.

MORRISON, HENRY C. *The Curriculum of the Common School*. Chicago: University of Chicago Press, 1940.

O'CONNER, D. J. *The Philosophy of Education*. New York: Philosophical Library, 1957.

PHENIX, PHILLIP H. *Philosophy of Education*. New York: Henry Holt & Co., 1958.

————. *Education and the Common Good*. New York: Harper & Bros., 1961.

RAUP, R. BRUCE, GEORGE E. AXTELLE, KENNETH D. BENNE, AND B. OTHANEL SMITH. *The Improvement of Practical Intelligence*. New York: Harper & Brothers, 1950.

RICKOVER, HYMAN G. *Education and Freedom*. New York: E. P. Dutton & Co., Inc., 1959.

RUGG, HAROLD. *Culture and Education in America.* New York: Harcourt, Brace & Co., 1931.

STANLEY, WILLIAM O. *Education and Social Integration.* New York: Teachers College, Columbia University, 1953.

THAYER, VIVIAN T. *Formative Ideas in American Education.* New York: Dodd, Mead and Co., 1965.

U.S. Office of Education. *Vitalizing Secondary Education.* Washington, 1951.

ULICH, ROBERT. *Philosophy of Education.* New York: American Book Co., 1961.

WARNER, W. LLOYD, ROBERT J. HAVIGHURST, AND MARTIN LOEB. *Who Shall Be Educated.* New York: Harper & Brothers, 1944.

WOODRING, PAUL. *Let's Talk Sense About Our Schools.* New York: McGraw-Hill Book Co., Inc., 1953.

Index

Date Due

FORM 109